D0208064

Policing Soviet Society

Policing Soviet Society is the first book to look in depth at the Soviet militia, one of the most vital elements of control within the Soviet state. The book will be a crucial aid to understanding the authoritarianism of the communist system and its legacy for Russia and the successor states.

The militia was created immediately after the Russian revolution, and throughout the communist period played a central social, political and economic role in directing and controlling a highly centralized socialist state. It held an important political position during the Stalinist period. Following Stalin's death, crime control became a more serious concern, but the militia remained a key tool of the party and the most immediate form of control over the lives of Soviet citizens. As the communist regime began to collapse, the militia was increasingly thrust into the front line of political conflict, a task it was not suited to perform. Despite the efforts of *perestroika* to reform it, the collapse of the Soviet state also led to the collapse of morale within the militia.

Louise Shelley deals with questions central to our understanding of recent history and the likely future for Russia and the successor states. Why, she asks, were the militia and the rest of the sophisticated Soviet control apparatus unable to prevent the collapse of the USSR? Does Soviet law enforcement provide an undemocratic legacy for the successor states? This fascinating book fills a vital gap in literature on the Soviet legacy.

Louise I. Shelley is Professor at the Department of Justice, Law and Society and the School of International Service at the American University, Washington, D.C.

Policing Soviet Society

The evolution of state control

Louise I. Shelley

London and New York

HV
8224
S376
1996

First published 1996
by Routledge
11 New Fetter Lane, London EC4P 4EE

Simultaneously published in the USA and Canada
by Routledge
29 West 35th Street, New York, NY 10001

© 1996 Louise I. Shelley

Typeset in Times by
Ponting–Green Publishing Services, Chesham, Bucks

Printed and bound in Great Britain by
Mackays of Chatham PLC, Chatham, Kent

All rights reserved. No part of this book may be reprinted or
reproduced or utilised in any form or by any electronic,
mechanical, or other means, now known or hereafter
invented, including photocopying and recording, or in any
information storage or retrieval system, without permission in
writing from the publishers.

British Library Cataloguing in Publication Data
A catalogue record for this book is available from the
British Library

Library of Congress Cataloguing in Publication Data
A catalogue record for this book has been requested

ISBN 0–415–10469–6
ISBN 0–415–10470–X (pbk)

LIBRARY

BUNKER HILL COMMUNITY COLLEGE
CHARLESTOWN. MASS. 02129

This book is dedicated to my son, Richard Graves, who was born on Soviet Militia Day, 10 November 1982.

LIBRARY
BUNKER HILL COMMUNITY COLLEGE
CHARLESTOWN, MASS. 02129

Contents

Tables & Figures

TABLES

FIGURES

Acknowledgements

Numerous individuals provided me with assistance during the many years in which I researched and wrote this book. I would first like to thank Cathy Cosman, Cathy Fitzpatrick, Murray Feshbach, Paul Goble, Eugene Huskey, Amy Knight, Peter Maggs, Gordon Rocca, Blair Ruble, the late T. Sadowski of the Library of Congress, Peter Solomon and Ger van den Berg for their advice and encouragement over the years. I thank Konstantin Mirozhnik for his help in arranging interviews with former militia personnel in Israel, Lidia Voronina for her assistance with transcriptions, my assistants at the American University – including Michael Beckelhimer, Kira Nakhutin, and Forrest Nielsen – for their help in locating many materials for my research, and my research assistant Sherry Norris for her assistance in preparing the bibliography.

I would also like to thank the many friends, students and colleagues who read various parts of the manuscript and gave me sound content and editorial suggestions. I am particularly grateful to Menachem Amir, Paul Chevigny, David Fishman, the late Joe Kirchheimer, Terri Kominers, Gary Marx, Angie Musolino and Ugljesa Zvekic for advice which helped me to refine the arguments I make in this book. I also wish to thank Joe Serio, who succeeded in having a member of the USSR Ministry of Internal Affairs in Moscow read the manuscript and provide me with detailed comments.

I am indebted to the John Simon Guggenheim Foundation for providing the initial support that allowed me to consider the problem of policing in the USSR and to the National Council for Soviet and Eastern European Research for subsequent research support. Vlad Toumanoff and Bob Randolph at the National Council gave me sound advice and perceptive comments on the project in its formative stages, for which I thank them.

I am enormously grateful to Gianmaria Ajani and Ernesto Savona for inviting me to the Università di Trento in Italy; they gave me the encouragement in a wonderful setting that allowed me to finish the book. My residence in a continental law school in Italy greatly enhanced my comparative perspective on Soviet policing; I particularly thank Christina Boglia for her perceptive comments in this vein.

Great thanks are also owed to Gordon Smith, my editor at Routledge, who has been a source of both substantive and editorial advice over several years. In addition, I thank Peggy McInerny for her superb editing work in preparing the manuscript for publication.

Finally, my heartfelt thanks are due my family, which has been very patient with me as I wrote and revised the manuscript many times in response to the numerous changes that occurred in the former Soviet Union during the course of my research. Special thanks to Donald Graves for his help on the fine points of Sovietology.

Louise Shelley
September 1994

Notes on transliteration

The text of this work follows the Library of Congress system of transliteration for spelling Russian words in English, with the exception of sources that use a different transliteration system, such as publications of the Foreign Broadcast Information Service and the Joint Publications Research Service (e.g., *USSR: Daily Report* and *USSR: Political and Sociological Affairs*), as well as English-language versions of such Russian newspapers as *Moscow News*. Other exceptions include proper names of cities and individuals that have acquired a more or less standard spelling in English; for example, Yerevan (instead of Erevan) and Boris Yeltsin (instead of El'tsin). In all other cases, transliterated text conforms with the Library of Congress system.

Introduction

The quality of policing is the quality of ruling.[1]

Otwin Marenin

My research on the militia, or non-security police, in Soviet society began in 1984, after the death of Leonid Brezhnev but before the advent of Mikhail Gorbachev and *perestroika*. At that time, the Communist Party and the Soviet state were still firmly in command of the society and economy of the USSR. By the late 1980s, the authority of the Party and its control apparatus lay in ruins – victims of Gorbachev's failed policy to reform the Communist Party and reinvigorate the Soviet state. The rapid decline of militia power during this crucial period suggests that state control in the Soviet Union had not been as great or as deeply rooted as previously thought.

Prior to *perestroika*, political and social order was dictated from above by the Communist Party; it did not originate in an institutionalized legal order. The power of the state manifested itself not only in governmental institutions, but in all parts of society. Militia personnel were key actors in the imposition of order from above, forcing citizens to comply with the state's ideological objectives. While the regular police worked to prevent the emergence of a civil society that would allow citizens to escape the ideological control of the Party, citizens were also complicit in their own control – obeying a police force that appeared impossible to oppose.

Crime rates were lower in the USSR than in other societies at comparable levels of economic development for most of its history. From the outside, the Soviet Union appeared to have achieved the impossible: a well-ordered, urbanized, multi-ethnic state. The labor unrest present in almost all industrialized societies was nearly unknown, private economic activity was suppressed and political protests and ethnic violence were infrequent. Much of the rural population lived in a feudal condition, tied to their agricultural collectives by the passport controls administered by the militia.

The order of the Soviet state was, however, realized at the cost of both economic stagnation – even decline – and the absence of civil liberties known in western societies, a cost that became more apparent as the regime entered its seventh decade. In an effort to revive the economy and political structure of the country, Gorbachev instituted his policy of *perestroika* in 1987. The reforms of the *perestroika* period would, contrary to Gorbachev's expectations, actually undo the structure of the Soviet state and prepare the way for its dissolution.

Gorbachev sought to promote citizen initiative in the Soviet Union, a goal that could be achieved only by diminishing police controls and Communist Party domination of daily life in Soviet society. Gorbachev naively believed that he could achieve two incompatible objectives when he promised his population democratization and order. Instead, he ended up rescinding the social contract that had provided the basis for consensus in Soviet society. Whereas the Soviet state had previously guaranteed its citizens concrete, if minimal, social benefits (including education, housing and medical care) and a social order secured by a pervasive militia apparatus, under *perestroika* the state not only reneged on its promise of full employment, it could not even guarantee the personal safety of its citizens.[2]

No social safety net was ever established for Soviet citizens dislocated by dramatic change in social and economic policy under Gorbachev. Compounding the problem of social dislocation, the limited democratization introduced in the USSR during the late 1980s permitted civil society, strangled by the Communist Party and its control apparatus for over seventy years, to reemerge in the Soviet Union. Democratization unleashed powerful forces in Soviet society: social and economic change accelerated, political and social order declined, organized religion revived and private economic activity, once controlled by the militia, was no longer suppressed.

Lacking resources and equipment and straining to operate in a more democratic fashion, the militia could neither control the emerging forces of civil society nor the rapidly expanding organized criminal activity of the late 1980s and early 1990s. Order in Soviet society proved elusive as crime increased in frequency and severity, labor strikes became common, unregulated economic activity proliferated and ethnic violence broke out with regularity. In contrast to its well-ordered past, the USSR had seemingly regressed to the Hobbesian state of nature where every man was in a continual state of war against his fellow man.

By the late 1980s, the Soviet state could no longer rely on the militia, whose morale and effectiveness had been destroyed by the corruption that had accompanied years of unlimited power. Throughout the decade the regime attempted to reinvigorate the militia apparatus by purging corrupt personnel, increasing police budgets and enhancing militia powers. Yet these efforts did little to increase the authority of the regular police or to improve it as an institution. By 1990, citizens had even less confidence in the militia than they had in the discredited Communist Party.[3] The militia, moreover, proved incapable of profoundly democratizing as Soviet society began to shed its authoritarian ways, remaining a tool of a state ideology that no longer commanded the respect of the populace. Lacking legitimacy and authority, policemen became victims of the very violence they sought to suppress.

Certain police leaders, unwilling to accept their loss of institutional authority, engineered the coup attempt of August 1991 in a desperate attempt to recover by force the authority lost by the control apparatus during *perestroika*. Because Soviet citizens no longer feared the control apparatus, however, the bungled effort of these leaders was doomed to failure before it began. In the absence of effective repression and a genuine basis for social cohesion, the Soviet state could not survive and rapidly dissolved following the failed coup.

The demise of the Soviet Union cannot, of course, be attributed exclusively to the collapse of the regime's control apparatus. Many experts had long contended that the socialist state was condemned to failure due to its failed ideology, unworkable economic system and legacy of massive repression. Yet the disintegration of the militia apparatus during *perestroika* facilitated the end of the Soviet state far earlier than acute observers, both inside and outside of the Soviet Union, had anticipated. Understanding the role the militia played in the Soviet regime is thus crucial to understanding the collapse of the Soviet state in 1991, as well as its perpetuation in power during the preceding seven decades.

Western scholars have yet to fully analyze the role of the Soviet militia in the formation and perpetuation, much less collapse, of the Soviet state. In the highly controlled society of the USSR, the militia represented the most immediate level of Communist Party and state control over the citizen, a control far more visible to the population than that exercised by the more frequently studied security police and military. If one accepts Otwin Marenin's maxim that an examination of the nature of a state requires analysis of its police and policing,[4] the role of the everyday police in the Soviet Union can tell us as much, or more, about the Soviet regime as can the functions of the KGB and the Soviet Army.

The KGB was a pervasive *political* presence in a society that kept virtually all individual expression in check. KGB personnel defended communist ideology and imposed the political will of the Soviet state on the citizenry, causing millions to die of starvation during the forced collectivization drive of the 1930s and millions of others to die in labor camps over the life of the regime, to mention but a few results of its work. Complementing both the political power of the KGB and the military might of the Soviet army were the everyday powers of the Soviet militia. Although the power of the militia was not as deadly as that of the security police or the armed forces, in many ways it was more pernicious because the militia continually monitored the minutiae of each citizen's daily existence, perpetually interfering in their economic, political and social lives.

The heart of police power in the USSR lay in the passport and registration system administered by the militia – making the regular police a more tangible presence in the lives of most Soviet citizens than the KGB. Police controls affected every aspect of Soviet citizens' daily lives: individuals could not move, take a vacation, travel abroad, register their cars or obtain a driver's license without authorization from the police. Prior to *perestroika*, no real impetus existed to change the authoritarian regulation of daily life in the USSR; almost until the end of the Soviet period, militiamen retained the right to intrude into many details of citizens' private lives, while citizens lacked adequate legal protection against police abuse.

Although the worst abuses of the security police of the Stalinist era were eliminated in the 1950s and 1960s, pervasive police controls of the militia were not addressed in a similar fashion. Consequently, the legacy of the Soviet police state is often more apparent in the daily policing which occurs in the successor states to the USSR today than in the structure and activities of their respective security police forces.[5]

This book surveys the role of the militia in the Soviet Union from the Bolshevik revolution of 1917 to the dissolution of the USSR in 1991, examining the structure, functions and operations of the regular Soviet police and its impact on Soviet society. The book seeks to prove that, far from being a question of purely historical or academic interest, the nature of Soviet policing is critically important to understanding the authoritarian legacy of the Soviet state in the newly independent states of the former USSR and the formerly communist nations of Eastern Europe.

The analysis of the evolution and operations of the militia presented in this book depicts Soviet police practice as a distinctive form of authoritarian policing. As Chapter 1 suggests, the Soviet militia combined the traditions of continental, colonial and communist policing in a mandate that exceeded that of police in most democratic and even traditional authoritarian societies. Backed by the power of the Communist Party, the Soviet militia not only suppressed individual rights, but imposed a specific state ideology on the population for over seven decades. As a tool of state ideology, the Soviet militia had more in common with the police of fascist states than those of nations without proclaimed ideologies. The analogy with fascist policing cannot go too far, however, because communist ideology assigned the regular police different functions than those awarded to the police by fascist ideology. The consolidation of the state and the economy in the USSR, for example, required police regulation of more aspects of everyday life than was the case in fascist societies.

Studies of twentieth-century policing have generally examined police in democratic societies, focusing either on police–state relations or police–citizen relationships.[6] Such analytical paradigms are possible because citizens in democratic societies enjoy an autonomy from the state that permits scholars to make a distinction between these two relationships. In an authoritarian society like the USSR, by contrast, the citizen did not enjoy autonomy from the state. Thus in order to explain the nature of policing in Soviet society, one must examine both the relationship between the militia and the Soviet state and the ways in which militia operations directly affected citizens in their everyday lives.

The natural temptation of scholars to overestimate the importance of their subjects is not an exaggeration in the case of the Soviet militia. The militia did not just control crime in the Soviet Union, it policed the entire society by means of far-reaching functions that touched the life of every citizen. In addition to shaping police practice throughout the expanse of the Soviet Union, the militia also served as the prototype for the police forces of the socialist countries of Eastern Europe. Although significant variations did exist among the police forces of socialist countries depending on a country's ethnic composition, the extent of permissible private economic activity and property ownership and the degree of political control exercised over civil society, all police forces in the Soviet bloc were structured on the model of the militia in the USSR.

Intricately tied to national politics, each General Secretary of the Communist Party of the Soviet Union established a different tone to policing. The militia were totalitarian in the Stalinist period (inspiring many theories of the twentieth-century police state), became authoritarian in the post-Stalinist period of Khrushchev, and attempted to democratize under Gorbachev. Although the USSR was far less of a police state under Brezhnev than under Stalin, the level of social and political control enforced by the Soviet militia was nevertheless greater than in most other industrialized societies during the Brezhnev era. Soviet citizens were simultaneously subordinated to a centralized, one-Party state, a state-owned and directed economy and an official ideology that sanctioned a higher degree of control over everyday life than is possible in most authoritarian regimes.

While the highly controlled Soviet state described in this book has now passed into history, the ultimate failure of its control apparatus – including the militia – to sustain the state does not diminish the influence and power wielded by the militia for the seventy-odd years of the Soviet Union's existence.

SOURCES

This study is heavily dependent on Soviet sources of the *perestroika* period. The reliance on Soviet materials was more or less a necessity, as western research on the militia has been extremely limited and direct access to original sources was impossible to arrange. In the mid-1980s, research for the manuscript depended heavily on interviews with émigré militia personnel living in the United States and Israel (see Appendix, p. 202 for descriptions of interviews and sample interview questions). The Communist Party archives of Smolensk *oblast'*, seized by the Germans in World War II, provided an understanding of militia conduct in the 1920s and 1930s and *samizdat* publications (unofficial writings circulated illegally in the Soviet Union) helped the author's analysis of the political dimensions of militia work. The author also combed libraries in the United States and Europe for scarce materials on militia structure, legislation and operations.

During the initial stages of the author's research, original source materials proved to be a particular problem because the Soviet regime considered the militia a taboo subject. Most research on the regular police conducted in the USSR was classified and Soviet newspapers were prevented from providing objective analyses of law enforcement. These conditions changed radically after Mikhail Gorbachev initiated his policy of openness known as *glasnost'*. Once a forbidden topic, the militia and its activities rapidly became issues of central concern to the Soviet public. Literally thousands of articles were published on policing in the USSR during the late 1980s, both in order to acquaint Soviet citizens with the violations of individual rights by policemen, as well as to pressure the militia to comply with the rule of law. Soviet journalists began to frankly discuss the difficulties of reforming a corrupt institution that consistently failed to observe legal norms, while foreign journalists were allowed to follow and film militia investigators for the first time.

During *perestroika* it became possible to conduct interviews with high-level militia personnel, as well as to obtain previously-classified legislation on the militia and to read militia periodicals and books previously inaccessible to foreigners. During visits to the USSR in 1987 and 1989, I found retired and active militia personnel willing to discuss their work and their research in the Ministry of Internal Affairs, the parent organization of the militia. The declassification of the Soviet militia magazine, *Sovetskaia militsiia*, also provided valuable information on the history of the militia, its operations and the attitudes of militiamen towards their work. Many of the researchers who were publishing in *Sovetskaia militsiia* in the late 1980s had access to archives that were closed to the author; their research provides the foundation for a great deal of the discussion of the militia's historical development found in this book.

ORGANIZATION OF THE BOOK

This book is divided into three parts. The first chapter seeks to establish a comparative framework within which one can usefully analyze the regular police of the Soviet Union. This chapter argues that the militia was highly successful as an agent of social control because it combined continental, colonial and communist police traditions – all of which emphasized the rights of the state over those of the citizen. Supported by an ideology that stressed the necessity of centralized state control, the structure, functions and operations of the Soviet militia were all conducive to maintaining the power of the Communist Party in the diverse regions of the former USSR.

Part I discusses the historical development of the militia since its creation immediately after the revolution and focuses particularly on militia–state and militia–Party relations. Chapter 2 discusses the birth of the militia under Lenin and Stalin, when regular policing was at its most political. Chapter 3 analyzes the important changes that occurred in policing during the post-

Stalinist period and looks at developments in law enforcement during the Khrushchev, Brezhnev and Gorbachev periods.

During seventy-four years of Communist rule in the USSR, the militia evolved from a small body that helped to establish the Soviet regime to a massive bureaucracy corrupted by years of nearly absolute power. Ultimately, it could not preserve the Soviet state. The historical discussion in chapters 2 and 3 nevertheless reveals that a capacity for institutional change existed even in the centrally controlled and hierarchical structure of the militia.

Part II focuses on the structure and personnel of the militia. Chapter 4 is devoted to the organization and management of the body – its internal structure, allocation of police responsibilities among the different branches of the militia, the mechanics of Party control and the militia's institutional response to *perestroika*. Chapter 5 examines the recruitment, training, pay and perquisites of militia personnel, paying particular attention to the ways in which the Communist Party controlled the work of militiamen and the reasons for endemic police corruption.

Part III focuses on the all-encompassing functions of the militia and their impact on the citizenry. Chapter 6 is a study of the law enforcement body at work and analyzes covert and overt policing, together with the variations in militia performance that were visible in different republics and among different ethnic groups. An examination of militia attitudes towards the rule of law, as well as police operations generated by a system in which the police was accountable to the Communist Party rather than to the citizenry, is also presented in this chapter.

Chapter 7 analyzes the militia's role in daily life and its responsibility for enforcing pervasive state regulations. The passport system, for example, was the central component of militia intervention in daily life, but this intervention was further expanded by means of licensing functions and controls over individual expression. Chapter 8 focuses on the control of the so-called "deviant" in Soviet society and the militia's efforts to make the citizen conform to the desired image of "Soviet man." As this chapter relates, deviants in the USSR included not only alcoholics, drug addicts, prostitutes and juvenile delinquents, but special categories created by the communist system such as "parasites." Chapter 8 makes clear that in the decades before *perestroika*, the significant powers of the Soviet militia contributed to the population's apparent conformity with the norms of behavior decreed by communist ideology.

Chapter 9 analyzes the diverse activities of the militia to control crime in the Soviet Union. The broad Soviet definition of criminal activity ensured that the police controlled not only internationally recognized forms of criminal conduct, but such activities as private enterprise and religious worship. This chapter argues that the low crime rates characteristic of the USSR for many decades were sustainable only when the social, political and economic controls of the communist system functioned, demonstrating that *perestroika* produced a sharp increase in criminal conduct and the number of organized criminal organizations.

Chapter 10 examines the political functions of the militia, particularly in the post-Stalinist period, focusing on how the militia used criminal law to curb religious practice, labor and ethnic protest, nationalist movements and human rights dissent. In the increasingly polarized society of *perestroika*, the militia could no longer rely primarily on criminal law, however, and resorted to increasingly futile, violent measures to control political activism.

The communist system that developed over many decades in the Soviet Union and Eastern Europe largely collapsed in the short period between 1989 and 1991. Yet the institutions which developed during the years of communist rule did not necessarily collapse along with the political system. Soviet police practice endures today in the structure, functions, operations and personnel of the law enforcement bodies of the newly independent states. The conclusion analyzes the social and political consequences of this legacy for the post-Soviet states and predicts that, by perpetuating the power of the state at the expense of the rights of individual citizens, the traditions of Soviet policing will impede democratization in many of these nations for years to come.

Part I

A comparative framework

1 The sources of Soviet policing

The study of the exercise of power and the establishment and maintenance of authority lie at the very heart of the historiography of empire.[1]

Law enforcement in the Soviet Union represented a unique form of authoritarian social control in which the police practices of continental European, colonial and communist societies were combined. The degree to which the Soviet militia intervened in the daily lives of the diverse peoples of the USSR can be explained by its amalgamation of these three distinct types of policing, making it a powerful instrument of state power. Its authority rooted in a single, centralized Party that enjoyed a monopoly of power, the militia undermined citizen autonomy and destroyed indigenous legal cultures throughout the USSR for over seven decades. As in many other authoritarian and colonial societies, however, the impunity of the Soviet police bred widespread corruption and inefficiency that mitigated its power.[2]

Viewed in comparative perspective (see Table 1.1), the communist police system of the USSR does not differ markedly from the police systems of continental European and colonial societies. Although Soviet police practice was in sharp contrast to the Anglo-Saxon model that developed in the United States and Britain, the wide-ranging functions and legitimacy of the militia were consistent with police practice in continental European societies of previous centuries. Accountability was to a central ruler – in the Soviet case, to the Communist Party rather than a ruling monarch. Communist policing also shared many attributes of the police tradition of western European empires, in which colonial police imposed imperial rule by force on foreign populations, often in regions less economically developed than the imperial center.

Rooted in both the continental and colonial traditions, communist policing nevertheless represented a unique type of policing whose scope and authority far exceeded that of earlier historical models. In contrast to these police models, the Soviet militia represented and enforced conformity with a state ideology that proscribed a wide range of human activity and justified a single party's monopoly of power. The ideological imperatives of state intervention in everyday life, as well as state ownership of the means of production, made the Soviet militia the defender of a broader range of state interests than

Table 1.1 Models of police systems

	Communist	*Anglo-Saxon*	*Continental*	*Colonial*
Legitimacy	Communist Party	Local government; based on law	Central government, ultimately the ruler (prior to twentieth century)	Colonial authority
Structure	Centralized; armed, militarized force	Decentralized; armed in US, unarmed in England	Centralized; armed, militarized force	Partly centralized; armed force
Function	Crime control only one function; primary emphasis on political and administrative functions; enforced state ideology	Crime control, order maintenance, some welfare and administrative responsibilities*	Crime control only one function, emphasis on political and administrative control	Crime control subsumed by concern for political/administrative control

* Whether or not the police should be assigned welfare responsibilities is a highly contested issue in the United States

Source: Adapted by the author from Table 2.1 in R.I. Mawby, *Comparative Policing Issues* (London: Unwin Hyman, 1990), 30, with additions on communist and Anglo-Saxon policing by Louise Shelley

existed in absolutist European states or empires. Curiously, after an initial period of great violence during which an immense police apparatus was established, Soviet police power was largely sustained by citizen complicity in police control – a characteristic that differentiates communist policing from earlier police models.

As John Locke understood, Soviet citizens lacked independence from the state in the absence of private property. Law in the USSR functioned not to grant rights to citizens, but to reinforce central state power. Moreover, communist ideology interpreted the Marxist dialectic to view conflicts as being inherently irreconcilable, with every situation bearing only one "right" and one "wrong" resolution. Such an interpretation both exacerbated social conflict and encouraged state suppression, often by force (that is, by the militia), of groups the state considered ideologically "wrong" and, hence, hostile to its interests.[3] Behavior that transgressed prescribed ideological norms was perceived as threatening the state; a great number of areas of life thus became criminalized and, consequently, subject to police authority.

THE HERITAGE OF CONTINENTAL POLICING

Of the three sources of Soviet policing – continental, colonial and communist – the continental tradition was the most important, providing the basis for the structure, mandate, and operational procedures of the Soviet militia, as well as its relationship to state authority. The police were first established as an institution when political power remained concentrated in the hands of absolute rulers in Europe, beginning with Louis XIV of France, who in 1667 sought to create an institution to "strengthen royal authority in all fields of activity."[4] The legitimacy of continental police did not derive from the people, as in a democracy, but from the authority and power of the ruler – usually a king or an emperor. These police were a centralized, militarized force subordinate to a state which, at least in principle, enjoyed a total monopoly of policing. (This monopoly endured until the mid-twentieth century, when private policing began to take hold in western Europe.)[5]

Continental police represented precisely the kind of absolutist power against which the American colonists, inspired by the ideas of the Enlightenment, rebelled. Influenced by such philosophers of the French Enlightenment as Voltaire and Montesquieu, the colonists attempted to create a democratic legal system devoid of the political controls wielded by the absolutist state. The balance of powers – the basis of the American legal system – was written into the American Constitution by the nation's founding fathers specifically to prevent the concentration of police power that existed in France prior to the French Revolution. From its inception, therefore, the decentralized institution of the American police was in structure and function fundamentally different from the continental police model adopted by Russia and, subsequently, by the Soviet Union.

The French Revolution eliminated authoritarian policing in France only temporarily; the centralized police power associated with French kings was soon supplanted by that of Napoleon. Other continental European rulers, sobered by the French revolution and subsequent revolutions on behalf of democracy which occurred throughout the nineteenth century, also sought to reinforce their power by means of the police. Monarchs such as Franz Joseph and the Russian tsars developed centralized police forces in order to maintain their power over ethnically diverse populations spread over large geographical areas. Knut Sveri describes rulers of such states as wanting "strong states with obedient and docile subjects . . . the police in states with these ideas were not servants of the law, but of the state."[6]

The Soviet Union inherited the absolutist police tradition of eighteenth- and nineteenth-century western Europe; unlike western European states, however, it failed to democratize its policing in the face of industrialization and urbanization. The police in the USSR was not simply a body responsible for crime control, but a vital component of the apparatus of the state. Consequently, the Soviet militia acquired much greater powers than those accorded police in Anglo-Saxon societies. As is discussed in depth in the following chapter, the Bolsheviks early laid the groundwork for an extensive militia bureaucracy, establishing numerous divisions to regulate diverse aspects of Soviet life. These functional divisions were similar to those which characterized German and French police of the nineteenth century and encompassed law enforcement duties with respect to political, social, economic and religious life.

From the German police tradition, the Soviet militia acquired such functions as inspections, public works planning, framing regulations for the public conduct of citizens and oversight of public assemblies and meetings. From the French police tradition, the militia acquired responsibilities regarding public health and hygiene, the control of dangerous substances, fire prevention and the monitoring of food quality and supplies.[7] While both German and French police monitored markets and food supplies, the Soviet regime greatly expanded the economic functions associated with traditional continental policing to accommodate the administration of an economy completely owned and managed by the state.[8]

The Soviet militia similarly inherited a highly politicized notion of policing which the tsarist police had originally borrowed from the French model. Like the French king and the Russian tsar, the Communist Party of the Soviet Union used the police as a guarantor of centralized state power. In the USSR, this notion translated into a legal requirement that the regular police assist the security police in whatever manner deemed necessary by the state. The militia's most fundamental tool of social control – registration of the population – was also derived from the police traditions of France and Germany.[9] First adopted by the tsar in the nineteenth century, the practice of population registration was subsequently refined by Stalin in the 1930s, eventually providing the militia with the power to control the movement of Soviet citizens.

With the Soviet militia assigned to control citizen mobility, crime, sanitation, markets and political activity – not to mention registration of printing presses and typewriters – virtually all citizen activity fell within the legitimate purview of the police (see Table 1.2). Such wide-ranging police functions enabled the Communist Party to maintain a monopoly of political and economic power and to control cultural and religious life.

OPERATIONAL PROCEDURES

Not only did the Soviet militia acquire its functions and structure from the police of absolutist continental European states, it acquired their mode of operations as well. The Soviet police, like its tsarist predecessor, followed the French model and relied on informers as the basis for the prevention and disclosure of crime.[10] Unlike France, however, Russia and, subsequently, the USSR did not go on to incorporate the legal ideals of the Enlightenment into its philosophy of government, thereby failing to establish a legal framework to regulate covert policing. Offered powerful inducements to comply and severe punishments for disobedience, few citizens of the USSR were capable of resisting the power of the police. Ultimately, most believed resistance to be futile as the police

Table 1.2 Functions of the Soviet militia as per 1973 USSR statute

1 To maintain order on streets, public places, highways, train stations and at mass gatherings.
2 To protect socialist property and the rights and interests of citizens, enterprises and organizations.
3 To take measures to prevent crime and other legal violations; to implement other measures such as searches and arrests; to counteract crime and reveal its causes.
4 To inform citizens and responsible persons of crime commission; to register and record crimes.
5 To take measures to suppress crime and initiate criminal cases and the *doznanie* (inquiry) into cases.
6 To fulfill requests of procurators and investigators and to help them in their investigations; to guard those arrested and detained; to provide convoy service for the arrested.
7 To fight alcoholism and drug addiction in cooperation with other governmental organizations; to inform an individual's place of employment regarding his/her misuse of drugs or alcohol.
8 To detect and enforce laws against antisocial and parasitic elements of Soviet society.
9 To license and enforce laws on guns, printing devices, seals and stamps and radioactive substances.
10 To administer the passport and registration system; to grant Soviet citizens permission to travel and reside in border zones.
11 To control address and information bureaus.*
12 To issue passports to Soviet citizens travelling abroad and register foreigners visiting and/or living in the USSR.
13 To locate individuals evading court sentences, parties to civil cases, draft evaders and missing persons; to cooperate with the Red Cross.
14 To maintain street and highway traffic control; to register and inspect automobiles.
15 To supervise exiles and those returning from exile; to aid in the job placement of former prisoners returning from labor camps.
16 To assist the security police in the battle against anti-state crime and undertake other measures to protect state security.
17 To assist military commissariats in draft registration and call-up for military service.
18 To assist victims of natural catastrophes.
19 To assist health organizations and veterinary surveillance organs in instituting quarantines.
20 To assist victims of crimes and accidents.
21 To find and return lost documents to citizens.
22 To enforce sanitary measures in streets, courtyards, public places and beaches.
23 To prevent poaching and violations of hunting and fishing regulations.
24 To promote legal propaganda among the population concerning the Soviet social order and the militia's fight against crime.**

* In the absence of published telephone directories, the militia maintained information bureaus where citizens could request the address and/or telephone numbers of other individuals.
** Militia members provided education to community members on Soviet law and on crime prevention, a responsibility that involved visits to schools, places of employment and housing complexes.
Source: 1973 statute on the militia, *Svod zakonov SSSR*, vol. 10 (Moscow, 1980), 238–41

apparatus would eventually prevail. Faced by such a massive system of social control, they were largely prevented from forming a civil society independent of the state.[11]

In contrast, civil liberties in France remained very much alive despite police reliance on informers. As Jean-Paul Brodeur has noted, such a strategy may threaten civil liberties, but it does not abrogate them. As articulated by Rousseau in *The Social Contract*, the concept of civil liberties was based on the idea that power should never be exercised in the absence of law.[12] Civil liberties formed a vital part of the legal framework that developed in France following the revolution of 1789 and served to protect citizens from unlimited state power.

In neither Russia nor the USSR did concepts of civil liberties and individual rights evolve into legal constraints on state power. Although various Soviet constitutions granted citizens of the USSR numerous rights – the Stalin constitution of 1936 was a model liberal document – these rights were not unequivocal. As Article 39 of the 1977 USSR constitution stated, the social-economic, political, and personal rights of citizens should not damage the interests of society or the state – an elastic provision that provided the militia tremendous discretion to protect state interests at the expense of the individual.

ACCOUNTABILITY

In the absolutist European states that gave rise to centralized policing, there existed a permanent imbalance between the rights of the state and the rights of the citizenry. The hierarchical continental police tradition consistently weighed power in favor of the state at the expense of the citizen. Over time, however, this imbalance became tempered by notions of law and civil liberties.

Fosdick, an early analyst of comparative policing, commented about German policing prior to World War I:

> The autocratic spirit of the German government is reflected in the imperviousness of the police to public opinion. The police department is a specialised institution in the details of which the people are held to have no proper interest.[13]

The idea of the *rechtsstaat*, a rule-of-law state, was a fundamental concept of nineteenth-century German jurisprudence. According to this legal model, individuals and institutions were subordinate to the written law. However impervious to public opinion, the police, as part of the administrative apparatus of the German state, were subordinate to the written law and were expected to follow it precisely. The authoritarian German police were accountable to the law but not the citizenry; the Soviet militia were accountable to neither.

There was no expectation in the USSR that officials or state institutions would adhere to the law and no enforcement mechanism to ensure compliance with the law or to protect the legal rights granted to citizens in the constitution. Only in the final years of the Soviet regime did the Communist Party leader Mikhail Gorbachev and other Soviet legal officials begin to advocate the ideal of a rule-of-law state. Yet even then, they did not propose a pure *rechtsstaat*, but a socialist *rechtsstaat* in which observance of the law was delimited by the needs of the socialist state.[14]

If the Soviet militia was not accountable to the law, however, it was accountable to the Communist Party, a party which promised its citizenry a greater degree of order than existed in western societies – one achieved at significant cost to the rights of the individual citizen. Prime among these costs was the denial of the right to choose a governing party; Article 6 of the USSR constitution granted hegemony to the Communist Party, making the party the leading and guiding force of Soviet society.[15]

In a *rechtsstaat*, knowledge of and access to the law are essential in order that the citizenry can hold the state accountable to its own laws. Such a situation did not prevail in the USSR, where Soviet officials enhanced their power by enacting laws known only to law enforcement bodies. Thousands of laws and regulations were published in the USSR "for official use only," many of which affected such aspects of daily life as the practice of religion, mobility and the registration of housing.[16] In a state where checks and balances on the exercise of state power were almost nonexistent, the presence of classified laws further expanded the power of the state at the expense of the citizenry. By controlling not only the institutions of coercion, but also access to the law, the Soviet state acquired a disproportionate advantage over the individual citizen. Laws enforced by the Soviet militia thus became the foundation of the so-called "administrative command system," making all Soviet subjects subordinate to the unknown and overarching authority of the state.

THE EVOLUTION OF CONTINENTAL POLICING

Although tsarist Russia was slow to change its norms of policing, three major developments of the nineteenth century had a profound impact on continental policing in western Europe: the rise of state paternalism, the advent of industrialization and urbanization and the birth of the modern bureaucratic state. All of these processes occurred earlier in western Europe than in Russia and their implications for policing were felt only during the final years of the tsarist autocracy. The Soviet militia began to respond to these phenomena in the early post-revolutionary period, but in a manner that further centralized rather than devolved state power.

The reaction of many nineteenth-century European monarchs to the challenge of the French revolution was state paternalism. Increasingly aware that the state must provide for its citizenry, enlightened monarchs determined that their citizens had to be protected, social welfare enhanced and society improved – all by means of state intervention.[17] Unlike democratic societies, the monarchs and not the citizens determined the services the latter would receive from the state.

The Soviet Union inherited this paternalism in its core ideology; the Marxist injunction "to each according to his needs, from each according to his ability" made the state the inevitable arbiter of the needs of its citizens. In order to realize this ideological objective, the Soviet state intervened in the lives of individual citizens to a significant degree, an intervention accomplished primarily by the militia apparatus in the name of public interest.[18]

In sharp contrast to the American constitutional tradition, no wall separated the citizen from the state and no area of personal activity remained outside the permissible scrutiny of the state. The Enlightenment concepts of citizenship and citizens' rights were never incorporated into communist ideology along with those of social welfare and societal improvement. As one Hungarian scholar describes the traditional police state, "[it] was not characterized by the under-regulation of life circumstances, but . . . by over-regulation and the principle *'regis voluntas supreme lex'* (the will of the emperor is the supreme law), which made it impossible for the subordinate to rise to citizen."[19]

Ideologically committed to a policy of rapid industrialization, the Bolsheviks faced the same challenge encountered by highly centralized western European governments in the previous century: maintaining centralized control in a period of rapid social change. Early Soviet leaders sought to industrialize their society rapidly without devolving power from the central state to the working class or industrial managers. Continental policing, with its combination of broad regulatory functions and a coercive centralized bureaucracy, suited their needs in the same way it had suited those of nineteenth-century European monarchs. The all-encompassing militia apparatus that emerged in the immediate postrevolutionary period proved an ideal instrument for maintaining centralized control over Soviet society when Stalin launched his drive for rapid industrialization in the late 1920s. Whereas western European states did not exert hegemonic control over the forces of economic development and were forced to accommodate the interests of a rising working class, the powers of the Soviet militia – particularly its power over citizen mobility – prevented the rise of an autonomous working class and enabled the Soviet state to control the processes of industrialization and urbanization to a greater degree than was the case in Europe in the 1800s.

Although industrialization would change political conditions, the paternalism adopted by western European monarchies was initially achieved without a devolution of state power. On the contrary, the state's assumption of such responsibilities as public health, market supervision and banking regulation in the nineteenth century extended state control to areas of life previously outside the reach of central governments and marked the advent of the modern bureaucratic state. By assigning many of the functions of the new bureaucratic state to police forces directly subordinate to them – especially those concerning the regulation of commerce and industry – European rulers were able to enhance their authority at a time when the state was challenged by competing sources of power in the form of industrialists and the urban working class.[20]

With the collapse of the last great empires and the demise of fascism in the twentieth century, European political systems moved towards decentralized state power, a change that significantly influenced police practice. The legacy of absolutist policing remains evident in the centralized and hierarchical nature of western European police forces, but the range of police functions has been reduced and their accountability to the citizenry increased. The French and Dutch police, for example, retain a wider range of functions than do their Anglo-Saxon counterparts, but these functions are far fewer than in previous centuries.[21]

The continental police model never went through a similar transition in the USSR, remaining intact until the day the Soviet Union collapsed in August 1991. The intrusive police power of the Soviet state first came into question during the last years of the Soviet regime, only to unravel the power of the central government.

COLONIAL POLICING

In addition to its continental heritage, Soviet police practice incorporated many important elements of colonial police tradition. The enduring influence of the conquest phase, the type and quality of recruit attracted to the service and colonial attitudes towards race and political matters all colored police behavior in the non-Slavic areas of the USSR.[22] It is important to note that this aspect of communist policing was not universal within the communist bloc. Absent in Poland and East Germany, colonial police attitudes were nevertheless present in the USSR, the multi-ethnic state of Yugoslavia and, to a lesser extent, Bulgaria with its considerable Turkish minority.

The blending of continental and colonial police functions in the USSR permitted a hierarchical, centralized police system to execute orders through a vast territory populated by numerous – and diverse – ethnic groups. Precisely because the Soviet militia represented the most immediate point of contact between the central state and the citizenry, analysis of its role in the non-Slavic areas of the USSR, and even in the non-Russian Slavic republics, is crucial in order to achieve an accurate understanding of the Soviet state and its exercise of power.

The Soviet Union occupied very much the same territory as did the Russian empire. Although non-Russian areas of the tsarist empire were clearly occupied territory, the consequences of tsarist colonialism were less dramatic than those of Soviet colonialism. The nature of the tsarist state and the absence of the technology that facilitated control over so vast a territory in the twentieth century meant that indigenous cultures, legal systems and local elites of occupied territories were largely left intact. The Russian empire represented a traditional absolutism in which the relationship between citizen and ruler entailed fewer benefits and fewer obligations than the authoritarianism of its Soviet successor.

When the Bolsheviks reconquered the vast empire of the tsars in the 1920s, a fundamental change occurred in these territories. Residents of Central Asia, the Caucasus and the Far East were no longer merely ruled by Slavic occupiers, they became citizens of the Soviet state and subject to the same social contract as all other Soviet citizens. Against their will, they exchanged personal liberty and the preservation of their native cultures for the benefits of the communist state: education, medical care and full employment. The costs of integration into the Soviet state were extremely high; for some peoples, such as the Kazakhs, it resulted in the elimination of 40 percent of their native population.[23]

Although it inherited the Russian imperial tradition, Soviet colonialism differed in key respects from traditional colonial models. In the first place, colonial police of European powers such as Britain operated outside of the home country, generally in occupied areas not contiguous to the imperial center. (The British first developed a colonial police force in Ireland and subsequently applied this model to such distant parts of the empire as India and Africa.[24]) The Soviet militia, by contrast, operated as a colonial police force within the home country (Russia) and in areas contiguous to it. Second, colonialism in the USSR had two distinct components, one ideological and one nationalistic: colonial police in the Soviet Union enforced both Marxist ideology and Great Russian dominance.

Despite these crucial differences, the functions of the Soviet police were markedly similar to those of the police in European empires of the previous century. As R.I. Mawby has noted with respect to the British empire, law enforcement in the USSR was "transplanted . . . to delegitimise indigenous customs, to impose centralised social control and to incorporate local society as a branch of imperial society."[25] Similar to other imperial police forces, the Soviet militia focused less on preventing and detecting crime in "colonized" non-Russian areas and more on protecting state property and maintaining social and political control. Because all threats to the political order were perceived as impinging upon the power of the imperial state, law enforcement in these areas became highly politicized. In areas where it operated as a colonial police force, the continental character of the militia thus became even more pronounced. Militia in these areas were uninterested in policing by consent and openly served the interests of the central state. Indigenous legal customs were outlawed, Islamic leaders who meted out traditional justice were purged and traditional customs alien to Marxist ideology were banned. Most significant, perhaps, emphasis on central control resulted in the elimination of traditional means of dispute resolution.[26]

The authority of the Soviet state was maintained outside of Russia by means of both legislation and an administrative structure that incorporated the various Soviet republics into the Slavic legal culture of the imperial center. Soviet law did not accommodate the indigenous cultures of the USSR in the least; local societies were forced to acquire and observe the legal norms that emanated from the center. The entire legal apparatus of the USSR was headquartered in Moscow, where all policy was developed and communicated to the republics. All legislation adopted throughout the Soviet republics had to conform to the Fundamental Principles of Legislation promulgated at the all-Union level, with the principles of criminal, labor, and corrective labor law of the USSR, together with the USSR statute on the militia, adopted almost without modification at the republic level.

Soviet policing can be characterized as colonial not because the militia imposed alien legal norms on foreign populations, but because police leadership on the republic level followed a conscious personnel policy that favored Slavs. The central government in Moscow appointed Russians or Russified Slavs to key positions in all governmental, Communist Party and legal agencies throughout the country. These positions were part of the *nomenklatura* system of Party-controlled appointments that required approval by senior Party officials in Moscow, who supervised even routine appointments of law enforcement personnel in the republics. One such appointment was a Deputy Minister of the Interior (the ministry responsible for the militia), a post always filled by a Slav. This key individual controlled personnel appointments and communications with Moscow, ensuring that the local staff and policies of the police in that republic adhered to the policies and laws promulgated in Moscow.

CONSEQUENCES OF COLONIAL POLICING

Colonial police suffer from the same problems of legitimacy which plague police in any divided society. As Ronald Weitzer has noted with respect to British police in Northern Ireland: "the police may be able to mechanically reproduce order and control, but they do not enjoy the confidence of one or more sections of the society."[27] In a colonial society, the dominant (ruling) group sees the police as upholding their values (and supremacy), while inhabitants of occupied territories see them as the oppressor – an accurate description of the situation in all republics of the former Soviet Union except Russia. Yet even in Russia, autonomous republics and areas inhabited by non-Slavs felt themselves subject to colonial rule. Russians or Russified Slavs assumed an important role in law enforcement in every part of the USSR and, typical of imperial elites, saw themselves as representing a superior culture.

The effects of colonial policy in the USSR were similar to those observed in other empires: destruction of traditional legal cultures and forms of social control, together with rapid growth in corruption. Deprived of their native legal cultures, corruption became an effective means by which indigenous populations could resist the domination of the central state. Just as provincial cities in France under the *ancien régime* acquired some degree of independence from Paris by, in Mawby's words, "buying the offices of lieutenant-general and appointing their own officials."[28] Central Asian republics acquired a certain autonomy by bribing high-level officials of the Ministry of Interior during the Brezhnev era. The large bribes proffered to the Deputy Minister of Interior, Iurii Churbanov (Brezhnev's son-in-law) helped these republics secure a degree of independence they could achieve in no other manner. The investigation of Churbanov and the Central Asia "mafia" that followed Brezhnev's death signalled, in the opinion of many analysts, an attempt to reinstate the control of the central government over colonial areas whose subordination had been seriously eroded by corruption.

Militia power collapsed in many parts of the former USSR prior to the dissolution of the Soviet state because the police proved incapable of maintaining order in regions of interethnic conflict. As was the case in other empires, once the power and resolve of the imperial center began to wane, colonial police became physical targets of the hostility of native populations. In the Soviet case, this hostility was directed against Marxist ideology as well as Russian domination. Oblivious to the resentment many national groups bore the central state, the Soviet government was unprepared for violent assaults on the militia. Its failure to withdraw law enforcement personnel from arenas of overt hostility made the transition away from communism more violent than was otherwise necessary, both before and after the collapse of the USSR.

COMMUNIST POLICING

As noted earlier, the communist state did not accept the Enlightenment idea that the state represents the will of its citizens;[29] instead, it molded its subjects into the desired citizenry. As agents of Soviet ideology, the militia enforced an all-encompassing view of society in which political, economic, social and cultural activity was subordinate to the state. Despite intense efforts to create the "new Soviet man" out of the ethnically diverse populations of the USSR, many citizens remained loyal to their respective national traditions instead of the Marxist-Leninist ideology promulgated by the imperial center. In the absence of conformity to the socialist ideal, the Soviet state relied on the militia and the threat of criminal law to induce it. The enormous role of criminal law in the Soviet legal and law enforcement systems is a distinctive characteristic of communist policing and can be directly traced to the emasculation of civil law and property rights achieved by the socialization of the means of production.

The Soviet regime abolished most forms of individual property known in capitalist societies following the October 1917 revolution and imposed strict limits on the property it did tolerate. Individuals were proscribed from owning more than one home and were permitted to farm only small private plots of land, with sharp limits on animal ownership. Soviet citizens were thus deprived of one of the most important protections that citizens of western

European states enjoy against the power of the central government: private property.[30]

Following the Enlightenment, law in many European societies expressed individual rights and limited the power of the state *vis-à-vis* the individual. In communist states, by contrast, law became an instrument of state power: the legal system was concerned not with the division, but the concentration of power in the state. Lenin himself was primarily concerned with the efficacy of law – a notion at odds with western understanding of the rule-of-law state – and Soviet law enforcement emphasized results (arrests and prosecutions) rather than application of established legal procedure.

The fundamental tenet of Marxism – that private property is the basis of capitalist exploitation – came to justify the single-party rule of the Communist Party and the enormous expansion of state power associated with this rule. The centralized, hierarchical structure of the Party shaped the organization of law enforcement in the USSR and left no room for decentralized policing or local autonomy. As executors of the ruling party, the Soviet militia functioned first to create and then preserve the political and economic systems of the communist state.

Because the state owned and managed the entire economy, functions that are entrusted to administrative bodies in capitalist societies became the responsibility of the militia in the USSR. The militia's enforcement of laws regulating the economy resulted in a more passive citizenry than is the case in societies where individuals do not depend on the state for employment and, consequently, unemployment is not punishable by law. Law, or more precisely criminal law, became a more important vehicle of the police in the Soviet Union than in countries where the state does not enjoy such a startling combination of economic and political power.

Central to Marxism is a vision of society in class terms, a world in which human relations are defined by individuals' social origins and not their personal attributes. Law enforcement in the USSR was permeated by this perspective; through the prism of dialectical materialism, the state viewed the world as polarized, conflict irreconcilable, and compromise impossible.[31] Force rather than negotiation became the primary legitimate means of resolving conflicts of interest in the communist state, transforming the militia into a mechanism for the suppression of conflict.

Marxism's antipathy towards religion similarly influenced communist policing. When atheism became the official philosophy of the Soviet state, organized religion was suppressed and the practice of religion and religious education were severely circumscribed. The Soviet militia was required to arrest religious figures who conducted unauthorized services, seek out and confiscate unauthorized printing presses used for religious purposes and even locate parents who provided their children religious educations (sometimes going so far as to initiate proceedings to deprive religious parents of their parental rights).

Cultural life in the USSR likewise came under the control of the state and, consequently, fell under the jurisdiction of the militia. Artistic expression was not intended to be free, but to serve the state and express the socialist ideal. After Stalin adopted socialist realism as official state policy in 1934, art, literature and other forms of cultural expression were forced to conform to the criteria of socialist realism; those who deviated from these standards were subject to sanctions. While the state had numerous means at its disposal to enforce conformity short of law enforcement, the militia was occasionally used to punish, or harass, artists who strayed from forms of expression authorized by the state.

CONCLUSION

By adding an ideological imperative to the defense of state power on which the continental and colonial police traditions were based, communist policing represented a unique form of authoritarian social control. More ideological than the police of most authoritarian societies, the Soviet militia served not only to maintain social and political control, but to enforce citizen compliance with communist ideology. Covert policing and pervasive militia penetration of daily life meant that little social activity occurred outside the scope of state regulation. Although Soviet law enforcement shared many similarities with that of ideological fascist regimes – both fascism and communism intervened in religious life and many spheres of civil society – the Soviet system required far greater controls over economic life.

The history of the USSR demonstrated that an authoritarian state can be perpetuated without the use of great force if the individual has already been denied autonomy. In contrast to the police forces of other authoritarian regimes, the Soviet militia became less brutal over time. As the terror of the Stalin years receded, citizens became complicit in their own control, thereby sustaining police power and making duplicity the heart of the state–citizen relationship. Despite the unprecedented array of police power amassed by the Soviet state, police controls eventually proved powerless before nationalism, failing to prevent the dissolution of the last remaining empire of the twentieth century.

Part II

The historical development of the militia

2 The formation of the militia

> The militia is a mirror of Soviet power through which the population can judge Soviet rule.
>
> M.I. Kalinin

The evolution of law enforcement in the first decades of Soviet rule would determine the organization and activities of the militia until the dissolution of the Soviet state. The initial populism of the early Bolsheviks soon gave way to the realities of maintaining power and, early in the postrevolutionary period, a structured police force emerged whose personnel and functions reflected the state's socialist ideology. A crucial relationship between the state and the citizen was established at this time: the state, in the guise of the ruling Communist Party, assumed responsibility for the regulation of the lives of its citizens. This relationship produced a pattern of state intervention in citizen activity that would characterize Soviet policing in subsequent decades and leave an important legacy for the post-Soviet states.

Although the institution of the tsarist police was destroyed after the revolutions of 1917, a new police force was established along continental lines almost immediately. In addition to preserving the continental character of the tsarist police, an element of colonial policing was soon introduced as the Bolshevik government began to assert its domination over the reconquered territories of Central Asia, the Caucasus and Siberia.

From its earliest days, the militia acted as an accomplice to the security police – known in its earlier incarnations as the Cheka and GPU (State Political Directorate). Both police organizations worked to uphold the rule of the Communist Party, then a small organization challenged simultaneously by political and ethnically-based oppositions. The militia did not lead the attack on the political opposition after the revolution, nor did it take charge of the campaign to liquidate kulaks and collectivize agriculture in the late 1920s. Nevertheless, it participated in mass repressions at these crucial moments of early Soviet history, gaining wide-ranging institutional authority which it used to shape the population to the demands of the state.

LENIN YEARS AND THE NEW ECONOMIC POLICY

The first years of the Soviet regime (1917–26), marked the birth of the militia under Lenin and its early development during the New Economic Policy (NEP), which commenced in mid-1921. This period saw the Bolshevik leadership create a new police apparatus that was ideologically different from, but similar in purpose and status to the institution it replaced.

The Bolsheviks did not step into a policing vacuum. After the overthrow of the tsar in 1917, the Provisional Government attempted to establish a democratic, accountable police system, an effort soon quashed by the Bolsheviks. Attempts to replace the tsarist police were initiated as early as February 1917, when the Mensheviks began to form militias at factories, using a ratio of 100 militiamen for every 1,000 workers.[1] These worker police units, which cooperated with the paramilitary detachments of the Red Guard, soon spread from their point of origin in Petrograd to other major industrial cities.

During the first months of 1917, the new police force operated in a multiparty state. The government attempted to democratize the force by establishing strict controls on the use of arms, banning tsarist police agents and establishing community-oriented policing.[2] The latter was implemented by urban patrols that used residents to maintain law and order in their immediate neighborhoods: idealistic young people devoted to the new order engaged in such community policing. This transitional police force markedly differed from the Soviet force that would soon develop, its populist, community-oriented approach dissolving in the face of opposition to Bolshevik rule.

The first legal act of the new state, issued only days after the Bolsheviks assumed power, established the *raboche-krestiianskaia militsiia* (workers' and peasants' militia).[3] This immediate attention to the formation of a police force reflected the emphasis the Bolsheviks would subsequently place on police power. Bolshevik expectations of the militia were greater than those the autocracy had had of the tsarist *politsiia*. Whereas the tsarist regime viewed the police as merely maintaining the status quo, the Bolsheviks had an activist view of policing and saw the militia as an agent of social change.[4] Despite the importance attached to the militia, during the Civil War and the 1920s the Bolsheviks were unwilling and unable – for ideological as well as financial reasons – to commit the human and material resources necessary to acquire a distinguished militia force.

Law enforcement personnel after the revolution came from the lowest rung of the social and educational ladder.[5] The rank-and-file Russian police of the autocracy had also come from the lowest element of tsarist society, not far removed from those they controlled. Poorly educated, often drunk and of dubious moral character, police personnel with whom citizens had the most contact gave the repressive tsarist police a deservedly bad name. (Supervisory personnel, by contrast, were often drawn from the large Russian noble class.)

The sudden name change from *politsiia*, the title of the dreaded tsarist institution, to the workers' and peasants' militia altered neither the quality of policemen nor the fundamental relationship between the police and the state. The tsarist legacy remained: the militia was a part of the political control apparatus of the state; it simply executed the mandate of a dominant party rather than a hereditary monarch.

Although a new police force was established immediately after the October revolution, the institutionalization of a large standing militia was not an immediate objective of the Bolshevik leadership. Consistent with the ideological premise that the state and its institutions would wither away under communism, the government first made efforts to involve large numbers of private citizens in policing (a tradition subsequently revived by Khrushchev and reenforced by certain of his successors). In Petrograd, for example, *druzhinniki* (auxiliary citizen militia) worked under Red Guard supervision. Serving six-month rotations, these armed citizens tried to liquidate armed gangs, burglars and other categories of criminal offenders. Men aged 18 to 40 helped fulfill other militia responsibilities, but, like the community patrols, they were unable to maintain social order.[6]

Combined efforts of the Red Army and the Red Guard – the other approach to non-professional policing attempted by the Bolshevik regime – also failed.[7] Serious problems of order, the great demands of the Civil War period and the requirement of steady service made many Red Guard and military personnel ill-suited for the demands of ordinary policing. Many performed their duties reluctantly; others turned out to be criminals who had volunteered in order to legitimize their status. Lack of professional policing only aggravated already serious problems of social order in rural as well as urban areas. Seeking law enforcers more willing to serve in the countryside, the government suggested that rural militia personnel be elected rather than drafted. This populist approach proved unsatisfactory because elected personnel did not show sufficient vigor in combatting the kulaks and speculators whom the regime defined as the principal opponents of Soviet rule.

The greatest drawbacks to these makeshift law enforcers were their political unreliability and inability to maintain order in either the cities or the countryside. Even Moscow militia and Red Guard units failed to respond forcefully to anarchist groups. In Tambov in the spring of 1918, Red Guards supported the anti-Bolshevik city government.[8] Given such unreliable police performance, the communist leadership concluded that private citizens, even under Red Guard supervision, were unsuited to instill order in areas of great social unrest. The idea of a popular police, responsive and accountable to the local community, was abandoned. Instead, a complex, centrally controlled organization was founded and grew rapidly. In 1918 the Bolsheviks established a full-time police force, building on the force created by the Provisional Government and the strong militia organizations that had formed at major urban factories.[9]

THE STRUCTURE OF SOVIET POLICING

To enhance its reliability, the militia was militarized in 1919; military training was introduced and forces were made available for the Civil War front. As Neil Weissman has observed: '[t]he April 1919 militarization, which was carried even further by subsequent decrees, indicated the degree to which the Soviet government had moved away from its original intent in ultra-democratic policing by the citizenry itself.'[10] Rather than institute citizen policing, the government returned to the continental police tradition that had characterized the tsarist regime.

The state then took major steps to give the newly formed militia the kind of structure needed to instill order in the shattered society of postrevolutionary Russia. With only limited modifications, this initial structure survived the entire Soviet period. The mid-1918 congress of the representatives of state executive committees (at which Lenin was the keynote speaker) assumed a decisive role in the development of the militia apparatus; the congress adopted a resolution authorizing the establishment of the militia on all territories of the Russian Federated Republic, including cities and rural areas.[11] At this time the militia, initially under the control of the local Soviet of Workers' and Peasants' Deputies, came under dual subordination – reporting to both the local governmental structure and the Commissariat of Internal Affairs (NKVD). The NKVD was granted responsibility for overall direction of militia activities (see Table 2.1). In a pattern common to the continental police tradition, however, central ministerial and Party control proved far greater than that exercised by local governments.

Table 2.1 The formation of the militia (1917–26)

1918:	Popular policing abandoned.
	Dual subordination of militia to central ministry and local government.
	Hierarchical structure and specialization of militia established.
	Territorial and transport militias created.
	Criminal investigative unit (*ugolovnyi rozysk*) established.
1924:	Departmental guard established.
1925:	All militia responsibilities consolidated in NKVD (People's Commissariat of Internal Affairs).

Following the 1918 congress, a complex system of command was established. In the USSR function followed organization, reflecting the great importance attached to centralized control and command in the Soviet system. The intense centralization of the state, already apparent in the immediate post-revolutionary period, resulted in the central militia administration being established in Moscow. In this respect, the Soviet experience was similar to that of other centralized absolutist states. In Imperial Japan, as David Bayley has observed, the police also developed from the "top down by explicit acts of central government."[12]

Although control was centralized, police regulation extended into the immediate residential district of every Soviet citizen. A complex chain of command descended from the national headquarters in Moscow to the republic level, the regional level and, finally, the local level, with the latter divided into districts that could be more manageably policed. The thirty-six people who initially ran the central office in Moscow with responsibility for criminal investigations, information and supplies would have difficulty imagining the size and complexity of the militia organization that would soon exist.[13]

In its initial organizational period the militia was divided into two particular forms: territorial and transport militias. Specialization was by function as well as by geographic area. By 1920, five specialized types of militia units existed: urban, rural, river, criminal investigative and industrial and railway (transport) militias (see Table 2.1).[14] The first centralized unit to be created was the *ugolovnyi rozysk* (criminal investigative branch), established in late 1918. The formation of this unit was the logical reaction of a society in which revolution and civil war had made crime a viable means of survival for many citizens. A merging of social and political functions was evident in this body, whose responsibilities included not only the fight with ordinary crime, but also politically motivated banditry. For example, the militia was charged with attacking such capitalist activities as speculation (the purchase and resale of goods at a profit) and black marketeering. In this manner, criminal law was used to institutionalize the socialist economic system.[15]

Despite the growth of the state's administrative bureaucracy at this time, the Russian Soviet Federated Socialist Republic (the name of the country prior to the establishment of the USSR in December 1922) was in such chaos that it had little money to run even the most essential of state operations – the army and the Cheka (security police). The militia, an organization of much lower priority, received some funding from the People's Commissariat of Internal Affairs, but relied mostly on local budgets for its support. Yet financial obstacles did not necessarily hinder its growth; the departmental guard (*vedomstvennaia militsiia*), for example, formed in 1924 to protect state institutions and restrict access to state installations, was funded by the organizations it protected. In 1925, the militia and the security police were merged in the nearly omnipotent NKVD and crime control was subordinated to political functions.[16] Despite the merger, however, the militia retained an explicit crime control function.

STAFFING THE MILITIA

State ideology determined the staffing of the militia, committing the state to a police by class origin would represent the desired socialist order. The initial formation of the militia out of Provisional Government police forces and organizations at factories gave the Soviet government the needed personnel. In accordance with Lenin's initial plan, 95 percent of the militia were of worker or peasant origin, with some regions having a higher percentage of workers, others of peasants.[17] There was no expectation, as there is in democratic societies, that the police would identify with the values of the many in the community. Instead, the militia functioned to impose the ideology of the central state on the citizenry.

Most militia leaders in this early period lacked law enforcement experience; the selection of leaders evidenced the body's militarization. Those chosen for supervisory positions had distinguished themselves in the fight against political opponents and armed criminals during the first years of the postrevolutionary period. Some tsarist police officials were even allowed to serve on the new force, as only they had the expertise to fight the criminals who were undermining the social order – a fact the Soviet leadership did not publicize. Even after the creation of the Soviet militia and the criminal investigation service, however, the security police apparatus continued to be used to fight crime.[18] Not until the Stalin years did a professional and entrenched Soviet-trained bureaucracy govern the militia.

The new militia was urban based and many rural areas remained unserved by the police. Rural areas and territories recently freed from the Whites (supporters of the tsarist regime) suffered particularly acute staffing problems as the fragile Soviet state had difficulty manning both an army and a militia. In 1919, when numerous militia cadres left for the front, women communists and former factory workers joined the militia, first in Petrograd and then in other cities. Archives reveal that women substituted for men without arousing citizen complaints.[19]

Law enforcement personnel during this initial period were expected to be sensitive to community opinion; they were instructed to be polite to citizens, to avoid hounding them when verifying documents and to help the blind across the street. Yet at the same time they were ordered to show little tolerance for the possible offender, as respect for the enforcers of Soviet law was too important to be jeopardized.[20]

The links between the militia and the military were evident from the earliest years of the Soviet period. During the Civil War period (1917–21), one-third of the Moscow militia went to the front; the corresponding figure for Petrograd was one-quarter. Militia ranks expanded to several hundred thousand individuals during the war as the law enforcement body assisted the army in suppressing political opposition to the Bolshevik regime. Demand for new cadres escalated and the Soviet state was not in a position to be selective. Party members remained few in number and the majority of militiamen were illiterate. Despite the initiation of basic educational programs among militia personnel, poor living conditions and calls from the front limited the potential for improving personnel qualifications. The militia had trouble retaining the few qualified members it had – distinguished personnel were often transferred to "more important work" in the security police.[21]

In 1921 the Civil War terminated in the western regions of the Russian Soviet Federated Socialist Republic, permitting the diminution of militia ranks, a financial necessity in light of the limited resources of the new Soviet

state. Drastic personnel reductions ensued. According to the national archives, the 1992 militia was 60 percent smaller than that of 1920.[22] Even after
these reductions, however, a significant militia force remained. As Neil
Weissman has documented, "[i]n 1921 the government mandated reductions
first to 333,665 and then to 210,000;" at the lower figure, this force was still
approximately 20 percent larger than that which existed in the United States
at that time.[23]

These cadre reductions permitted the purging of counterrevolutionaries and
criminal elements. When the militia was subsequently rebuilt, the state
acquired a more educated force by recruiting demobilized Red Army soldiers.
Unlike hiring practices in democratic societies, ideological concerns determined personnel selection in the Soviet militia; class background was more
important than individual qualifications. In 1921, 10–15 percent of the militia
force was estimated to be illiterate and an additional 35 percent, semi-literate.
After training programs were initiated, the NKVD reported in 1922 that
complete illiteracy in the militia had been reduced to 2.6 percent and semi-
illiteracy to 11 percent.[24]

After the Civil War, the Soviet authorities could again consider, in
Weissman's words, "their commitment to a professional police and begin to
address the issues of peacetime law enforcement."[25] Training programs
served not only to improve literacy rates, but to inculcate Party values.
Political domination of policing, an issue of concern in many democratic
societies, was intentionally institutionalized within the law enforcement
structure. Political commissars were used in the militia, as in the military, to
spread communist ideas and enhance political control. With ideological
control thus institutionalized, the militia was forced to be responsive to the
demands of the Communist Party. Yet few Party members actually joined the
militia because the Party still could not spare its limited cadres for work in
bodies of less political centrality than the military or the security police.
Byelorussian statistics reveal that in 1925, only 10 percent of the militia
bureaucracy were Party members and only a further 2 percent belonged to
the Komsomol.[26]

In 1922, funding of the militia was transferred to local governments and
central government support was reduced.[27] The average monthly wage of a
militiaman in a provincial city in 1924 was 22 rubles (at the official exchange
rate of that time, USD 11), while that of an industrial worker was 55 rubles
(USD 27.50). Low pay and difficult work conditions resulted in high
personnel turnover and poor health. Illness demonstrably increased with a
militiaman's length of service; nearly 40 percent of those on the Moscow
police force for more than a year were chronically ill.[28]

FUNCTIONS OF THE MILITIA

The militia functions articulated in the first years of Soviet rule remained
constant throughout the entire Soviet period. These functions were to prevent

crime, maintain social order, ensure the population's adherence to the ideology of the socialist state, repress political opposition, enforce sanitary and health measures, conduct legal education, perform regulatory functions and oversee citizen registration (see Table 2.2). These varied duties, as described in depth in Chapter 1, represented a combination of the functions of continental, colonial and communist police. Territorial units of the militia performed the full range of militia functions in cities, settlements and highways, whereas the responsibilities of the transport militia were more circumscribed. The latter was assigned social order and crime control responsibilities on trains, boats and air transport, but lacked the educational and licensing functions of the territorial militia.[29] Special branches were established within both the territorial and transport divisions to perform the diverse duties assigned to them.

Table 2.2 Functions of the militia as of February 1925

---

1 To preserve revolutionary order, protect citizens and their property.
2 To execute decrees, laws and directives.
3 To guard places of confinement.
4 To fight crime.
5 To fight unsanitary conditions in residential areas.
6 To serve the population: to give out identification documents, to certify identity, receive money orders and packages and replace lost documents.
7 To implement administrative laws and impose fines.
8 To register and train village officers.
9 To ensure observation of cattle-grazing rules.
10 To provide assistance to:
    a) The People's Commissariat of Agriculture, to prevent lawless cutting of forests and illegal hunting and fishing;
    b) The People's Commissariat of Army and Navy, to register horses, military transport and maintain order at assembly points;
    c) The People's Commissariat of Finance, to combat violations of excise rules and aid in the collection of taxes;
    d) The People's Commissariat of Foreign Trade, to assist in customs functions;
    e) The People's Commissariat of Justice, to execute court sentences in civil cases, deliver notices and summons, levy fines and court costs, execute sentences and carry out bans on residence in particular areas; and
    f) The People's Commissariat of Railroads, to impose fines on individuals without tickets.

Source: M.N. Eropkin, *Razvitie organov militsii v sovetskom gosudarstve* (Moscow: Vysshaia Shkola MOOP, 1967), 44

As this list indicates, the political and economic functions of the Soviet militia predominated in the early postrevolutionary period. From the first days of the Soviet regime, the newly constituted militia worked alongside the army and "was at the disposal of the local Chekas (special organs of repression) insofar as it was essential to the discharge of their responsibilities."[30] This statement of Robert Conquest indicates that from the moment of its inception, the militia was tied to the worst repressions of the Civil War and Stalinist period. Bolshevik leadership, fearing foreign intervention as well as domestic opposition from the Whites and the Basmachi (a Central Asian Islamic-based opposition), used the militia – together with the secret police – as a fundamental weapon against its opponents. This strategy supports David Bayley's insight that "[c]riminal insecurity does not impel police into politics; only political insecurity does."[31]

A fundamental difference exists between the politicization of the Soviet militia in this period and the use of police in democratic societies for repressive political action. The militia was established by the Soviet regime with the overt intention of having this body assist the political police and support the interests of the central state. Repressive political actions were also committed by American police personnel during the era of American patronage politics in the second half of the nineteenth century, when policemen often intimidated political opponents for the benefit of political bosses, brutally suppressed labor unrest and even killed strikers. This repression was, however, highly directed and did not constitute an explicitly stated function of the police. Ultimately, such political functions could not be sustained because the police were required to focus on the interests of the majority and uphold the institutions of representative democracy.[32] Bolshevik leaders had no such constraint – their primary concern was to acquire and retain power. To achieve this goal, the Communist Party sanctioned the elimination of class enemies and political opponents by the police apparatus on a large scale, eliminating civil society in an effort to place business, religious and cultural life under its domination.

"Class struggle" dominated the work of all militia personnel, even those who did not participate in the Civil War. Horse brigades under the direction of the Ukrainian militia liquidated many kulaks (wealthy peasants) in the early 1920s, foreshadowing the massive collectivization campaign conducted by the army and militia later in the decade. As mentioned earlier, the criminal investigative division also had political functions during the Civil War. Even as it struggled against ordinary crime and administrative violations, its activities exhibited clear political overtones: the responsibilities of this division extended to the suppression of counterrevolutionary activity, sabotage and speculation – all of which required close cooperation with the Cheka.[33]

The militia, working closely with the Red Army, was also part of a colonizing force that shaped entire antagonistic regions to the will of the central state in Moscow. As in other colonial states, "[t]he blending of military and civilian roles in colonial police services tended to reinforce the position of the policemen as the colonial state's first line of contact with the majority of the populace."[34] Militia personnel were trained to combat political opposition to the regime, an opposition often linked to a specific ethnic identity. The Bolsheviks not only defeated the White opposition during the 1920s, but reconquered areas that had been part of the Russian empire.

Their conquest of these areas, however, differed from that of the tsarist period, as it resulted in the suppression of local legal and religious systems as well as traditional economic activity – all of which had remained more or less intact under the tsars.

When Party power became secure in one area, members of the militia moved to other parts of the country to combat domestic opponents of the Soviet regime. In 1920, for example, 8,000 militia personnel and commanders were sent from the general administration of the police of the Russian Soviet Federated Socialist Republic (RSFSR) to the northern Caucasus, Turkestan and Ukraine. This pattern of transferring militia personnel who were experienced in the suppression of domestic political opposition from the Russian Federative Republic to areas still under siege was repeated throughout the 1920s. By the middle of the decade, the militia was assisting the army in its effort to defeat opposition in Central Asia.[35]

Virulent political conflict ended in the western Russian Federative Republic in the early 1920s, but raged on in other parts of the country, particularly Central Asia, throughout the decade. Russian forces, like colonial police in other parts of the world, tried to recruit policemen from among the local population in order to improve its assault against resistance in the region. Yet the militia in Central Asia remained understaffed because the local population was unwilling to suppress its own members. As Great Britain had encountered in its own empire, "[t]he uncertain legitimacy of the colonial state in the eyes of many of its subjects added to the problems of recruiting reliable constables from among the local population."[36] To combat such resistance, the Soviet regime introduced conscription and drafted men from multi-son families. Families reluctantly surrendered only the least desirable of their offspring, providing the militia with many drug addicts who were weeded out only after the Soviet government established domination in the region.[37] To compensate for local manpower inadequacies, detachments from other republics were sent to the area.

Soviet officials in Central Asia tried not only to occupy these territories, but to mold its peoples according to the state's ideological objectives. Hence physical conquest was accompanied by an attempt to dominate the minds, religions, legal systems and family structures of Central Asian society. Law enforcement efforts to outlaw polygamy, bride purchase and other Islamic family traditions in the 1920s exacerbated already conflictual relations between the authorities and the citizenry. Domestic life, for example, was disrupted as the militia pressured husbands with several wives to assume monogamous marriages. Undesirable wives were often ejected from their homes; penniless, some turned to crime for survival, producing yet another problem for the militia.[38]

Despite these attempts to mold Islamic society, Soviet rulers were unable to immediately wipe out local justice because tsarist rule had never eliminated local governance in the region.[39] According to former Soviet law enforcement personnel, Islamic courts based on the *shariia* (traditional Islamic law) continued to operate in Central Asia in large numbers well into the 1930s. Equally reflective of the tenacity of local traditions of justice, citizens often would not report crimes to Soviet officials.

Although particularly intense in Central Asia, armed political opposition to Bolshevik rule also existed elsewhere. The militia, the army and the Cheka suppressed the White opposition that had relocated to Siberia after being routed by the Red Army in western parts of the country. Policing social conflict had fatal consequences for many militia personnel, replicating the colonial experience in Russia itself. When militia forces ambushed bandits, many policemen perished at the hands of these gangs, armed by opponents of the Bolshevik regime.[40] Using the militia in such social conflicts also had long-term institutional consequences: because its role in armed clashes was fundamentally political, the militia became identified as a symbol of state oppression. Consequently, towards the end of Soviet rule, militia personnel were frequently attacked and even killed by citizens of non-Slavic republics.

The end of the Civil War and the increased security of the Communist Party permitted the militia in western parts of the Russian Federative Republic to turn its attention to social and economic functions. The militia proceeded to try to control crime, a symptom of the prevailing social disorder, but could not affect the fundamental conditions responsible for the veritable crime wave. Militia anti-crime activity was, however, directly tied to political objectives. A major prohibition campaign waged throughout the 1920s bore strong political overtones (unlike Gorbachev's aggressive 1985 anti-alcohol drive, which was motivated by economic objectives). Those recruited for the Soviet campaign were required to be energetic and highly class-conscious, as the anti-alcohol drive was intended to trap the Party's enemies – merchants and kulaks (rich peasants) – who were blamed for illegal alcohol production.[41] The strong political component differentiated Soviet efforts to ban alcohol from the temperance-based prohibition enforced by American police during the same period.

Evidence that ordinary crime was a secondary consideration at the time was, in Peter Juviler's words, "[the] debacle of the Soviet drive against delinquency and homelessness."[42] Tens of thousands of poverty-stricken urban youths lived a life of crime in cities that had been partially deserted by residents who had fled to the countryside in search of nourishment. No attempt was made to alleviate the conditions giving rise to these problem youths; the militia merely rounded up many such young people and thrust them into overcrowded detention centers.[43]

Regulation of economic activity, a function the Soviet militia had inherited from the continental police tradition, was compounded by the regime's ideological commitment to state ownership of the means of production. Militia participation in the economy was a distinctive element of communist policing and was closely tied to the state's political objectives. The new government could not remain in power at first unless it could feed its supporters and protect its urban power base. Consequently, even before the

Soviet regime consolidated its hold over the economy the militia was assisting special food requisition units (military units headed by Party personnel) to provide food for urban residents. In 1921 the militia helped such units requisition grain from the peasantry and escort it to cities on the verge of starvation. Following Party instructions, the militia used whatever steps were deemed necessary to confiscate peasants' grain.[44] Given its experience in brutalizing the peasantry, it is hardly surprising that the militia was later enlisted in the forced collectivization campaign at the end of the decade.

THE STALIN YEARS, 1926–53

When Stalin assumed the post of Communist Party Secretary in 1926, two distinct organizations policed Soviet society: the ordinary police and the political police. These forces were housed in separate institutions. Ordinary criminal offenses came under the jurisdiction of the People's Commissariat of Internal Affairs (NKVD), while political crime was the responsibility of the OGPU (Unified State Political Administration). This separation of political and regular policing was short-lived; a concentration of police power accompanied Stalin's increasing hold on power (see Table 2.3). In 1931, the militia was divided into national and local militias, with local governments retaining some supervisory functions over their police forces. This arrangement also proved temporary – Stalin was bent on increasing the control of the central government without input from the local level.[45]

Table 2.3 Militia structure in the Stalinist period (1926–53)

1931:	Dual subordination of militia ends.
1932:	Consolidation of all police functions; NKVD placed under OGPU (Unified State Political Administration).
1934:	OGPU absorbed by expanded NKVD.
1937:	Establishment of OBKhSS (service to combat theft of state-owned property).
1941:	NKVD divided into two commissariats, the NKVD and NKGB (People's Commissariat of State Security); militia remains under NKVD.
1946:	NKVD and NKGB renamed as Ministries (MVD and MGB).
1950:	Militia transferred to MGB.
1953:	MVD absorbed into MGB.

The massive police apparatus associated with Stalin was created by the consolidation and expansion of the security police and the militia in one massive organization. In 1932, the infamous OGPU (renowned for its purges of specific social classes such as priests and kulaks in the 1920s) absorbed the NKVD. Security and militia functions were not, however, merged: a chief administration of the workers' and peasants' militia was established within the new agency. Further tuning of the control apparatus followed in 1934, when an expanded NKVD (housing all police functions) in turn absorbed the OGPU.[46] In 1935, a new statute on the militia defined the activities and responsibilities of the regular police.

In the newly constituted NKVD of 1934, notes Conquest, "the Soviet police forces reached their full development and the USSR finally evolved the widespread system of police controls."[47] This body was able to acquire such extensive authority because its head reported directly to Stalin, who closely supervised its activities. As a law enforcement agency, the NKVD represented the antithesis of democratic policing, and its structure and activities were the inspiration for theories of totalitarianism.[48]

The earlier incarnation of the NKVD, organized on a republican basis, had been subject to some direction by both local and republican governmental authorities. The later organization, by contrast, had direct control over all NKVD activities in the republics. Even the Party was subordinate to the NKVD, whereas the reverse was true for all other Soviet organizations. Party archives show that Party officials were forbidden to interfere in NKVD work at this time and could not summon its employees to do their bidding.[49] Moreover, the NKVD had control over its own personnel appointments and was subordinate to no governmental agency or Party structure. Unlike other state institutions, whose key positions were staffed according to the *nomenklatura* system of Party-controlled appointments, the NKVD suggested the appointment and/or dismissal of district and regional personnel and the Party merely confirmed these internal NKVD decisions.[50]

The police apparatus, constantly reshuffled in this most insecure Soviet period, stabilized only when Stalin's hold on power was cemented in the late 1930s. Even then, all police power remained consolidated in the NKVD. As the Soviet state matured and its control over the economy solidified, economic policing ceased to be the responsibility of every militiaman. The formation in 1937 of the OBKhSS (Service to Combat Crimes Against State-owned Property) concentrated economic law enforcement in a specialized law enforcement agency, as is the case in other industrialized societies.[51]

The maturation of institutions of governance is generally accompanied by a stabilization in leadership. Yet Stalin, fearing all who might challenge his power, repeatedly purged the leadership of this most powerful of Soviet institutions. Between 1934 and 1938 there were three leaders of the NKVD: Yagoda, Yezhov and Beria. The first two, Yagoda and Yezhov, suffered the same fate as the numerous victims of the purges they had overseen. Yezhov, in power from 1936–38, was nearly as brutal to his staff as he was to the millions of prisoners in the labor camps under his control. Not only did he retaliate against his own subordinates, militia personnel also suffered arrests and sanctions for failing to record all reported crime during these years.[52] Only blood-thirsty Beria, a fellow Georgian and close associate of Stalin, survived in power from his appointment in 1938 until the dictator's death in 1953. Beria directly headed the Ministry of Internal Affairs from 1938 to 1945 and his survival can largely be attributed to his personal qualities.

The entire police apparatus was changed once again during the Second World War, a reflection of the renewed insecurity of the Soviet state. Threatened by the Germans and seeking to enhance state control over the populace, Stalin again altered the structure of the law enforcement and security apparatus, splitting the NKVD into two commissariats in 1941 (see Table 2.3 above). The Commissariat under Beria retained the title NKVD, that under his crony Merkulov was named the NKGB (People's Commissariat for State Security) and specialized in political policing. This division lasted six months; the two commissariats were reunited with the outbreak of war in 1941, only to reemerge as separate entities under the same leadership in 1943, an arrangement that would last until the end of the war.[53]

In 1946, the activities of the NKVD were handed over to Kruglov, but Beria continued to supervise the agency's work. Unlike Beria, Kruglov did not have Stalin's ear; in his seven years as minister, he saw Stalin only four times. His correspondence with Stalin was also more restrained and official than that of Beria. The difference can be explained by Stalin's great interest in security police activity and relative disinterest in the daily work of the militia.[54]

Following the war, the NKVD and NKGB were in 1946 renamed as ministries, becoming the MVD and MGB (ministries of interior affairs and state security) respectively.[55] The wartime division of responsibility between the two organizations prevailed until 1950, when yet another significant shift occurred. The MVD, which had previously controlled most law enforcement activities, then lost several of its most important components. Between 1949 and 1953, the militia was transferred from the Ministry of Internal Affairs to the Ministry of State Security. In accordance with Stalin's wishes, the former was concerned with the construction of massive correctional facilities of all types during this period: labor camps, labor colonies, prisons and labor settlements.[56]

In 1953, Beria again assumed control of the Ministry of Internal Affairs for a brief period before his arrest. The forty volumes of documents prepared for his trial in 1953 reveal a man of superior organizational ability but of great physical cruelty, which often manifested itself during interrogations that he chose to conduct personally.[57]

MILITIA PERSONNEL IN THE STALIN ERA

The quality of militia personnel did not improve in the Stalinist period. Although training programs were expanded and militia schools were opened to provide staff for entry- and advanced-level positions, these institutions did not obtain the best available recruits – they were siphoned off to the security police. Interior Minister Dudurov, commenting on this Stalinist legacy, disclosed in 1956 that almost one-half of all militiamen had only a primary-school education; an additional 42 per cent had below-average educational levels. This meant that close to one-half of the militia force was nearly illiterate.[58]

The least qualified personnel, who filled the rank-and-file positions in the militia, labored under the most difficult conditions. The Soviet film, *Moi drug Ivan Lapshin* (*My friend Ivan Lapshin*), released in the 1980s, provided a vivid and realistic illustration of these men's working conditions. The film chronicled the daily life of a militia unit fighting criminals in a small Russian town during the mid-1930s. Criticized for its dismal view of Soviet life, the film showed a militia group living at subsistence level in crowded, poorly heated dormitories in a city along the Volga River, eating badly and drinking excessively. Only in one sense did the movie distort reality: unlike their real-life counterparts, the cinematic militiamen were adequately dressed and shod. There was nothing refined about these small-town militiamen – their educational level was low and they relied on great force and native intelligence to pursue the criminal population bravely. Unlike their Brezhnev- and Gorbachev-era counterparts, however, they were not corrupt and their lives and activities were permeated by patriotic and ideological slogans.

The Smolensk Party archives, records captured by the German Army during World War II, depicted daily militia life in much the same manner. Party minutes of the 1920s and 1930s for this western region reflect the difficult physical conditions, poor pay and scanty provisions of militiamen. There was no glamour to early Soviet militia work, only long hours under harsh conditions.[59]

STALINIST POLICE ACTIVITIES

The political functions of the militia remained pronounced in the early 1930s. Stalin's collectivization drive in which all farm land and animals were appropriated by the state placed great demands on the institution of the regular police. The ignominious role of the army and the Cheka in subjugating the peasantry and eliminating so-called "kulaks" in the 1930s has been carefully chronicled, but the important militia effort in this campaign and the purges remains unacknowledged.[60] In the words of Soviet historians, militia personnel, together with specialized criminal investigative units, "[s]truggled decisively for the elimination of all anti-Leninist groups" during these years.[61] Political education was intensified among militia personnel at this time so as to ensure their ability to distinguish enemies of the state, usually defined as "peasant resisters". Militia staff consequently brutalized political rebels operating as bandits and anyone who disrupted the *kolkhozy* (collective farms) because both groups were perceived as threatening local Party domination. According to the Smolensk archives, militia personnel worked with such intensity to promote collectivization that they literally fell asleep wherever they landed.[62]

The initiation of the collectivization drive in 1929 led to a mass exodus of the peasantry from the countryside, fleeing slaughter and starvation. Citizens flocked to cities, leaving the newly constituted collective farms understaffed. To combat the urban influx, the passport system was introduced in 1932 and responsibility for its enforcement was assigned to the militia. An internal passport and registration system had been a major tool of social control in the continental police forces of France, Germany and pre-revolutionary Russia. Lenin had sharply criticized the system for limiting personal movement and it was eliminated after the October revolution. A mere two years before its reintroduction, the *Small Soviet Encyclopedia* had described it as an instrument of police coercion, commenting that "Soviet law does not know the passport system."[63]

The reintroduction of the passport system was justified by the need for heightened social order and state security, as well as for improved enumeration of the population. Initially issued only to residents of cities, workers' settlements, state farms, and construction sites, passports quickly deprived collective farm members of their mobility. Since peasants were ineligible for passports, those who dared to move to cities without permission were subject to a militia-imposed fine of 100 rubles, then a significant sum of money. Repeat violators were subject to criminal penalties.[64]

The passport system curtailed the mobility of millions of people and bound many rural residents to the land. At the time of Stalin's death in 1953, 42 million Soviet citizens did not have passports – roughly one-third of the adult population. Of these 42 million, 12 million had lost their passports after entering labor camps;[65] and most of the remaining 30 million represented the immobilized peasantry.

The constant and extensive repression in the Stalinist years carried out by the army, the security police and the militia diminished visible opposition to Communist Party rule. With the effective subjugation of both peasant and ethnic opposition to Soviet rule and state domination of the economy, in the latter half of the 1930s the militia relinquished some of its political responsibilities to the increasingly professionalized security police and turned its attention to non-political forms of social control. Anderson and Killingray have noted that, typical of a colonial society, "[a]s patterns of authority, of accountability and of consent, control and coercion evolved in each colony the general trend was towards a greater concentration of police time upon crime."[66] Until the onset of World War II, the principal responsibilities of the militia after collectivization were combatting such offenses as banditry, embezzlement, *kolkhoz* disorder, appropriation of *kolkhoz* harvests, the abuse of power by officials and the usual array of criminal activity.[67] As crime was defined in class terms, however, many of these offenses had strong political overtones.

The intense repression of the Stalinist years resulted in both political conformity and low crime rates. The removal of professional criminals to labor camps for lengthy sentences also contributed to the low incidence of crime. (The high degree of social order attained at that time is remembered nostalgically by many people in post-Soviet states today.) The major remaining challenges to social order were the numerous homeless youths and so-called "*déclassé*" individuals. Products of years of internal strife, these people formed armed gangs and became the primary targets of the militia, who sought to isolate rather than reintegrate them into Soviet society.

THE WAR YEARS

The Soviet Union's entry into World War II in June 1941 placed new pressures on the militia apparatus. Soviet military forces, caught short by Stalin's miscalculations, recruited heavily from the militia to bolster army units demoralized by heavy casualties and leadership losses from the purges. Many members of the militia were sent to the front lines to defend crucial Soviet cities from the German onslaught. Soviet authorities, dismally short of police personnel, again turned to women to fill militia positions – even pensioners were assigned more sedentary law enforcement functions. Citizens complained of militia shortcomings, but pressing problems of national security overshadowed such concerns. Only the war's conclusion and Stalin's death permitted the restaffing of the militia apparatus.[68]

The militia's military role was complemented by its heightened involvement in domestic politics: militia personnel were expected to root out spies, saboteurs and those undermining the Soviet war effort. Their expanded jurisdiction included a mandate to track down such diverse and ill-defined offenders as deserters, resisters, marauders, "panickers" and rumormongers, particularly in border areas.[69] Additional political functions were added to their mandate after the USSR annexed the Baltic states, western Ukraine and Moldavia in 1940. As the Soviet legal system was imposed on 23 million new citizens, the colonial character of communist policing once again became evident.[70] The memory of militia mistreatment during these years remained strong among citizens of these territories; verbal and physical attacks on the militia in the Gorbachev period were one legacy of this repression.[71]

Newly added political functions did not, however, exempt the militia from responsibility for proactive measures to prevent crime. Wartime conditions exacerbated crimes against the socialist system and the militia conducted crackdowns against black marketeering and theft of state-owned property using techniques that were even harsher than usual.[72] After the USSR entered World War II, already minimal standards of justice for ordinary offenders were further abridged in an effort to expedite the judicial process.

The dislocations of wartime endowed the militia with yet another additional responsibility: that of controlling the *bezprizornye* (homeless and parentless youth).[73] These youths existed in large numbers in areas crippled by civilian losses; given the Party's need to maintain strict control over the domestic population, the militia once again found itself responsible for such people.

The politicization of the militia continued in the post-war period, when the massive demands placed on the total law enforcement apparatus both within the USSR and in Eastern Europe created more work than the security police alone could adequately handle. The militia mandate consequently expanded to include the reestablishment of internal political order and supervision of the creation and training of police forces throughout the Soviet bloc.[74] The popular uprisings in Eastern Europe in 1989 were in part a reaction to the repressive policies instituted by these Soviet-trained police and their counterparts in the security apparatus. As former USSR Foreign Minister Shevardnadze is purported to have said, the Soviet Union lost Eastern Europe not because of its policies in the 1980s, but because of its actions in the late 1940s.

CONCLUSION

The Soviet militia was highly effective in achieving its objectives. Under Stalin, the state achieved political and economic control over the population and civil society was virtually eliminated. A well-ordered state resulted in which crime rates were low and ethnic conflicts repressed. This state was the consequence not only of sweeping police powers and brutal investigative techniques, but of a massive labor camp system that confined ordinary criminals for lengthy periods. The militia was an important component of state control in this society.

The structure and general functions of the early Soviet militia derived from the continental police model. Its role in the subjugation of the Central Asian republics and Siberia during the 1920s, and of regions newly annexed to the USSR during World War II and the Eastern European states during the postwar period reflected the colonial relationship that existed between Moscow and the rest of the USSR and the Soviet bloc as a whole. The important role played by the militia in collectivization and the suppression of embezzlement, speculation and theft of socialist property reflected its role as an agent of control of the communist system. The regular police of this period can easily be compared to their Prussian predecessors, prototypes of continental European police forces who, in Clive Elmsley's words, were "first and foremost, instruments of the state."[75]

Police legitimacy in this period was not based on the rule of law, but on the individual power of the supreme dictator. The militia enjoyed a sweeping mandate from Stalin, allowing them to intervene in many aspects of political, economic and daily life. Police in democratic capitalist societies are re-strained by constitutional controls on their authority and held accountable for their behavior.[76] Under Stalin, the militia did not abide by the law and its primary function was to enforce compliance with the state's political and ideological objectives. The enlightened Stalinist constitution, ignored by the leadership, offered citizens no protection from arbitrary militia authority. The police were not accountable to the community – all state institutions were subordinate to the Party and, ultimately, to Stalin.

When Party ranks were decimated by arrests in the authoritarian police state of Stalin, the police became, as Chapman has observed, "the leading apparat of the state, assuming the Party's role of ultimate guardian of ideological purity."[77] This ideology was then transformed and routinized into bureaucratic regulatory militia measures easily understood by the populace. In such circumstances, the militia destroyed all that it should normally uphold: law, morality, justice and safety,[78] creating a self-destructive legacy for the Soviet state.

3 The post-Stalinist militia

Without providing itself with an effective means of securing observance of its laws, no community succeeds in maintaining its existence for any appreciable length of time.[1]

The post-Stalin period saw a sharp break with the policing of the Stalin years. Many years later, reformers of the *perestroika* period would assert that the political changes of the late 1980s were dwarfed by those which rapidly followed the death of Stalin in March 1953. The dramatic changes in law and policy that occurred in the USSR during the 1950s revealed that significant political change was possible even within an authoritarian state.

Khrushchev, who became First Secretary of the Communist Party of the Soviet Union in September 1953, sought to reform the country's justice system. His prime objective was to reduce the scope of criminal law and eliminate the harsh penalties and extra-legal procedures that had characterized the criminal justice system during the Stalin era. As de-Stalinization required ending the rule of terrorist law and reestablishing Communist Party control over law enforcement, discrediting the Stalinist police apparatus was a necessity.[2] Unlike Gorbachev, Khrushchev did not seek to promote a new conception of society – his reforms profoundly changed Soviet society, but altered neither the fundamental objectives of Soviet law enforcement nor Soviet attitudes towards legal authority. The basis of law enforcement under Khrushchev remained an amalgam of continental, colonial and communist police traditions.

Khrushchev did achieve certain institutional changes associated with democratic policing, such as increased community involvement, greater professionalization of the regular police, and increased observance of legal norms. In contrast to democratic societies, however, the legitimacy of the militia during the Khrushchev and Brezhnev periods continued to derive from the Communist Party, not the authority of criminal law or a constitution.

It is important to note that the major social changes wrought by de-Stalinization did not significantly affect those militia functions associated with colonial and communist policing. Whereas Khrushchev sharply curtailed police repression and attempted to strengthen legal procedures in the USSR, neither he nor Brezhnev implemented policies that undermined the militia's capability as a police force. Gorbachev, on the other hand, instituted reforms that compromised both the authority and legitimacy of the regular police. The development of extensive private economic activity and the loss of credibility of communist ideology in the late 1980s made it impossible for the militia to successfully enforce the norms of the socialist system. Centralized control weakened during *perestroika* as different republics sought greater autonomy and, in many regions of the USSR, the militia came to resemble a colonial police during the last days of empire. Although the move away from colonial and communist policing was not intentional, it was nevertheless a direct result of Gorbachev's conscious decision to move law enforcement towards the rule of law. Before law enforcement in the country could be overhauled, however, the consequences of his reforms led to the dissolution of the Soviet state.

THE KHRUSHCHEV YEARS, 1953–63

Major changes in the structure, personnel and functions of the militia occurred under Khrushchev. The purpose of these reforms was not to separate the militia from politics, but to reassert Party control over the bureaucracy that policed Soviet society. Under Lenin and Stalin, the political functions of the militia took precedence over social and economic functions. Under Khrushchev, these priorities were reversed: crime control and enforcement of economic regulations became more important than political duties. This shift in emphasis was accompanied by the reestablishment of Party control over both the militia and the security police. Leaders of Stalinist law enforcement agencies were eliminated, replaced by Party professionals without ties to the police apparatus. Criminal law and procedure were changed, providing citizens greater protection from arbitrary police power and a police more accountable to the community. As de-Stalinization progressed, professionalism increasingly replaced sheer force in Soviet law enforcement as a whole.

The death of Stalin closed a chapter in militia history. Both the security police and the militia enjoyed extraordinary power until his demise, but the new leadership's rejection of terror would soon drastically reduce their authority. In order to begin a new political era, the leaders of Stalin's vast law enforcement apparatus had to be eliminated and, although his henchmen initially survived the dictator's death, their own crimes rapidly led to their political and personal undoing.[3] Theirs was almost the only blood shed during this major political transition. Unfortunately, although Stalin's police leaders perished, their influence endured in the personnel and the ingrained institutional disregard for the rule of law they left behind.

Stalin's death seemed to propel Beria – chief of the police apparatus – to the pinnacle of power. Along with Georgii Malenkov, who was named Prime Minister, and Viacheslav Molotov, who was renamed Minister of Foreign Affairs, Beria became a member of the ruling triumvirate that assumed power in March 1953. When Beria once again took control of the enlarged MVD (consisting of the security police and militia),[4] his power base temporarily expanded. Fearing concentrated power in his hands, Communist Party rivals orchestrated a dramatic palace coup, ordering the Soviet Army to surround the security police headquarters and cordon off parts of central Moscow. A *perestroika* newspaper later claimed Defense Minister G.K. Zhukov "led the entire arrest operation and played a most direct part in it."[5]

In an attempt to justify their actions against Beria, the Central Committee discussed his crimes in July 1953, only four months after Stalin's death. Chief among the accusations made against him was "that he aspired to control the Soviet government by establishing the MVD [Ministry of Internal Affairs] as an organ free from scrutiny by the Communist Party."[6] Together with several of his associates in the security apparatus, Beria was subsequently tried and executed.[7] His execution was not, however, announced until December 1953.

Trials and executions of other police leaders continued for the next three years, during which time the courts were used to promote a political transition. Revenge and retaliation were channeled through legal proceedings – extra-legal "justice" was to be associated only with the Stalin era. Yet revelations from these trials were hidden from the public, their contents so potent as to undermine Communist Party credibility in the eyes of the population.

The transformation of the militia was not achieved by democratic means, but orchestrated from above. Once again, the police body reflected critical changes in the evolution of Party and state authority in the USSR. The last holdover from the Stalinist leadership, Sergei Kruglov, proved to be only a transitional leader once the MVD was de-Stalinized. Removed from the worst abuses of the Stalinist period, he was not an immediate target of the new leadership. Already an ill man by his mid-forties, Kruglov had been weakened by the grueling work style of the Stalinist era and did not present a major threat to Stalin's successors. Looking for a pretext to replace him, Khrushchev found fault with his execution of decrees. Kruglov's ouster from the MVD in 1956, three years after Stalin's death, however, did not lead to his immediate downfall, which came only in 1960, when he was expelled from the Party. Reduced to penury after the loss of his apartment and official pension, he survived a sick man until his death in 1977.[8]

Kruglov's replacement, Nikolai Dudurov – trained in Party work and inexperienced in law enforcement – was representative of the new generation of MVD leadership. Previously a construction official, Dudurov was chosen for his administrative abilities and previous lack of contact with the militia and the military. (Khrushchev managed to resist Defense Minister Zhukov's pressure to place a military man at the head of the militia apparatus.) Dudurov was appointed on the eve of the twentieth congress of the CPSU in 1956, long celebrated for Khrushchev's secret speech condemning the crimes of Stalin. According to his memoirs, the Central Committee demanded that Dudurov recount the activities of his MVD predecessors prior to the congress, no matter how awful these actions had been. Dudurov followed orders and provided gruesome revelations of special torture chambers personally used by his predecessors to extract confessions from high-ranking Party officials.[9] The personal involvement of the police leadership in Stalin's excesses was so damaging that, at the time, such revelations were confined to a small group of the Party elite and became public only during the *glasnost'* era.

Stalin's successors arrived at the same conclusion as that reached by the French at the close of their revolution: the police are the enemy of democracy. This view held that the police, while a necessary and inevitable institution of society, must be firmly controlled. The Party thus took various steps to ensure that the militia apparatus provided no further threat to its preeminence.[10] Among the most visible of these steps was the appointment of trusted Party personnel to posts in the militia leadership, a policy that reinstated Party dominance over the institution in the short term, but led to crippling corruption in the long term. Another key step was the reshuffling of the entire law enforcement apparatus in order to prevent the reemergence of a hegemonic police (see Table 3.1). In 1954, for the first time in three decades, the KGB (Committee on State Security, or security police) was separated from the MVD (Ministry of Internal Affairs, or the regular police) – a major achievement of the de-Stalinization process. (As the population had become

Table 3.1 Changes in the police apparatus during the post-Stalinist period (1953–86)

1953:	Beria becomes Minister of Internal Affairs, is soon arrested, tried and executed.
1954:	Permanent separation of MVD and KGB.
1956:	MVD decentralized, Sergei Kruglov ousted as Minister. Nikolai Dudurov appointed Minister of Internal Affairs (serves until 1960); gives speech at twentieth congress of the CPSU on crimes of MVD predecessors.
1958:	*Druzhinniki* (People's Patrols) formed throughout the country.
1960:	USSR MVD dissolved, its functions transferred to the ministries of internal affairs of the union republics.
1961:	Vadim Tikunov appointed MVD Minister, serves until 1966. Political organs created within the MVD.
1962:	MVD changed to MOOP (Ministries for the Defense of Public Order). Soviet Militia Day initiated; new statute promulgated on the militia.
1966:	Nikolai Shchelokov named Minister of Internal Affairs, serves until 1982.
1968:	Recentralization of militia; MVD reinstituted as name of internal affairs ministry. Anti-crime campaigns initiated.
1973:	New statute issued on the militia.
1974:	Crime prevention units established.
1978–83:	New ministers of internal affairs appointed in 12 of the 14 union republics.
1982:	Minister of Internal Affairs Nikolai Shchelokov ousted; commits suicide in December 1984. November. Leonid Brezhnev dies; replaced by Iurii Andropov.
1983:	January. Vitalii Fedorchuk appointed Minister of Internal Affairs.
1983–86:	200,000 MVD employees dismissed, including numerous militia personnel.

submissive after years of intense repression, the resources of the KGB alone remained sufficient to maintain political control.)

The division of ordinary and political police functions achieved by the ministerial split was crucial to the depoliticization of the regular police, placing limits on the influence and size of the militia bureaucracy. In the United States, removing responsibility for political control from the jurisdiction of the regular police facilitated the latter's professionalism and enhanced police prestige;[11] yet in the USSR, improved status did not accompany growing professionalism. Leaders of the militia apparatus were no longer members of the preeminent Party body, the Politburo. Their consequent lack of political influence and autonomy outweighed any improvement in militia performance. Whereas the decline of political functions on the part of the regular police in the United States and England coincided with increased police autonomy from the political apparatus,[12] the militia in the USSR remained an arm of the Party apparatus despite a corresponding decline in its political duties.

RECONSTRUCTING THE POST-STALINIST MILITIA

As Stalin's successor, Khrushchev faced two formidable tasks: reconstructing the law enforcement apparatus and subordinating this apparatus to the Communist Party. During his years in power, the Party made every effort to ensure that the Ministry of Internal Affairs, which supervised the militia, did not become an independent kingdom, as it had under Beria. Legislation was enacted to improve the militia and formalize its position, helping to reverse the dramatic decline in militia authority that had begun to affect adversely its ability to maintain social order.[13]

In early 1956, Internal Affairs Minister Nikolai Dudurov addressed the pitiful state of the militia in a meeting with leaders of republican ministries of internal affairs: "[T]he organs of the MVD, in particular the militia and gulag [the labor camp system], and all their links work badly, are so incredibly bad ... that the MVD does not enjoy the population's appreciation."[14] Dudurov informed his subordinates that two personnel problems were particularly urgent: the inability of militiamen to effectively combat crime and the large number of criminals within the ranks of the militia itself.[15]

In 1956, the Central Committee made further efforts to combat the legacy of Stalin and decentralized the MVD. Regional-level militia and MVD organs were combined into administrations of internal affairs and subordinated to regional and local governmental bodies.[16] These local bodies exerted little influence over militia or MVD operations, however, because political power remained concentrated almost exclusively in the Communist Party apparatus at all levels. Yet the structural change did have a significant financial impact on the militia: it was now forced to compete with other local government agencies for scarce resources.

Concerned by opposition, Khrushchev wanted to diffuse the power of the central MVD bureaucracy. His efforts to decentralize the ministry were part of his overall attempt to reform the organs of the Communist Party and the Soviet government, visibly demonstrated in his 1957 *sovnarkhozy* (councils of the national economy) reforms and the 1962 reform of Party and government organs. In 1960, the Ministry of Internal Affairs was dissolved and its functions – including management of the militia – were transferred to the ministries of internal affairs of the union republics. According to a Soviet historian of the MVD, Dudurov was completely surprised by the decision to break up his ministry. Forced to leave his post, he spent the remainder of his uneventful career in construction.[17]

A former deputy to KGB chairman Aleksandr Shelepin, Vadim Tikunov, was appointed in 1961 to replace Dudurov as head of the newly decentralized MVD. The first lawyer to direct the (renamed) MVD, at 40 years of age Tikunov had already acquired a great deal of administrative experience. (He had spent the war years in the Komsomol (Communist youth organization) apparatus and was promoted to the Central Committee of the CPSU upon the war's conclusion.) A decisive person who sought to establish legal norms for militia work, he devoted much of his time to defining the responsibilities of the different branches of the ministry.[18] Tikunov's close personal ties to Shelepin, who left his post at the KGB when he became a secretary of the Central Committee, also in 1961, enhanced the political standing of the beleaguered MVD.

During his five years as head of the ministry, Tikunov took steps to streamline paperwork, provide personnel with better technical equipment, expand the ministry's relations with the media and study the police experience of other socialist countries. Attacking the bureaucratization of police work, Tikunov noted in one address to ministry personnel that from 1960 until mid-1961, the MVD had issued 515,000 different documents that had consumed 228 tons of paper! He urged the speedy adoption of a new statute on the militia, which became law in 1961. Under his direction, militiamen were authorized to use handcuffs, night sticks and tear gas, and a lengthy training program for senior personnel was initiated. Many of the social work functions performed by the Soviet militia were first introduced under Tikunov. A branch of the militia devoted to youth affairs – called the children's room (*detskaia komnata*) – was opened to improve work with adolescents; additional efforts were undertaken to deal with alcoholics, drug addicts and petty hooligans. Perhaps most significant, under Tikunov the Party strengthened its hold over the militia by founding political organs within the militia bureaucracy.[19]

Tikunov survived the temporary name change of his ministry in 1962 from the MVD (the dreaded name of the Stalinist period) to the Ministries for Defense of Public Order (MOOP). Yet his reformist outlook, characteristic of the Khrushchev years, proved incompatible with the cronyism of the Brezhnev era. Always loyal to the Party, Tikunov in 1966 willingly accepted his dismissal from the ministry and subsequent diplomatic exile to Romania, the Upper Volta, Burkino Faso and Cameroon. He died in 1980, weakened by years of service in Africa.[20]

The Khrushchev years were years of political relaxation. Following the trials of Beria and his associates, there were no major political trials apart from anti-parasite cases; the dissident movement had yet to emerge as a visible force in Soviet society. Consequently, many of the political challenges the militia would face in ensuing decades were still on the horizon. Its political activities were redirected towards general surveillance. Rather than isolate political offenders, for example, as it would do in the Brezhnev era, the militia under Khrushchev helped register millions of Stalinist prisoners released from labor camps in their new homes.[21]

Relieved of many of its political functions, the militia in the late 1950s could focus on the central elements of socialist policing: social and economic regulation. Economic functions of the militia, low-key during the initial Khrushchev period, reemerged with heightened importance in the 1960s, when new all-Union laws reinforced the state agricultural sector at the expense of private farming. These laws became the marching orders of the militia and newspapers began to feature reports on the arrest of people who shipped fruits and vegetables from private plots in the Caucasian republics to other locales, as well as stories about women who fed bread to animals.[22]

At the same time, the militia performed a key function of communist policing by enforcing the Marxist maxim "from each according to his labor" in Soviet society. Soviet citizens who did not work were not only excluded from the benefits of their society, they were subject to the coercive arm of the state. Under Khrushchev, the militia became the enforcer of the economic policy that required all adult males and unmarried women to work. Thousands of vagrants and beggars and other "antisocial individuals" – defined as parasites – became subject to militia-imposed discipline.[23] The militia also suppressed capitalist activity by arresting private entrepreneurs, many of whom were subsequently prosecuted in widely publicized trials.

Under Khrushchev, the citizenry was mobilized *en masse* to aid in law enforcement. Although scholars such as Carl Friedrich and Alex Inkeles have suggested that mass mobilization is characteristic of totalitarian societies, Khrushchev's efforts to popularize the militia recalled the early Bolshevik revolutionaries, who had envisioned the withering away of the state. In this context, his populist campaign represented more a move away from the totalitarianism of Stalin than its continuation.[24]

Beginning in 1958, millions of *druzhinniki* (auxiliary citizen militiamen) were recruited to aid the militia in its work. Lacking the volunteer nature of citizen watch groups or vigilante organizations in the west, the work of these recruits cannot be equated with the community-based policing that emerged in the United States during the 1970s. Unlike American groups, *druzhinniki* did not respond to law enforcement needs articulated by the community. Rather, they heeded the state's injunction to police a society which itself had never been consulted about the means or manner of its control. American vigilantes volunteer to aid law enforcement bodies and citizen watch groups tend to develop spontaneously. *Druzhinniki*, on the other hand, were drafted for community policing in campaigns orchestrated by the Communist Party and their place of work.

This populist approach to policing proved problematic, as militia personnel were often ignorant of the laws they were to uphold. Despite this drawback, an MVD historian writing for *Sovetskaia militsiia*, the journal of the Soviet militia, found that additional voluntary law enforcement personnel did help to reduce crime commission during these years.[25] The sheer number of citizens who participated in police work and their physical presence on the streets alone helped to eliminate many of the grossest police abuses of the Stalinist era. At the same time, however, many *druzhinniki* also abused their authority; some even exploited their new-found status to commit crimes.[26] Although mass citizen participation in police work continued until the *perestroika* years, the practice had become largely symbolic by the 1980s.

Citizen participation in law enforcement and a more critical press increased public scrutiny of the militia under Khrushchev. Newspapers, although not given the same latitude as they enjoyed in the Gorbachev era, were permitted to focus on certain aspects of militia misconduct. Neither the militia's efficiency nor their incompetence were hidden from the populace. Reports of militia personnel harassing private citizens, exceeding their authority and showing little respect for the law they were supposed to uphold appeared with regularity in major national newspapers during the Khrushchev era.[27]

At the close of this era, the authority of the militia had clearly diminished. Once it was separated from the secret police apparatus, the militia lost access to national policymakers and its effectiveness as an organ of social control was circumscribed. The downgrading of the militia, however, clearly went too far. In 1962, criticism of militia performance in the media was so rampant that *Izvestiia* found it necessary to reassure skeptical readers that the militia was still in the good graces of the Soviet leadership.[28]

Verbal assertions, however, meant little in a country where actions spoke louder than words. Consequently, despite his commitment to anti-Stalinism and concern about arbitrary police power,[29] Khrushchev in his last years as leader of the Communist Party took concrete measures to enhance the status of the militia in the eyes of Soviet society. Structural changes were made in the militia bureaucracy and a significant symbolic measure was implemented: "Soviet Militia Day" was made an annual holiday in 1962, as announced in a lead editorial in *Pravda*.[30] Banners, ceremonies and speeches by leading Party personnel would henceforth laud militia accomplishments on November 10th of each year, the anniversary of the militia's founding in 1918.

To conclude, the law enforcement apparatus in the Khrushchev era did not develop in accordance with a specific vision of Soviet society, but in reaction to the abuses of police power of the Stalin years. The Party thus sought a new legitimacy for the militia – one based on the authority of the Party rather than that of a single individual. Commitment to the rule of law, intrinsic to democratic policing, was conspicuously absent from the Khrushchev reforms.

THE BREZHNEV YEARS, 1963–82

The early Brezhnev years mark the beginning of the mature Soviet militia. Brezhnev upgraded the quality and image of the militia during the 1960s; increased professionalism and power were the hallmarks of his era. Militia morale recovered from de-Stalinization and populist policing policies, but was not yet subject to the corrosive effects of the stagnation of the late Brezhnev period. New and more educated personnel were recruited to improve the qualifications of those on the force and newly purchased equipment made them more effective. While the primary focus of the militia remained the maintenance of social and economic order, its role in controlling dissidents gave it a greater political mandate than that known in western democratic societies.

Militia leaders in the Brezhnev period were often not career law enforcement personnel, but individuals known to be loyal to the Party Secretary. Within two years of Brezhnev's assumption of power, the reformist Tikunov was dismissed as MVD minister and replaced by Nikolai Shchelokov, a graduate of a metallurgical institute with a long history of service in the Party apparatus. Shchelokov's association with Brezhnev dated to the pre-war period in Dneprpetrovsk; they ascended the Party ladder together in Moldavia. In appointing Shchelokov to this important post, Brezhnev ignored warnings of Party associates that his long-time friend was both stupid and incompetent.[31]

Although Shchelokov served as head of the Ministry of the Interior longer than any other Soviet official, his subordinates did not enjoy similar longevity in the ministry. Law enforcement officials in this period, according to one western student of the Soviet police apparatus, had often previously served

> in the Party apparatus (as heads of administrative organs departments, Party secretaries or in the Komsomol) or in some cases in the procuracy, prior to going to the MVD. Not infrequently, MVD cadres later move back into these positions. Of 28 MVD officials serving in leading posts at the republic or national level during the seventies, only six could be classified as "career" MVD personnel. This trend reflects the Brezhnev regime's deliberate policy of bringing in Party apparatchiks to serve in the MVD, a policy that was begun in the late 1960s in an effort to strengthen the Party's supervision over the MVD.[32]

Brezhnev strengthened not only Communist Party but familial control over the MVD apparatus, appointing his son-in-law, Iurii Churbanov, First Deputy Minister of Internal Affairs in 1979. (Churbanov was promoted over colleagues with more seniority.) This appointment, as well as the placement of Brezhnev cronies in other powerful militia posts, eventually proved the undoing of the Party Secretary himself and the upper echelons of the militia.

"Nepotism, string-pulling and servility, which increasingly ousted Party principledness, entered our life . . . . Thus the number of untouchables, protected by highly-placed patrons increased."[33] Widening corruption did much to undermine the credibility of Party rule in the late 1970s; by the end of the Brezhnev period, it was rampant at all levels of the militia apparatus and in all regions of the USSR. Scandals led to the top of the MVD, with Churbanov and other members of the First Party Secretary's family figuring prominently in cases of militia corruption.

Attempts to stem abuse of power by militia officials in the late 1960s were short-lived;[34] only when Brezhnev's power began to wane in the late 1970s was a major housecleaning initiated. A massive turnover at the top of the MVD ladder then ensued; between 1978 and 1983, new ministers were appointed in 12 of the 14 republican ministries of internal affairs (until the late 1980s, the RSFSR had no republican ministry). Only four of these appointments occurred due to natural attrition.[35] Upon Brezhnev's death in 1982, Iurii Andropov, the KGB chief with a reputation for integrity – not a Brezhnev protégé – assumed the post of Party Secretary.

STRUCTURE AND FUNCTIONS OF THE BREZHNEV MILITIA

Brezhnev dismissed Khrushchev's belief that public order and social safety could be maintained by ordinary people without a special police force. In contrast to his predecessor, he set out to rebuild and refinance the internal affairs ministry, which had been renamed the Ministries for the Defense of Public Order in 1962. Even before the appointment of Shchelokov as head of the decentralized internal affairs ministry in 1966, national police ranks were augmented by 35,000 additional personnel, militia salaries were increased and better uniforms were introduced. Once his trusted friend Shchelokov was in place, Brezhnev initiated a significant reorganization of the ministry, allocating 220 million rubles to upgrade the militia apparatus alone.[36]

Khrushchev's structural changes were undone by Brezhnev (see Table 3.1, p. 41) and the militia was returned to a continental police model. The regular police was recentralized once again and the onerous name of the Stalinist police organ – the MVD – was reinstituted in 1968. Other personnel and legislative changes placed Brezhnev's stamp on the militia apparatus. In the early 1970s, new legislation on the MVD, the militia and the internal affairs organs of local governmental committees combined to augment militia authority.[37] A new statute on the militia itself, issued in 1973, expanded the administrative and data collection responsibilities assigned to the militia in the earlier statute of 1962.[38] In line with Brezhnev's law-and-order orientation, the militia's right to administer penalties and handle drunks was expanded.

The procuracy, formerly the principal investigative body in the Soviet criminal justice system, ceded much of its investigatory responsibilities to the militia at this time. The new division of responsibilities gave the militia jurisdiction over the majority of criminal investigations conducted in the judicial system. Proactive investigatory units were added in 1974 and housed within the criminal investigative branch of the militia.[39] Unfortunately, numerous problems resulted from this reorganization that impeded actual day-to-day police work.

Under Shchelokov's leadership, crime control became the prime responsibility of the militia. In this respect, the regular Soviet police resembled its counterparts in other developed countries. Yet the broader mandate of the Soviet militia included reintegrating released offenders into Soviet society; fighting recidivism among released convicts; protecting state property; cooperating with the community; and combatting hooliganism, alcoholism, narcotics and problem youth.[40] The following chapters devote much attention to the militia mandate of the Brezhnev years and demonstrate how modes of enforcement, as well as political and economic responsibilities, set the militia apart from the police forces of capitalist societies, making the regular police a central component of the authoritarian–command system of the USSR.

The human rights movement, ethnic unrest and religious activism all grew under Brezhnev.[41] Consequently, the militia's role in regulating political activity became far more pronounced than had been the case in the Khrushchev period. Whereas the KGB had primary responsibility for monitoring and controlling "deviant" political behavior, the militia actively participated in searches of dissidents' apartments, fined priests who performed unauthorized services and even arrested political activists on trumped-up criminal charges. Detention facilities manned by the militia held many political and religious activists, especially during official visits by leading foreign dignitaries. The pervasive militia presence in the community and its readiness to subdue nonconformist behavior clearly established the limits of permissible political conduct in Soviet society.

Renewed faith in the competence of the militia in the 1960s caused the Party increasingly to use the MVD to address fundamental economic problems in Soviet society, a pattern that repeated itself in the post-Brezhnev period. Beginning in 1968, a wave of anti-crime campaigns was initiated in support of the socialist system. These campaigns sought to combat the lack of discipline and drunkenness among workers, as well as to eradicate economic crimes and embezzlement at the workplace. Pressure mounted on MVD personnel to perform such tasks effectively; some were found deficient and dismissed.[42]

Yet enforcement of economic controls over the population was inconsistent. The Soviet underclass, represented heavily in official statistics on "parasites," was subject to extensive militia surveillance in the early years of the Brezhnev period. Small-time black marketeers were similarly subject to close scrutiny by militia personnel. In contrast, the Party elite, deeply involved in corruption and illegal business activity, had minimal contact with the law enforcement community as Party status granted such individuals immunity.[43]

Although the Party apparatus sought more effective law enforcement during the Brezhnev era, Party domination of local and republican MVD bureaucracies remained a fundamental obstacle to objective law enforcement. Improvements initiated by the Party in the areas of investigation, patrols and forensics were limited by the non-autonomous character of the police.[44] Despite better training, militiamen remained executors of Party policy rather than professional enforcers of the law. As during the American era of political policing, when local police served the interests of political party machines, police officers were often, in the words of Samuel Walker, "tools of local politicians . . . not impartial and professional public servants."[45]

The diminished political agenda of the militia reduced tensions between the community and the regular police, but had a long-term debilitating effect on militia morale. The KGB, by contrast, retained its prestigious role as the protector of national security and enjoyed an unjustified reputation for incorruptibility until the post-Soviet period, when this image was over-shadowed by revelations of illegal foreign currency trading and other corrupt activities.

During the almost twenty years of the Brezhnev period, the institutional structure of Soviet society stagnated while beneath the surface, society evolved. The schism between the control apparatus and the population was exacerbated by policies that did little to accommodate a changing social reality. Brezhnev's patronage system, moreover, led to pervasive militia corruption that undermined the policing authority of the Soviet state. One consequence of this deterioration was the populace's visible lack of confidence in the militia, apparent already in the early 1980s and publicly recognized by Soviet officials at the time:

> Unfortunately, public opinion cannot conceal its suspicions about the honesty of some personnel of the law enforcement organs . . . We are especially concerned about the militia's authority . . . Ten years ago the MVD had a name that was synonymous with honesty, principle and steadfastness. The people believed in the militia's authority and depended on it in the struggle for law and order . . . . It is astonishing and regrettable sometimes how easily and in how short a time one can lose that which took many years of dedication and toil to gain.[46]

THE IMMEDIATE POST-BREZHNEV PERIOD

The leaders who assumed control after Brezhnev's death had a rapid and immediate impact on law enforcement (see Table 3.2). The new leader of the Communist Party, Iurii Andropov, former chief of the KGB, had built his reputation on efficiency and incorruptibility. As General Secretary, he immediately initiated a major drive against corruption in Soviet trade organizations and in all branches of the justice system, including the militia. The anti-corruption drive was a dramatic reversal of past policy. As Minister

Table 3.2. Major events affecting the Soviet militia during the final Soviet period (1982–91)

1985:	May. Anti-alcohol campaign launched immediately after Gorbachev becomes General Secretary of the Communist Party.
1986:	Vitalii Fedorchuk ousted, Aleksandr Vlasov appointed Minister of Internal Affairs.
1987:	OMON, special-purpose militia detachments, established.
1988:	Vadim Bakatin replaces Vlasov as head of MVD.
1988:	Policing privatized – private detective services and guard cooperatives created. Motorized divisions of militia created to deal with political demonstrations.
1988–89:	Nine-month-long trial of ex-MVD Deputy Minister Iurii Churbanov (Brezhnev's son-in-law) ends with his conviction and 12-year sentence.
1989:	April. Georgian militia defends peaceful demonstrators against Soviet Army troops in the capital of Tbilisi.
1989:	RSFSR Ministry of Internal Affairs created.
1990:	Baltic states attempt to establish autonomous ministries of internal affairs. December. Bakatin dismissed as head of MVD; Boris Pugo appointed Minister of Internal Affairs, Boris Gromov appointed Deputy Minister.
1991:	January. KGB and MVD awarded enhanced powers to search businesses; joint army–MVD patrols instituted. August 19–21: coup attempt fails. Baltic states achieve independence following coup, police power transferred from USSR MVD to ministries of internal affairs of new states.

of Internal Affairs Aleksandr Vlasov explained: "The stagnant phenomena of the 1970s–1980s led to ugly negative processes . . . within agencies of the Ministries of the Interior, which found themselves above criticism."[47]

The cronyism of the Brezhnev era, severely criticized during the Gorbachev years, had its most visible manifestation in the militia. Not only did Shchelokov and Churbanov have close ties to Brezhnev, but similar close relationships between First Party Secretaries and their MVD chiefs existed in the union republics. Such personal associations permitted gross abuses of individual rights that went almost entirely undisciplined. These problems came to the surface just one month after Andropov became Party leader, when *Pravda* reported that a Politburo meeting had discussed public complaints about widespread corruption and growing crime. Laying the groundwork for a major change in the ministry, the article commented: "The procurator's office and the MVD have been notified of the necessity of taking steps to improve law and order."[48] The following day, Moscow radio announced that Shchelokov had been deprived of his post as USSR Minister of Internal Affairs.[49]

Speculation about Shchelokov's successor was short-lived. Less than a week later, Vitalii Fedorchuk, Andropov's successor as head of the KGB merely six months before, was assigned to the post of Minister of Internal Affairs. Fedorchuk had served in the state security organs since 1939 and had acquired a reputation for being tough while chief of the Ukrainian security apparatus.[50] The transfer of a KGB man to the MVD was a familiar strategy to aid the beleaguered militia and placed the MVD in a clearly subordinate position to the security agency.

In his new role as MVD chief, reported *Pravda*, Fedorchuk quickly initiated major changes in order "to eliminate shortcomings in the performance of internal affairs organs."[51] MVD personnel subsequently complained that he used KGB tactics within the ministry, including surveillance, denunciations, secret dismissals and unjustified arrests. According to a *perestroika*-era article on the subject, such methods weeded out not only corrupt elements, but also snared thousands of competent professionals in traps.[52]

The next Minister of Internal Affairs, Aleksandr Vlasov, reported that in 1983 161,000 MVD personnel were fired at all levels of the MVD hierarchy throughout the USSR. The crackdown against corrupt personnel in trade organizations (distribution centers for food and consumer goods) in Moscow was intensified, with 15,000 individuals arrested by 1984. Many of those arrested for corruption were later linked to the militia apparatus.[53]

Fedorchuk examined MVD archives and discovered ample evidence of Shchelokov's abuse of his power: acquisition of antiques and other valuables by his family; maintenance of dachas for his vast entourage, remodelled at the MVD's expense; acquisition of a Mercedes for himself and other cars for family members. Among his most egregious offenses was Shchelokov's establishment of a special store that sold tape recorders, televisions and furs for the exclusive use of his relatives. Shchelokov's relations spent 50–70,000 rubles daily in the store on scarce consumer goods that were subsequently resold at considerable profit. Fedorchuk passed documentation on these crimes to the chief military procurator.[54]

Shchelokov's position unravelled rapidly after his dismissal in 1982. Deprived of his rank as general in November 1984, he was expelled from the Communist Party the following month. His disgrace was made complete when the Presidium of the Supreme Soviet deprived him of all Soviet medals and his designation as a "hero of socialist labor," also in December 1984.[55] Faced with the possibility of a trial, he committed suicide later that same month. (His wife had earlier committed suicide in February 1983.)

The purge of MVD personnel that began in 1983 continued for three years. Approximately 5 percent of the MVD and an even larger proportion of the militia force was dismissed. The most visible victim of the purge was Iurii Churbanov, Deputy Minister of Internal Affairs, who, along with his Central Asian associates, was accused of large-scale corruption and bribery. The joint trial of Churbanov and several leading Uzbek MVD officials in Moscow was the focal point of the anti-Brezhnev campaign. The trial lasted nine months, concluding in December 1988 with convictions for all defendants and a twelve-year prison sentence for Churbanov. A challenge to the political authority of the Brezhnev period, the trial and its conclusion were anxiously awaited by the entire population.[56]

Long-term associates of Shchelokov also suffered. In the spring and summer of 1983, two of the eight deputy ministers of the MVD were forced into early retirement at the age of 61; their replacements came from the KGB. In major appointments at the republic level, close to one-half of the republican ministers of internal affairs were purged in an effort to root out corruption and strengthen law enforcement.[57] Many of those ousted were members of the indigenous nationality of their republics, whereas a number of the newly appointed republican MVD ministers were Slavs. A similar pattern of personnel replacement at the top of the Communist Party leadership followed the Russification of the MVD leadership. The number of Slavs on the Politburo, for example, was increased at the expense of other ethnic groups. Introduced by Andropov, the policy was sustained by Gorbachev.[58]

The anti-corruption campaigns left the militia critically understaffed. New, more mature cadres preselected by their workplaces were often used as unwilling replacements. The infusion of Party personnel, many of them Slavs, into the supervisory ranks of the militia in turn aroused resentment among career law enforcement professionals and adversely affected militia–community relations.[59] Although the appointment of Slavs to leadership positions at the local level succeeded in reducing local control over the militia, it increased tensions between the republics and the central Soviet government. In subsequent years, many republics accordingly sought full control over their own law enforcement agencies.

Perhaps the most significant element of the restructuring achieved by Andropov and Fedorchuk was the introduction of political organs in the MVD. Reporting directly to the Central Committee of the Communist Party of the Soviet Union (CPSU) and acting only on its instructions, these bodies were instituted in order to combat collusion between local Party and MVD officials.[60] These units were dedicated to maintaining central ideological and personnel control over the ministry, thus preserving the basic elements of continental and communist policing at a time of great instability.

Konstantin Chernenko, a Brezhnev associate who assumed the post of General Secretary upon Andropov's death in 1984, only slightly tempered his predecessor's efforts to revitalize the militia; the major shake-up that had already been initiated could not be halted. During Chernenko's sole year in office, Fedorchuk continued his attempts to improve militia performance by streamlining militia administration – a much-needed response to the proliferation of bureaucratic divisions that took place under Shchelokov. The number of operational police divisions was significantly reduced and patrol posts were restructured in towns and cities in order to make the militia more responsive to community complaints.[61] These changes laid the groundwork for more fundamental reforms that Gorbachev, Andropov's heir apparent, would initiate after assuming leadership of the Communist Party in 1985.

THE GORBACHEV YEARS, 1985–91

Gorbachev's desire to change the militia exceeded that of Andropov. His objective was to reduce corruption and use the law as a vital instrument of change. Like the American Progressives of the early twentieth century, Gorbachev had a vision of reform. As part of his program of *perestroika*, or reconstruction, of Soviet society, he sought to establish a socialist *pravovoe gosudarstvo* (law-based state) in which the Communist Party and its institutions would be subordinate to the law and individuals would enjoy greater legal protections *vis-à-vis* the state.

This vision of Soviet society had very specific implications for the militia. Inspired by western legal models, Gorbachev wanted to shift the source of militia legitimacy from the Party apparatus to the law. This transition would follow western European practice, which had seen continental police made more accountable to the law over time. According to Gorbachev's plans, militia personnel were to be made subordinate to legal codes and act first and foremost as law enforcement professionals, not servants of the Party apparatus. Ironically, Gorbachev's effort to reshape the militia was preceded by the anti-alcohol campaign, one of the most disliked operations ever mounted by the Soviet state in its later years. The campaign served to alienate citizens from the militia, which had been responsible for instituting alcohol restrictions.

The militia, a taboo topic for many decades, became a prime subject of the Soviet press during the *glasnost'* era. Between 1986 and 1988, 2,500 vivid revelations of militia brutality, violations of individuals' rights and bribe-taking appeared in the press.[62] Newspapers depicted the militia as not only brutal but ineffective, reporting declining clearance rates for offenses. In 1987, crime statistics were made public for the first time in sixty years, documenting escalating crime rates in Soviet society that reflected poorly on the police. Such revelations of corruption and incompetence severely tarnished the militia's prestige.[63]

To address these weaknesses, Gorbachev attempted to restructure the militia by adding new branches for municipal policing and organized crime. Other new units included renewed workers' detachments and the OMON (special-purpose militia detachments created in 1987). OMON troops were first deployed against demonstrators in 1988; they were later used with great visibility in the Baltic republics.[64]

Although Gorbachev appointed several chiefs to the MVD in order to accomplish his reform objectives, he never freed the ministry from Party domination. His first two ministers of internal affairs were both former Party officials. Aleksandr Vlasov, a former first secretary of an *obkom* (*oblast'* committee of the Communist Party) and member of the CPSU Central Committee, became head of the MVD after Fedorchuk's dismissal in January 1986.[65] (Fedorchuk was subsequently demoted to the Inspectorate of the Soviet Army.[66]) Vlasov served until his appointment as chairman of the RSFSR Council of Ministers in 1988, when he was replaced by Vadim Bakatin, a man from the same mold. Prior to becoming Minister of Internal Affairs, Bakatin had also served as an *obkom* first secretary in the RSFSR. He subsequently distinguished himself as minister by his sharp criticism of MVD practices and commitment to the rule of law, making him many enemies among Communist Party conservatives who sought to preserve the status quo.

The Gorbachev years also saw the state relinquish its monopoly on law enforcement. For the first time in Soviet history, private detective agencies and guard services were legally established as part of the newly authorized cooperative movement. This privatization of policing moved the USSR closer to the police practice of its western neighbors and away from the concentration of police power characteristic of the continental police model. In the USSR, however, many private policemen were drawn from the ranks of those dismissed from the militia and no legal regulations existed to govern their proper conduct. Absence of such legal safeguards thus meant that democratization of policing was achieved in form and not substance.

Operational changes in the militia accompanied its reorganization. Militia personnel were instructed to tolerate thousands of informal social groups, limited private business and greater diversity in citizens' public appearance.[67] Particularly in the largest cities, the militia ceased to defend state-established norms in dress and hairstyle. As the state sought to encourage economic initiative in Soviet society, greater tolerance was likewise exhibited towards individual entrepreneurs operating in farmers' markets and newly formed cooperatives. This new-found tolerance represented a break with ideological values of communist policing that had been inculcated in the militia both individually in training and during long years of Communist Party rule.

Another significant change in policing during *perestroika* saw the Party cease to demand that the militia clear 95 percent of all crimes – an unattainable performance standard in any society. Once pressure to meet such unrealistic targets diminished, the militia cleared far fewer crimes than it had in past years, although its clearance rate still exceeded the American rate of 25–30 percent. Declining performance reflected not only reduced conviction targets, however, but also inadequate technical equipment and greater legal protections for the citizenry.

Law enforcement in the Gorbachev era changed largely due to specific instructions to personnel rather than through the development of the legal culture required to realize a more democratic militia. In other words, democratization in the political arena was ordered. As an officer policing a

Moscow version of Hyde Park remarked on what he considered his restraint at the time: "Now we have *perestroika*."[68] It is important to note here that militia tolerance of nationalist, anti-Semitic groups such as *Pamiat'* in the late *perestroika* years reflected the innate conservatism and lack of legal consciousness among policemen more than their evenhanded tolerance of a variety of social groups.[69]

The Soviet state ultimately could not survive the challenges of *perestroika* and the revelations of *glasnost'*. Increased free enterprise, decentralization of political power to the republics and diminished fear of the state on the part of the populace produced fundamental changes in Soviet society. The response of the MVD to this rapid social change was chaotic and unco-ordinated, with the regime learning only belatedly that its control apparatus could not be liberalized within the existing state structure. Once a formidable element of the state's social control apparatus, the MVD proved unable to combat the widening nationalist conflicts, rising crime and increasingly powerful organized criminal groups that resulted from the policies of *perestroika*.

THE FINAL YEARS OF THE SOVIET STATE, OR DECOLONIZATION REVISITED

As MVD troops joined Soviet Army recruits in repressing nationalist resistance to central rule, the colonial functions of the militia again came to the fore. Mirroring the final years of the British empire, the Soviet govern-ment's lack of faith in the local police and eventual reliance on the military did irreparable damage to the legitimacy of the central government.[70] The situation differed markedly from those years during which the militia helped to consolidate Soviet power; in several republics during the late 1980s, local militia personnel turned against the national leadership in favor of local interests, enhancing the drive for sovereignty. When Soviet troops were flown to Tbilisi, Georgia in April 1989, for example, they attacked peaceful demonstrators with shovels, only to face Georgian militia personnel who intervened to protect Georgian citizens.[71] Similarly, when Soviet troops laid siege to Baku in the neighboring republic of Azerbaijan in January 1990, local militia personnel again sided with the populace.

The drive for increased political autonomy in many Soviet republics eventually broke the central government's hold over the administration of internal affairs. In Moldavia, the Caucasus, and the Baltics, leaders of national movements took increasingly bold steps to assert control over the ministries of internal affairs of their respective republics. Lithuania took the most dramatic stance by establishing its autonomy from Moscow in all areas of government administration, with Latvia and Estonia not far behind.[72]

In Latvia, severe conflict developed within the republican MVD after a man loyal to the national popular front was appointed internal minister. Many Russian militia personnel loyal to the central MVD administration protested this attempt to establish regional control over local policing.[73] In late 1990, the Estonians prepared a draft law for the creation of a "police" in place of the militia. The legislative mandate for the new body completely de-politicized law enforcement and curtailed many of the social control functions exercised by the Soviet militia. Moldavia followed suit with a law establishing a depoliticized police subordinate only to the republican leadership.[74]

Before Bakatin's ouster from the USSR MVD in late 1990, work had nearly been completed on a union treaty. The treaty, intended to be signed by all republican interior ministries, would have decentralized law enforcement in the Soviet Union.[75] Although his removal temporarily slowed official acknowledgement of it, decentralization proceeded unofficially throughout 1991. Full autonomy of republican police forces was achieved in the Baltic states after the failed coup of August 1991; similar autonomy followed in the other Soviet republics after the dissolution of the USSR.

In its final years in power, the Communist Party came to rely on the political organs and Party cells within the MVD. These structures became the primary focus of democratic reformers, who sought to eliminate them as symbols of Party power.[76] Removal of Party influence from this key institution of state control was seen as a prerequisite to enhanced civil rights. Under these conditions, even members of the MVD apparatus understood the waning utility of the Party's presence within the militia. After the constitutional guarantee of the Communist Party's monopoly on power was eliminated in 1990 – when Article 6 of the USSR Constitution was repealed – the deputy chief of the political administration of the central ministry explained: "MVD employees will soon belong to different political organizations, not just the Communist Party."[77]

Depoliticization of the militia did not, of course, proceed uniformly throughout the Soviet Union. The process met strong resistance in some parts of the country and was the subject of sharp controversy among militia personnel.[78] Many regions of the USSR were still grappling with the problem on the eve of the coup; the subsequent banning of the Communist Party by Russian President Boris Yeltsin soon made such debates irrelevant in Russia. Depoliticization was further complicated by militiamen's participation in emerging democratic political processes in Soviet society. Law enforcement personnel, for example, were elected to national parliaments in the majority of the republics. Women police officers, together with figures who had gained visibility in the campaign against racketeers and corruption, represented the majority of those elected.[79]

At the same time the central MVD was trying to maintain control over the crumbling Soviet empire, Minister of Internal Affairs Bakatin was trying to force his subordinates to observe the rule of law. In 1989, 83,500 people were dismissed from the MVD, including 37,700 commissioned officers.In 1990, 6,000 militia personnel were brought up on criminal charges and 30,000 were dismissed, many for work-related misconduct.[80] In October of that year, the state took "urgent measures" to protect citizens' rights and security, when Nikolai Ryzhkov, chairman of the USSR Council of Ministers, presented a package of measures to strengthen law enforcement. These measures included an increase in the number of militia personnel and the purchase of squad cars, radios and other equipment. Ryzhkov also proposed closer coordination between the KGB and the MVD.[81]

Bakatin, in the latter half of 1990, was repeatedly criticized by Communist Party conservatives for his failure to put an end to ethnic disorder in the USSR. In what proved to be a great political mistake, Gorbachev in December 1990 bowed to pressure from conservatives in the Supreme Soviet and dismissed the relatively liberal Bakatin from the MVD, replacing him with Boris Pugo, the former KGB chief of Latvia. Despite this swing to the right, the Supreme Soviet in the same month rejected Gorbachev's proposals to create a special police force that would have assured the execution of official decrees.[82] Pugo and his first deputy, Boris Gromov, a former foreign military commander,[83] attempted to shift the direction of the MVD. Their appointments essentially subordinated the internal affairs ministry to the KGB; closer coordination with other branches of the state's control apparatus would soon follow.

The consequences of these personnel changes were immediately apparent. In late January 1991, Gorbachev issued a decree that gave the militia and KGB forces broad new authority "to inspect 'without hindrance' the properties, supply stocks, cash accounts and ledger books of all domestic and foreign businesses in the country."[84] At the same time, the ministries of defense and internal affairs announced that joint street patrols of army troops and militia personnel would commence in major cities as of 1 February 1991, a policy that shortly spread to 86 other Soviet cities. Finally, OMON contingents were repeatedly deployed in the Baltics and other republics to quell unrest. In 1991, OMON and Soviet Army units attacked the Lithuanian television station in Vil'nius and numerous Lithuanian border patrol posts. To support these new initiatives, the MVD budget was substantially augmented with funds provided by both the central government and the republics.[85]

The actions of President Boris Yeltsin of the Russian republic frustrated Pugo and Gromov in their efforts to reverse the direction of *perestroika*. Yeltsin increasingly challenged the authority of the conservatives and Soviet President Gorbachev himself, applying constant pressure on the USSR government for a new state structure for the country. In July 1991, he banned all primary Party organizations in state institutions of the RSFSR, thereby accelerating the collapse of the Communist Party. Unwilling to acknowledge the changing reality of the USSR, the leadership of the MVD joined other conservative elements to restore Party hegemony over state institutions. In August 1991, MVD Minister Pugo, together with military leaders, the Vice-president of the Soviet Union, the head of the KGB and leaders of the military–industrial complex initiated a coup.[86]

Soon after the coup began on 19 August, the Ministry of Internal Affairs split. While Pugo ordered his subordinates to support the coup, Deputy Minister of Internal Affairs A. Dunaev refused to follow orders and actively instructed militia units to ignore Pugo's instructions. Soviet television and radio, commandeered by leaders of the coup, transmitted messages in support of the *putsch* while Dunaev communicated Yeltsin's appeals to Russian citizens and local offices of the MVD through other channels. Many MVD personnel willingly responded to these carefully worded appeals to remain loyal to Yeltsin and the USSR constitution.

N.S. Myrikov, chief of the Moscow militia, also played an instrumental role in the militia's resistance to the coup. Dunaev sent encrypted messages to the heads of militia schools in many Russian cities instructing them to proceed to Moscow on 21 August, yet when they arrived, all approaches to the city were controlled by the Moscow militia. Dunaev then informed Myrikov over a secure phone line that several hundred fighting men would break Myrikov's defenses. The latter opened the roads and MVD cadets loyal to Yeltsin entered the city. Although Pugo had by then retracted his threat to shoot Dunaev, the cadets proceeded according to plan and headed for the "White House" (the Russian parliament building) where Yeltsin and his supporters had taken refuge.[87]

The coup foundered at critical moments because not only the militia, but part of the KGB resisted orders. The Alpha Division, a super-secret crack unit of the KGB, was commanded to storm the "White House" on the night of 21 August. The unit's own reconnaissance of the situation, however, made clear that Yeltsin's headquarters could not be taken without serious loss of blood. The division refused to attack, telling KGB chief Vladimir Kriuchkov they would not "fight against their own people" and the legitimate Russian government.[88]

The coup attempt collapsed within three days and its leaders were quickly arrested, although Pugo committed suicide before he could be detained. One militiaman standing guard at the parliament building summed up the reason for its failure: "Gorbachev's problem all along was that he trusted the wrong people. He never had any trust in us."[89] Within months of the ill-conceived coup, the Soviet state had collapsed and law enforcement had been transferred from the USSR MVD to the ministries of internal affairs of the respective successor states.[90]

CONCLUSION

The militia changed dramatically with the development of the Soviet state, although it always remained the executor of the will of the Communist Party. The latter's demands, however, changed over time, as Bolshevik power became institutionalized and the state ceased to fear for its survival. When that security vanished in the late 1980s, the militia once again found itself on the political front lines. During seven decades of Soviet rule, the militia was transformed from a militarized force that suppressed political opposition to a law enforcement body responsible for social and economic order, only to return to its initial mission of maintaining political order.

None of these transformations were gradual. The most dramatic shift in policing occurred in the interim between the Stalin and Khrushchev periods. After Stalin's death and the dramatic arrest of his secret police lieutenants, a major overhaul of law enforcement leadership was instituted – its leaders were changed from the "enforcers" of a dictator's brutal will to Communist Party functionaries implementing Party-conceived policies. Major functional changes in Soviet police practice also occurred during this watershed period. The militia ceded many of its political functions to the KGB and began to focus on those activities most closely associated with police forces of other industrialized societies: crime control and the maintenance of order. Yet even at the close of the Soviet period, the scope of Soviet police activity was far broader than that of police in capitalist societies, where the state regulates but does not control the entire economy.

Although the political functions of the militia diminished after the death of Stalin, the regular police retained a diverse set of functions associated with continental, colonial and communist police models. In contrast, the United States and much of western Europe saw a dramatic narrowing of police responsibilities during the post-World War II period. The contraction of police functions in the United States occurred in part because the police ceased to serve local political machines exclusively and were increasingly required to fulfill the law enforcement needs of entire communities.[91] In Europe, reaction to the fascism of World War II prompted many countries to reduce the power of the state. In the Soviet Union, however, the state never ceded its paternalistic role and the militia consequently continued to act as an agent of general social control rather than an ordinary law enforcement body.

Gorbachev's goal of establishing a socialist law-based state sharply deviated from the political and legal practice of seventy years of Soviet rule, but the Soviet leader never intended to make the Soviet militia resemble its western counterparts. As Gorbachev understood *perestroika*, the Soviet Union would retain the principal components of state socialism (state control over the means of production and centralized planning), meaning that state control over the economy and the labor force were to be maintained. The militia, like the socialist law-based state, would thus have continued to intrude into citizens' everyday lives to a greater degree than is the case in western democratic societies.

A significant change in the distribution of power within Soviet society was necessary to restore the credibility of the militia in the late 1980s. Such a change did not occur.[92] Under such conditions, the militia did not reflect the changing balance of forces within Soviet society, nor could it reestablish its credibility among Soviet citizens. In the absence of a major devolution of power, the USSR proved unable to weather the political crisis and the militia, a prominent symbol of the regime, fractured along with the Soviet state.

Part III

Structure and personnel of the militia

4　The organization and management of Soviet policing

> Traditions of police centralization will be created where state and nation-building are accompanied by violent resistance."[1]
>
> David H. Bayley

The USSR Ministry of Internal Affairs (MVD) was responsible for the maintenance of order in the Soviet Union. Grounded in the ideology of Marxism–Leninism, its mandate was to control crime, isolate political opposition (including political and nationalist movements), and combat economic activity outside the state sector. Like other ministries, the MVD was highly centralized. Its massive apparatus extended into every corner of the USSR, consisting of several functional branches: the militia, the internal troops (*vnutrennye voiska* or VV),[2] the departmental and extra-departmental guards, the fire service, and the prison and labor camp systems. Together with the KGB and the procuracy, the MVD long enjoyed a monopoly of policing functions in Soviet society.

Until the Gorbachev era, the MVD remained an extremely powerful – and seemingly unshakeable – instrument of state control, despite occasional changes in its name and scope of activities. The restructuring of the Soviet economy and Soviet society, however, as well as the rise of nationalism in the republics during the *perestroika* years, gradually undermined the institutional integrity of the ministry. The following discussion focuses on the organization and management of policing in the Soviet period and the critical role played by the police in the final period of the existence of the Soviet state.

THE ORGANIZATION OF THE MVD

Throughout the Soviet period (1917–91), the militia had a quasi-military, centralized structure. This structure was a legacy of both the tsarist period and the continental police tradition, as well as the violent first years of the Soviet state. Bayley's thesis that policing becomes centralized due to early, violent resistance to the state is well illustrated by the Soviet experience. Opposition to Soviet rule in many regions reenforced the Bolshevik tendency towards centralized authority; a highly centralized law enforcement apparatus, used to defend the authority of the state and suppress political resistance, resulted. Rather than a contractual model of policing, a statist model developed in the USSR.

The police apparatus was centered in Moscow, where administrative chiefs determined policy for the entire country. The main directorates of the USSR MVD (see Figure 4.1) corresponded to its principal operational functions and consisted of the criminal investigative division (*ugolovnyi rozysk*), the OBKhSS (the division for crime against state property), the division of social order, the GAI (State Automobile Inspectorate), the internal passport division, the OVIR (division of foreign passports and emigration), the departmental and extra-departmental guards, the division of correctional labor (which encompassed the labor camp system), and the fire service.[3] Only the first five of these divisions were considered parts of the militia.

The USSR MVD determined policy, monitored law enforcement, compiled statistics and was responsible for budgeting, medical and educational programs and last, but certainly not least, political work and the selection of cadres. Prior to the movement towards autonomy in various republics during the late Gorbachev years, all major appointments in the MVD went through Moscow. Like the Communist Party, the MVD structure had deputies with specific organizational responsibilities: the first deputy MVD chief in each republic, like the second Party secretary of the republic's Communist Party organization, was a Russian whose primary responsibility was personnel.

The diverse responsibilities of the MVD were supervised by a board, headed by the Minister of Internal Affairs, which consisted of deputy ministers (usually three to five), directorate heads and other ministerial management personnel. The composition of the board, which met once or twice monthly, was approved by the Council of Ministers upon presentation by the Minister of Internal Affairs.[4] The board considered the plans and regulations that were to be implemented by the Ministry, but could not act autonomously of the decision-making process of the Communist Party.

The USSR MVD directly managed all subordinate organizations, including schools and institutes for training entry-level personnel in different republics and advanced training institutes and programs at the republic and national levels. As was the case with all other institutions in the Soviet state, the militia and other MVD organizations were guided by work plans developed by the ministerial headquarters staff, who oversaw the implementation of the numerous directives and instructions that emanated from the all-Union ministry.[5]

The militia, through a system of dual subordination, was subject to two masters: the MVD and local governmental bodies, the latter consisting of legislative bodies (*soviety*, or councils of workers' deputies) and executive bodies such as the *oblispolkom* (the *oblast'*, or regional, governmental executive committee) and *ispolkom* (the executive committee of the lowest-

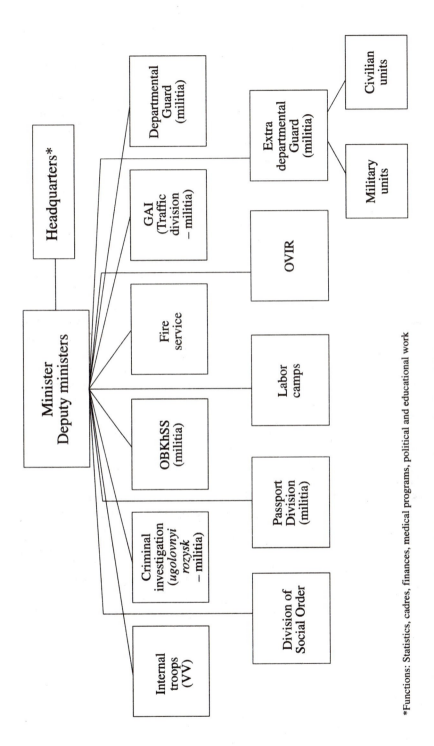

*Functions: Statistics, cadres, finances, medical programs, political and educational work

Figure 4.1 Main directorates of the USSR Ministry of Internal affairs (MVD)

level unit of local government).[6] This system of dual subordination meant that, while national law enforcement policy was decided by the Politburo or the Central Committee of the Communist Party and administered throughout the country by the USSR MVD, local input and oversight was still possible within established guidelines. The MVD thus fulfilled law enforcement policies of the national Soviet leadership as well as the personal demands of local Party leaders, who pressured militia personnel through Party and governmental channels.

Beneath the central headquarters in Moscow, the MVD was divided into republic, regional (*oblast'* or *krai*), district (*raion*) and city administrations. Each of these administrations reported to the Party organization and the executive committee at their respective administrative level, in addition to the next-higher level office of the MVD. The militia existed at each level of the MVD structure (see Figure 4.2). With the exception of the RSFSR (Russian Republic), each Soviet republic had a long-established republican Ministry of Internal Affairs. (The RSFSR, generally equated with the Soviet government, lacked a republican-level ministry until 1989. This ministry later came to inherit many of the resources of the former USSR MVD.[7])

The responsibilities of republican ministries were in many respects analogous to the USSR MVD, except that the jurisdiction of the former was confined solely to their respective republics. In autonomous republics and republics with autonomous regions (usually an area inhabited by a particular national group), the administrative structure was similar. Responsibilities of internal affairs organs at lower levels were, of course, much more limited, as they simply supervised the operational activities of regional and city MVD units.[8]

Each republican ministry contained the following divisions of the militia: criminal investigation, the OBKhSS, administrative services (this division performed patrol post, passport and licensing duties)[9] and the GAI (automobile inspectorate). These branches existed at all administrative levels within the republic, with the relevant militia division subordinate to the corresponding internal affairs administrative unit at every level of government. In small republics such as Lithuania, Latvia and Estonia, which were divided into districts rather than the larger *oblasti*, the MVD was divided into units at the city and regional level (i.e., *gorispolkomy* and *raiispolkomy*). In larger republics that contained several *oblasti*, the MVD had an intermediate unit of administration at the *oblast'* level. In Georgia and Armenia, which were divided into both autonomous republics and *oblasti*, the MVD of each autonomous republic or *oblast'* reported to the republican MVD.[10]

The militia itself was divided between transport and territorial militias, whose structures differed. The transport militia was not subject to dual subordination – each branch was subject only to the higher link in the MVD chain of command. The main link in the system of the territorial militia, however, was the *gorispolkom* or the *raiispolkom* (i.e., the city or district executive committee), which existed in all rural areas, cities, districts of big

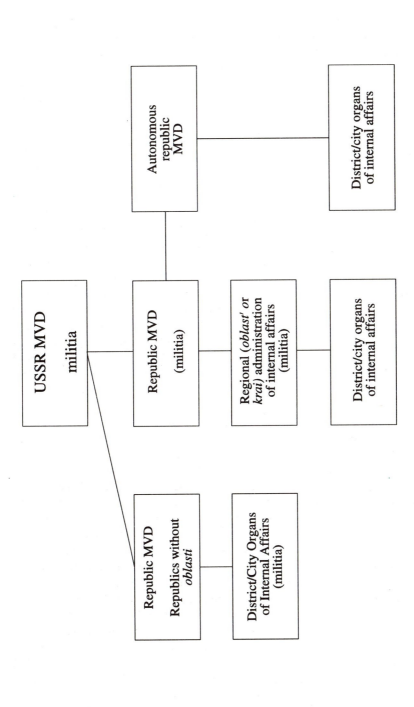

Figure 4.2 Organization of the militia

cities and territories that were divided into administrative regions. The size of the area policed determined whether the city or district unit was higher within the institutional hierarchy. In Moscow, the district branches of the militia were subordinate to that of the city, whereas in less populous areas, city units fell under the administration of the district.

In several large cities (Moscow, Leningrad, Kiev and Novosibirsk, for example), the territory of each city district was further divided into sectors that were served by militia units subordinate to the department of internal affairs of the *raiispolkom*. In the post-Stalinist period, a typical district in Moscow was divided into six sectors, each of which was served by its own unit of the militia. Such administrative divisions also existed in some mid-sized and smaller cities. After Gorbachev launched his program of *perestroika*, some 1,500 outdated orders and instructions were changed in an effort to decentralize administrative control, giving city and district organs of internal affairs broader independence and rights.[11] These changes were sufficiently extensive to satisfy the aspiration of many municipalities to enhance their control over policing in their own cities.

The management of municipal policing was difficult. In a typical city, each unit of 150 to 200 personnel might have as many as 20 different subunits, each divided into approximately 10-person squads. The senior administrator of the 200-man militia unit, known as the "commander," had at a minimum two deputies.[12] The deputy chief for operations supervised those militia divisions responsible for ordinary crime, crime against state property, traffic regulation and the maintenance of order. This pattern of personnel assignment made coordination difficult and led to inadequate staffing in important areas. For example, in 1990 there were only 17 people in the narcotics division of the city of Moscow,[13] the main transit point for drugs in the entire USSR. Other citywide and local units lacked needed manpower because personnel spent so much time behind their desks.

Many smaller communities and rural areas did not need great numbers of specialized personnel and had only one or two individuals working in the criminal investigative unit or the OBKhSS. Other communities had a precinct inspector (*uchastkovyi inspektor*) who had personal responsibility for a particular beat and acted as a direct link between the militia and the community.[14]

Administrative and political divisions complemented operational units at the city level. These units oversaw personnel matters, political education of the militia force and propaganda among the citizenry. At the *oblast'* and republic levels, militia administrative units had additional responsibilities, such as investigating Communist Party members and the conduct of militia personnel. These higher-level units handled sensitive matters and were somewhat analogous to the internal affairs units of American police departments; such units had more contact with the procuracy and the KGB than did militia units at lower levels of the administrative hierarchy.

Crime statistics were registered with the First Special Division of the republican militia, the department responsible for maintaining statistics on the regular police.[15] The lack of routinized procedures for collecting and tabulating statistics at the local level made the consolidation of crime figures difficult. Moreover, there was little scrutiny of this data before renewed publication of crime statistics in 1987.

The *spetsmilitsiia* (special militia), which served "closed" institutions and cities that comprised part of a special court system within the USSR, were a part of the territorial militia administrative structure.[16] No published statute discussed the activities of this militia, but interviews with both practicing and former Soviet lawyers suggest that its jurisdiction rather than its function differentiated it from other militia divisions. Other specialized units also existed within the territorial militia. The guard services employed approximately 200,000 men, of which nearly 80,000 were employed by the departmental, or institutional, guard (*vedomstvennaia okhrana*). In existence for over six decades, this force was assigned to guard state institutions such as the USSR State Bank, territories, economic enterprises, airports and reservoirs. Subordinate to the USSR MVD, the departmental guard operated under the militia statute. In Moscow, this guard was employed by the metro, the exhibition of economic achievement (*VDNKH*), the Lenin Library and the Ostankino radio and television tower.[17]

A more sophisticated, extra-departmental guard (*vnevedomstvennaia okhrana*) existed in both civilian and military forms.[18] Created in 1952 as part of the militia's external administrative division, the functions of the civilian units of it resembled U.S. private guard services. Working under contract, this force guarded enterprises, construction sites, and such organizations as clinics, hospitals, pioneer camps, children's nurseries in cities, worker settlements, and district and regional governmental and Party centers. During the *perestroika* years, it provided guards to more than one thousand church buildings.[19] Non-departmental guards also supervised the transportation of goods, especially *spetsproduktsiia* (special products), that had to be protected from public scrutiny for political reasons.

The internal troops of the MVD were separate from the military units of the extra-departmental guard. Unlike militia personnel, rank-and-file soldiers of this force were not long-term employees of the MVD, but conscription call-ups.[20] Commissioned officers of the internal troops, however, were permanent MVD employees. Separate from military units and reporting directly to the head of the MVD, the internal troops were always on call to control special situations such as strikes, ethnic conflict or outbreaks of violence at sports events. Originally a special supplementary force used as convoy defense or guards at strategic installations – yet never a part of the transport militia – the internal troops were increasingly called upon to quell unrest in the USSR during the late 1980s.

New legislation on the internal troops (drafted by the MVD) was adopted in 1990 that divided the troops into two bodies, one subordinate to the central government and the other, a specialized motorized militia, subordinate to the local government at the republic level. Remarking on the organizational change, the commander of the USSR MVD internal troops rejected the suggestion that these troops be transferred to republican command, claiming that such a transfer would weaken the authority of the national government.[21] Also in 1990, approximately six divisions (about 65,000 men) were added to the internal troops, which already numbered 300,000. Many of these troops were subsequently sent to suppress nationalist movements or curb ethnic conflict in Azerbaijan, Nagorno-Karabakh, Tajikistan and the part of the Fergana Valley located in Uzbekistan.[22] In such situations, these units fulfilled the role envisioned for them at the time militia troops were first created early in the postrevolutionary period.

THE DIVISION OF POLICING FUNCTIONS IN THE SOVIET JUDICIAL SYSTEM

The militia shared investigatory police functions with the KGB and the procuracy. The latter, the principal prosecutorial agency in the Soviet judicial system, not only investigated and prosecuted certain categories of serious crime, but represented the state in civil cases and exercised oversight over the investigative branches of the militia and the KGB. Although the USSR code of criminal procedure delineated a clear division of responsibility between the procuracy and the militia, it was less specific about the investigative functions assigned to the KGB. The KGB had exclusive jurisdiction over anti-state crimes, yet its mandate included smuggling, violations of rules on financial transactions (e.g., trading in currency, precious stones and metals),[23] and, prior to *perestroika*, certain crimes involving foreigners. (The MVD had responsibility for investigation of homicides, armed robbery and crimes of deception involving foreigners.) Depending on the nature of the case, two or even all three of these investigative bodies might work together; such complex investigations, however, were often hindered by jurisdictional conflicts.

At one time the procuracy conducted most criminal investigations in the USSR, but after the enactment of new legislation in the early 1960s, the MVD assumed between 65 and 70 percent of preliminary investigations for all categories of crime. Following further legislative changes in 1965, the MVD became responsible for 80 percent of all preliminary criminal investigations, while the procuracy retained sole investigatory responsibility for certain serious offenses such as homicide, rape and abuse of authority by state and Party officials.[24] See Table 4.1 for a breakdown of functions among the three agencies.

Although it officially ceded a number of its investigative functions to the militia, the procuracy officially maintained the upper hand in investigatory work by authorizing searches and detention and verifying the legality of militia work. It preserved its control unofficially by secretly instructing investigative personnel how to proceed in a case, as well as failing to

Table 4.1 Division of investigative responsibilities between the militia, the procuracy and the KGB in the USSR[a]

Crimes investigated by militia and procuracy:

- Stealing or damaging state property (Articles 89–91, 93, 94, 96/2, 98, 99, 100 of the RSFSR Criminal Code)
- Crimes against the person: infliction of bodily injury, torture, infection with venereal disease, pederasty, evasion of child or parental support (Articles 108–11, 113–15/1, 121–3, 125)
- Crimes against personal property of citizens (Articles 144–50)
- Economic crimes: trading on the black market, deception of purchasers, issuance of poor quality goods, engaging in trade, timber or mining violations (Articles 153, 154/1, 155–57, 159, 162/2, 165, 167)
- Crimes against justice: escape from medical–labor clinics, unwarranted return to residence from which one has been banished, escape from place of confinement (Articles 186–8)
- Crimes against the system of administration: stealing or forging documents; hooliganism; threatening injury to another person; fencing goods; violation of vehicular safety regulations; violation of firearms and dangerous substance regulations; narcotics violations; maintaining a brothel; making or marketing pornography; desecrating graves or cultural monuments (Articles 194–6, 206/3, 207, 208, 211–13/1, 217–20, 224–6, 228–30)

Crimes investigated solely by the procuracy:

- Crimes against the state: warmongering, banditry, disrupting labor camps, draft evasion (Articles 71, 74, 77, 77/1, 80–2, 85)
- Crimes against state property: negligent use of agricultural equipment (Article 99/1)
- Crimes against the person: homicide; illegal abortion; rape; statutory rape; abuses of guardianship; illegal deprivation of freedom; leaving a person in need of immediate assistance in danger; defamation (Articles 101–7, 116–20, 124, 124/1, 126–9, 130/2–3)
- All crimes violating the political and labor rights of citizens (Articles 132–43)
- Economic crimes: violation of plant and animal regulations (Articles 151–152/1, 160, 161, 164)
- All crimes concerning the abuse of official power and bribery of officials (Articles 170–5)
- Crimes against justice: violations of criminal procedure (Articles 176–80)
- Crimes against the system of administration: anti-Soviet slander,[b] resisting or insulting a militiaman, illegally displaying the Soviet flag (Articles 190/1, 191–3, 197/1, 202–205/1)
- Crimes against public security: drawing minors into crime; violation of safety and construction rules; violation of medical and pollution regulations; performance of religious ceremonies (Articles 210, 214–16, 221–3, 227)
- Crimes constituting the survival of local customs that contradicted Soviet legal norms, such as bride purchase (Articles 231–5)
- Military crimes (Articles 238–58)

Crimes investigated by the KGB:

- Especially dangerous and other crimes against the state: treason; espionage; anti-Soviet activity;[c] divulgence of state and military secrets; smuggling; mass disorder; illegal entry and exit (Articles 64–70, 72, 73, 75, 76, 78, 79, 83, 84, 259)
- Economic crimes:[d] violation of financial transactions (trading in currency, precious stones and metals), theft of state property on a large scale or through the abuse of one's position (Articles 88, 92, 93/1)

Table 4.1 continued

a This table cites the Criminal Code and the Code of Criminal Procedure of the RSFSR because no criminal or procedural codes existed at the national level in the Soviet Union. USSR law consisted solely of "Fundamental Principles" concerning different categories of civil and criminal law; actual codes were adopted at the republican level only and were fairly uniform across republics.

b Article 190/1 specified that investigations of anti-Soviet slander be conducted by the procuracy, when in reality they were conducted by the KGB. At the close of the Soviet period, prosecutions on this charge were halted and inmates charged under this article were released.

c Prosecutions on this charge were halted at the end of the Soviet period and inmates so charged were released.

d The procuracy and internal affairs organs could be asked to assist the KGB in its investigation of economic crimes.

Source: Article 126 of the RSFSR Code of Criminal Procedure, as translated in Harold J. Berman, *Soviet Criminal Law and Procedure: The RSFSR Codes*, 2d ed. (Cambridge: Harvard University Press, 1972), 241–2

prevent other governmental bodies from intervening in the investigatory process.[25] Dependent on the procuracy for their welfare, the militia could not act independently. An illuminating example of this dependence was demonstrated by an incident in which a group of hooligans stormed the fifth precinct of the Moscow militia; police officers at the precinct were able to use clubs against their attackers only after receiving authorization from the procuracy.[26]

The procuracy's surveillance function also extended to KGB investigations. In this case, however, oversight was more pro forma than real. As the procurator who oversaw the investigative functions of the KGB in Leningrad once explained to the author: "In twenty-three years of overseeing their work, I have not found errors."[27] The procuracy did not automatically provide such positive evaluations of militia work, and occasionally even served as a check on militia illegalities, particularly during the *perestroika* era. For example, procurators might not sanction the detention of a suspect or might drop cases initiated by the militia. Yet Party pressure to produce convictions meant the procuracy was not a disinterested arbiter of legality during most of the Soviet period, and its oversight was thus inherently limited.

Glasnost' brought the structure of the investigatory process under severe attack for failing to ensure the independence of the investigator and, hence, the rights of the defendant. Because the criminal investigative branch of the MVD both supervised undercover work and investigated individual criminal cases prior to prosecution, investigators often could not be objective – their participation in both processes put operational information at their disposal. No genuine separation of powers existed when the procuracy investigated crimes, reviewed militia cases and represented the state in court.

Some reformers considered the reorganization of the investigatory process a primary objective of *perestroika* and proposed alternative structures to the existing investigative organs.[28] Reluctant to lose its authority and power, the MVD suggested that the investigative and operational branches of the militia be separated within the MVD structure, a position supported by a resolution of the nineteenth Communist Party conference in June 1988. Those who sought more dramatic change suggested the creation of a new investigatory body that would combine militia, procuratorial and KGB investigators in one organization subordinate to the USSR Supreme Soviet or Council of Ministers.[29] Such an arrangement would have freed criminal investigators from MVD pressure to clear crimes and procuratorial pressure to ensure convictions. KGB investigators, however, who retained a reputation for greater integrity and competence, were not eager to mix with militia investigators of inferior standing. The unwillingness of each of the three investigatory organs to surrender power inhibited efforts to reform the Soviet criminal justice system during the *perestroika* era. In the end, no change in the investigatory process was successfully implemented prior to the collapse of the Soviet state in 1991.

CONTROL AND COORDINATION

The MVD responded to the commands of both the government and the Communist Party. Yet, in law enforcement, as in other policy areas, the government (i.e., the Council of Ministers) exercised little control. The Party, more specifically the administrative organs department of the Central Committee (renamed the state and law department during *perestroika*), truly managed the MVD. It was assisted in this task by the KGB. According to an MVD general, the KGB had a uniform system for monitoring the activities of the Ministry of Internal Affairs in every republic, district and city.[30] After Boris Pugo, a KGB man, became the Minister of Internal Affairs in 1991, a committee for law enforcement organs was created within the MVD to systematize MVD–KGB cooperation.[31]

Party guidance occurred in several important forms. The Central Committee's administrative organs department oversaw personnel appointments and the implementation of Party policy, as did subordinate administrative organs at the provincial and regional levels.[32] When the Party apparatus began to shrink under Gorbachev's campaign to reduce its power, effective Party supervision of the MVD also declined. As this decline became apparent, attempts by local and republican governments to assert more control over law enforcement grew in number. Interestingly, Party control was not financial. Although all policy decisions were ultimately made by the Communist Party, funding for the militia was provided by the government via the Ministry of Internal Affairs, which had a vast, and secret, budget. Only towards the close of the Soviet period did local governmental organizations begin to supplement the budgets of their militia administrations.

Prior to the collapse of its authority in 1990–91, the Party also coordinated the activities of the various law enforcement agencies. Representatives of the courts, procuracy, customs, the Ministry of Justice and republican ministries of internal affairs met regularly with Party representatives to discuss policy. Party direction of the MVD itself was considerably more intrusive and included: evaluation of militia performance by Party commissions and organizations; written instructions; participation of Party members in internal MVD meetings; presentation of reports by internal affairs personnel at Party meetings; and examination of citizen complaints and press criticism of MVD improprieties.[33] These diverse forms of management brought the MVD into constant contact with the Party apparatus, permitting the ministry to fine-tune its operations to the demands of the Party.

Control was ensured from within as well as from above. Although political organs were instituted in the MVD only in the early 1980s, by 1988 the Minister of Internal Affairs Aleksandr Vlasov claimed there were 10,000 primary Party organizations and 17,000 political workers within the MVD system, including a total of 500,000 Communist Party members.[34] Many individuals joined the Party because promotion was curtailed without Party membership. And, while many line personnel were not Party members, one-half of all militia officers belonged to the Party; membership was nearly universal among the upper echelons of the ministry due to the *nomenklatura* system.[35]

Party organizations at all levels, ranging from the district to the CPSU Central Committee, had their own *nomenklatura* appointments.[36] A clearly systematized process determined appointments and subordination within this system (see Figure 4.3): the head of the USSR MVD as well as the heads of republican internal affairs ministries were *nomenklatura* appointments of the Central Committee. Individuals appointed to these positions were nominated at the highest levels of the Party apparatus, with an internal political process determining the selection of appointees; selected officials reported directly to the CPSU Central Committee. The central committee of each republican Party organization controlled the appointment of the deputy minister of internal affairs for the republic, as well as those of the directors of internal affairs at the *oblast'* level. Each Party organization – whether at the republic, *oblast'*, *raion* or city level – appointed not only the deputy chief, but as many as five supervisory personnel (the exact number varied by republic). Subordination of each level of supervisory personnel to both the immediate and higher level of the Party structure ensured that the militia received instructions from both local and superior Party authorities. As promotion occurred through the Party apparatus rather than through the ranks, militia personnel did not need to be responsive either to the community or to those below them in the institutional hierarchy. The system thus worked to buffer elites from their subordinates, spawning endemic corruption and widespread abuse of individual rights.

Party control was maintained on a regular basis by means of Party

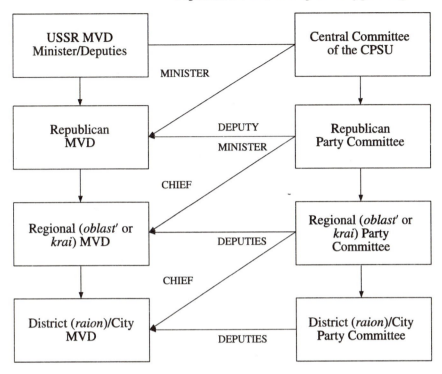

Figure 4.3 The *nomenklatura* (Communist Party appointments) of the MVD

meetings and educational seminars, both of which communicated Party policy directly to the MVD bureaucracy.[37] Political organs, reintroduced under Andropov for the first time since Stalin's death, were seen, as a major means of reasserting Party control over the ministry after Brezhnev's death, when its extensive corruption first came under public attack.[38] These organs were intended to provide stronger Party direction than that provided by the political education departments subordinate to the ministry, which had previously conducted ideological indoctrination among MVD personnel.

The new political departments reported directly to the Central Committee of the CPSU and acted on its instructions alone, supposedly enabling them to combat more effectively the incidence of collusion between Party and MVD officials at the local level. Before these organs were created, political officers, like their counterparts in the armed forces, helped to socialize personnel, maintain morale and even find housing for members of the militia. The creation of political departments, however, brought career Party personnel into the militia bureaucracy who did not budge from their offices and never interacted with the rank and file. Recruitment also continued along parallel lines: as late as 1988, there was still an intense effort to hire

Komsomol members into the militia in order to improve the ideological qualifications of its employees.[39]

Political organs, political officers and the role of the Party in militia work became heated topics by 1990, discussed within the militia itself as well as by democratic forces that sought the depoliticization of all state institutions. The declining prestige of political workers, a symptom of Soviet society's overall attitude towards Party work and Party personnel, was clearly discerned by militia personnel.[40] Consistent with the democratization occurring in legislative bodies, proposals were made to secretly elect rather than appoint political officers in the MVD. Some officers even spoke in favor of disbanding Party organs in the militia while supporting the right of militia personnel to join the Communist Party or any other political party.[41]

In September 1990, Gorbachev issued an order to restructure the political organs in the MVD, KGB and the military so as to emphasize principles of loyalty to the state, not the Communist Party. By the end of the year, the USSR MVD had abolished its political administration and established a main personnel department in its place.[42] This was the first step of a depoliticization that was never fully achieved in the Soviet period. At the same time, the role of the central Party apparatus in the administration of the militia was abolished: the administrative organs department of the Central Committee ceased to oversee law enforcement and its oversight over the MVD and KGB was assumed by the USSR Supreme Soviet Committee on Defense and Security. Internal Affairs Minister Vadim Bakatin proclaimed that "[t]here is not, nor will there be in future, any structure within the CPSU Central Committee that controls the Soviet legal system."[43]

Although control was seemingly transferred from the Communist Party to the government, the members of the Supreme Soviet committee were leading representatives of the military, the security apparatus and the military–industrial apparatus, many of whom subsequently participated in the coup.[44] Sadly, the advent of governmental control over the police in the USSR did not go hand in hand with the democratization or depoliticization of policing.

The move to substitute governmental for Party jurisdiction encountered similar problems in other areas of political life in the Soviet Union. Former KGB Major General Oleg Kalugin, spymaster turned whistle-blower on the Soviet secret police, commented,

> Despite power technically being transferred from the Party to the soviets (local government), the chiefs of the Leningrad KGB and MVD, for example, report to the first secretary of the *oblast'* and city Party committee, Boris Gidaspov, rather than to Leningrad Soviet Chairman A. Sobchak . . . [45]

Even when elected to city government, democratic politicians were unable to wrest control of the administration of law enforcement from the Party apparatus in cities throughout the USSR. Despite efforts to curb Party control, the Party's commands were still communicated to its millions of members within the law enforcement structure. In July 1991, President of the Russian Republic Boris Yeltsin sought to fully depoliticize the Russian governmental apparatus by banning all Party personnel from state organizations within the republic. Similar policies were under way elsewhere – in certain republics, individuals were forced to choose between Party membership and continued employment in the militia.

Boris Pugo, head of the MVD, joined the coup specifically to restore Party hegemony over the Soviet state and its institutions. The federal treaty scheduled to be signed by the central government and the republics in August 1991 gave, in his view, too little power to the MVD.[46] A month after the unsuccessful coup, the Communist Party of the Soviet Union was disbanded and direct Party influence over the institution of the police became a thing of the past.[47]

THE ADMINISTRATIVE RESPONSE TO PERESTROIKA

The central MVD leadership searched for enhanced powers until the dissolution of the Soviet Union (see Table 4.2). Throughout the late 1980s and into 1991, there was constant conflict between mandated openness (*glasnost'*) and the MVD's attempt to restrain fundamental changes occurring in the USSR as a result of increased free enterprise, decentralization of political power and diminished fear of the state on the part of the Soviet populace.

In 1988, the Sixth Administration of the MVD was established to fight

Table 4.2 Changes in militia structure following Brezhnev's death (1983–92)

1983:	Political organs departments institutionalized.
1987:	Establishment of OMON, special-purpose militia detachments.
1988:	Establishment of private detective services and guard cooperatives.
	Motorized militia divisions created to police political demonstrations.
	Sixth Administration of the USSR MVD created to combat organized crime.
1989:	RSFSR Ministry of Internal Affairs established.
	May. Administration of Preventive Services of USSR MVD created.
1990:	Political administration of USSR MVD closed, replaced by Administration for Personnel Work.
	Baltic states attempt to establish autonomous ministries of internal affairs.
1991:	March. New USSR statute on militia adopted by USSR Supreme Soviet.
	OBKhSS division of the militia (responsible for crimes against state property) converted into a service to combat economic criminality.
	MVD Sixth Administration, formerly responsible for organized crime, transformed into Main Administration to Combat the Most Serious Forms of Crime, Organized Crime, Narcobusiness and Corruption.
	August. Transfer of militia power from USSR MVD to the ministries of internal affairs of newly independent Baltic states.
	December. Yeltsin attempts to combine MVD and KGB.
1992:	January. Russian Constitutional Court finds presidential decree combining MVD and KGB unconstitutional.

organized crime. Its 1,200 employees were, however, woefully insufficient to control the increasingly pervasive organized criminal organizations in the USSR. Leading militia officials thought that a national organization – a Soviet FBI – might be the answer to their problems, but the state's budget crisis prevented the creation of such a body.[48] In mid-1991, in recognition of the increasing severity of the organized crime problem, the Sixth Administration was transformed into the Main Administration to Combat the Most Serious Forms of Crime, Organized Crime, Narcobusiness and Corruption; ten republics subsequently created such bodies within their territories.[49]

The MVD also responded early to the ethnic conflicts that threatened the Soviet state, strengthening a force that had first been created for the Olympics in 1979. The formation of a special Moscow militia division, the Special-Purpose Militia Detachments (OMON), was hidden from public scrutiny.[50] This militia division – distinct from the internal troops of the MVD – had originally been part of the patrol service of the Division of Social Order (see Figure 4.1, p. 65), a service that maintained public order during meetings, demonstrations, exhibitions and sports events. (The OMON, discussed further in Chapter 10, were later used in the Baltic republics primarily for political purposes: that is, its troops were used to intimidate national movements in these republics. More recently, in 1994, OMON troops have been used against organized criminal organizations in Russia.) Finally, the establishment in 1989 of a proactive militia unit, the Administration of Preventive Services, was another major structural response of the militia to the social conditions created by *perestroika*.

Among the functions of the latter division was the supervision of worker detachments and other volunteer and citizen groups that were assigned to assist the militia. Worker detachments were first established in the industrial city of Gorky (now Nizhnii Novgorod) to supplement understaffed militia units and substitute for personnel sent to areas of unrest, such as Nagorno-Karabakh.[51] Such units subsequently spread to Uzbekistan, Kazakhstan, Ukraine, Moldavia and fifteen different *oblasti* around the USSR. Their rapid expansion was ascribed to the encouragement of the department of state and law of the CPSU Central Committee. The then Russian Minister of Internal Affairs Vadim Bakatin viewed worker detachments as a way of reviving the voluntary people's militias of early postrevolutionary days.[52]

Worker detachments consisted of factory workers released on a temporary basis from their enterprises for militia service. Even though such units took much-needed workers away from enterprises, the level of community insecurity made many Soviet citizens willing supporters of this new initiative. Paid substantially better than militia employees, these individuals began to patrol after receiving only 32 hours of training, as compared with the 4 months received by professional militia personnel. Without appropriate training in the legal norms they were to enforce or effective restrictions on their right to enter residential areas in pursuit of trespassers, many people feared these units were a force for establishing order rather than a law-based state.[53] The Gorky force operated only in conjunction with actual militiamen, providing citizens some assurance that worker detachments would observe the law. Yet the creation of a parallel police force equipped with truncheons that could be used to suppress informal groups aroused concern among people pressing for democratic reforms. The tendency of certain Party *apparatchiki* to see these forces as an antidote to nationalism gave the latter further cause for concern.[54]

Worker detachments were just one form of supplemental law enforcement that compensated for the void in the federal law enforcement apparatus during the final years of the Soviet regime; other such forms included municipal and private security services. The establishment of municipal militias in different cities reflected the failure of worker detachments to impose order in many areas as well as the desire of local authorities to become responsible for law enforcement in their communities. The desire for local control over policing was evident in many parts of the country; local militia forces were established in areas of Central Asia, the Crimea, Siberia and European areas of the Russian Republic. In Dushanbe, the capital of Tadjikistan, for example, a 500-man city militia funded by local firms and individual contributions was formed after citizen self-defense groups helped restore order in the city following major riots in February 1990. During the riots, the militia had protected government installations in the city center, ignoring the needs of citizens under attack in more outlying areas of the city.[55]

Arrangements varied among municipalities. In Kuibyshev, formerly a closed city in the RSFSR, the municipal government decided that 40 individuals should be recruited from city enterprises and 24 from state and collective farms to improve order in the city. In rural areas, individuals generally aided precinct inspectors, receiving in return special privileges from their workplaces such as a place in nursery school for their children or a place on the waiting list for housing. Some locales allocated large sums to establish their own militia forces. In Simferopol, 300,000 rubles were set aside from the local budget to found a police force that would regulate traffic, investigate minor offenses and handle other questions of daily life. Even more money was budgeted in Volgograd, where the city government allotted two million rubles to finance a 2,000-man militia.[56]

In Spring 1991, the control and financing of the Moscow city militia became the subject of a power struggle between Gorbachev and the newly elected democratic leaders of Moscow. The Moscow leadership did not want to bear the expense of the militia force if it could not determine police policy. Gorbachev ruled in March that the Moscow militia would be subject to the jurisdiction of the national ministry, the USSR MVD, creating a single administration of internal affairs for Moscow and the Moscow *oblast'* and placing it under the direction of a hard-liner. The actual purpose of Gorbachev's maneuver was to curb popular demonstrations in support of Boris Yeltsin, then Chairman of the Supreme Soviet of the RSFSR.[57] The Russian legislature, however, rejected Gorbachev's decision and placed the Moscow militia under the control of the Russian government. The conflict culminated in April 1991 when the Moscow city government established an autonomous militia with Moscow officials rather than MVD management personnel in charge.[58]

Private detective and investigative services were further proof of the diminishing control of the central authorities. In 1988, the MVD was telling its personnel to have nothing to do with such services. By 1990, their approach had changed completely and policemen were permitted to work for such organizations on the side. Those who moonlighted were able to augment their incomes by at least 250 to 300 rubles a month, an income supplement that helped stem attrition in certain locales.[59] By 1990, literally hundreds of private police, detective and guard organizations were in existence. These services performed a variety of functions including security for cooperatives, personal security, escorting shipments, spying on spouses, searching for runaways and missing children and installing security systems. Even though their services were expensive, citizens turned to them because overburdened militia investigators could rarely provide them assistance. A national convention of private police groups was even held in 1990, at which such organizations sought to establish links with similar groups abroad.[60]

In western societies the emergence of large private security forces is generally seen as a threat to democratization. In the Soviet Union, however, the emergence of such forces was initially viewed as a sign of privatization and democratization because they diminished the state's monopoly of social control. Although their challenge to Party and state control of law enforcement was seen positively, such private forces also represented a potential social threat as they were not subordinated to any ministry or regulated by law. Often staffed and run by former MVD or KGB personnel, many agencies either worked directly for or were managed by organized criminal groups. Numerous guards recruited into private police services lacked moral character; some had even committed murder.[61] A serious problem of professional ethics thus accompanied the privatization of policing in the USSR and Soviet citizens criticized private police services for the same reasons as have American and British citizens: their operations are accountable to no one.[62] Rather than represent a new form of policing, privatization merely continued the worst of Soviet policing practices while freeing private police forces from legislative and institutional controls.

Privatization of the economy had other effects on policing. The transformation of the OBKhSS division into an economic crime service in 1991, initiated by Minister of Internal Affairs Pugo, was an attempt by the state to obtain some control over and the right to intervene in the burgeoning private sector.[63] Special units were established within local divisions of the Moscow militia, ostensibly to protect traders from racketeers, with the need to provide consumers with food cited as justification for the initiative.[64]

In conjunction with structural changes within the militia, the late 1980s also saw serious discussion of a changed mandate for the militia. A new

USSR draft statute on the militia, published in June 1990, was widely debated before a final draft was adopted in March of the following year. Much of the debate focused on such issues as the political status of policing; its relationship to governmental bodies; the use of firearms; the relationship between the center and the periphery (i.e., between local governments and the central ministry); and which governmental bodies had the right to deploy militia detachments in different parts of the country.[65]

The pull of sovereignty in the republics, the increasing autonomy of local governments and the greater vulnerability of the militia itself were all reflected in the new legislation. Although it did not reduce the range of militia functions, the draft law differed from previous statutes on the Soviet militia in certain important respects. For the first time, legislation governing the regular police reflected the importance of accountability (to the community), depoliticization and the independence of law enforcement. Despite the lengthy development of the new law, its adoption in March 1991 came too late to be of much effect; the legislation remained a transitional document of a failing state.[66]

These developments in Soviet policing were a response to the decline in social and political order and the beginnings of a market economy in the USSR. Typical of democratization in the Soviet Union as a whole, the MVD's institutional response to *perestroika* represented a curious mix of enhanced controls and greater autonomy for law enforcement bodies. Symptomatic of the organizational flux in which policing found itself at the end of the Soviet regime was the attempt of Russian President Boris Yeltsin to merge the security apparatus with the internal affairs ministry. His December 1991 decree uniting the KGB and the MVD was opposed by many legislators who feared the reunification of these law enforcement bodies, last united under Stalin. Fortunately, Yeltsin's attempt to combine these powerful ministries – a tactic to secure his power within the Russian republic – ran counter to democratic trends in Russia and was found unconstitutional by the Russian Constitutional Court in January 1992 in its first major decision.[67]

CONCLUSION

Until the final years of the Soviet period, the MVD was a primary organ of state control in the USSR. Accountable neither to the population nor to the government, it remained a tool of the Communist Party of the Soviet Union (under Stalin, it served the Party leader directly). Created in the first decades of Soviet rule, the militia was designed to serve the demands of a command economy and a nearly omnipotent dictator. When it became apparent that the structural demands of a highly centralized system were not conducive for democratization, both its mission and effectiveness came under siege during the *perestroika* era.

By the advent of *perestroika*, the USSR Ministry of Internal Affairs employed three million employees engaged in various law enforcement, correctional and public safety duties. The diverse and often conflicting responsibilities of the ministry made it difficult to reform and, towards the end of the Soviet regime, a marked division of responsibility existed within the MVD: republican ministries (and local organs) devoted themselves to crime control, while the central USSR MVD concerned itself with "internal and state security tasks."[68] Whereas the militia and correctional authorities were instructed to humanize their activities under Gorbachev, increasing ethnic conflict caused more frequent deployment of MVD internal troops in the republics. Although state security responsibilities were not explicitly part of the 1962, 1973, or 1991 statutes on the MVD, deployment of the OMON (and its strict military discipline) were evidence that the militia did indeed act in defense of the Soviet state.

The organization and management of the militia in the USSR had always been the responsibility of the Communist Party, a single ruling party that succeeded in imposing a homogeneous institutional structure on the world's largest country. Yet neither the central control maintained by the system of *nomenklatura* appointments, nor the structure of the Soviet militia itself, was able to adequately accommodate the problems posed by the diversity of the USSR's population and the vastness of territory – a fact that became abundantly clear as the process of democratization proceeded under Gorbachev.

Efforts to transfer the management of policing from Party to governmental institutions during the *perestroika* era were eventually outpaced by the course of political events in the country. In the end, the Ministry of Internal Affairs could not effectively respond to growing centrifugal forces within the USSR. Like colonial forces in other collapsing empires, the Soviet militia found that local conditions on the ground were more compelling than policies developed by the imperial center.[69]

5   Allocation, recruitment and training of militia personnel

> The higher is the general intellectual development of our militiaman, the better the standard-bearer he will be of Soviet power.[1]
>
> M.I. Kalinin

Western observers of policing have suggested that the quality of a police department is dependent on the character of the individual police officer.[2] The collectivist ideology of the Soviet state and the nature of communist policing precluded a focus on the individual: the militiaman was valued solely as one part of a state-organized institution. There was little concern for the professional development of the individual within the militia bureaucracy – individuals' needs were addressed only when their neglect might impinge upon the effectiveness of law enforcement. Militiamen in the USSR were recruited not for their personal attributes, but their ability to conform to and execute the demands of the Soviet law enforcement apparatus. Obedience to superiors was the expectation within its militarized, hierarchical structure.

Apart from the KGB, whose primary function was to protect state security, no alternatives to the militia existed for those who enjoyed law enforcement. Given the unified national structure of law enforcement in the USSR and the state's monopoly of policing, those who sought promotion had to conform to the organizational objectives of the MVD. There was no possibility of obtaining alternative work experience in another police body – lateral movement existed only within the confines of the Party apparatus and its related law enforcement bodies.

The early Soviet militia did not meet even minimal standards for a professional police, defined by David Bayley as "[r]ecruitment according to specified standards, remuneration sufficiently high to create a career service, formal training and systematic supervision by superior officers."[3] True, the poorly paid, often illiterate and superficially trained militiamen of the 1920s were eventually replaced by adequately paid personnel with high school educations and some law enforcement training. Yet the rank and file of the post-Stalinist militia never became fully professional because they lacked other important attributes of a genuine profession: education, political neutrality and the use of modern technology. Although more educated than their predecessors, policemen in the post-Stalinist era had less education than the norm in Soviet society; the police training they did receive was more ideological than professional, and ideological preparation and subordination to the Party meant militiamen were not impartial professionals. Lack of technical equipment also prevented them from meeting professional performance standards.

In contrast to police forces in democratic societies, the Soviet police operated in an authoritarian legal environment where the rule of law was devalued and the Soviet constitution was never considered a fundamental legal document.[4] Whereas in American society, the role of the police is to see that popular conceptions of order are maintained,[5] in Soviet society the militia enforced citizen compliance with state objectives (see Table 5.1). Accountable to the Communist Party rather than to the law or the citizens, corruption flourished throughout the militia apparatus, ultimately eroding its authority.

Table 5.1 A comparison of the American and post-Stalinist Soviet police

	American police	*Post-Stalinist Soviet police*
Recruitment	Voluntary (occasionally induced in some locales*)	Conscripted (only in the 1920s); induced; recruited
Nature of personnel	Lower to middle class; often from rural backgrounds	Worker and peasant; often from rural backgrounds
Education	Educated and poorly educated	Educational levels less than societal norm
Training	Physical and police techniques	Physical, militia and ideological training
Pay	Average	Less than average
Benefits	Average	Good
Leadership	Administrative training	No administrative training
Basis for promotion	Examinations	Political reliability; job performance; training

* In 1968, soldiers in Vietnam who agreed to join the Washington, D.C. police force were allowed to end their service six months early.

MILITIA SIZE AND ALLOCATION OF PERSONNEL

Sir Leon Radzinowicz, a distinguished historian of crime and justice, has commented that crime could be reduced if a society had a policeman on every corner. Visitors to Moscow for many years witnessed the validity of this insight. The visibility of militiamen, particularly in central Moscow, contributed to a high degree of order. To a certain extent, however, appearances were deceiving. The showcase cities of the USSR were beneficiaries of a policy that allocated enhanced law enforcement capabilities to major cities, leaving many rural residents and those in remote areas of Soviet republics without the rudiments of militia protection. This distribution of law enforcement resources was typical of a colonial society in which policing is concentrated in the most settled areas.[6] Such unequal distribution of militia resources contributed over time to declining social order in the Slavic countryside, a reality that in time fueled Russian nationalism.[7]

The disproportionate police resources showered on the major Slavic cities shortchanged newly established cities in the Soviet Far East and Far North. Although rates of crime commission were much higher in the latter,[8] their militia forces lacked adequate means to maintain order, let alone properly investigate the large number of offenses common to these cities. Many of the Soviet republics, who had little input in developing national law enforcement policies, also found themselves critically short of militia resources. In contrast to underserved urban and rural regions in Russia, however, indigenous populations of these republics – particularly in Central Asia and the Baltic states – did not regret the absence of militia personnel. Crime rates in these republics (at least until the late 1960s) were generally low, and the Slavic-dominated militia was generally perceived as a tool of Russification by their native populations.

The allocation of law enforcement resources and the total size of the USSR militia were hidden from the Soviet populace until *glasnost'* freed information dissemination in the country. In 1988, Interior Minister Aleksandr Vlasov reported that approximately 3.5 million personnel were employed by the MVD, of which approximately 700,000 were militia personnel assigned to police a population of 280 million.[9] These numbers translated into 1 militiaman for approximately every 400 citizens in the USSR, a slightly lower police-to-citizen ratio than existed in urban areas in the United States at the time, where the ratio was approximately 1 policeman to every 454 citizens.[10] National figures for the Soviet militia did not, however, account for the pervasive traffic police nor the departmental guards visible at numerous Soviet enterprises and organizations. (Nationwide, 1.3 million individuals worked as enterprise guards.[11])

As already noted, police personnel were distributed very unevenly in the USSR. In 1987, 56,000 policemen were assigned to Moscow, a city only slightly larger than New York, which in 1992 had a police force of only 28,000. With roughly 3 percent of the nation's population, Moscow commanded 8 percent of the nation's police force. Even if the transit population of approximately 3 million daily were added to the total population count, the capital still received a vastly disproportionate share of the militia protection available in the country.[12] The allocation of militia resources was a conscious national policy to maintain a greater degree of order in the capital. Residents of Moscow thus long benefited from a favorable distribution of consumer goods and cultural opportunities as well as the less tangible benefit of greater personal security. In the second-largest city of Leningrad, the norm was 1 militiaman to every 1,500 people; in Leningrad *oblast'*, 1 to 2,500. The provincial city of Gorky, later renamed Nizhnii Novgorod (the city where Sakharov was exiled), also had an approximate ratio of 1 militiaman to every 1,500 residents.[13]

The overall size of the militia was reduced after Brezhnev's death, when Andropov and his successors purged almost 200,000 individuals from the MVD. Most of these dismissals occurred in the GAI and the militia, with the share of militiamen dismissed in the Central Asian and Caucasian republics outweighing all others. Only a small percentage of those removed were incarcerated. Many were forced to retire early or to seek alternative employment. Some former militiamen found work in private detective and guard services, dismissed officers with legal training often became legal advisors within Soviet enterprises or members of the bar – all too frequently a dumping ground for corrupt legal personnel. (In Uzbekistan, those dismissed from the militia were later accused of fomenting interethnic violence.) Many militia personnel also left the force voluntarily at this time. Replacements were never found for many of these positions, creating a particular shortfall in the militia's investigative division. The replacements that were found were frequently young and inexperienced in police work.[14]

It is important to note that the number of full-time militia employees did not determine the capabilities of the Soviet law enforcement apparatus. In addition to the sizeable guard services, thirteen million civilians served as unpaid auxiliary militia (*druzhinniki*), a large number of informants assisted the militia in its work and, during the late Gorbachev years, army units staffed numerous militia patrols. These voluntary and official organizations complemented control mechanisms that were already strongly ingrained within Soviet communities.

RECRUITMENT

Militia personnel were recruited in a number of ways. Some were assigned to the police, others induced to join and still others volunteered. Although the Soviet militia followed the continental model, it did not hire the quality of personnel recruited by the German, French or Italian police forces, where higher educational levels are usually required of entry-level personnel. Throughout the Soviet period, the major attraction of the militia remained the privileges rather than the salaries offered by police work.

Forced conscription of militia personnel, which occurred in the 1920s, disappeared with the maturation of the Soviet state. Specific recruitment instructions were eventually developed by the Main Administration for Personnel and Educational Institutions of the USSR Ministry of Internal Affairs. Recruits were expected to be decisive, brave, demonstrate initiative and discipline, and be able to establish rapport with strangers. According to senior militia officials, however, these instructions were a "fiction, a fig leaf," as no system of staff selection existed: the militia took the recruits it could get.[15]

Political reliability was *the* key criterion for selecting personnel – both the Communist Party and KGB personnel scrutinized appointments to the local militia force.[16] When applying for employment with the militia, rank-and-file personnel submitted to the city militia administration the *kharakteristika* (character reference) required for employment in the Soviet Union. (Most individuals obtained this document either from the army or their former workplace.) Many applicants were needlessly weeded out as the result of an extensive questionnaire completed by all potential militiamen. As two Soviet journalists noted: "[a]ll they had to do was find some relative who violated the law in the 1940s and even if the man were a genius, the path to militia employment was shut."[17] Publicly criticized by senior-level militia personnel in the late 1980s, including Internal Affairs Minister Vadim Bakatin, these questionnaires nevertheless remained in use until the collapse of the Soviet regime.

Recruitment throughout the Soviet Union was closely monitored by the central bureaucracy in Moscow – no republic had control over hiring decisions for its Ministry of Internal Affairs. The head of the MVD in each republic belonged to the dominant national group; his deputy – the official in charge of cadres – was always a Russian. Through this key appointment, the center ensured that local appointments suited its preferences and that the militia remained under Moscow's command.

Former conscripts who had completed their term of military service were a major source of lower-ranking militia personnel. The quasi-military structure of the militia was attractive to those who had just served in the armed forces and had no definite educational plans. For many, particularly those seeking to escape drab factory or sedentary work, there was a certain attraction to militia work. Many rural conscripts did not want to return to their home communities; those from collective farms wanted to obtain an internal passport – the key to escaping impoverished farm life. As a result of secret regulations, the MVD in many major cities offered recruits an internal passport, a residence permit and a place in line for coveted state housing.[18] Until 1987, 70 percent of new militia recruits in Moscow were non-residents, attracted by the possibility of a residence permit rather than by a genuine interest in policing. When he served as first Communist Party secretary of Moscow, Boris Yeltsin banned non-residents from the force in an effort to curb such corruption; a severe shortfall in militia personnel followed.[19]

Most officers entered the militia either from law school or the extensive MVD educational apparatus. While many of these individuals were committed to a career in policing, others were simply attracted by the possibility of collecting lucrative bribes. Some people even paid bribes to enter the traffic police, an apolitical branch of law enforcement that came in contact with the affluent more frequently than with criminals.

Law schools themselves were rampant with corruption during the Brezhnev era, a phenomenon the regime attempted to curb after Brezhnev's death. The dean of the law school at Moscow State University – the premier law school in the USSR – for example, was ousted in 1984 for accepting bribes for admission. In Azerbaijan in the early 1980s, first Party secretary Geidar Aliev closed the republic's law school to the offspring of certain legal personnel in a purported effort to curb a self-perpetuating elite based on corruption.[20]

At times of reformist zeal, other means were used to obtain militia staff. Under Khrushchev, special efforts were made to identify honest, competent young men in the Komsomol and the Party and direct them to join the militia. Other preferred candidates were directed to militia work after initial employment at factories or construction sites. Similar measures were tried repeatedly in succeeding decades whenever new blood was needed in the lower ranks.

The Soviet administrative apparatus was able to channel individuals towards law enforcement work when the Soviet command system worked, yet by the late 1980s individuals were no longer intimidated by the state and many resisted dangerous militia assignments. In 1987, for example, 2,250 employees of different enterprises were directed by the city Party organization to join the Moscow militia, but only 600 showed up at their new work assignments.[21] To meet its personnel needs, the Moscow city government subsequently reached an agreement with the Ministry of Defense that allowed 3,000 conscripts to serve in the capital's militia each year.[22] This solution to staffing problems recalls the situation in Washington, DC, during the late 1960s, when policing in the United States reached its nadir. At the time, U.S. soldiers in Vietnam could be discharged several months early if they agreed to join the police force in the capital.

STAFFING CITIZENS' AUXILIARIES

Recruitment patterns for part-time, unpaid *druzhinniki* were very different from those for the militia. Whereas the military was the prime recruiting ground for the militia,[23] enterprises, factories and institutes were given numerical quotas of *druzhinniki* they were to provide the militia. Alas, Soviet citizens were often unwilling to donate their time for boring patrols and intrusive raids to verify the internal passports of other citizens. Laws introduced during the Brezhnev period required employers to provide citizen auxiliaries with additional paid leave, but this proved an unsatisfactory inducement. Many managers were forced to provide more benefits to *druzhinniki* than officially required by the state simply in order to fulfil the militia quotas for their organizations.[24]

Research among Soviet émigrés in the United States in the mid-1980s revealed that only about one-tenth of those surveyed had served as *druzhinniki*, hardly a high level of citizen mobilization. Those who did "volunteer" failed to regularly attend training courses and lectures at which anthologies of relevant legislation were disseminated and explained. This behavior was true of both higher- and lower-level professionals.[25] Large numbers of volunteer militia were thus rounded up, but lacked the commitment desired by the Soviet state. The willingness of people to join citizen militia groups in the 1990s stands in sharp contrast to their reluctance to work as state-controlled *druzhinniki*. Their readiness to join self-defense groups cannot, however, be explained solely by fears for their personal safety. People were, rather, more willing to serve in militia groups when they felt a national affinity for their fellow members and had some kind of individual control over the organization.[26]

RANKS AND SALARIES

The militia was divided into a hierarchy of ranks (see Table 5.2). Although ranks in the militia officer corps resembled those in the military, all ranks in internal affairs organs had special titles that indicated that an individual served in the militia. (An officer was, for example, a militia sergeant or a militia captain.) Commissioned militia officers were paid significantly more than privates and non-commissioned officers.

Table 5.2 Ranks and titles in the Soviet militia

1 Ordinary *militsiia* personnel
2 Lowest officers: sergeant to *starshina* (petty officer)
3 Middle officers: junior lieutenant to captain
4 Senior officers: major through colonel
5 Highest officers: major general and above

Source: V.G. Kutushev, *Sotsial'noe planirovanie v organakh vnutrennykh del* (Saratov: Izdatel'stvo Saratovskogo universiteta, 1983), 12

Significant privileges existed at the top of the militia bureaucracy and members of the Party apparatus were often appointed to these high-ranking positions. Part of the Party's administrative cadres (the *nomenklatura*), they were shifted to different parts of the state bureaucracy as needed. At various times, these injections of Party personnel assumed significant proportions. In the mid-1980s, for example, thousands of Party personnel were added to the MVD. These employees had no background in law enforcement, yet earned more than other members of the militia and often treated their subordinates without respect, fostering great resentment among career employees.[27]

At the beginning of the Gorbachev period, the senior internal affairs official of a major city earned between 350 and 400 rubles a month.[28] His salary, however, comprised only a small share of his income; such an official had access to special stores that sold difficult-to-obtain food and consumer items at reduced prices. In addition, such an official usually resided in special housing built especially for senior MVD and KGB officials and had the use of a summer home. A car and chauffeur would be at his personal disposal. Finally, a senior militia officer could significantly enhance his income by accepting bribes.

In the late 1970s an ordinary militiaman earned about 150 rubles a month (approximately USD 250 at the then highly inflated rate of exchange) – more than an ordinary doctor but slightly less than a skilled factory worker, who then earned about 180 rubles a month. In the 1980s militia salaries fell further behind those of enterprise workers. In 1982, for example, the average wage of militia personnel was 177 rubles. The base monthly pay of militiamen in the late 1980s was only 165 rubles a month, with additional sums paid for further education. A five-ruble raise was awarded after every two years of service; thus after 15 years of service, a militiaman would receive a monthly wage of 215 rubles. Militiamen also enjoyed the fringe benefits available to militia personnel: housing within the community, free uniforms, no-cost vacation trips and free public transport. Special food packages might be ordered for personnel during holidays and access to special stores might be arranged for an event such as a marriage. Until the tax reform of 1990, all militia members were exempt from taxes, a perquisite that netted them approximately 20 rubles more in monthly take-home pay.[29]

Militia salaries at the lower ranks were too meager to deter corruption. A precinct inspector, for example, who stood at the lower end of the middle officer corps, earned only approximately 300 rubles a month in 1987. In the late 1980s, a survey of militia personnel attitudes concerning their compensation revealed that 64 percent of militia employees in Kazakhstan, 63 percent in Georgia and 83 percent in Latvia were dissatisfied with their salaries.[30]

Subsequent pay increases alleviated this problem to a degree, but galloping inflation made survival on state wages difficult. In a move that cost the government over one billion rubles, in 1991 salaries for employees of the organs of internal affairs were raised to an average of 510 rubles per month, making them equal to those of armed forces personnel. Yet even then, this pay did not match that of private guard services, which already in 1989 were paying employees 600 rubles a month (then three times the pay of an average militia employee).[31] With the state unable to compete effectively with the private sector, the only financial benefit of state service was the greater possibilities it offered for illicit income – low salaries meant that militia officials accepted bribes.

Many of the benefits supposedly available to militia personnel were in fact unobtainable: there were continual shortages of places in nursery schools and long waiting lists for apartments. One former militiaman with many children became a squatter in Novosibirsk because he had waited so long for housing; members of the city's militia apparatus sympathized with his plight and refused to evict him. In 1990 there were 1,100 militia personnel waiting for apartments in Moscow and the 58 dormitories for militia personnel and their families in the city were full. Political officers, expected to focus on group morale, were often forced to spend their time placing children in schools and securing housing for families who had spent years on waiting lists. The housing situation for lower-level officers was not much better than that of their subordinates. In the Moscow criminal investigative branch, for example, one out of every four employees lived in a communal apartment (the approximate norm for Moscow) in which four individuals typically inhabited a 162-square-foot room and shared a kitchen and bathroom.[32]

The pay and benefits available to militia personnel reflected their ambivalent status in the eyes of the Communist Party. Viewed as necessary, they were nevertheless paid significantly less than their counterparts in the KGB with whom they compared themselves. As one officer explained:

> Paradoxically, even in the MVD, everything connected with the militia is second-rate. Even the highest rank in the militia is only lieutenant-general. Salaries and pay according to rank are lower than in the internal troops and the KGB. It recalls the absurdity of long ago when horses of the local militia received 100 grams of oats less than the horses of the security police or the cavalry.[33]

In earlier periods it might have been inappropriate to compare the salaries of the militia with those of the internal troops and the KGB, as the latter two bodies were primarily engaged in national security tasks. During the *perestroika* era, however, the militia was on the front lines of conflict, evidenced by the large number of militia officers wounded and slain in the line of duty. Although not reflected in salary levels, the danger of militia work was acknowledged in a retirement policy that allowed militia personnel to retire earlier than other government employees. Female militia employees could retire at age 45, males at 50; both retained full pension rights. Higher retirement ages were set for senior militia officers. Those serving at the rank of lieutenant up to that of lieutenant colonel could retire at 50. Colonels, however, were required to wait until 55; generals, until 60.[34] The differential in retirement ages appeared to acknowledge the increasingly sedentary nature of militia work at higher bureaucratic levels.

PROMOTION

The militia was not a route to political power. The only individual to reach the top of the political hierarchy from the MVD was Eduard Shevardnadze, foreign minister of the USSR under Mikhail Gorbachev, who had previously served as MVD chief of his native Georgia. Ambitious individuals within the militia apparatus could generally expect to rise only within their organization or be transferred to another part of the law enforcement apparatus.

Promotion in the militia was not based on examinations; rather, Party reliability, educational training and job performance determined advancement. The first criterion was the most critical, prompting career militia personnel in the days of *glasnost'* to regret that careerism and not professionalism led to promotions.[35] Desk work and Party activities earned rewards, not results in the field. Individuals could not rise to the top through competence alone; but with appropriate training and political reliability competent individuals could rise to the top. Yet the emphasis on Communist Party criteria meant that incompetent but well-connected individuals often rose to leadership positions in the MVD.

Rules for promotion within the militia were governed by a series of unpublished regulations.[36] Promotions at the lowest ranks were determined by local supervisory personnel; at the middle officer rank (militia lieutenant) and above, advancement was decided by the USSR MVD. All promotions to *nomenklatura* positions required Party as well as MVD approval, prompting reformers to contend that change could not come from above in the law enforcement body. The rapid turnover of ministers of internal affairs in the post-Brezhnev period offers evidence that new leadership at the top was indeed insufficient to reshape policing in the Soviet Union.

COMPOSITION OF THE MILITIA

Law enforcement in the USSR was primarily a male profession. Men dominated the organization not only in numbers, but in their nearly complete monopoly of supervisory positions. Women obtained positions in the lower and middle ranks of the militia officer corps, yet no women were present in the top ranks of the republican and national MVD administrations. As in other countries, women were segregated into less dangerous areas of policing where their "female" qualities might be used to advantage – dealing with juvenile delinquency, for example. At the close of the Soviet period there were 96,000 women in the militia, representing approximately 15 percent of total militia personnel. Apart from work with problem youth, women were concentrated in the traffic and investigative divisions (many female law graduates worked in the latter).[37]

Slavs dominated law enforcement both at the national level and in many regions of the country. Although some non-Slavs managed to reach high positions in the USSR MVD, many individuals viewed relocation to Moscow as an undesirable promotion. Native presence in the militia increased in many republics over time, but in numerous areas the local population refused to join the regular police. The significant presence of Slavs in the militia was therefore not simply the consequence of a deliberate policy decision by

Moscow, but also of the unwillingness of non-Russians to participate in their own policing – an experience not uncommon to colonial police forces in other empires.

The Slavic presence was most apparent in the militia and the OBKhSS. In some Baltic states, 80 percent of republican militia employees were Russians, Byelorussians and Ukrainians.[38] Elsewhere in the USSR, the militia was also primarily Slavic; the majority of Soviet German émigrés interviewed in U.S. interview projects during the early 1980s reported that in their home communities in Kazakhstan and other areas of Central Asia, Slavs outnumbered all other ethnic groups in the militia. A Slavic-dominated militia was nevertheless impossible to achieve in rural areas of Central Asia, where few individuals were sufficiently conversant in Russian to be policed by Slavs. In these areas, local militia cadres had be drawn from the native population, working to the detriment of centralized law enforcement. The Soviet press in the late Brezhnev period was still reporting, for example, that Central Asian militia personnel were unwilling to arrest individuals who engaged in long-outlawed traditional practices such as bride purchase and polygamy. During the Gorbachev era, members of the Uzbek militia even joined local residents in attacking members of minority groups when, in June 1989, ethnic conflict broke out in the part of the Fergana Valley located in Uzbekistan.

Towards the end of the Soviet period, predominantly Slavic militia forces caused serious problems in areas where strong opposition to Soviet rule existed. In Latvia, for example, members of the republican militia allied themselves with the USSR MVD in the late 1980s rather than support emerging political leaders in the republic.[39] Following the Latvian example, other republics also tried to establish autonomous ministries of internal affairs that would permit the titular nationality to control police personnel decisions; such policies often led to the removal of Slavs and their replacement, when possible, by local staff.

TRAINING AND EDUCATION

Many people who joined the militia were graduates of the educational system administered by the Ministry of Internal Affairs. Those who entered the body following military service went through a comparatively brief training program. During much of the post-Stalinist period, for example, recruits were given four months of training in both basic law enforcement techniques and the political indoctrination considered essential for militia work. The training period provided limited exposure to criminalistics and ballistics and even less to the legal principles that normally provide a basis for law enforcement. Although the reformist zeal of the *perestroika* period resulted in the training period being extended to nine months, many militia officials felt the lengthier period still fell far short of the twenty-one months received by police privates in Japan – a program Minister of Internal Affairs Vadim Bakatin considered a model for the Soviet militia. As he noted in 1990: "The question of training and retraining cadres remains probably the most urgent."[40]

The Ministry of Internal Affairs initiated its educational program in the early postrevolutionary period; the first militia school was founded by 1918 in what was then Petrograd. By the end of the Soviet period the educational apparatus of the ministry encompassed a wide range of institutions, ranging from the fifty militia schools that covered the last years of high school and first years of post-high school education to the MVD Academy in Moscow that provided postgraduate degrees. In between were sixteen militia institutes throughout the country that granted the equivalent of a college degree.[41] During the twenty-five years of the Khrushchev and Brezhnev periods, 82,500 individuals graduated from MVD educational institutes, insuring that almost all supervisory personnel above the city–regional level had specialized educations.[42]

In the first two decades of the post-Stalinist period, most prospective MVD officers were sent to two-year militia schools. After many of these schools were closed in the 1970s in an effort to upgrade militia training, officers began to be educated primarily at MVD institutes and state law schools. All schools in the MVD system provided a fundamental education in investigative and criminalistics techniques, Soviet law and Party subjects. A rigorous program of physical training and emergency techniques complemented the academic program.[43] A significant share of the educational program was devoted to ideological studies that included the history of the Communist Party of the Soviet Union and Marxism–Leninism. The concentration of instruction time in these subjects indicated the central importance of a political education in performing militia work, a major attribute of communist policing. Even in short training programs, approximately one-half of total class time was spent on ideological instruction, thereby limiting training in police techniques and legal subjects.

Specialized militia schools prepared individuals exclusively for militia employment, whereas college-level institutes of the MVD prepared students for work in the correctional system, the fire service and the militia. During the late Gorbachev years, efforts were made to develop a more general educational curriculum in these schools which blended training in law with the specific skills needed for militia work. Yet graduates of both the militia schools and the higher institutes of the MVD received the rank of lieutenant, an inconsistent policy that provided students no incentive (in terms of money or enhanced rank) to pursue two years of further study at an MVD institute. The contradiction in policy, hotly contested by MVD professionals, was never resolved during the Soviet period.[44]

The institutions of higher learning of the MVD system were much more expensive to operate than their civilian equivalents. Expenditure per student in the civilian sector was 8–10,000 rubles in the late 1980s; the comparable figure for students in MVD institutes was 20–30,000 rubles. Students attending educational institutes of the militia received 30-ruble monthly stipends, outstanding students 60-ruble stipends. These stipends represented only a minimal level of support, one generally supplemented by students' families. By the final stage of their studies, when they were already working in internships, students might receive as much as 250 rubles per month (at that time more than a worker's monthly income).[45]

Despite the high cost of their maintenance, the 104 institutions that comprised the MVD educational system suffered from the same shortages that hampered the militia itself. Thirty-three did not have firing ranges, 24 lacked dining halls, 12 lacked gymnasiums and 77 had dormitories that did not meet acceptable sanitary conditions. Instruction equipment was also sorely lacking. Thousands of students dropped out of these institutes each year because the paucity of equipment meant they could not learn the basic skills needed for a militia career – how to shoot or employ self-defense techniques, for example. Many could not stand the living conditions. It thus comes as no surprise that many MVD professionals referred to themselves as the beggars of the bureaucratic–command apparatus.[46]

A survey of militia personnel in eleven different regions of the USSR during the *perestroika* era concluded that, for 80 percent, their educations had not prepared them for the contemporary situation.[47] Like their counterparts in other Soviet educational institutions, many militiamen had received training so specialized that it was difficult for them to work outside very narrow fields. Political officers and firemen, for example, were unprepared to fill existing vacancies in criminalistics. Nowhere in the academic program were there courses in administration, not even among the special training classes given to officers already employed in the militia. In fact, militia personnel spent so many hours in the field carrying out the commands of the Party apparatus and local governmental authorities that there was little time left for a program of formal education.[48]

Although militia personnel were usually educated within the republic in which they would eventually serve, many republics lacked MVD educational institutes and sent their officer corps to be trained elsewhere. Baltic personnel, for example, were trained in the higher militia school in Minsk, Byelorussia, and some Central Asian republics sent personnel to the higher school in Tashkent, Uzbekistan.[49] These higher MVD institutes often provided reliable, Slavic supervisory cadres to the ethnically diverse Soviet republics.

Overall, the educational programs of the MVD gave members of the Khrushchev and Brezhnev militias a higher level of education than personnel of the Stalin years had possessed. At the end of the Brezhnev period, 90 percent of ordinary and lower-level MVD supervisory personnel nationwide had secondary educations, while 84 percent of the officers had received a higher or a specialized secondary education. The most educated personnel were found in the OBKhSS division, which demanded a degree of economic knowledge and, often, accounting skills.[50]

As the data in Table 5.3 demonstrate, there were noticeable variations in

Table 5.3 Educational levels of militia personnel (Based on a 1983 survey of 4,680 employees in the Urals, Siberia, the Soviet Far East, Central Asia and the Baltics; in percentages. Hereafter, the 1983 poll)

	1979	1980	1981	1982	1983
Higher and high school educations, combined	67	72	76	79	85
By category:					
Higher education	16	17	18	18	20
Specialized high school only	17	18	20	21	24
General high school only	34	37	38	40	41

Source: V.G. Kutushev, *Sotsial'noe planirovanie v organakh vnutrennykh del* (Saratov: Izdatel'stvo Saratovskogo universiteta, 1983), 87

the level of education among militia personnel in the USSR. In a country that placed a premium on education, militia personnel attained a level of education slightly lower than the national norm, further confirmation of their relatively low status in Soviet society.

THE MVD ACADEMY

Those seeking to advance their militia careers or to do research might enter the MVD Academy. Founded in the mid-1970s under the progressive administrator Major General Sergei Krylov, the Academy sought to develop a wide humanitarian perspective among future militia leaders. According to Arkady Vaksberg: "[Krylov's] first directorial order specified that every student should acquaint himself with the works of Aristotle, Plutarch, Theophrastus, Montaigne, La Bruyère and Montesquieu."[51] A progressive, Krylov managed to survive in the Academy after the fall of Khrushchev because he was the principal speechwriter for MVD Minister Nikolai Shchelokov. Many mid-level employees of the ministry who trained at the academy appreciated the director's objectives. (Brezhnev's son-in-law Iurii Churbanov, by contrast, hated Krylov and accused him of embezzling a rug and housing an academy refrigerator at his dacha.) Ousted from the MVD Academy in the late 1970s, the "dreamer-general" Krylov committed suicide thirteen days after his dismissal, shooting himself at his office at the Academy.[52]

Both the Academy and the three MVD research institutes developed significant research capacities; the four institutions employed over 1,100 researchers with advanced degrees who studied the administration of criminal and administrative law, various categories of criminality and the effectiveness of punishment.[53] Yet even during the *perestroika* era their work was determined by a state plan and sensitive topics remained impossible to pursue. In the late 1980s, for example, no research was conducted on the use of force, policing ethnic conflict or the impact of *perestroika* on militia performance.[54] At the same time, however, numerous publications devoted to the enforcement of administrative and criminal law were published and disseminated throughout the country.

One of Gorbachev's ministers of internal affairs, Aleksandr Vlasov, concluded that existing educational programs produced personnel unsuited to a law-based state.[55] After reformist tendencies in the militia educational system were destroyed in the Brezhnev period, it proved difficult to develop a new approach in an apparatus dominated by staff trained without respect for legal norms. Given the ideological and personnel constraints, little could be done to establish a militia education grounded in legal norms during the final years of the Soviet regime.

JOB PLACEMENT

Upon completion of militia institutions, MVD students, like their peers in institutions administered by the Ministry of Education, were assigned to jobs by means of a system intended to place individuals in regions of the country and in specializations where they were most needed. Initial assignments were decided by the Ministry of Justice in consultation with a school's instructors.[56] Although many graduates were able to circumvent undesirable placements, others found transfers to a new work location difficult to arrange and spent years at their first postings.

The assignment system was a direct reflection of the authoritarian-command system that characterized Soviet society. Only a small proportion of law school graduates were assigned to work in the militia, as the state allocated the limited number of such graduates to more prestigious work in the procuracy and the security apparatus. When assigned to the militia, law school graduates might try to influence the assignment process to secure a position in a desirable location or a division where the possibility of illegal gains was greater, such as the OBKhSS or traffic enforcement. Despite the allure of sizeable illegal incomes, however, most law school graduates disdained militia assignments due to their low prestige and the subsequent difficulty of obtaining employment outside of the MVD.

Theoretically, assignment to the militia was based on an individual's personal attributes. Students who had completed internships in the investigatory organs in their final semesters of law school might, for example, be assigned to jobs in law enforcement. Those identified as particularly reliable might be sent to do passport work, those with some economic training and skills, to the OBKhSS. As noted earlier, female graduates were generally assigned to work with youth and to the traffic and investigative divisions.

Until the *perestroika* period little emphasis was given to legal education in the Soviet Union. Approximately two dozen law schools existed in the country and their class sizes were limited; few full-time students graduated from these schools. There were ten to fifteen applicants for every slot in Soviet law schools, but only 1.6–1.8 applicants for every slot in the higher schools (the equivalent of college-level institutes) of the Interior Ministry.[57] Most people who sought a legal education, often after a few years of employment, were forced to study in evening sessions or correspondence schools where educational standards were much lower than in full-time university programs. Such students were not subject to the system of job assignments because they had not been supported by state stipends during years of full-time study and were thus relieved of the obligation to settle in remote locations. Their inferior educations, however, made them less desirable employees; many of the more attractive legal careers were closed to graduates of these courses. Upon graduation, they were often hired for positions in the militia that required legal training, but for which no suitable employees had been found.

Although graduates of law correspondence courses often acquired positions as investigators, critics within and without the militia bureaucracy pointed out that they were deficient in both field experience and formal legal training. Many such officers were responsible for the major human rights abuses committed by the Soviet militia. Even despite the recruitment of substandard lawyers, however, less than one-third of the employees of the criminal investigative branch had a legal education, a necessity in a division that played a more formal legal role than that played by the detective divisions of U.S. police forces.[58]

Once on the job, rooky militia learned the difference between instruction and practice. Little respect was paid to the law in militia operations, a far cry from the teaching of many MVD institutions. Although the same complaint about the dichotomy between law enforcement education and practice is made in the United States, in the USSR this dichotomy was aggravated by the absence of an established legal culture among both the militia hierarchy and ordinary citizens.

As part of an effort to enhance the professional qualifications of the militia, junior militiamen were often assigned to senior personnel for guidance and on-the-job training. Young militiamen were also provided with a conduct manual that gave them instructions as to appropriate behavior towards respectable citizens. One such manual smuggled to the west in the mid-1980s instructed law enforcement personnel to be respectful to "ladies." Needless to say, most Soviet citizens did not receive such polite treatment at the hands of the police.[59]

SOCIALIZATION AND MILITIA SUBCULTURE

The authoritarian militia subculture of the post-Stalinist period was distinctly different from that of the Stalinist period. Although respect for legal norms increased after the mid-1950s, the militia never operated in the kind of legal culture that characterizes western democratic societies. As Samuel Walker has noted of western police forces, police subcultures arise out of the "constant possibility of danger and the need to assert authority in the face of often overt resistance."[60] As in western nations, the pressure to produce arrests and convictions in the USSR forced the police to bend the law to obtain evidence and/or confessions that produced results.[61] If, as police expert Jerome Skolnick has argued, police subculture and police norms are at odds with the rule of law in the United States,[62] this was acutely the case in the USSR, a country in which the rule of law was never institutionalized and only came to be appreciated under *perestroika*. Unlike their western peers, however, militia personnel were not compelled to hide mistakes or cover up the use of physical force because the Soviet justice system tolerated such behavior.

Militia personnel of the post-Stalinist period were acutely aware of the absence of the rule of law and the perpetuation of the authoritarian–command system in their work. Even before these faults were pointed out to the general public under *glasnost'*, militiamen in the late Brezhnev period were telling MVD researchers that their most serious problems were unresponsive supervisors and the absence of input from below. Nearly 40 percent of rank-and-file militiamen surveyed in the 1983 national poll of 4,680 militia personnel (see Table 5.3 above) felt their superiors were too tolerant of illegalities,[63] evidence of a significant generational difference between personnel trained in the Khrushchev and Brezhnev periods and those trained during the Stalin era. While many old-guard militia officers regretted the declining authority of both the Communist Party and the social control apparatus during the final years of the Soviet state, much of the middle generation of law enforcement personnel looked abroad for innovation and training techniques that could promote a militia system more responsive to a new legal order.[64]

Socialization into the militia was a gradual process; both militia and investigative personnel considered the first two years the most difficult. It was during this period that militiamen learned the mores and culture of the militia work environment. A more formal division between work and private life exists in western societies than was the case in the USSR. Although western policemen also acquire formal policing skills and assimilate into a police subculture, no organized, intentional state intervention disturbs their non-working hours.

By contrast, in the Soviet Union the state regulated its citizens' working lives and, through the provision of social services at the workplace, touched their private lives directly as well. Soviet militia personnel received housing and vacations from their place of employment and their children attended work-related nursery schools. Numerous voluntary police activities such as police athletic leagues and "big brother" organizations that in democratic societies are run by police forces themselves were orchestrated and financed by the state in the USSR. Militia personnel could not develop independent social and recreational organizations because the state intentionally restricted the development of civil society, sponsoring militia sports teams, choirs, dance groups and orchestras.

Many militiamen tried to develop associations outside their work and to pursue more individualistic pursuits in their spare time. Interviews with both practicing and émigré Soviet police personnel indicated that they had a more diverse pattern of associations than their western peers. Like many of their fellow Soviet citizens, they sought to find a haven from state intervention and spent their free time in a variety of ways that removed them from collective activity. In the previously cited 1983 poll, the largest percentage of MVD personnel surveyed (48 percent) reported spending their free time on "intellectual activities" such as avid movie attendance and reading; 17 percent participated in sports activities and hunting and 35 percent reported that they socialized with friends, attending sports events and going to restaurants and cafés.[65] These research findings affirm that MVD personnel did not allocate their free time any differently from the average Soviet citizen.

State control over free time and organized recreational activities did not mean that members of the militia did not develop an organizational culture. The militia subculture was characterized by bonds of friendship, a common world outlook and a behavioral style in which extra-legal practices were frequent and corruption endemic. As in other countries, the distinctive attributes of police work – the high degree of stress, the strain of irregular hours and the constant pressure to achieve results under difficult conditions – led militia personnel over many decades to form close friendships at work. In the same 1983 poll, 90 percent of those surveyed reported having friends at work. Of these, 47 percent claimed the basis of these friendships was common interests and life views; 32 percent, a common social life; and 16 percent, similar hobbies.[66] Letters from wives of militia officers in the Soviet magazine *Sovetskaia militsiia* often revealed a familial commitment to law enforcement. Until the final, precarious days of the Soviet Union, many wives evidently accepted the dangers and irregular hours of their husbands' jobs because they appreciated the role these men played in the Soviet state and the satisfaction they derived from law enforcement.

As in western societies, divorce rates among policemen in the USSR were higher than the societal norm. Many militia personnel believed that increased contact with other militia families would enhance familial relations and regretted that the state did not organize more family-based social activities.[67] Despite the need for family support, the state generally mobilized militia personnel for group recreational activities apart from their families (see Table 5.4).

While police in many democratic societies need to be attuned to the political currents of local and even national politics, they are precluded from performing an explicitly political role. By contrast, Soviet militia were expected to perform political tasks such as providing a political education to citizens within their communities. Yet as Table 5.5 reveals, feelings of obligation rather than personal commitment generally motivated militiamen to perform such work.

The willingness of these survey participants to admit to utilitarian reasons for political activities reflected a common understanding of the realities of Soviet life held by MVD researchers and the interviewees alike.

Table 5.4 Family recreational activities of militia personnel
(How often are recreational activities organized for members of your collective and their families?) 1983 poll; in percentages

Often (at least once a month)	Frequently every 2–3 months)	Rarely (once every 6 months)	Very rarely (once a year)	Don't organize	Can't answer
4.8	15.2	21.2	25.0	32.8	1.0

Source: V.G. Kutushev, *Sotsial'noe planirovanie v organakh vnutrennykh del* (Saratov: Izdatel'stvo Saratovskogo universiteta, 1983), 146

Table 5.5 Line and service personnel's motivation for participating in political activities (1983 poll; in percentages)

Feeling of obligation	25.8
Want to know my city or collective better	18.2
Love this work	16.5
Obligation to participate	9.2
Increases my authority	6.6
Somebody needs to participate	3.7
Don't want to be criticized for passivity	3.3
Can't advance without doing this work	2.6
Difficult to answer	3.8
Don't know	10.3
Total	100.0

Source: V.G. Kutushev, *Sotsial'noe planirovanie v organakh vnutrennykh del* (Saratov: Izdatel'stvo Saratovskogo universiteta, 1983), 122

CORRUPTION

Socialization of militia personnel involved not only friendships and common activities, but widespread participation in corrupt practices and frequent violation of the law. These problems are by no means unique to the Soviet system. As Richard J. Lundman, an American student of policing, has commented: "[p]olice work is exceptionally rich in opportunities for corruption . . . supervision is minimal." And to this is added "citizen willingness to corrupt the police."[68] Other American criminologists have pointed out that in many societies, structural pressures on police agents promote infractions in regulations and obstruction of legal proceedings.[69]

The corruption of the Soviet militia can only be explained by examining the political, economic and social structure of Soviet society. Mechanisms that in other states work to protect citizens and the state from police corruption were absent in the USSR; a one-party state that enjoyed economic and political hegemony left no room for an independent center of power to check militia misconduct. As recent corruption scandals in Japan, Mexico and Italy have demonstrated, corruption is particularly pronounced in societies where a single political party dominates the political process for an extended period of time. In the United States, political corruption has been most marked in urban areas long governed by a single political party. The USSR was ruled by one political party that became increasingly corrupt over time. Militia corruption eventually flourished on a national level because corrupt relationships between the ruling party and those engaged in criminal economic activity became institutionalized. Communist Party politicians who gave themselves license to commit crimes with impunity had no choice but to grant the same privilege to those who had the right to enforce the law against them. Militia personnel were thus in a position not only to passively receive bribes, but to actively seek payments as well.

Powerful incentives for corruption existed for Soviet citizens and policemen alike. The severity of the Soviet legal system and the absence of legal safeguards led citizens to use whatever measures were necessary to avoid entering the judicial system. Even if innocent, individuals had scant expectation of being freed from the judicial system, as few cases were dropped and acquittals were rare.[70] When threatened with arrest, even law-abiding citizens would resort to bribery to escape exposure to the system. The need to bribe a police officer was accordingly greater if one were guilty of a serious offense.

Similarly, police violations of legal procedures were more pervasive and severe in the USSR than in most other societies, a problem that failed to diminish even after the massive purges of law enforcement personnel in the mid-1980s. As one MVD spokesman commented, even after spectacular dismissals and prosecutions the state of corruption remained "extraordinary all the same."[71] Militia personnel ran car theft and pornography rings, trafficked in confiscated documents, violated currency laws on a massive scale and dealt in stolen merchandise. As noted in Chapter 3, Deputy Minister of the MVD Iurii Churbanov both accepted enormous bribes and acted as an accessory to the organized criminal activities of Central Asian political leaders. In sum, the volume of legal violations committed by the Soviet police was as disturbing as the character of their offenses. Infractions did not end with property and economic crimes, but extended as far as murder: in one year in the late 1980s, militiamen were found responsible for 57 murders.[72]

The extensive economic role played by the militia in the communist state also contributed to its corruption. In western economies, the market for illegal goods and services is significant but necessarily limited, inherently curbing the extent of probable police corruption.[73] The militia in the Soviet Union, however, did not regulate illicit goods and services, but basic consumer items that were in constant short supply. Regulation of such licit markets made the potential for militia corruption enormous, as almost any Soviet citizen would willingly engage in corruption to obtain goods and services that he or she deemed necessary for his or her survival.

PERESTROIKA AND THE MILITIA

The policy of *glasnost'* destroyed any illusions the Soviet citizen might have had about militiamen. The 1960s and 1970s press image of the militiaman as always alert, courteous, efficient, never exhausted and sensitive to the needs of his community was abruptly substituted by one of a corrupt, inefficient, abusive thug unwilling to obey the law. The state in turn attempted to address the serious problems plaguing the militia by depoliticizing the appointment process throughout the MVD hierarchy, disciplining personnel and holding militiamen accountable to legal norms. The public and work collectives were both brought into the selection process for militia employees most closely involved with the citizenry (i.e., precinct inspectors, juvenile commissioners and GAI employees) and the appointment of the USSR Minister of Internal Affairs was made subject to confirmation by the newly constituted Supreme Soviet. The latter took the appointment process seriously, as evidenced by the serious discussions that preceded the confirmation of Minister Vadim Bakatin in 1989.[74]

Employment guarantees that had existed prior to *perestroika* ceased to function as the state became unable to guarantee its employees physical or financial security. As a senior militia official in Minsk noted: "We need to honestly recognize that we are no longer in the situation where we can defend our employees."[75] Many militiamen resigned reluctantly, remaining loyal to the militia and the USSR, but feeling deserted by the state apparatus and made physically vulnerable by existing militia regulations. Compounding their difficulties, the law – once weighted in favor of the state and its employees – began to tilt in favor of the citizen. Militia personnel complained, for example, that citizens who cursed, spat in their faces or hit them were no longer incarcerated, but merely fined. As one officer explained: "In 1988, I already submitted my letter of resignation, but then I reconsidered and decided that it was not honest to leave at these difficult times. I thought maybe something would change. It is clear I was mistaken."[76]

The crisis in morale was plainly visible: in 1989 alone, nearly 200 militia personnel were killed and another 200 committed suicide. The killing of a militia officer in Leningrad that same year prompted an unprecedented public demonstration by policemen in the city's central Palace Square, when approximately one hundred officers with placards demanded higher wages, better housing and guarantees of greater personal safety. Leaders of the demonstration were subsequently dismissed from the militia, to be reinstated only after Bakatin was appointed Interior Minister. This protest by individuals charged with upholding public order was a rude awakening for Soviet authorities. Faced with militia insubordination and mass protests by miners that MVD personnel refused to subdue, the USSR Council of Ministers accelerated the drafting of anti-strike legislation that had been in secret preparation for several years. A draft strike law prohibiting militia, military and transport personnel from striking was published in August 1989. Although to vital state personnel the denial of the right to strike resembles a similar distinction drawn in American strike legislation, the need for such legislation in the USSR had been inconceivable only a few years before.[77]

The decline in state revenues during the *perestroika* era meant less resources for militia operations and worsening work conditions. Significant attrition occurred as the demoralized quit and the competent, particularly those with technical and bookkeeping skills, were lured from the police force by more lucrative positions in the burgeoning private sector. In the United States, policing generally competes with the private sector by offering greater job security rather than higher wages. In the USSR under Gorbachev, the Soviet militia was unable to offer either. People left the force in droves. In 1989, 500 investigators requested discharges because their increased work-load required 12–14-hour work days – shifts that violated Soviet labor laws. Unlike western practice, no overtime pay was available for such shifts in the USSR. Investigators were not alone in quitting the militia; in 1989 a total of 50,000 individuals left the militia for personal reasons and an additional 33,000 were dismissed.[78]

Turnover was so great as a result of purges and resignations that by 1990, only one-quarter of all criminal investigators, OBKhSS employees or precinct inspectors had five to ten years of work experience. The collapse of the militia force demoralized those policemen who remained on the job; in 1990, 87 percent of militia personnel interviewed in an MVD opinion poll in Kazakh-stan, 76 percent in Georgia and 91 percent in Latvia indicated that they did not want their children to follow their career paths.[79]

Recruitment also suffered. Although new personnel could be socialized into the formal militia structure, they lacked their predecessors' commitment to enforcing communist ideology. The increasingly political nature of militia work and the assertion of national autonomy on the part of many Soviet republics also made many potential militiamen unwilling to serve.[80] In 1988, only 1,200 people joined the MVD, yet the ministry's annual requirement was 3–3,500 new workers. That same year in Lithuania, the militia force was 700 employees short because individuals could not be found to work for low wages in a body that had been discredited for having suppressed peaceful demonstrations in the republic.[81] In Azerbaijan, many new recruits were drawn from Azeris who had been evicted from Armenian-held territory in Nagorno-Karabakh; their presence on the militia did much to exacerbate tensions in the city of Baku.

Significant changes occurred in the militia during the *perestroika* era as a consequence of deliberate social policies adopted by the state as well as the inadvertent – and massive – social, political and economic changes caused by these policies. Caught between the state's futile effort to reshape the regular police and the accelerating forces of social disintegration, Soviet militia subculture began to break down in the late 1980s due to massive resignations and consequent demoralization among the ranks. Only after the dissolution of the USSR would the newly independent states of the region be able to tackle the systemic problems of Soviet law enforcement made apparent by *glasnost'* and *perestroika*.

CONCLUSION

The centralization of law enforcement in an ethnically diverse society had a direct impact on the staffing and allocation of militia personnel in the USSR. The Slavs who supervised the Ministry of Internal Affairs in Moscow were more concerned with maintaining control of the vast Soviet law enforcement apparatus than with improving policing standards. Despite efforts to upgrade the militia in the decades up to and including *perestroika*, militia personnel never became fully professional because their training was as ideological as it was specialized. Nearly as much time was devoted to educating militiamen in Marxism–Leninism and Communist Party history as in the legal norms and law enforcement techniques essential for executing police functions.

Militia personnel were socialized into a subculture in which obedience to the Communist Party was emphasized over the observance of legal norms. The lack of legal consciousness among policemen and Soviet society in general exacerbated the problem of corruption present in any police force. By the 1980s, these problems were so acute as to undermine morale and severely reduce police effectiveness in the USSR. Rather than develop into a professional force, the militia changed in the manner of the Soviet state. As the population became more educated, so, too, did militia personnel. When de-Stalinization occurred, militia subculture changed in response, making policemen, like the society around them, more sensitive to legal norms. In the final thirty years of the Soviet regime, militia corruption simply mirrored that of the Communist Party.

As the Soviet state began to disintegrate under Gorbachev's leadership, many militia personnel felt themselves victims of a society that was changing faster than they themselves could change, and of a state that could not guarantee their personal safety. Personnel relations became strained by increasing ethnic tensions, financial hardships and the constant loss of colleagues to injury and death. Today, the police forces of the post-Soviet states suffer from the personnel and structural legacies of the Soviet period. The lack of legal culture, the low level of professionalism and rampant corruption among policemen remain problems for these states as they seek to create more accountable and competent law enforcement bodies.

Part IV

Soviet militia operations

6 Militia Operations

Lawlessness was not simply a fact of life in the relationship between state and citizenry but an institutionalized principle, the quintessence of the system.

Richard Pipes[1]

This chapter will examine militia operations in the USSR, including operational styles and methods, patrols, undercover work and variations in police behavior. It will also survey the changes in militia operations that resulted from *perestroika* and Gorbachev's attempt to subordinate militia operations to the rule of law in the late 1980s. The four chapters that follow will focus on specific areas of militia operations: the policing of daily life, the deviant in Soviet society, crime and the political functions of the militia.

Influenced by tsarist tradition, shaped by a system of centralized planning and directed by a single political party, Soviet militia operations reflected a distinct authoritarian style. Police activities in the USSR were far more encompassing, intrusive and freer of legal constraints than are police operations in democratic societies. In fact, many militia functions were governed by secret and unpublished laws – neither known nor accessible to the general population. Orchestrated campaigns against hooliganism, black marketeering and alcoholism formulated at the Politburo and Central Committee level of the Communist Party became the marching orders of the militia even in remote communities. Similarly, millions of citizens were mobilized country-wide to staff street patrols and assist in police investigations and crime prevention activities.

An adage of western policing is that the more nasty the reputation of the police, the less nasty the police has to be in practice.[2] This tenet of American policing did not, however, apply to the USSR – the Soviet militia earned its terrible reputation. Apart from a brief period during the Khrushchev years when certain kinds of militia misconduct were punished, police in the Soviet Union operated with almost total impunity until the death of Brezhnev. Illegal investigative techniques such as unauthorized wiretaps and physical abuse of defendants and witnesses were the rule, producing results that were accepted without challenge in court. Although field techniques improved over time as less brutal ways were found to extract information from law-abiding citizens and criminals, endemic corruption within the militia was partially explained by the fear the police instilled in Soviet citizens.

MILITIA WORK PATTERNS

Like all Soviet agencies, the militia functioned according to a plan – often formulated several years in advance. Each year an assigned number of educational lectures had to be given and a certain percentage of reported crimes had to be cleared; every three years a plan to maintain community order had to be presented.[3] (Such community plans discussed required daily militia activities as well as the function of the police at sport events and mass gatherings.) As is typical of a centrally planned economy, the large number of law enforcement personnel in the country were not used efficiently because managers had no idea how best to deploy their personnel. As Minister of Interior Vadim Bakatin confessed in 1990: "We have no idea of the proper workload per investigator or detective, whether it should comprise 20 or 80 cases. What should the militia density be? How should it be measured? Who knows. Per capita? Per square kilometer?"[4] Police resources were generally allocated without consideration of the specific geographic area or local customs prevalent in a given region; even militia patrols were not as visible as their numbers suggested because bureaucracy and extensive paperwork kept militiamen from spending enough time on the streets.[5] Most patrol officers worked a 9 a.m. to 6 p.m. shift with a one-hour lunch break. After morning check-in, daily patrols were planned with the supervising officer, a routine familiar to American policemen. Following the duty officer's report on the events of the past evening, a patrol of the courtyards, apartment complexes and stores in the district routinely followed.

Militiamen were stationed at movie houses, bus stations, stores and other places known for a high volume of traffic. They were also highly visible in some open-air markets, where they attempted to deter pickpockets and black marketeers and maintain public order. In addition, officers were routinely sent to liquor stores at closing time to control outbursts by customers who consumed alcohol on the streets. Just as store managers usually knew the militia personnel assigned to their stores, citizens also knew where to turn for assistance if they needed a police officer. Responding to changes wrought by *perestroika*, patrol personnel in the late 1980s began to man newly established markets where individuals traded in arts and crafts and hand-manufactured clothing. Such unauthorized markets had once survived only due to bribes; during the *perestroika* era, however, thousands of citizens gathered undisturbed by the militia to look, sell and buy at such exchanges.[6]

Militia resources were concentrated on daylight hours. Round-the-clock patrols – taken for granted in American cities – were instituted in the Soviet

Union only in 1970, following an increase in crime rates. Militia posts were manned by a *dezhurnyi* (duty officer) in the evening hours, yet this shift was far from calm, as 90 percent of all crime was reported during this period.[7] Without adequate staffing or logistical support, however, the militia could not cope with the high volume of calls in the evening, when heavy evening drinking led to public disorder, domestic conflict and crime commission.

Like police in other countries, much of militiamen's time was spent on administrative offenses and the maintenance of public order. Police operations helped to enforce sanitary and passport regulations, restrict public drunkenness and narcotics use and identify parasites and petty hooligans. Combing the streets and relying on informers, the militia dealt with over one million administrative violations annually throughout the country. In 1987 alone, for example, militia personnel in Moscow located 80,000 unemployed individuals, 71,000 of whom were placed in jobs.[8]

USE OF ARMS

Militia personnel patrolled with arms that were distributed daily, receiving their arms at check-in and relinquishing them at the end of their shift. It was forbidden for off-duty patrolmen to be armed, a regulation designed to prevent the misuse and theft of weapons. Increased assaults on militia personnel in the final years of the Soviet period, however, led many law enforcement personnel to call for greater access to arms and fewer restrictions on their use.[9]

The Soviet militia's use of force differed sharply from police in certain authoritarian societies of Latin America. In the recent past, for example, the regular police in several Latin American nations committed a significant share of total homicides, killing political activists as well as impoverished urban residents. In the USSR, by contrast, the militia rarely openly killed individuals after the close of the Stalin era, maintaining its power not so much through outright force, but through all-encompassing operations. Recent evidence suggests that the militia practice of killing suspects in confinement may not, in fact, have abated in Russia.[10]

The nearly two-pound Makarov pistol – the standard weapon of the Soviet militia – was carried on an officer's right side where it could be readily stolen, particularly on crowded public transport vehicles. In order to assure his or her personal security, a militiaman thus had to violate regulations on carrying weapons. Yet in the end, militiamen rarely used their pistols because they had to prepare a written report every time a shot was fired, a rule that was often overlooked if no one had been injured or killed. Casualties were even rarer because a militiaman who did use his or her weapon was required to precede the discharge of a gun with a warning cry, a precaution sometimes carried to an absurd degree by militiamen in order to escape disciplinary action.[11] Internal investigations might be launched if militia employees misused their arms; personnel were even dismissed for such violations under various post-Stalinist leaders. Until the *perestroika* period militia personnel were more likely to fire in the air than into a crowd.

With such strict regulations on the use of guns, militiamen more often than not used nightsticks against suspects and disruptive citizens. Although a beating with a nightstick could be just as deadly as a gunshot wound, the use of the former aroused much less public hostility in the Soviet Union. Beatings and rough physical treatment of suspects occurred frequently because the militia labored under a technical disadvantage; handcuffs, for example, were rarely used because, for many decades, they were associated with capitalist policing.

CONTROLLING THE COMMUNITY: THE PATROL

The local community was policed in two different ways: through overt and covert policing. As in the United States and Western Europe, militia personnel in the USSR patrolled neighborhoods on foot, by car and by motorcycle. These patrols, often using one or two individuals, were more reminiscent of European police patrols than those of the authoritarian police of certain Latin American societies, where helmeted groups of individuals patrolled in groups – instilling fear by numbers.

The parameters of patrol and post work in the USSR were developed in the 1920s, when militia personnel walked or used horse-drawn transport for their patrols. By the final decades of the Soviet regime, however, most patrols in major cities were conducted in radio patrol cars and/or on motorcycle. Militia personnel patrolled individually on foot; two-man patrols were generally reserved for cars. In downtown areas of Moscow a militiaman or GAI inspector might be found on every corner because the use of single officers on street patrols allowed the militia to stretch its resources and maximize its visibility. With strict gun control laws and the elimination of many high-crime neighborhoods through the arrest and imprisonment of professional criminals, militiamen could walk a beat safely on their own prior to *perestroika*. Yet, in the late 1980s and early 1990s, rising crime rates caused militiamen to fear patrolling certain neighborhoods individually and many began to opt for patrol cars over foot patrols.[12]

Soviet cities were divided into a large number of *uchastki* (a small geographical unit of several blocks) that were patrolled by individuals assigned to a militia post, an entry-level position. The division of the public order effort into small, immediate community units in the USSR sharply contrasted with urban law enforcement practice in the United States, where city neighborhoods are divided into a few relatively large police precincts. Despite the immediacy of the Soviet system, it did not share the success of the Japanese *koban* system.[13]

The inefficiency of the Soviet patrol system was in part attributable to the fact that one-quarter of Soviet precinct officers had no housing, offices or telephones. A typical Moscow precinct, for example, had less than one-half of the patrol cars needed to cover its assigned routes. The situation was even worse in rural areas, where proportionately fewer operational cars and poor-quality roads often prevented militiamen from reaching their assigned communities. Although patrols improved slightly after 1985, when direct oversight of precinct officers was introduced in the militia, few jurisdictions had sufficient resources to purchase or maintain adequate equipment for local police units.[14]

Assisting the militia in its patrol functions were mobile militia units, or "points," auxiliary citizen patrols (*druzhinniki*) and Komsomol *druzhinniki* units (hereafter Komsomol units). Mobile units made the militia more accessible, quicker to respond to citizen complaints and better able to coordinate *druzhinniki* activities. Founded in Kazakhstan in 1983 to maintain social order, they subsequently functioned nationally, serving the GAI, the fire service, the OBKhSS and local communities. In Moscow, mobile divisions pursued gamblers, manned markets and were occasionally on call for domestic disputes.[15]

In the Brezhnev era over 400,000 adults participated in auxiliary patrols in cities and rural areas every day.[16] In some areas with high crime rates, such as the Far East and the Far North, their services were appreciated, but in many large communities they had little impact largely due to improper supervision. *Druzhinniki* assigned for daily duty gathered at the local militia precinct and might be given a special assignment, particularly if a law-and-order campaign was under way. As with reserve police in the United States, they were often used during periods of peak demand generated by athletic events. If they did not receive special assignments, *druzhinniki* were generally divided into groups of four to six people and instructed to follow a route under a delegated leader. Militia inspectors, however, often failed to properly instruct these "volunteer" details, and routes were frequently left unchanged for months.[17]

Patrolling *druzhinniki* were permitted to stop only those people violating public order, but this rule was interpreted quite loosely. Many auxiliary personnel stopped anyone who displeased them and brought them back to the station house. Prior to *perestroika*, hippies and punks were repeatedly subject to the arbitrary power of *druzhinniki*. Alas, harassment of youth was not the worst of the excesses committed by auxiliary militia personnel. In the 1960s, the Soviet press reported that some *druzhinniki* violently attacked private citizens, a practice that continued at least into the 1970s, despite efforts to curb such abuse.[18]

The main purpose of Komsomol detachments was to interact with defiant peers and provide them proper direction in life. Although such units conducted joint raids with the militia to locate unsupervised and unemployed youths as well as school dropouts, they, too, received minimal direction from police authorities. Active at one time in such major cities as Leningrad, Kiev, Alma-Ata and Kazan', it became increasingly difficult to mobilize such units once the authority of the Komsomol began to decline during the late Brezhnev era.[19]

Komsomol patrols were completely under the control of the local militia and were often exploited to the latter's advantage. The following story was recounted to the author by an émigré militia officer who had used his position and his Komsomol assistants to ruin another man's career. While such accounts were once obtainable only from émigrés, similar tales surfaced in the Soviet press of the *glasnost'* era. While patrolling a neighborhood restaurant in the company of two members of a Komsomol unit, the militiaman was humiliated by an insult from a drunken patron. The militia officer immediately summoned a squad car and had the man arrested. The drunk was a man of some position – a factory engineer and a Party member, but lacked sufficient Party status to protect himself from the officer's revenge. The officer subsequently falsely accused the engineer of assaulting him; members of the Komsomol patrol testified at his behest that a fight had ensued when in fact no more than an insult had passed the drunken engineer's lips. Their testimony was sufficient for the man to lose both his job and his Party membership.[20]

Cognizant of problems caused by inadequate supervision of auxiliary militia detachments, the Soviet government adopted legislation in the late 1970s that required increased oversight of Komsomol units. These controls were adopted in certain areas at the local and regional level in subsequent years, but proved difficult to implement.[21]

Komsomol patrols often had political as well as social order responsibilities. Patrols assigned to academic institutes, for example, searched for *samizdat* publications (unofficially published and disseminated literature) and other signs of anti-Soviet activity among members of the student body. In Moscow, members of such units were assigned to "protect" members of the foreign press corps and to greet delegations of foreign students at airports and train stations.[22]

Druzhinniki and Komsomol units also manned stations known as "community points for the maintenance of order" (*obshchestvennye punkty okhrany poriadka*), which began operating in Soviet apartment complexes during the 1970s. Reminiscent of the Japanese system of community law enforcement centers mentioned earlier, these *punkty* were as dreary as most Soviet housing complexes. Militia personnel were well represented on the councils that managed these units, with the latter maintaining close ties with local law enforcement bodies. Such *punkty* worked at the direction of local Party committees and were highly visible in the Brezhnev period in both urban and rural areas.[23]

During the final years of the Soviet regime, when neither ideology nor the coercive power of the state could compel citizens to participate in volunteer militia units, other means of supplementing police patrols had to be found. One such means, discussed in Chapter 5, was to have enterprises pay groups of factory workers to assist militia patrols. After conservatives gained control of the USSR MVD in 1991, army–militia patrols were initiated throughout the country. Joint patrols of four men soon operated in 450 cities, ostensibly to control crime but also to enhance political order. (In eastern Siberian cities, Cossack units supplemented such joint patrols.) In areas seeking greater autonomy, such as western Ukraine and the Baltic states, political leaders managed to resist these joint patrols with some success.[24]

CITIZEN ATTITUDES TOWARDS THE MILITIA

Citizens often did not receive adequate assistance from militia patrols, as a disproportionate number of policemen were concentrated in Moscow and a few other large cities. In some locales, the problem of insufficient patrolmen was remedied by joint patrols of military and militia personnel even before *perestroika*. Although additional personnel were assigned to patrol work in the 1980s, the uneven allocation of militia manpower led many citizens to complain about the scarcity of policemen on the streets. Outside of major cities, some people claimed to have never seen their local militia inspector. The manpower crisis worsened at the end of the Soviet period due to high turnover, a problem further aggravated by inadequate supervision of recruits.[25]

Considering the deployment of militia resources, it is hardly surprising that even before the revelations of *glasnost'*, citizens openly expressed their dissatisfaction with daily militia performance, as documented in a 1979 survey of 1,530 citizens in Gorky *oblast'* and the Uzbek republic conducted by Soviet legal researchers (Table 6.1):

Table 6.1. Inadequacies of militia work (in percentages)

Slow reaction to violations of social order	29.0
No preventive action against social disorder	22.4
Inadequate use of comrades' courts, *druzhinniki*, and housing and street Party committees	26.1
Little consideration given to public opinion	20.7
Rudeness and bureaucratic attitude of militiamen	35.5
Insufficient operations	17.3
Poor quality of legal propaganda	19.9
Inadequate number of militia personnel on evening patrols	49.6
Other shortcomings	3.0

Source: E.P. Petrov, R.A. Safarov and S.S. Strel'nikov, "Obshchestvennoe mnenie i sovetskaia militsiia," *Sovetskoe gosudarstvo i pravo*, no. 7 (1981): 75

A survey of émigrés conducted in the United States in the early 1980s revealed similar citizen attitudes toward the militia. Only a small percentage of the 2,042 émigrés interviewed for the survey believed the militia possessed either integrity or competence. Militia personnel surveyed at the same time in the USSR perceived the need to pay attention to public opinion and the need for accountability to the community. Obligations to the Communist

Party and local governments, however, as well as an inability to retain their humanity once in uniform, made militiamen incapable of bridging the obvious divide between the police and the community.[26]

SPECIAL OCCASIONS

Special occasions placed extra demands on the militia, at which time policemen ignored legal norms even more than usual. During special holidays or state visits by American presidents, additional militia personnel were generally brought into Moscow from different parts of the country to augment municipal patrols. At such moments the militia would also round up known troublemakers and place them in militia detention cells or "export" them from the city for a period of time. The Soviet press itself reported that seventy prostitutes were removed beyond a 101-kilometer line from Moscow prior to the commencement of the 1980 Olympic Games. (Alas, this number represented only a fraction of the prostitutes operating in the city.) Thorough "cleansing" of undesirable elements, complemented by police saturation of the streets, dramatically reduced the recorded crime rate during such special occasions.[27]

The practice of locking up troublemakers at such moments was not confined to ordinary Soviet deviants; dissidents were also locked up, often on trumped-up administrative charges. In such cases, the militia performed the work of the KGB. One former dissident recalled being detained by the militia during an American presidential visit to the USSR because she had planned to participate in a Jewish seminar. After her arrest, she was taken to the local precinct station where she and another Jewish activist were placed in a room with a woman picked up for black market activities. KGB officers arrived a few hours after her arrest and proceeded to criticize the arresting militia officer for not having isolated the Jewish activists from ordinary criminals. The militiaman's resentful reply, characteristic of militia attitudes towards the security police, was: "Where else should I have put her?"[28]

ANTI-CRIME CAMPAIGNS

As in western societies, militia operations in the USSR swayed with political trends and Party-orchestrated campaigns were launched periodically to address certain forms of crime.[29] Just as the United States declared a war on drugs, the Soviet Union initiated campaigns to combat black marketeering, parasitism and *samogonovarenie* (home brewing). While the American drug war is unique in the attention and resources it has garnered, Soviet society was regularly mobilized on a large scale to fight one or another type of offense.

As federal and state law enforcement bodies work together in the United States, so joint operations related to anti-crime campaigns were conducted by different branches of the militia. Sometimes all branches of the internal affairs ministry conducted sweeps of cellars and dens where so-called "low life" gathered. At other times, members of the criminal investigative and passport divisions of the militia jointly visited apartment complexes in order to detain undesirables, drifters and the unemployed. In similar fashion, OBKhSS and automobile inspectorate staff stopped trucks travelling on highways in coordinated operations designed to detect crimes and vehicular violations.[30]

Anti-crime campaigns generally lasted two years, but their intensity usually diminished after the first several months. Campaigns were formally announced in the Soviet press and nothing was left to chance: following initial militia briefings at the commencement of a campaign, law enforcement personnel were required to sign papers agreeing to execute the Party's mandate. All militiamen then focused on this form of misconduct. Minor violations that would have been tolerated at any other time resulted in arrests, thereby improving militia performance indicators. Thus, for example, petty theft from the workplace that might have been ignored by an enterprise guard under normal circumstances became grounds for arrest during a Party-initiated campaign against embezzlement of state property. Likewise, individuals might trade western records on a Moscow street corner for months, untouched by militia personnel, until a campaign was launched against black marketeering. During such periods, even a generous bribe to the arresting officer or militia investigator might not free a black market trader from the clutches of the law.

Procedural safeguards, never a primary concern of the militia, were treated with even more abandon during such campaigns, when policemen relied heavily on raids to trap targeted offenders. Often militiamen would lead forays to locate offenders in places where criminals and deviants were known to congregate. In one case recalled by an émigré defense counsel, a retired colonel was arrested during a Khrushchev-era campaign against individuals who resisted militia personnel. The colonel, who was drunk, was arrested after being overcharged by a taxi driver who took his recalcitrant customer to the precinct station. While in his cell, he shouted, "Fascists! Gestapo! I am a war veteran." A case was then initiated against him for resisting the militia and insulting Soviet power. Eventually the case was dismissed because the retired colonel never touched an officer nor resisted arrest, yet the defense attorney had a very difficult time having the charges dropped. As he explained: "The procurator, the judge – they all knew that once a campaign was on, it was impossible to go against the flow."[31]

The advent of *perestroika* did not eliminate anti-crime campaigns, but for the first time questions of civil liberties began to be raised concerning their execution. One major advocate of legal reform, Yuri Feofanov, wrote extensively in these years about the moral and legal responsibilities of militiamen who ruthlessly carried out such campaigns.[32]

UNDERCOVER OPERATIONS

Both the militia and security police of the Soviet Union inherited a long tradition of undercover work dating to the tsarist period, if not before. As Russia shifted from one authoritarian tradition to another after the Bolshevik revolution, it maintained its reliance on covert policing to control crime and ensure political conformity. Throughout the Soviet period, the militia relied on undercover work much more extensively than do police in democratic societies. Today, the legacy of dependence on undercover work is creating significant difficulties for post-Soviet states in their attempt to move towards more democratic societies.[33]

Although the functions of undercover work changed with the nature of the state, in all periods of Russian and Soviet history the purpose of undercover operations was not only to detect crime, but to uphold the political order. During the tsarist period, covert police work helped to maintain an absolute monarchy long after most European countries had moved away from authoritarian government. In the postrevolutionary period, undercover work helped to establish, and subsequently maintain, the hegemony of the Communist Party.

In democratic societies, undercover work is considered a necessary evil that is an important, but not primary, means of combatting crime.[34] Societies based on the rule of law closely scrutinize undercover work to ensure that citizens possess adequate protections against arbitrary police authority. In contrast, undercover work in a non-democratic society like the USSR was perceived as a fundamental means of pursuing criminals. Due to the premium the Communist Party placed on political and social order, no operational technique or undercover operation capable of controlling crime in the USSR was considered off limits. Although in many societies undercover work involves technology as well as informers, the use of individual informants took precedence over technological surveillance in the former Soviet Union and other socialist states. The degree of citizen mobilization in undercover police in these countries was simply unknown in democratic societies.

There were no safeguards – constitutional or legal – against the use of undercover techniques during the Soviet period. While constitutional and legislative restrictions do not hinder most American undercover work, Gary Marx has pointed out that "the major control over this kind of work – the exclusion of evidence – applies equally to covert and overt methods."[35] In the Soviet Union, where the courts rarely excluded evidence, neither the law nor the judiciary acted as a check on undercover police operations.

Americans value privacy and autonomy, and police techniques that contravene these values are viewed with particular suspicion.[36] In Soviet society, however, there was no legal or social concept of privacy, nor any demarcation between the lives of citizens and the right of the militia to monitor their lives. Autonomy was an alien value in a society that expected state intervention into daily life. Undercover work thus did not challenge central societal values; the use of listening devices, surveillance and hidden cameras were almost taken for granted by the citizenry. (For some reason, however, militiamen were not allowed to record conversations in their patrol cars.) Only in 1990, when members of the Supreme Soviet voted down a proposal on militia wiretaps did the nation begin to reject its Stalinist past.[37] Sadly, with the growing seriousness of organized crime, there is again a strong societal motivation to use undercover techniques against criminals in contemporary Russia.

Certainly, many criminals were detected in the USSR through overt police methods, yet they were located through the complex system of informants just as frequently. Undercover work is in many ways actually easier, more effective and often no more costly than overt policing techniques. Yet reliance on covert techniques in the USSR prevented the development of a more open system of policing. While overt techniques improved after Stalin's death, they did not develop to a sufficient degree to address the serious crime problems of the late Soviet period – contradicting the popular wisdom that overt and covert methods develop in tandem.

Covert policing eclipsed overt operations in the USSR largely because so many individuals worked at the disposition of the government and the Communist Party. Nevertheless, there were limits to co-optation and these limits were evident to citizens and law enforcers alike. Whereas individuals were easily subordinated to police aims in authoritarian states of previous centuries, fascist states of the mid-twentieth century and under Stalin's brutal regime, it eventually proved difficult for the industrialized Soviet state to force a highly educated population to continue to act as its tool.

THE INFORMANT SYSTEM

The recruitment of citizens into undercover police activity began almost immediately after the Bolshevik seizure of power in October 1917. A decade and a half later, the Smolensk Party archives revealed that fully 10 percent of the Soviet population had been recruited as full-time informers.[38] Although the level of citizen participation in police undercover work declined after the Stalin era, commentary of the *perestroika* and post-Soviet periods suggests that 30, perhaps even 60 percent of the population were forced to cooperate in the undercover work of the security police, with a smaller percentage similarly co-opted into militia undercover operations.[39] The high percentage of the population compromised by involvement in undercover police work – whether such operations were run by the KGB or the militia – was not confined to the Soviet Union alone, but was common in all the socialist regimes of Eastern Europe.

An elaborate system was used to develop informants in the USSR. (In many ways, the extensive use of informers was more reminiscent of eighteenth- and nineteenth-century continental European societies than of contemporary industrialized nations.) Informants in the Soviet Union were recruited from different pools of recruits, with different inducements and for different purposes. Because it had more resources at its disposal, the KGB was able to use more positive inducements than the militia. The security agency tended to recruit "respectable" citizens to help it promote its objectives of enforcing political conformity and maintaining Soviet power. The MVD, on the other hand, drew most of its informants from a more limited social sphere: the criminal world, the trade sector and the administrative staffs of apartment houses, dormitories and hotels.

The one feature all informants had in common was that the KGB or the militia generally possessed compromising material on them.[40] Many informants were, in fact, members of the criminal population who faced criminal prosecution. Charges against them would be dropped in exchange for future services and reinstated for failure to comply with militia requests for information. Given that the scope of criminal law in the Soviet Union was so broad, a great number of individuals who would be considered law-abiding citizens in other societies found themselves in compromising positions, making them potential recruits for informant work.

The militia recruited successfully among young adults and school dropouts attracted by the romanticism of police work. Ex-offenders who had lost the right to reside in a major city after receiving five-year labor camp sentences were often wooed with the much-coveted registration permit that allowed them to return to their home communities. Members of the criminal underworld who became informants were often excused from previous offenses and, under the cover of their service to the police, committed crimes such as theft with impunity.

In addition to recruited informants, there was also a category of ordinary informants – people whose job responsibilities required cooperation with the militia, such as building commandants, doormen (*dvorniki*) and watchmen (*storozhi*).[41] Their services complemented those of community and residential apartment committees under the supervision of local Communist Party organs. Close cooperation between doormen and the police was not a Soviet innovation; doormen have historically played such a role in many societies and acted as major informants for the tsarist police in the imperial Russia.[42] The unique twist to such collaboration in the Soviet Union was that it was required by law.

In less settled rural areas where an established informant infrastructure did not exist, militia personnel relied more on individual informants. Yet the informant system worked better in anonymous urban environments than in close-knit rural communities since individuals there, continuing a tradition of tsarist times, often relied on community justice. (A similar situation existed in certain Central Asian republics where Islamic justice often regulated crime in rural communities.)

Developing informants was a basic qualifying skill for criminal investigative work in both the KGB and the militia. Learning how to turn ordinary citizens and criminals into informants and provocateurs was a key component of investigative training in the latter. Convincing an individual to inform sometimes required cunning as well as money; a manual even existed to help officers succeed in the endeavor.[43] Investigators were often assisted in this task by their local district inspector, who often detained on a pretext individuals who might prove useful as informants.

Recruitment was a formalized process. Prior to recruiting an individual, an officer filled out a form and submitted it to his division chief. After five to ten days, the officer received a response concerning the suitability of the proposed informant. Contractual agreements between the militia and the agents it recruited were of long standing in the Soviet regime – the Smolensk archives reveal that the OGPU–NKVD created official conditions for the services of informants in 1927. Like those of later years, these contracts stipulated that, under threat of prosecution, the informant could not give out state secrets.[44] With a signed agreement, a militia informant might be given a code name and even sent to briefing sessions.

Although militiamen routinely paid 10 to 25 rubles for useful information, they, like police everywhere, preferred to obtain information for free. Even if paid, informants were rarely placed on the militia payroll. By finding a suitable individual in a compromising situation – or by using an individual with a checkered past and an uncertain present – militia personnel could sometimes escape paying for tips. A law-abiding citizen found drunk and disrupting public order might, for example, be convinced to serve as an informant rather than be penalized for his or her misconduct. If the subject hesitated, the individual might be confined for a period of two to three weeks until he or she consented, although certain stalwarts resisted despite the threat of prosecution.

Officers in the criminal investigative unit typically developed six to twelve regular informants. Employees of the OBKhSS relied on informants more heavily than any other category of militia investigator. Responsible for investigating embezzlement and corruption in state enterprises, they tried to develop several reliable informants in various branches of each organization. Identities of informants were hidden not only from their colleagues at work, but usually from other militia personnel as well.

Certain categories of individuals were not considered appropriate for informant work. Juveniles were rarely employed because they often proved unreliable, but were nevertheless occasionally enlisted to provide information on youth gangs. Although some militia personnel used prostitutes, others found them unsuitable due to serious alcohol and drug problems that impaired their reliability. Finally, Party and Komsomol members could not be recruited without special permission and, as such authorization was notoriously difficult to obtain, were rarely enlisted in undercover work.

DEPLOYMENT OF INFORMANTS

In the mid-1960s, informant work was routinized and classified into several categories including prophylactic, surveillance, operational and observational. Prophylactic work was used primarily among juveniles to redirect behavior, provide grounds for arrest or isolate troublemakers. Surveillance was used to keep track of inmates recently released from prison and those suspected of significant criminal activity. Ex-offenders listed as potential dangers to the community on militia records could be quickly returned to labor camps through the agent system. Operatives were used to obtain information under different guises. Informants might, for example, pose as electrical employees or utility personnel in order to enter apartments and elicit information from neighbors. Observational informants did not always consciously serve the militia; recidivists, for example, were often granted liberty only to be used as decoys for fellow gang members. The militia would observe contacts made by these criminals in the community and then return them to prison along with other gang members.

Although informants' reports focused primarily on crime, surveillance took place not only in the political and criminal arenas, but also in daily life. Informants residing in apartment buildings might report on domestic violence, alcohol abuse or violations of passport regulations. Housing personnel, a backbone of the Soviet system for maintaining public order, were rarely compensated for their tips, yet often had much to report in the way of violations of passport and registration laws. The informant system was, however, far from fully effective in this area. Towards the end of the Soviet regime, approximately one million citizens were managing to reside illegally in Moscow without being expelled by the militia by routinely bribing superintendents or guard personnel of apartment complexes not to inform on their unauthorized residence.

Informants reported exclusively to one officer, either by telephone or at personal meetings held in special apartments maintained for such encounters. Several "safe" apartments were located in ordinary residential buildings in every large urban area and officers generally tried to avoid using the same apartment consistently. Every effort was made to mask the functions of these apartments from neighbors, with one officer often pretending to reside there, always appearing in civilian clothes. Informants who could not be met in an apartment might be met in corridors, movie houses, stadiums or other populated areas where such a meeting could not easily be detected.

Nasedki, the special class of informant used in prison investigation cells to obtain information and extract confessions from suspects during their detention, often spent much of their day performing such tasks. Their professional identity was usually known only to the militia investigatory division and not to law enforcement personnel working in their immediate residential neighborhoods. In one case recounted to the author by an émigré defense counsel, a man was brought in on parasitism charges (a crime defined as the failure to work) by local militia authorities. Not forewarned about his identity, the judge repeatedly asked the defendant "What do you do?" The man replied that he worked for the militia. The perplexed judge replied, "In what capacity?" The accused man's response – "I sit in jail all day and then recount all" – was greeted by general laughter.[45]

ANONYMOUS TIPS AND DENUNCIATIONS

The militia also detected crime through the undercover technique of anonymous tips. During the Stalin era, Soviet citizens were urged to denounce their compatriots for misconduct. The practice unfortunately did not disappear entirely following the dictator's death. According to Ukrainian *samizdat*, for example, residents of Kiev in 1981 received postcards requesting that they report anonymously to a council of the public order (a neighborhood body) the names of parasites, alcoholics, problem families and adolescent dropouts. The growing awareness of democratic values that preceded *perestroika* in Moscow caused concern among certain government officials about this operation. Early the following year, an article appeared in *Izvestiia* criticizing the Kievan request for anonymous denunciations.[46]

The furore over anonymous denunciations never abated in late post-Stalinist Soviet society and became even more vocal with the advent of *glasnost'*.[47] Rather than diminish, however, denunciations to the police increased in the late 1980s. The procuracy and the MVD defended their necessity, claiming that the 25 percent of serious crime would remain undetected without the use of anonymous tips. Such tips did not, however, bear the fruit that law enforcement personnel claimed they did. Of the 50 percent of the inspections made by the OBKhSS (occupying 30 percent of their time) based on such sources, for example, only 1 to 2 percent of the tips panned out. Critics contended that the value of such sources was oversold and unnecessarily encroached upon the individual's rights.[48]

The increasingly sophisticated technology available to law enforcement personnel in industrially developed nations poses a growing threat to the rights of citizens in general.[49] This phenomenon is especially problematic in modern authoritarian societies like the former USSR, where citizens do not enjoy legal safeguards and policemen lack a sense of the rule of law. Thus, in spite of its content, the Supreme Soviet's adoption of a law in 1990 authorizing militia investigators to use videos, films and tape recordings actually represented an effort to regulate police behavior previously outside the reach of Soviet law. The law stipulated that phone lines could be tapped only in cases where legal proceedings have been initiated and only after receiving the procurator's approval or on the court's decision.[50] Unfortunately, the legislation failed to resolve many problems associated with undercover policing because it did not institute enforcement mechanisms to ensure police compliance with the law.

OPERATIONAL BIASES AND VARIATIONS IN MILITIA BEHAVIOR

Leninist policy, reenforced by Stalin, centralized political power in the USSR and ignored essential differences among the various nationalities in the country. Every attempt was made to standardize law enforcement across regions inhabited by different ethnic groups with distinct political, social, cultural and religious traditions. Given the Soviet regime's ideological commitment to equality, the government sought to eliminate not only regional, but social differences from policing. Yet equal treatment before the law was unattainable in such a diverse society. Moreover, a very real discrepancy existed between professed law enforcement goals and day-to-day policies in the USSR. From the first days of Bolshevik rule, differential treatment of citizens was institutionalized by means of special privileges for Communist Party members that, in effect, exempted many high-ranking members and their families from arrest and prosecution.

Militia personnel could initiate an investigation of a high-ranking Party member only after obtaining permission from the relevant Party organization; suspects could be brought to trial only after being expelled from the Party. The repeated refusal of Party organizations to expel members often gave them immunity from white collar offenses and crimes related to the abuse of office. In the Central Asian republics and the Caucasus, immunity sometimes extended to such serious crimes as rape and homicide. Investigators who initiated proceedings against well-placed Party members without first obtaining Party approval often found themselves, and not the actual criminals, defendants in criminal trials.[51]

Glasnost' allowed legal critics to advocate equal treatment of all citizens before the law and the elimination of Communist Party members' exemption from prosecution. Although this privilege did not officially disappear until the dissolution of the CPSU after the August 1991 coup, it was abridged in 1989 when the USSR Supreme Soviet made intervention in the legal process by Party members a criminal offense.

In contrast to the political elite of the Soviet Union, who enjoyed special legal treatment, ordinary citizens such as flower vendors (who lacked social status), might be repeatedly harassed by the militia, as the following story makes clear:

> From time to time . . . a militia squad arrives . . . and starts chasing the old women with their flowers. Then one of them goes round all her friends and collects one ruble from each. The money that is collected is handed over and the squad departs . . . . Sometimes there are two raids on the same day. "But we've already paid," the flower sellers complain. "Nothing to do with us," the militiamen reply, "they were probably from another precinct."[52]

Dissimilar treatment of low- and high-status individuals by the police is common in most societies. As criminal justice scholar James Q. Wilson has noted, in certain American cities in the past "the precinct station . . . may have acted benevolently toward friends and party faithful."[53] Unlike most contemporary western societies, however, political party membership rather than individual wealth procured preferential police treatment in the USSR. Whereas such preferential treatment is generally situational in democratic societies, in Soviet society – a society ideologically committed to equality – preferential treatment was, ironically, institutionalized.

Variations in Soviet militia behavior across the USSR differed sharply from the variations in U.S. police behavior identified by Wilson. Two of the three styles of U.S. policing he distinguishes – legalistic and service – did not exist in the USSR; the militia had neither an obligation to uphold legal norms nor an interest in serving the community.[54] Soviet militia operations were more reminiscent of Wilson's third *modus operandi* – the watchman style, as Soviet militia "watched" a great deal of behavior that was essentially private and therefore beyond the purview of American police. This style, which broadly characterized the functions of the regular Soviet police, did, however, assume different forms in the socially and culturally diverse cities, regions and republics of the country.

According to Soviet specialists who studied the regular police, militia personnel themselves employed one of two operational styles: careerist or pragmatist.[55] The careerist style characterized militiamen who were interested in applying the law, not in using their discretion. The pragmatist style was common to policemen who were most interested in processing cases efficiently. The pragmatist was interested in the opinion of his superior, who would ultimately decide the case, and remained unconcerned by whether or not he was a reliable executor of the law or responsive to the community.

Urban policing in the USSR also differed according to neighborhood and city. Although cities in the USSR were not as clearly segregated by income level or social class as are most western cities, clearly identified neighborhoods of workers and intellectuals did exist in major Soviet urban centers. Working-class neighborhoods – where fights were more likely to break out – were, for example, often policed with less civility than those inhabited by individuals with higher social status and Party connections.

Variations in police operations among different republics were also striking. It is telling that such differentiation existed even during the Stalinist period, when efforts to achieve uniform law enforcement policies were strongest. Despite nearly uniform criminal law, long-standing cultural, social and religious differences among the Soviet republics made it impossible to implement consistent militia operations. Legal violations, for example, were more frequent in remote Slavic areas and the Central Asian republics than in the Baltic republics and more westernized parts of the USSR, where law enforcement more closely adhered to written legal norms. Personal ties between militia personnel and community members, particularly in Central Asia, also contributed to police operations that violated Soviet legal norms. Extensive bribery of employees of the USSR Ministry of Internal Affairs during the Brezhnev era actually placed many of these republics outside of the control of the central militia apparatus altogether.

The colorful case of the Kurbanov family, who resided in Turkmenistan in the mid-1960s, is illustrative of the geographic discrepancies in law enforcement in the former USSR. In accordance with traditional Islamic custom, Kurbanov, a lieutenant and precinct militiaman, kidnapped a minor as a bride for his younger brother. The kidnappers and the prospective bride were sheltered by another Kurbanov family member, himself a former militia worker. An *Izvestiia* article later indicated that responsibility for this misconduct did not lie with the Kurbanov family alone; at the time of the paper's exposé, the local militia had neither investigated the criminal nor his collaborators.[56]

Significant geographical differences in policing existed even in the Russian republic. In the absence of adequate infrastructure, housing and recreation facilities in the "new" cities of Siberia and the Soviet Far North, for example, alcohol abuse was frequent and crime rates were high among populations with disproportionate concentrations of young male workers.[57] Militia operations in these cities were consequently more aggressive and crisis-oriented than in older, more established cities of the Russian republic. Yet, even in newer regions of established cities like Moscow and Leningrad – neighborhoods that were generally inhabited by recently arrived workers – crime rates were higher than the city norm and militia behavior was closer to that known in newer Soviet cities.

Prior to *perestroika*, police operations were not normally defined by the nationality of the militia officials involved nor that of the citizens subject to their authority. In many ethnically diverse regions of the country, militiamen did not always immediately seek to determine the nationality of an individual. (It became clear, however, as soon as a citizen presented his or her internal passport.) Nevertheless, stereotypes did affect law enforcement in the country. Slavic policemen, for example, might be harder on individuals from the Caucasian or Central Asian republics. The Georgian selling fruit at a market in the Russian republic was often stereotyped as a "speculator" by the militia, whereas a visiting Moldavian or Ukrainian would escape the pejorative label. Interestingly, nationalities were not subject to the same stereotypes in all regions of the country; ethnic Germans, for example, might face discrimination in Central Asian republics, but were treated favorably in the Russian republic.

Law enforcement personnel in multi-ethnic regions often discriminated either in favor of or against certain ethnic groups. Native policemen in the Baltics, for example, might give the benefit of the doubt to a fellow Balt. One former Latvian OBKhSS inspector reported that while he might release a Latvian suspected of embezzlement at a warehouse, the same man might be prosecuted if a Russian militia official checked the inventory.[58] As Jewish and German émigrés attested in two surveys conducted in the early 1980s, certain distinct minority groups were also subject to differential treatment. As former residents of the urbanized cities of Russia, the Baltics and communities along the Volga River, both groups believed that their nationality had or would have suffered harsher treatment by the militia in the case of arrest.[59]

Law enforcement became profoundly differentiated in many regions of the

USSR during the ethnic strife that shook the country during the late 1980s and early 1990s. In fact, blatant discrimination by militia units helped to fuel explosive situations in Azerbaijan and Armenia, two republics where law enforcement was rapidly subordinated to nationalist sentiment.[60] Total disregard for the rights of Armenian residents on the part of Azeri law enforcement personnel in Azerbaijan and Armenia ignited riots in both countries. Purges of law enforcement personnel who failed to protect Armenians from Azeri pogroms failed to quell the unrest.[61]

Differentiated law enforcement in the late *perestroika* period had far-reaching political implications for Soviet society. National groups could not reach consensus in areas where nationalist sentiment had been fired by militia abuses, and mistreatment of various ethnic groups only inhibited national reform efforts. These barriers to impartial law enforcement eventually constituted an additional cause of the dissolution of the Soviet state.

CONCLUSION

Soviet militia operations demonstrated certain marked similarities with police operations in other societies. The militia used a combination of overt and covert activities to deal with deviants and criminals and often focused on particular forms of criminal activity in response to governmental priorities. A superficial glance at the militia's patrols, safe houses and covert techniques might suggest that the Soviet militia differed little from the police of western societies. Such superficial similarities, however, masked fundamental differences. Without essential procedural guarantees of the rights of citizens, the law remained on the side of the Soviet militia, which readily imposed its will on both criminals and law-abiding individuals.[62] Citizens, moreover, were compelled not only to inform on others, but to participate in their own policing as "volunteers."

Until *perestroika*, citizens had scant legal protection and often failed to exercise those limited rights they enjoyed. Defense attorneys did not have access to clients until the criminal investigation had been completed. Few institutionalized checks existed to control militia operations. Evidence that should have been inadmissible in court was used, testimony of unreliable informants was accepted and forced confessions occurred to an extent unknown in societies that provide greater protection to defendants.

Although not uniform across the USSR, police operations in all regions of the country were characterized by lack of respect for legal norms. Gorbachev's attempt to reverse this situation by creating a law-based state was immediately frustrated by the Soviet state's use of the regular police to more aggressively control crime and to halt the centrifugal forces of the collapsing regime in the late 1980s and early 1990s. In the end, the militia, at a crucial juncture in Soviet history, failed the basic test of policing: it could no longer control the country's citizens.[63]

7   The militia and daily life

The militia watches out for me.

Vladimir Mayakovsky

Ordinary Soviet citizens had more frequent contact with the police than do citizens of democratic societies. In the west, the patrol is the heart of police work and the most frequent point of police–citizen contact. In the Soviet Union, by contrast, the vast majority of citizen encounters with the police took place outside of the daily militia patrol. Law-abiding citizens in the USSR were constantly forced to consider the militia as they planned their day's activities. Adult citizens who left their homes without their internal passports were subject to police sanction. Individuals who went on weekend car outings would invariably be stopped by the ubiquitous traffic militia. A Soviet television camera crew that attempted to film the homes of the nation's political elite would be stopped by militia guards. Even in the Gorbachev period, people who listened to political speeches in downtown Moscow could not help but notice a massive police presence in the city center. In all these situations, the militia acted as a reminder to Soviet citizens that they did not inhabit a free society and that their personal movements and routine activities were the object of state scrutiny.

The militia annually handed out administrative sanctions to approximately one-quarter of the adult population, an indication of the degree to which police controls pervaded daily life. In 1987, Soviet citizens lost 25 million work hours attending to passport requirements alone.[1] Administrative sanctions in the USSR were not on a par with the parking tickets awarded to careless drivers in western societies and often involved stiff fines and/or short-term imprisonment. Sanctions could be imposed for such minor infractions as the failure to buy a local transport ticket, their consequences extending far beyond the original penalty. Militia records of citizen transgressions could, for example, cause individuals to lose their place in line for state-subsidized apartments. Defendants who faced administrative charges enjoyed even fewer legal protections than those who faced criminal charges; until 1985, they were denied the right to counsel and any right of appeal. Powerful demonstrations of the militia's control over everyday life, administrative sanctions left citizens unable to challenge decisions that bore significant ramifications for their private lives.[2]

As the following two chapters illustrate, policies of the *perestroika* era changed the militia's relationship toward the deviant and the criminal in Soviet society, permitting the former greater latitude in personal expression and the latter greater legal protection. Curiously, police controls such as the passport system endured throughout the Gorbachev reform period, despite their condemnation by both liberal legislators and representatives of the Soviet legal establishment.

After political revolutions swept through Eastern Europe in 1989, many democratizing states of the region moved rapidly to dismantle police controls that had been modelled on the Soviet system and imposed by Soviet-trained police. The Czechs, Slovaks, Hungarians and Poles all viewed the removal of such controls as an immediate and necessary prelude to the establishment of civil society and a market economy. In the USSR, however, numerous components of the system of social control imposed by Stalin survived for at least five years after the advent of *perestroika*. Subordinate to the Communist Party of the Soviet Union, the militia was unable to extract itself from numerous functions that inhibited the development of civil society in the USSR. A number of police restrictions over daily life described in this chapter remain in existence today in the post-Soviet states; there is little hope that this well-established police apparatus will be dismantled anytime soon.[3]

PARAMETERS OF CONTROL

The Soviet citizen lived in a country where his private life, residential community and workplace were all regulated by a vast network of police controls. Regulation of daily life in the USSR reflected both an authoritarian–command system and the state paternalism of a continental state. The key to the system lay in Soviet citizens' complicity in their own control. Dependent on the state for housing and employment, they were forced to observe police regulations in order to assure their welfare, becoming participants in their own policing. As Clifford Shearing and Philip Stenning have noted concerning social controls that are embedded in a given environment:

> A critical consequence ... of embedding control ... is that control becomes consensual. It is effected with the willing cooperation of those being controlled so that the controlled become, as Foucault has observed, the source of their own control.[4]

This formulation accurately described Soviet society until the era of *perestroika*.

Strict police direction of daily life in the USSR was formally established in the immediate postrevolutionary period. The Bolsheviks copied the tsarist system of precinct inspectors (*uchastkovye*) and issued an inspectors' handbook in the 1920s that, in most respects, remained valid up until 1991.[5]

Within a decade of the revolution, the NKVD developed an 800-page compendium of regulations, circulars and decrees governing daily life that were far broader than any legislation at the disposal of American police.[6] Internal disorder and police illiteracy initially made these copious regulations of little use, but as the Soviet system evolved, the militia was gradually able to apply the extensive social controls so skillfully assembled in the regime's first decades.

The mandate of the militia did not aim merely at preserving peace and preventing crime, but at subordinating personal privacy to the larger interests of the state. Aided by housing committees, janitorial personnel and informants, the militia kept track of citizens from birth to death. Among other functions that touched the individual directly, the militia monitored family relations, regulated disputes among neighbors and administered the massive passport system. Regional internal affairs offices even maintained centralized files on all residents who had ever violated the public order[7] – a practice that would be considered an invasion of privacy in the United States. Unable to change residences or go on an extended trip without informing the local militia, the Soviet citizen was never far removed from police scrutiny.

Administrative functions of the Soviet police spanned a wide variety of other activities, including registration of housing; hunting, fishing, and vehicle licensing; and control over petty speculation, minor hooliganism, trafficking in contraband, drunkenness and fire safety. The encompassing nature of the legal provisions that assigned such duties to the police, as well as the latter's intrusion into private life, were evident in the conduct Soviet law defined as criminal, such as "leading a juvenile to drunkenness by parents or other individuals," "receiving poached game" and "negligent care of the land."[8]

The militia performed many regulatory functions that in western nations are performed by administrative agencies. Community controls enforced in the United States by such agencies as the public health service, the Bureau of Tobacco and Firearms and the Fish and Wildlife Service, for example, were enforced by the militia in the USSR. Thus territorial militia units implemented medical, veterinary and sanitary measures; licensed hunting weapons; protected natural resources and dealt with the consequences of natural disasters.[9] Such far-reaching and demanding responsibilities complemented the militia's visible presence in every urban and rural community of the country in the form of patrols, posts and the local precinct inspector.

Although the militia performed extensive educational activities with respect to administrative laws – visiting schools, factories and other work sites to acquaint people with pedestrian safety rules, criminal law and the citizen's obligations to the state – no citizen could comply with all regulations governing daily life. The scope of the law, particularly administrative law, was simply too broad to permit genuine law-abiding behavior. Whereas the criminal code was published and compliance with criminal law was thus nominally possible, citizens could not observe all administrative laws because not all were published,[10] including many that directly affected their personal lives. Citizens trying to establish residence in Moscow, for example, might find the militia uncooperative and intransigent, when militiamen were only enforcing classified regulations barring new settlers in major urban centers.[11] This system of *sub rosa* legislation pervaded daily life and exacerbated universal problems of arbitrary and subjective law enforcement, a fact publicly recognized only with *glasnost'*.[12]

Just as the Soviet citizen could not comply with all administrative laws, neither could the militia in fact regulate every aspect of daily life – its mandate was too broad and its numbers too few. Although called to task by the Communist Party whenever family discontent resulted in destructive violence or young people committed brutal crimes, Party pressure to achieve unrealistic levels of order strained militia capabilities and undermined its credibility in the community.

THE INTERNAL PASSPORT AND REGISTRATION SYSTEM

The militia did not issue internal passports to citizens until they reached the age of 16. This document contained all vital information about an individual, including his or her nationality and address. The permanent residence specified in the passport was the only place a Soviet citizen was permitted to live. Additional entries might indicate a previous labor camp sentence or past failure to pay child support.[13] Citizens were required to carry their internal passports at all times and retained them until death, when the documents were returned to the militia for safekeeping.[14]

Militiamen could command citizens to show their passports at any time or place – an individual's appearance was sufficient to trigger a body search in the USSR. (Because searches were not subject to any legal constraints, no citizen was immune from a document check.)[15] To cite just one example of the intrusive nature of these checks, militiamen and *druzhinniki* often conducted joint raids in apartment complexes and dormitories solely in order to detect individuals who were not registered with the police. As a professor at an MVD institute noted in 1988, such actions contradicted the USSR constitution, which held the Soviet citizen's home to be inviolable.[16]

In order to reduce the resentment caused by the passport system, the regime created rituals that made the passport an integral part of daily existence. The issuance of passports at age 16, for example, was accompanied by a militia ceremony that in another culture might be interpreted as a ritual of manhood. When new passports were issued in conjunction with newly issued legislation in 1974, the regime enlisted Party, trade union, Komsomol and social organizations to help the militia exchange passports in a mass campaign characterized by much publicity and great patriotic display.[17]

As mentioned in Chapter 2, passports were originally awarded only to restricted categories of urban residents; unpublished passport laws adopted after Stalin's death in 1953 only slightly expanded the categories of individuals eligible to receive this crucial document.[18] As late as 1974, a much-heralded new law failed to grant full passport rights to collective farm members. Although these farmers did receive passports, specialists on Soviet law pointed out that the legal position of these people (i.e., being bound to the land) remained unchanged, as their passports bore "secret indications that their owners belonged on the farm."[19]

The passport system thus established two classes of citizens. Urban residents could travel freely domestically and even purchase airplane tickets merely by alerting militia authorities – both locally and at their point of destination – of their travel plans. (Only trips of less than three days' duration did not require registration with the police.) Collective farm residents, on the other hand, lived in a feudal state and enjoyed second-class status. They could not buy plane tickets without the authorization of their *kolkhoz* director and were often forced to sleep in railway stations when travelling because they could not be admitted to a hotel without an internal passport.[20]

Many Soviet citizens chose to ignore the registration requirements when they travelled, yet disregard of these rules made them vulnerable to militia harassment and fines, a vulnerability that diminished only during the *perestroika* era. Failure to register a visit with relatives or a stay at the beach with the local militia could incur penalties – an administrative fine for the first violation and criminal penalties for subsequent offenses.[21] Dissidents specifically targeted by the militia were sometimes returned to labor camps for violating passport rules, as were numerous ordinary ex-offenders.[22]

Residential permits represented a major power the militia held over Soviet citizens. Any change in one's permanent residence required the permission of the passport division, a regulation that annually brought many citizens into contact with the militia.[23] Husbands and wives from different cities could be denied the residence permits that would allow them to live together; relatives from other communities could be denied permission to live with ill or elderly family members living in major cities; citizens could lose their jobs if they lacked the required registration permits.[24] In Leningrad, three passport officers were needed in each precinct to handle the volume of passport work.[25] Overall, administration of the passport system represented a significant share of the total legal work performed by the militia.[26]

It was impossible to move to a major urban center in the USSR if it were a *rezhimnyi* city closed to new residents (e.g., Moscow, Leningrad or Kiev). Unpublished regulations determined citizen registration not only in large cities, but also in specific regions of the country. Specific regulations, for example, prohibited the militia from registering Crimean Tartars, Meskhetian Turks and other peoples expelled from their native lands in the 1940s if they returned to their homelands. These rules were still being strictly enforced in the early 1990s when exiled Meskhetian Turks found themselves subject to pogroms in the communities of Central Asia to which they had been exiled.

Refugees posed a difficult challenge to registration regulations. By the end of 1991 there were nearly 800,000 internal refugees in the USSR;[27] many were Russians and Armenians who had fled the Caucasus to seek safety in Moscow. Registration requirements, however, precluded the long-term residence of refugees in the capital and many of these people soon found themselves threatened with expulsion from the city. Although ordinary citizens might be able to bribe militia personnel to obtain a residence permit, this option was not available to refugees and exiled nationalities.[28]

By means of such police controls, the USSR managed to limit the growth of major cities that ordinarily would have attracted numerous new residents. Such *rezhimnye* cities generally had populations that were older than those of other urban communities, particularly those which did not limit the population of young male residents. (Many young men were forced to settle in new towns on the outskirts of major urban centers.) Only in October 1990 did the Committee for Constitutional Supervision of the USSR Supreme Soviet rule that residence permits violated Soviet citizens' civil rights, declaring that domicile registration was permissible, but the obligation to obtain a residence permit was not.[29] Unfortunately, the committee had no enforcement mechanism at its disposal and this decision was never implemented. Even in mid-1992, almost a year after the Soviet state had collapsed, Muscovites interviewed in a public opinion poll did not believe that residence permits would be abolished or that one day they would be able to live where they chose.[30]

Until the Gorbachev period, Soviet citizens had no legal recourse when denied a residence permit by the militia. Accordingly, a new 1987 administrative law that permitted individuals to challenge acts of official malfeasance or injustice on appeal was heralded as a sign of genuine *perestroika*. Unfortunately, the complaints law was largely ineffective, permitting citizens to appeal against only individual decisions, whereas almost all Soviet decision making was collective. Nevertheless denial of a residence permit was the decision of an individual militia officer and citizens with sophisticated lawyers were able to successfully challenge refusals of residence permits in several parts of the country in the early 1990s.[31]

Permit regulations enabled the militia to restrict changes of residence not only between, but within cities. A militiaman might not authorize a citizen's move within a locality if he or she believed that the individual's interests conflicted with those of the state or, as in the following case, with the state's idealized view of family life. A member of the passport branch of the Tallinn militia in Estonia hesitated in the 1980s to register a man in a new apartment across town from his elderly mother. Only after the officer received the son's assurance that the distance would not impede his performance of filial duties did the militiaman authorize the move.[32]

Despite their pervasive intrusion into daily life, passport controls in the Soviet Union were far from infallible. In the mid-1970s, the late dissident Andrei Amal'rik – author of *Will the Soviet Union Survive until 1984?* – was confined to Moscow under militia surveillance after his release from labor camp. A pair of dissident friends invited Amal'rik to join them on a much-needed vacation in the Baltics. The dissident triumvirate could not register with the local militia, as revelation of Amal'rik's concealment might have had severe consequences for them all. After their fresh-air vacation, they returned to Moscow, their illegal sojourn apparently unnoticed either by the militia or the KGB. Amal'rik subsequently emigrated and his hosts joined the Moscow Helsinki group that monitored human rights violations in the USSR. Despite Soviet authorities' efforts to disband this group, the un-registered travel of these political activists remained a secret and was never used against them.[33]

Strict passport laws and militia harassment also did not succeed in stopping people from migrating to the larger cities of the USSR. According to the estimates of Soviet authorities, close to one million individuals resided illegally in Moscow at any given time.[34] Whereas several thousand citizens were harshly penalized for violating passport regulations each year in the USSR, by 1990 the Moscow militia had nearly ceased to impose such penalties. Prior to *perestroika*, however, periodic campaigns were launched to improve citizen compliance with the passport laws.[35]

Once a campaign had begun, both landlords and illegal residents were subject to sanction, as the following story indicates. To capitalize on the shortage of hotel space in the city, one Muscovite routinely housed visitors in her apartment. Because such visitors did not register with the militia, both their residency and her provision of accommodation were illegal. The local precinct inspector several times tried to view the woman's apartment, but the proprietor categorically refused to open the door. When summoned to the local militia station for an explanation, she did not appear.

Eventually the woman was called to attend a meeting with the local housing committee and delegated community members, where she was warned that failure to respond to the militia would result in criminal prosecution. Following this warning, the woman allowed militiamen to enter her apartment, where they found two individuals residing illegally. The illegal visitors – from central Russia and Erevan, respectively – were invited to the local militia station to explain their lengthy unregistered stay in Moscow. In the end, both were given 72 hours to leave Moscow and Moscow *oblast'*; the landlady was fined 10 rubles for having violated passport regulations.[36]

The collaboration of the militia, housing authorities and community members to regulate daily life in the USSR is clearly demonstrated in this story.[37] While the penalty ultimately imposed on the apartment proprietor was quite mild, only the threat of criminal prosecution made her comply with regulations. Such joint militia–citizen efforts can be said to have had one positive impact: they prevented Moscow and other large cities with in-sufficient housing from becoming even more overcrowded.

Typical of the centralized Soviet system, enforcement of the passport laws often proved counterproductive to the interests of both the state and the community. Collective farm chairmen burdened with elderly populations, for example, often could not meet their production quotas without contracting groups of *shabashniki* (wildcatters) to increase their harvests. These migrant laborers were given seeds and agricultural equipment and granted use of the land in exchange for delivering a set volume of crops at harvest time. *Shabashniki* worked on the farm from dawn to dusk, lived in swinish conditions and suffered untold hardships. As their income depended on the fruits of their labor at the end of the season, they worked far harder than collective farm members. Yet, despite the fact that collective farms could not meet production quotas without them, *shabashniki* frequently ran afoul of the passport laws administered by the militia.[38]

After 1976, temporary residence permits for rural areas were prohibited and individuals could work in the countryside only for six weeks before becoming subject to administrative penalties. In order to produce crops, however, temporary laborers had to work an entire season on a farm. Militiamen were reluctant to move against such productive citizens and complained about having to take action against them. Farm managers adamantly opposed militia enforcement of permit laws against them, but militiamen often had no choice but to fine *shabashniki*. Thus laborers indispensable for feeding the Soviet population were fined for violating the most fundamental provision of the passport laws: the requirement to obtain a registration permit.[39]

Interestingly, the passport system was able to adapt itself to the social and political changes of *perestroika*. In 1990, for example, a new use was found for the internal passport when certain price controls were lifted: preventing runs on food stores. Following measures already adopted in the Baltic republics and Leningrad, the Moscow city council in May 1990 enacted a temporary rule that required prospective customers to show their passports before entering a food store in the city – proving that they were Moscow residents. At the same time, regular militiamen together with GAI and OBKhSS personnel were instructed to monitor cars, railroads and airports to prevent the export of food supplies from Moscow. Similarly, even before the food situation became acute in Siberia, militiamen in Tiumen' were under orders from the regional Soviet executive committee to control the exodus of food from the region. As one militia official in the city commented: "We had to organize special checkups at railway stations and airports, i.e., to 'take measures'. But isn't that a violation of the law?"[40] As was the case in the 1920s, when the militia confiscated food in rural areas and protected food reserves in major cities, the role of the militia in protecting food supplies was very much in place at the end of the Soviet period.

RECORD KEEPING

The internal passport system did more than simply monitor the domiciles and movements of Soviet citizens. Because each citizen was in contact with the militia from birth to death, the police were able to maintain records essential to the command economy of the USSR. Data gathered by the passport division permitted the state to plan trade volumes, the production of consumer goods, transport systems and the construction of educational, cultural and medical facilities.[41] The files of this division also aided citizens, the army, the KGB and the militia in locating people (among other functions, the militia was responsible for missing persons).[42] Such files located draft-age young men and supplied data to the address and information bureaus that citizens used to locate community members, lost relatives and former husbands and/ or lovers who failed to pay alimony. Civil and criminal justice professionals used the files to locate witnesses needed to testify in court. Finally, these records also fulfilled a surveillance function, as the passport division reported suspicious individuals to operational divisions of the militia apparatus.[43]

Despite the all-encompassing registration system, the militia did indeed lose track of people, a problem that only worsened with *perestroika*. In 1976 there were 23,000 missing persons in the USSR; by 1989 the figure had more than quadrupled to exceed 94,000.[44] This figure did not include those individuals who had not been declared missing by friends or relatives and managed to elude militia detection. Although small in comparison to the total population of the USSR (then approximately 290 million), the latter number was an indication of the difficulty of closely monitoring such an enormous population in the absence of full computerization.

OTHER MEANS OF CONTROLLING PERSONAL MOBILITY

The militia's control over individual mobility reached far beyond passport regulations and residence permits, extending to the highways, the movement of foreigners within the USSR and the ability of Soviet citizens to travel abroad. The constant vigilance of the far-from-polite traffic police, for example, provided Soviet citizens and foreign nationals alike a strong disincentive to travel within the country. The GAI (State Automotive Inspectorate) not only administered driver education courses and granted driving licenses, it stationed its men along all main thoroughfares and highways. Although GAI inspectors frequently stopped cars to maintain vehicular safety, check passports and apprehend suspects, they often also stopped vehicles simply to elicit bribes. In one case documented in the western press, different GAI officials stopped one man several times on his way from Sheremetevo airport to downtown Moscow (approximately an hour's drive), ostensibly to check his documents, but in reality to extract their standard three-ruble payoff.[45]

The passport division also controlled the mobility of foreigners in the country, approving concrete travel itineraries, authorizing domestic car travel and registering visitors at their hotel or place of residence. Although the militia often prepared the formal paperwork documenting foreigners' stays in the USSR, it was usually the KGB which actually followed foreigners and scrutinized their contacts. In fact, the militia granted foreigners authorization to travel within the country only after consultation with the security organs.[46]

Among its other duties, the passport division granted foreign passports to Soviet citizens who travelled abroad as tourists, diplomats or on other official business.[47] The OVIR (visa and registration administration of the Ministry of Internal Affairs) awarded citizens permission both to travel abroad and to emigrate from the USSR. Again, the militia did not have the ultimate say in such decisions, simply fulfilling the paperwork requirements of decisions made by the KGB. Nevertheless, OVIR personnel were highly corrupt and themselves posed a major obstacle to foreign travel.

The following story reflects the difficulties Soviet citizens regularly encountered when they attempted to travel abroad prior to *perestroika*. In the 1970s and early 1980s a retired war veteran and his wife frequently paid visits to old friends in East Germany (the German Democratic Republic, or GDR). Suddenly, a new chief of the OVIR division at the Frunzenskii *raion* in Moscow put a stop to their travel. While the OVIR official taunted them, the couple haunted his office for three months. The officer authorized, then refused them permission to travel, once going so far as to suggest that the man find a way to procure the officer a cheap car. The OVIR chief was removed after the husband wrote a letter of complaint, but a "brick wall" of refusals materialized in his place. Complaints to the office of the USSR Procurator yielded no results.

For three years, the couple attempted to obtain permission to travel, providing the militia complete documentation of their invitations to the GDR twice annually. Eventually, their persistence provoked a response: they were told that the man's previous participation in secret work barred him from travelling abroad. His certificates, however, attested that his employment had been of a non-classified nature. Subsequently the couple learned that the husband's colleagues of sixteen years previously had been forced to lie about the man's work status. The pair eventually appealed over the OVIR and sent letters of complaint to the Minister of Internal Affairs as well as the Moscow city Party committee (*gorkom*). The MVD never responded, but after four years of struggle, the head of the administrative organs division of the Moscow *gorkom* finally authorized the couple's trip to East Germany.[48]

By establishing legal procedures that reduced the possibility of arbitrary decisions by the MVD, *perestroika* had a significant impact on foreign passport matters. The chief of the OVIR division of the USSR MVD even began to accompany newly elected legislators on delegations abroad to discuss the fulfillment of Soviet human rights obligations under the Helsinki Accords.[49] New laws on foreign travel, particularly to countries of the former Soviet bloc, lessened the likelihood of militia corruption and diminished its discretionary powers. In addition, many individuals long refused permission to emigrate had such decisions overturned, purportedly by a commission within the Presidium of the USSR Supreme Soviet.[50]

REGULATORY AND LICENSING FUNCTIONS

Apart from the entire spectrum of personal mobility, the militia affected individuals' daily lives through its regulatory and licensing functions. The performance of what in other societies are considered public health functions by a coercive police apparatus demonstrated the essential authoritarian nature of the Soviet system. Together with the sanitation inspection division of the Ministry of Health, the militia was responsible for maintaining sanitary conditions in streets, parks, public places, homes and courtyards. In urban centers where many inhabitants lived in communal apartments and courtyards compensated for the lack of toilets, poor sanitation made enforcement of these regulations a major burden. In 1979 in the Byelorussian republic alone, the militia fined 400,000 individuals for violating sanitary rules.[51] Among the various medical responsibilities of the militia were the introduction of quarantines, isolation of citizens with venereal disease and the tracking of individuals who had contracted AIDS.[52]

The broad licensing authority of the militia dated to the early Soviet period and concerned guns, radioactive materials and other dangerous substances. Stringent controls required by law were never strictly observed, however, as implementation of such controls required a dedication to the public good that went unrewarded in the militia. Thus, long before *glasnost'*, Nikolai Shchelokov, Minister of Internal Affairs under Brezhnev, openly described a case in which unguarded radioactive materials had seriously harmed Soviet children.[53]

Both private citizens and state institutions needed militia authorization to keep guns, which were registered at the local militia station only after the owners presented a hunting license and a medical certificate. Individuals who failed to register weapons, or who improperly maintained or fired them, were subject to fines and/or imprisonment. Militiamen were required to confiscate weapons and ammunition from individuals who systematically violated public order, disrupted their home environments, abused alcohol or suffered from mental illness. Despite centralized registration, gun control in the country was not nearly as effective as these regulations suggested; numerous crimes were committed annually with hunting weapons and, increasingly, with arms stolen from the militia and the army. In the late Soviet and early post-Soviet periods, the latter category of arms was frequently used in interethnic conflicts in the Caucasus, Moldavia and Central Asia.[54]

In another sphere altogether, typewriters were also registered with the militia. Typewriters, printing presses, seals, stamps and photographic equipment all fell within the militia's licensing authority. Knowing the particular type of each machine made it possible for the militia and the KGB to monitor illicitly published documents and writings, such as religious and political literature. (Criminalistics teams devoted much effort to attributing *samizdat* materials to particular typewriters.) Printing equipment hidden from the authorities usually ended up being confiscated or destroyed by the militia.

Even during the final years of the Soviet regime, the acquisition of fax machines, computers and printers was a risky undertaking, as such equipment could be confiscated at the border or later seized by the militia during raids intended to impede the development of independent publications. Only in May 1990 did the Council of Ministers eliminate all controls on the acquisition and use of copying machines.[55]

Until its dissolution in 1991, the Communist Party proved far from ready to relinquish control over Soviet printing facilities.[56] During *perestroika*, regulations on duplicating and printing equipment were liberalized at different rates in different republics. The Baltic republics, where popular front movements managed to develop alternative presses, were the first to enjoy fairly liberal controls over the duplication of materials. As a Helsinki Watch report documented at the time: "the alternative press editors openly give their material to state-run printers and publish newspapers on web presses, rather than copying computer-printed material. Only rarely have the Baltic publishers been discouraged or harassed by inspections."[57] The Sajudis printing presses were later, however, physically seized by troops loyal to Moscow in January 1991; a similar seizure occurred in Latvia at the same time.[58]

In the RSFSR, members of independent social and political groups did not have access to state printing presses and turned instead to newly formed cooperatives. Although these businesses could legally duplicate materials only for official institutions, they regularly violated these regulations by taking on private work.[59]

Despite, or perhaps because a majority of democratic reformers were elected to the Leningrad and Moscow city councils in 1990, these councils came into increasing conflict with central Soviet authorities over the right to control state-owned printing presses. During the same period in western Ukraine, conflicts broke out between Communist Party organizations and emerging democratic organizations over the publication of republican newspapers and magazines.

DOMESTIC VIOLENCE

Although intervention in familial life was a central task of the militia, militiamen found it their most unpopular duty. Their unwillingness to intervene in family disputes resulted from several factors: the frequent futility of intervention, the potential volatility of such situations and the conflict between community mores and existing legislation. In many republics of Central Asia and the Caucasus, Soviet law had been imposed on Islamic societies, and traditional practices continued to prevail. (Such practices did, however, become less pervasive over time.) In Tadjikistan, for example, a Tadjik husband sent his wife and children away, only to marry again in their absence. Upon their return, he offered his original spouse the position of second wife. Although the husband had violated Soviet law by marrying twice, he had also violated Islamic custom by demoting his first wife.

Nevertheless, militia authorities failed to respond to the first wife's complaint, claiming no crime had taken place. Only several days later, when the man in question brutally murdered the woman who had reported his misconduct, were militia officials chastised for their negligence.[60]

Expected to address all signals of alarm emanating from their communities, militia personnel were criticized for failing to make sufficient preventative visits to apartment complexes.[61] Heads could roll if a domestic dispute escalated to the level of a criminal assault. In Donetsk, for example, a militia officer was dismissed after a drunken husband assaulted his wife with a knife. The reason cited for his dismissal: the precinct inspector had not heeded an MVD directive on preventing domestic violence.[62] Alas, scapegoating police personnel for failure to prevent a brutal crime was not unique to the USSR. In the United States, municipal authorities and the press routinely criticize the police when a child dies of physical abuse or a woman is killed in a family altercation. Yet in the absence of the kind of social service agencies common in western societies, the militia bore the brunt of such criticism.

INSTITUTIONAL CONTROLS

The militia maintained control over institutions and state property by means of access permits, oversight over shipments of dangerous substances and physical protection of organizations and enterprises. In force since the early 1920s, these controls revealed the foresight of early Bolshevik leaders, who created a complex administrative structure capable of controlling daily life in the country.[63]

Certain functions that were assigned to the militia and the departmental (*vedomstvennaia*) and extra-departmental (*vne-vedomstvennaia*) guard units in the USSR are generally performed by private police agencies in the west. (Both guard units protected Soviet enterprises and installations, but the latter were not bound to a single institution.) Yet the centralization of law enforcement in the USSR demanded that community and work life be policed by state bodies. Approximately 1.3 million individuals belonged to the guard forces, which were organized and overseen by the militia. These guards worked closely with regular militia units; those that protected sites with dangerous substances, for example, worked with members of the militia authorization branch who oversaw the storage and transport of dangerous materials.

Incompetence was a serious problem among departmental guards charged with patrolling shops, enterprises and institutions. These poorly trained personnel who sat at the top and bottom of metro escalators, monitored the premises of institutions, verified the *propuski* that granted individuals admission to installations, checked observance of internal institutional regulations and dealt with those who broke the law in their facilities[64] were often pensioners – a far cry from the youthful, energetic security personnel frequently seen in American stores and hotels. Poor training and equipment also made such guards inadequate guardians of the fish reserves, forests and natural resources entrusted to their supervision in rural areas.[65]

The division of responsibility between guard units and the regular militia produced conflicts similar to those between private and public police forces in western societies. In the west, private police bodies often operate outside the reach of the law and are not obliged to meet the same norms required of official police forces. As Albert J. Reiss, Jr., an expert on law enforcement in the west, has written of the United States: "privately employed police have greater discretionary powers to intrude upon private space than do our public police, who are constrained by . . . criminal law."[66] The dichotomy between public and private space did not arise in the USSR until the cooperative movement blossomed in the late 1980s. Until that time, both institutional guards and community militiamen were bound by state-established regulations[67] that enhanced, rather than limited, their ability to intrude on peoples' private lives, thereby greatly expanding opportunities for corruption.

CONCLUSION

The USSR managed to regulate daily life to a degree unknown in western societies because the state and the citizenry shared a general consensus that social order was a primary objective of Soviet society. This consensus between the rulers and the ruled compelled many Soviet citizens to become willing accomplices in their own control. Overt police controls and classified regulations governing daily life were introduced in the Soviet regime during the early postrevolutionary period and then institutionalized under Stalin, remaining in force until the dissolution of the Soviet state in 1991. Together, these overt and hidden controls produced the citizen conformity, public order and low crime rates for which the Soviet Union was long noted.

The heart of police power in the USSR lay in the passport and registration system administered by the militia – making the regular police a far more tangible presence in the lives of Soviet citizens than the KGB. Police controls affected every aspect of Soviet citizens' daily lives: individuals could not move, take a vacation, travel abroad, register their cars or obtain a driver's license without authorization from the police. Prior to *perestroika*, no real impetus existed to change the authoritarian regulation of daily life in the USSR – militiamen retained the right to intrude into many details of citizens' private lives and citizens lacked adequate legal protection against police abuse almost until the end of the Soviet period. Although de-Stalinization put an end to the most egregious excesses of the political police, many so-called "police state" controls remained intact after Stalin's death: notably, the passport system and the broad licensing powers of the regular police.

Just as the nature of police authority in the Soviet Union was arbitrary (citizens were not privy to all regulations governing their existence and had scant recourse to the law) so was the militia's exercise of this authority. Given its virtually unrestricted mandate, the full extent of which was concealed from the public, the militia in the USSR was in a position to make or break the law – a prerogative militiamen exercised on a daily basis. In the eyes of Soviet citizens, the police and the law came to represent arbitrary, not impartial, power and they accordingly sought to avoid, circumvent or transgress laws depending on the circumstances.

The mandate of the Soviet militia resulted in highly subjective law enforcement, corruption and inequality before the law – conditions incompatible with the law-based state that Mikhail Gorbachev sought to achieve. In fact, the limits of *perestroika* could be seen clearly in the policing of daily life: while Soviet society had once largely accepted all-encompassing police controls and served as their own best watchmen, the awareness that came with *glasnost'* made many citizens begin to question, and even resent, militia controls over their routine activities. Despite attempts to reform the police apparatus during the *perestroika* era, however, the militia never ceased to regulate such personal matters as where an individual could live or whether he or she could travel.

Police penetration of everyday life acted as a powerful barrier to the development of democracy in the USSR during the late Soviet period – only in republics that pushed for greater autonomy did any noticeable change occur in militia behavior prior to the disintegration of the Soviet Union. Many in the successor states acknowledge that the legacy of the Soviet police system and its travesty of the idea of law will long weigh heavily on the Soviet successor states as they attempt to build more accountable, democratic systems of governance.

8 Policing the deviant: social workers with sticks

The question concerns the very manner in which human life is to be lived.
Plato, *The Republic*, Book 1

Police are expected not only to maintain order and contain crime, but to establish the limits of permissible conduct in a society. In many societies the mandate of the police extends beyond the criminal to encompass the drunk, the prostitute, the delinquent, the ex-offender and the drug addict. The Soviet militia shared such an expansive mandate with its counterparts in other countries, yet several distinctive features characterized Soviet efforts to control and define deviance. Many activities that in other societies are entrusted to social workers or separate branches of the judicial system, for example, were performed by the militia and community organizations in the Soviet Union, making militiamen "social workers with sticks."

The Soviet militia used a more systemized approach to track deviants and delinquents in their communities than do western policemen, maintaining detailed files on individuals with known police records. Their designated counseling role allowed policemen to enter homes and schools in order to obtain information on deviants who had not yet violated criminal law without having to obtain prosecutorial permission. The supremacy of the state over the citizen – and concomitant lack of legal restraints – on the militia made many citizens in the USSR both willing and unwilling collaborators in police operations to identify and root out deviants. Militiamen's disdain for the deviants, moreover, who were most frequently handled by general and not specially trained police units, often led to outright abuse of suspects.

In the USSR, the state determined the needs and appropriate contributions of citizens to society. Translated into Soviet practice, healthy males and unmarried women who refused to work at jobs designated by the state were defined as parasites and subjected to police sanctions. For most of the Soviet period, this large category of deviant – non-existent in capitalist and many other socialist societies – incurred administrative and criminal penalties. Only in the late 1980s, when communist ideology was discredited and unemployment became an accepted reality, did arrest rates for parasitism drop sharply.[1]

The Soviet regime attributed its success in controlling social deviance to prophylactic law enforcement. Under *glasnost'*, however, Soviet commentators began to suggest that the suppression of deviance was a consequence of pervasive police intrusion into citizens' private lives. Until *perestroika*, people considered to be "deviants" in Soviet society were identified by the militia, constrained by the internal passport and registration system and subject without recourse to arbitrary law enforcement. In other words, deviants were controlled, not protected. Despite the fact that the control orientation of Soviet law enforcement remained intact throughout the *perestroika* era, increasing concern for the rights and welfare of the deviant eventually prompted Soviet militia specialists to seek more contact with western experts on how to deal with this social group.[2]

DEALING WITH THE DEVIANT

Operational techniques to locate and identify deviants in the Soviet Union reflected both nineteenth-century continental and twentieth-century communist police practice. While police in western societies regularly survey public gathering places of known deviants, their patrol techniques are rarely as formalized as those of Soviet militiamen. Raids, often conducted by several militiamen together with Komsomol auxiliaries and *druzhinniki*, were an important part of militia activity in this sphere and were conducted in public bathrooms, parks and other public places to detect speculators, homosexuals and drug addicts. (In raids to detect alcoholics at cafeterias and enterprises, a doctor specializing in alcoholism occasionally participated.)[3] In Central Asian republics, raids were used to detect and eliminate poppy fields and drug factories.[4] Whatever the venue, such brigades rarely returned to the station house empty-handed.

Information obtained on these maneuvers helped the militia maintain files (*uchëty*) on problem residents. Separate from the files of the passport division, these records were reminiscent of the practice of registering prostitutes in certain western European countries. Essential differences, however, existed between the two practices. First, Soviet militia files on deviants were not limited to prostitutes, but encompassed many other categories of individuals, such as alcoholics and ex-convicts. Prostitutes in West Germany may have been required to register with the police, but in the Soviet Union numerous categories of individuals were placed on militia lists without their consent or knowledge, thereby becoming subject to greater militia scrutiny than the ordinary Soviet citizen.

Such records were often quite detailed: cards on problem youth, for example, provided information about their families, school performance, emotional state, abilities and interests.[5] Such data were generally used solely for local operations, but the USSR MVD coordinated the information at the national level. Maintaining these records required a massive bureaucratic effort. In 1988 alone, the militia registered 130,000 narcotics addicts, 500,000 juvenile delinquents and over 4 million alcoholics nationwide.[6] (The MVD itself estimated that the adolescent registration system identified only 1 out of every 5 or 6 problem families. Other categories of deviants were equally underrepresented on militia rolls.) Some 80 to 90 percent of registered narcotics addicts were under 30 years of age and many were identified as parasites.[7] In addition to addicts and juvenile delinquents, the militia also registered ex-convicts.

Surveillance of the deviant did not always assume an unpleasant form. Youths placed on the *uchët* might be assigned a militia trainee as a big brother; like police athletic leagues in the United States, militia personnel used sports and other common interests to develop a bond with such juveniles. In one case, a former hooligan improved so dramatically that he was dropped from the police registry. According to a Soviet account of the story, rather than rejoice, the youth cried when he heard the news, dejected at the loss of a close relationship of the kind he had never enjoyed at home.[8] Alas, such happy outcomes were the exception rather than the rule in the USSR, as many Soviet delinquents were exceedingly difficult to reform. The militia, moreover, did not generally exhibit reformist instincts in its relations with deviants listed on its registries.

Just as individual cunning and an inefficient bureaucracy precluded the registration of all deviants in the USSR, so the state was unsuccessful in its attempt to solve the labor shortage in Soviet heavy industry (apparent already in the late 1960s) by assigning loafers and juvenile delinquents to industrial jobs. To cite but one example, the Chel'iabinsk metallurgical plant needed 2,000 workers in 1969, but could not staff these positions with "loafers" due to the cumbersome manual procedures used to identify parasites.[9] In the end, bureaucracy – not guarantees of civil rights – protected citizens from the full weight of militia authority.

THE MILITIA AND DRUGS

Although officially acknowledged only during *perestroika*, the Soviet militia had addressed drug abuse since the time of Khrushchev.[10] The drugs most frequently abused in the USSR were various opium derivatives such as heroin and hashish, as well as addictive pharmaceuticals.[11] *Toksimaniia*, or addiction to non-standard drugs (such as sniffing glue, smoking toothpaste derivatives and inhaling cleaning fluids), was also a serious problem in Soviet society.

Although the USSR served as a transit point for drugs cultivated in Afghanistan, most addicts in the country used drugs grown in the Caucasus and Central Asia, where vast poppy fields were regularly cultivated.[12] Drug addiction was a significant problem even before the Afghan War – according to a former high-level MVD official, many addicts were registered with the Leningrad militia already in the 1960s.[13] The war in Afghanistan (1979–1989) considerably worsened the problem, resulting in increased drug abuse in the Soviet Union for many of the same reasons that American drug usage rose during and after the Vietnam War, an analogy cited privately by many informed Soviet specialists. (Despite increased addiction rates, drug use in the USSR remained well below that of the United States and many northern European countries.)[14]

Many of the hundreds of thousands of Soviet soldiers who fought in Afghanistan were exposed to drugs and became addicted, carrying their addictions to their home cities and small towns upon their return. In the absence of reintegration and addiction treatment programs, many former soldiers did not abandon their drug habits and induced others to drug use, spreading the problem to remote communities where law enforcement personnel could not even recognize drug abuse, let alone combat drug trafficking.

Cognizant of the western war on drugs, Soviet militiamen realized that the police alone could not stop sophisticated drug dealers. Thus, when addicts became the focus of considerable media attention during the Gorbachev era, the militia introduced drug education programs for the first time. These programs gave citizens the opportunity to learn first hand about the consequences of drug addiction, an important prerequisite for prevention and citizen cooperation with the police.[15] Yet, despite the cooperation of middle-aged citizens, militia members in many communities lamented their inability to reach young people, who increasingly fell prey to drug dealers.

Increased interest in drug education and prevention under Gorbachev did not, however, change Soviet law enforcement priorities with respect to the drug problem. As in the United States, the militia concentrated on eradication and interdiction; the Communist Party began to actively launch large-scale comprehensive operations to stop the spread of drugs in the Soviet Far East and in the Islamic republics of Central Asia in 1989.[16] Such campaigns included massive MVD aerial eradication programs that bore a certain similarity to those sponsored by the U.S. State Department in South America. Just as U.S. programs increased anti-American sentiment in South American countries, so, too, did Soviet eradication campaigns exacerbate inter-ethnic relations in the USSR. Frequently executed by Slavic militia personnel, eradication efforts destroyed thousands of hectares of poppy fields – crops on which many Central Asian ethnic groups depended for their survival. The consequences of this approach were remarkably similar in both cases: seizures eliminated only a small fraction of the fields under cultivation, and rather than come to a halt, cultivation was merely transferred to more remote locations.[17]

Although stopping drugs at transit points and borders was the responsibility of the customs service, individual republics and metropolitan areas in the USSR retained considerable discretion in establishing individual anti-narcotics efforts. The militia in the Kuban, for example, established its own anti-drug unit; sensitized by enlightened drug researchers, the republic of

Georgia likewise established a coordinated commission under the MVD to deal with drug abuse.[18]

At the other end of the distribution chain, raids had only limited success in controlling drug dealers. In fact, narcotics dealers in the USSR did not generally come from the traditional criminal population: some were even medical workers who sold drugs stolen from the Ministry of Health. Others constituted a genuine and sophisticated drug mafia that cultivated and processed drugs.[19] Although law enforcement personnel successfully struck at certain large-scale drug rings by destroying crops, the militia was slow to act at the point of sale, be it on the street, in an apartment or in other locales.[20] Even when traditional raids were mounted on drug dens, inadequate technical equipment often impeded their effectiveness, as *Pravda* itself confessed in 1988.[21]

The increasingly severe drug addiction problem placed great demands on Soviet undercover work. Despite extensive use of informants, the proliferation of well-equipped organized criminal groups inhibited militia intelligence gathering. By 1989, Soviet officials publicly acknowledged that law enforcement efforts to reduce the trade and use of narcotics were as unsuccessful as those of western police agencies.[22] Analysts of drug trafficking in the post-Soviet states today fear that many former republics of the Soviet Union may soon become major exporters of drugs to western Europe in the same way that Latin American countries supply drugs to the United States. The preconditions for such an export network are largely in place: high unemployment and severe economic conditions in Central Asia; insufficient law enforcement resources; the absence of will to combat the narcotics trade and declining internal border controls.[23]

THE MILITIA AND ALCOHOL

While drug addiction is a relatively recent phenomenon, alcoholism has long been a scourge of Slavic societies. Alcoholism was so pervasive in many republics of the former USSR that many citizens did not consider it deviant behavior, and although the Soviet state did not officially tolerate alcoholism, many individual policemen looked the other way when confronted with a drunk. The indulgent attitude towards alcoholics did not, however, prevent the registration of drunks and control of alcohol-related crime from being major components of the average militiaman's workload.

Militia personnel removed drunks from the streets and placed them in sobering-up stations throughout the Soviet period, often assisted in these duties by police volunteers (*druzhinniki*) who helped to locate workers buying alcohol during work hours. *Druzhinniki* then reported on those arrested at their places of work, where they would be publicly criticized for their conduct.[24] Such auxiliary citizen police units also assisted the militia in rounding up drunken workers on collective farms. Despite the occasional moonshiner being sent to a therapy-and-labor rehabilitation center, however, many cases of illegal alcohol production in rural areas went unreported.[25]

Until the mid-1980s, the militia generally ignored the pervasive alcoholism, home brewing and public drunkenness that characterized Soviet society. Although the number of drunks actually apprehended by the regular police appeared large, it represented only a small percentage of individuals potentially subject to militia action. Yet anti-alcohol law enforcement activity took center stage in May 1985, when Gorbachev launched a prohibition campaign. The massive campaign, which sought to reduce production and consumption of alcohol in order to improve labor discipline, was launched against the advice of leading MVD personnel, who warned Soviet leaders that American prohibition had fostered organized crime and undermined police integrity. If the leadership did not listen to its own experts, neither did it learn from its own bitter experience of the 1920s: the language of the 1985 prohibition law (with the exception of style and orthography) was identical to a law of 1924. According to one Soviet expert, the major difference between the two campaigns was that the NKVD in the 1920s was more honest about recognizing its mistake in launching a prohibition campaign.[26]

The anti-alcohol campaign epitomized the punitive approach towards the alcoholic: the militia waged a moral war (one it did not, however, seek to fight) against the entire citizenry. Policemen checked people's internal passports at the entrance of liquor stores, noted excessive alcohol purchases and monitored the sobriety of individuals in public places. In the years 1986–88, ten million individuals were arrested annually for violating anti-alcohol legislation and hundreds of thousands were placed in miserable sobering-up facilities rather than being treated for what might have been, in many cases, a serious medical problem.[27] Detention in a sobering-up station could cause an average worker the loss of a month's wages, imposing a great financial burden on him and his family. Multiple visits to a sobering-up station could lead to an immediate court hearing. Militiamen often victimized individuals in these facilities, imposed heavy fines on those detained and reported arrests to citizens' places of work, where further penalties were sometimes exacted.[28]

The campaign served to intensify police intrusion into people's private lives. Whereas in the past this intrusion had often occurred with the cooperation of community members, large numbers of citizens refused to participate in the campaign to repress alcohol use.[29] The population in Moldavia, for instance, became enraged after militiamen destroyed grapevines that had been developed over decades of careful cultivation. Hostility towards the police also increased in the Russian countryside when militia units began to confiscate stills in large numbers, depriving many elderly citizens of a means to supplement their meager pensions.

Unable to acquire alcohol legally due to state-imposed limits on alcohol production, individuals turned to cologne and numerous other substitutes, prompting militia and *druzhinniki* units to monitor department store queues where perfume was sold.[30] Alcohol production, once dominated by the state, increasingly passed into the hands of sophisticated criminal entrepreneurs during the late 1980s. The campaign's ultimate cost to the Soviet state, estimated between 50 and 100 billion rubles (USD 80 to 160 billion at the time) in lost revenues,[31] was in large part transferred to organized criminal groups and the people they bribed. Loss of such significant state revenues greatly aggravated the national debt and contributed to the inflation of the late Gorbachev years.

The anti-alcohol campaign was largely abandoned by 1988–89 because it had proved wildly unsuccessful; knowledge of the personal costs of alcohol abuse had deterred neither the alcoholic nor the community in general.[32] As a result of its failure, some Soviet experts began to advise a treatment approach to alcoholism in place of the quasi-militaristic approach of the recent past. Once belief in God became acceptable in the USSR and citizens began to lose their fear of opening up to strangers, the long-rejected technique of Alcoholics Anonymous began to be adopted, with AA clubs opened in St. Petersburg and other cities.[33]

The total cost of the 1985–88 campaign was not only economic – the campaign severely exacerbated militia corruption. The demoralized militia, which enforced incredibly unpopular legislation,[34] became a procurer of alcohol during the campaign, just as U.S. police had become during Prohibition. The black market accordingly expanded and home brewing, once the domain of poor women pensioners who needed an income supplement, was taken over by young professionals frequently linked with organized criminal groups. Finally, the campaign left a legacy of aggravated citizen resentment of the police that contributed to the collapse of the USSR during the crucial period of Soviet history that followed.

PARASITES AND VAGRANTS

Before *glasnost'*, visitors to the Soviet Union might have seen individuals sleeping in railway stations or airports and presumed that they were citizens waiting for trains or planes. In reality, many of these individuals were Soviet vagrants – homeless people and individuals labelled "parasites" – without work or a place to live. During *perestroika*, acronyms were coined for such individuals, who became known as *bomzhi* (individuals without permanent homes) and *bizhi* (individuals without direction).

With their belongings spread out on mattresses in the waiting rooms of airports, these people formed communes and prepared food together. Militia personnel, cognizant that transport hubs were no place for these people to spend a month or even half a year, had no solution as to where they should go.[35] Such individuals existed on a day-to-day basis, having neither the inclination nor the resources to find housing or a community in which to settle. By the mid-1980s, Soviet authorities estimated that there were half a million such "parasites" and vagrants in the USSR.[36] Whereas such unfortunate individuals are often assisted by social agencies and religious groups in western countries, in the Soviet Union they were the exclusive responsibility of the militia.

Early in the Soviet period, the Russian Republic adopted legislation that required all citizens to work.[37] For seventy years – from the revolution until the early 1990s – those who did not work in the USSR were subject to sanction, a policy that ended only with the state's recognition of unemployment. Under the criminal code, individuals who refused to work after receiving three warnings were subject to imprisonment for a period of up to two years, three years for a repeat offense.[38] The unemployed did not, however, immediately fall into the clutches of the judicial system, as a fair number were placed in jobs by the militia in conjunction with local labor commissions.

Because they had no families, no documents, and no permanent place to live, many vagrants were not the responsibility of any particular militia unit. In Moscow, such people spent the night in manholes, basements and attics; if caught without a Moscow residence permit, they were either fined, expelled from the city or even imprisoned. Yet fines had little meaning for many vagrants, who were unintimidated by administrative penalties after having survived labor colonies. Indeed, by 1985, 90,000 homeless people had already been sent to special colonies where they had undergone special programs in social adaptation.[39]

Vagrants were more common in the southern provinces and the Far East of Russia as well as in Central Asia, where militia controls were less strict and itinerant labor was often needed. Many homeless flocked to Central Asia when cold weather descended upon other parts of the Soviet Union:

> Some of the migrants head straight for the Tashkent militia station, flowing from all corners of the country. They give themselves a month off. That's how long the militia will keep them to find out their identity. During this period they are guaranteed a roof over their heads and free meals.[40]

A sample of the individuals assembled at a Tashkent precinct in early 1988 included a senile woman who left home and never found the way back, a mentally disturbed woman with delusions of nobility and a man who left his home after discovering his wife's infidelity. The motley crew bore a certain resemblance to street people commonly found in American cities. Ex-offenders, however – who were thought to comprise approximately half of all Soviet vagrants – studiously avoided such militia detention facilities.[41]

At various railroad stations and in every city of the country the Ministry of Internal Affairs also maintained "special receiving and placement centers whose job [was] to determine whether vagrants and undocumented persons who have been detained by police are suspected criminals, beggars or men who have defaulted on alimony."[42] These vagrants, like parasites who resided permanently in a particular district, were hard to place and keep on a job. Many Soviet managers resisted hiring such individuals; when forced to accept them, managers frequently refrained from alerting the militia when they left their newly found jobs. An unemployed individual might consequently be listed as working on a militia registry and in fact be free to wander without being harassed by the police.[43]

A higher level of vagrant more consistently evaded the watchful militia. Such an individual might move in with a lonely, unattached woman for a short period, perform repairs, tend the garden and bring in money through occasional odd jobs. This kind of vagrant was very cautious and was described thus by a Soviet paper:

> He stays away from the train and bus stations, where police might stop a fellow like him – carrying no luggage – and ask to see his documents. The professional bum never drinks himself into a stupor and can spot the red band of a policeman's cap a kilometer away. On arriving in a new town, he heads for a market or a beer hall where he can gather all the information he needs – where to find temporary work, the location of liquor stores, police stations, etc.[44]

MVD concern about these individuals was not simply ideological – over one-third of all individuals officially warned about parasitic behavior (250,000–450,000 nationwide each year during the period 1985–88) were between 18 and 29, a group that could have actively contributed to the nation's economy. Parasites, moreover, were known to spread venereal disease and tuberculosis; many were released convicts unable to reintegrate into Soviet life, who returned to a life of crime. A sociological study of crime in Moscow *oblast'* during the 1980s revealed that one out of every three people charged with larceny, theft or robbery was a parasite. By 1985, 29.8 percent of all offenders in the USSR were so defined.[45]

Although the militia complained that it lacked adequate powers to control vagrants, it resorted to various underhand techniques to handle these people.[46] For example, vagrants were sometimes confined for lengthy periods while militiamen collected evidence against them, their lengthy confinement attributed to the absence of places in invalid centers and old age homes or the difficulties of finding them employment. The more accurate explanation for lengthy detentions, however, was the lack of specialized social service agencies, in whose absence detentions served as the functional equivalent.[47]

Ironically, the regulations enforced by the militia helped create many vagrants by denying them residence permits to live with their families. Once an individual was identified as a vagrant or a parasite, there was little chance that he or she could escape the lifestyle this label conferred on him or her. These lost members of society were handed over to "social workers with sticks," that is, militiamen unable and unqualified to assist them with their numerous problems. After disguising himself as a vagrant for six months in the 1980s, one Soviet journalist concluded: "Getting vagrants to adapt socially is too complex a problem for the police to handle by themselves."[48]

THE MILITIA AND PROSTITUTION

Like drug abuse, prostitution had always existed in the USSR, but was recognized officially only with *glasnost'*.[49] The ideological conviction that socialism would end the exploitation of women led the state to conclude that prostitution had withered away. Consequently, until 1987, prostitution was neither a criminal nor an administrative offense, although the word itself was not entirely excised from Soviet legal vocabulary (enticing minors into prostitution remained a criminal offense). Prostitution was never really decriminalized, however, and the militia regularly arrested, punished and converted prostitutes into informants.

Until prostitution became an administrative offense, the militia closely monitored the activities of numerous prostitutes who operated in streets and out of apartments and hotels (the latter serving high-class clienteles). Frequently targeted by the militia, brothels were often raided and closed down, yet a certain number survived due to the patronage of local Party officials or significant payments to local militiamen. In Moscow, the criminal investigative branch of the militia had a special unit that focused solely on prostitutes who served foreign clients and were paid in foreign currency. Ordinary prostitutes who served Soviet clients were often arrested on charges of stealing from their customers. As with brothels, however, individual prostitutes often escaped punishment by bribing militia personnel or by agreeing to serve as KGB or militia informants.[50]

Once prostitution was officially recognized in the USSR, militia tactics changed and policemen dealt more directly with the problem. In Riga (the capital of Latvia), for example, the militia established a registration system for prostitutes in order to control the threat of AIDS posed by the numerous foreigners who frequented the port city. Inspired by this step, other cities established morals divisions in order to maintain similar records. In Moscow, where prostitution had long been widespread – particularly in the downtown areas – such registries had been maintained for years. During the 1970s and 1980s, the operations chief of the 69th Precinct of the Moscow city militia collected the names of 3,500 prostitutes in an alphabetized registry. All had black marks on their record cards, indicating that they had received militia warnings to cease plying their trade.[51]

The concentration of prostitutes in this precinct was explained by the presence of three busy railway terminals. Ranging in age from 14 to 70, the prostitutes on the militia registry were classified into three different categories. First were the "downtowners," women who had formerly worked as prostitutes in central Moscow but had lost their looks and moved downward on the social ladder. Second were Moscow natives who had begun working as prostitutes at the railroad stations. Third were *bomzhi* without Moscow residence permits who frequented the train stations, often after being released from labor camps.[52]

In order to deprive the first two categories of prostitutes of their residence permits, militiamen in the 69th Moscow precinct had to apprehend them three times in the same year. In the absence of specialized morals squads of the type that existed during the 1980 Olympic Games, patrolmen were so occupied with serious criminals that they either could not or did not pursue prostitutes effectively. As one militia major explained,

> [E]ven if you're lucky and you've detained a certain individual the requisite number of times, the 69th Precinct won't do anything to move her out of the city. Papers are forwarded to her place of residence. Then the red tape begins, which leads you to realize that, although it's hard to get a residence permit for the city of white stone [Moscow], it's even harder to take someone's permit away.[53]

The process of prosecuting prostitutes on registration regulations was even more complicated in the case of *bomzhi*, as paperwork on such women had to be forwarded to other locales where militiamen were often not interested in instituting proceedings against individuals who were not creating a disturbance in their immediate districts.

Perestroika contributed to the spread of prostitution in the USSR by lifting certain social controls, increasing the flow of foreign visitors to the country and creating a new class of affluent Soviet businessmen. For many high school and vocational students, prostitution unfortunately became a prestigious occupation.[54] As in the NEP period of the 1920s, elegantly dressed girls became a fixture in restaurants frequented by the new wealthy class. Prostitution became so overt that the militia stationed outside prominent hotels in Moscow could be heard to chase young girls away from these buildings in the early hours of the morning. In the late 1980s, the Moscow militia even confiscated a book in Japanese about Moscow prostitutes, together with other catalogues of prostitutes in general circulation at the time.[55]

Raids on bars, cafés and restaurants began to be instituted in Baltic cities and other urban centers during which female prostitutes would be hauled off to local precinct stations, fined 100 rubles and inspected for venereal disease.[56] As in other societies, such round-ups had little impact on the problem of prostitution because the fines imposed by the police were insufficient to deter such women from practicing their profession. Vice squads, already constrained by Soviet law, were rendered even more impotent by bribes. Corruption was not only passive – in Estonia, militia personnel teamed up with prostitutes to deprive foreign tourists of money and prized possessions.[57] Even under the more open conditions of *glasnost'* and *perestroika*, policing the so-called "victimless crime" of prostitution had the same corrupting impact on police that it has had in the United States. Not only did the militia fail to deter or reform prostitutes, their enforcement of laws prohibiting prostitution aggravated corruption within the law enforcement body.

THE MILITIA AND PROBLEM YOUTH

The militia's dual function – as counselor and law enforcer – was never clearer than in its assignment with problem youth, which forced policemen to perform social welfare services for which they were ill-prepared and had little time. Militia efforts with underage offenders and delinquents centered on the children's room (*detskaia komnata*), an innovation of the Khrushchev era that provided youth-oriented services at the local precinct level. Children's rooms dealt directly with minor offenses committed by children under 14 such as fights, insults, petty speculation, misuse of transport services, gambling, vagrancy and curfew violations.[58] In addition, militia personnel in these centers performed surveillance on older problem adolescents and advised criminal operation units of their charges' criminal ties.

In Moscow in the 1980s, one militiaman was assigned to every 20,000 youth. Apart from the limited number of personnel allotted to such work, the fact that such posts were staffed by female officers indicated that *detskie komnaty* served an educational rather than coercive purpose. The main functions of these rooms were: to maintain registries of problem youth in their communities, monitor their behavior, work with the bureau of labor placement to locate work for dropout charges, maintain detention facilities and conduct community outreach programs in schools and among parents, teachers, pensioners and Komsomol members to prevent delinquency and aid problem youths.[59]

Every effort was made to keep juveniles within the community instead of sending them to correctional institutions. The work of militiamen who directed children's rooms took them out of the precinct into schools, youth community centers, parks and other locales where problem youths were known to congregate. Like all other aspects of policing, the work of such militia personnel was planned, down to the exact number of lectures that militiamen should give each year and the prevention programs and operational activities they should implement in order to detect and respond to crimes committed by adolescents and pre-teens.[60]

Most children's rooms had at least several hundred youths on their registries. In general, these were homeless youths, runaways (from individual homes as well as children's institutions), vagrants, gamblers, alcohol and drug abusers, returnees from special schools and juvenile labor colonies and children who were inadequately supervised at home.[61] Even after committing legal infractions, many youths did not make it onto militia lists because privileged parents often bribed officers to keep their children's names off the registry. School authorities, furthermore, did not provide the militia with all possible names of problem juveniles for fear of being labelled poor administrators. Understaffed militiamen did not always choose to follow up on all reports for similar reasons. As one Moscow precinct chief explained, he feared unfavorable comparisons with his peers and thus did not report all youth crime committed in his district.[62]

To ensure their charges' well-being, militia personnel were expected to find employment for problem youth by maintaining links with local bureaus of labor placement. Despite a labor shortage in many Slavic regions, placement of high school dropouts and troublemakers, like that of parasites and vagrants, was a challenge. Juveniles released from correctional institutions were particularly difficult to place – employers either refused to hire them or secretly dismissed them without informing the authorities; a great deal of recidivism occurred among this particular group of offenders.[63]

Youth commissions subordinate to local governments worked with children's room personnel and other community organizations to ensure the good conduct of underage offenders and older teenagers who had committed criminal offenses. Their cooperation represented another manifestation of the blending of social control between official state organizations and so-called voluntary community groups, an important prerequisite to the effectiveness of communist policing.

Young people registered with children's rooms were often assigned to visit local youth clubs several times a week after school. The head of the children's room was thus expected to work closely with the heads of neighborhood youth clubs, a relationship that functioned smoothly for many decades when a consensus on the appropriate ideological outlook for youth existed in Soviet society. After *perestroika* began, however, different groups sought to influence these clubs and conflicts began to break out among club volunteers, militia and Komsomol personnel charged with overseeing problem youth. In one case in Leningrad, volunteers tried to turn youth clubs into military–patriotic organizations instead of focusing on the primary objective of preventing crime among young people.[64]

Youth commissions also fulfilled educational functions and could impose restrictive sanctions on young people, short of depriving a youth of his or her liberty. In one case, a 15-year-old Uzbek boy on a militia registry had given up on school. After the local youth commission convinced the young man to return to school, he created a scandal by showing up drunk. The commission next gave the boy a warning and sent a letter to his parents' place of work. The letter formally criticized the father for educating his son poorly and instructed him to appear twice a month at his son's school.[65] Such intervention in the home and the workplace – unknown in western capitalist societies, where the state and the employer are generally not linked – was common in socialist systems, where all aspects of life were nominally under the control of the state.

Juvenile militia work became increasingly difficult in the post-Khrushchev period as spiralling divorce rates, maternal alcoholism and drug addiction created more and more neglected children. Once a youth was placed on the registry, children's room personnel were supposed to establish and maintain contact with the child's home and/or workplace. Militia officials were often so busy with the most serious delinquents on their registries, however, that they had little time to attend to neglected children or minor offenders.[66] When they did visit the homes of such children, they often discovered cases of physical abuse and neglect; children's room personnel would then work with militia district inspectors to initiate action against the parents to deprive them of their parental rights. Lacking the assistance of trained social workers, however, it fell to the militia to initiate proceedings against such parents, a rather paternalistic aspect of Soviet law. Unfortunately, few officers had the proper education to evaluate when to take such a step.[67]

In addition to running children's rooms, the militia also maintained special detention facilities where juveniles and underage youths from 11 to 14 could be held for limited periods. While younger offenders were the responsibility of children's room personnel, older juveniles were the responsibility of criminal investigative units, who conducted investigations of their offenses and could detain them for longer periods.[68] Abandoned children and those whose parents had been deprived of their parental rights were sometimes sent to these detention facilities as a last resort. The *glasnost'*-era press opened the public's eyes to the shocking conditions within such facilities, where drunken militia personnel sexually abused children, fed them soup with cockroaches, and confined orphaned children with delinquents. Sadly, press revelations addressed but did not remedy the problem of youths being abused by their designated guardians within the Soviet justice system.[69]

There was ample evidence of misconduct by youths in many regions of the USSR during the Brezhnev period, although a significant share of this misconduct did not constitute serious crime. Yet by the early 1970s, youthful offenders were already responsible for 21 percent of all violent crime in the country, a figure greatly in excess of its U.S. equivalent at the time. By the early 1990s, youth crime had reached serious proportions in many Soviet cities, where gangs of youth regularly terrorized residents. With mounting evidence of youth gangs and juvenile disorder, the militia was frequently called to task for inadequate performance.[70] Without training in counselling and social work, however, militiamen found it increasingly difficult to reconcile the functions of social worker and disciplinarian during the last decade of the USSR's existence.

THE MILITIA AND THE EX-OFFENDER

The juvenile offender was not the only class of offender under the purview of the local militia, which also handled ex-convicts and adults who had committed minor offenses, overseeing the parole and surveillance of the former and the fulfillment of work-related community sentences by the latter. In addition to their other duties, militiamen thus acted as both probation and parole officers. In accordance with the socialist ideal that valued the collective over the individual, Soviet citizens who had committed minor offenses were rehabilitated by their peers at work and their places of residence. Individuals sentenced to community-based sanctions by Soviet courts were entrusted to work collectives, where – overseen by the militia –

they performed corrective labor or worked their regular jobs at reduced wages. Like the charges of American probation officers, those sentenced to community-based sanctions were required to report to the internal affairs organs one to four times a month and were forbidden to leave their district without the permission of the police.[71] Many work collectives failed to pay attention to those entrusted to their care, however, or even tried to rid themselves of such undesirables.

In their role as parole officers, Soviet militiamen placed released offenders in jobs and saw to their social reintegration. As no community correctional apparatus existed in the USSR, once an offender was released from a penal colony, responsibility for his or her rehabilitation was transferred from the labor camp personnel to the divisional inspector and regular militia staff. When the offender arrived at his permanent place of residence from labor camp, the program was supposed to work as follows: "Such people go first to the militia. There they receive a passport and are registered and their first conversation about their future life and labor activity takes place. There they are met with advice and assistance."[72] Reality, however, was a far cry from this ideal picture. Militia personnel were not trained as correctional officers and existing conditions made it close to impossible for ex-convicts to find suitable housing, given that lengthy waiting lists of law-abiding citizens already existed for state-subsidized apartments. If ex-offenders did find work, management was often relieved when they no longer appeared and a year might pass before the authorities were alerted to their absence from work, a period during which many returned to crime. Precinct inspectors in the town of Nikolaev, for example, were so lax about released offenders in their care that in 1987, ex-convicts managed to commit 192 crimes before being rearrested. Placement of ex-offenders became even more difficult after *perestroika*, when state guarantees of employment and housing no longer held and enterprises began to lay off workers in order to improve efficiency.[73]

The militia had another function related to the ex-offender that had no equivalent in the United States or other western societies: *nadzor*, or administrative surveillance.[74] The essential difference between this sanction and parole was that the individuals affected had already completed prison sentences. *Nadzor* was a further penalty imposed on criminals who had not behaved well in prison or who continued to live antisocial lives after their release; it was mandatory for many former political prisoners and people convicted of serious offenses. Such surveillance of released convicts violated internationally recognized human rights norms; individuals who incurred *nadzor* had no right of appeal to Soviet courts or any other external body.

The restrictions imposed under *nadzor* were similar to those imposed under parole: curfews, travel restrictions, limits on an individual's personal associations and regular reporting to the militia. Once under surveillance, however, former political prisoners were more vulnerable to police harassment than were ex-convicts.[75] The militia could place an individual on *nadzor* on the basis of its own information or on the advice of labor camp authorities. The released offender was not privy to this limitation on freedom and had no way of challenging militia actions undertaken under *nadzor*. Often an individual remained under surveillance until his record was expunged – an indefinite period in some cases, as long as 3 to 8 years in others.

Those placed under *nadzor* were closely monitored, with the militia maintaining the right to enter their residences at any time of day or night. If an ex-convict violated curfew or travel regulations, he or she might be automatically returned to labor camp. Return to an institutional setting was common, as the restrictions imposed by local militia units were often so encompassing that offenders had trouble abiding by the law. In small communities *nadzor* was used effectively by local militia authorities to limit the contacts of exiled dissidents and/or return them to prison.[76]

ISOLATION OF THE DANGEROUS DEVIANT

The militia's consolidation of correctional and law enforcement functions had a significant impact on the offender. In the American criminal justice system, rehabilitation and reintegration of the offender in society are concentrated in correctional departments separate from the police. The primary duty of such departments is to place the individual in a job and help him secure a crime-free life. Personnel in these agencies contact law enforcement personnel only when they detect evidence of criminal activity on the part of a parolee or ex-convict. In the USSR, where these functions were consolidated in the militia, the state emphasized the isolation of dangerous individuals from the community rather than their reintegration into everyday life. This consolidation of functions was far from successful, with militia personnel having only limited success in reintegrating ex-offenders and rapidly returning released prisoners to penal institutions in order to rid the streets of threats to community order. (An estimated 25 to 30 percent of all crime in the USSR – actual and fabricated – was committed by previous offenders.)[77]

Reintegrating the ex-offenders into Soviet society had always been difficult, particularly due to the passport and registration system that kept them at the margins of society. In fact, many serious offenders lost the right to settle in any of 70 Soviet cities or any closed area of the USSR. As one vagrant explained:

In 1976, at age 18, I thoughtlessly went to prison for three years. My parents permanently lived in Moscow. When I was released I was denied a registration permit with my parents. I could not live at home, but in dormitories. I lived that way for five years. I wanted to see my parents but that was forbidden. For violations of the Moscow passport regime, I again was confined. I worked well in the labor colony and asked the administration about my registration permit. My mother had died, my father lived in Moscow with my sister and her young children. They needed my help. Appeals from my father, an invalid, were to no avail. I was sent to Kalinin, not so far from Moscow, but there I was also denied a registration permit. I have nowhere to live. Where am I to go? To prison?

He concluded ironically, "There, they register everyone."[78]

Forced to settle in smaller cities and rural areas, many ex-convicts settled in the countryside where they disrupted the formerly peaceful lives of the peasantry and came under the close watch of the local militia. This problem became magnified in the final years of the Soviet regime. In 1988, as efforts were made to humanize the corrections system, 450,000 offenders were released from Soviet prisons; registration requirements prevented 30,000 from returning to their home communities. In the freer atmosphere of *perestroika*, the MVD, long the enforcer of residence regulations, now proposed the removal of restrictions on residence permits and the outlawing of housing discrimination based on criminal records.[79] Despite the aura of reform, however, this stance seemed more an accommodation to Soviet realities than a reflection of a genuine desire for democratization.

PERESTROIKA, THE MILITIA AND THE DEVIANT

Once treated like nineteenth-century children – neither seen nor heard – deviants and protesters at the end of the Soviet period were plainly visible and their brutal treatment at the hands of the police no longer officially tolerated. In July 1987, for example, militiamen brought dozens of hippies who had been loitering in a park to the local station house. Two were then beaten so badly that they required hospitalization, an incident that received highly critical press coverage.[80]

Greater prevalence of deviant behavior did not, alas, reflect greater tolerance of the nonconformist among the general public. Survey research revealed that many citizens continued to be strongly antagonistic towards the deviant. In a 1990 survey by the Soviet Center for Public Opinion Research, for example, 27 to 33 percent of those queried wanted to "liquidate" prostitutes, drug addicts and homosexuals.[81] In addition to Soviet society's disinclination to tolerate such groups, the new legalism, with its emphasis on the rights of the deviant, prompted complaints from Soviet militiamen who had long used searches, eavesdropping and surveillance to combat problem members of society. Like their American counterparts, Soviet law enforcers resented restrictions on their efforts to control deviance. To cite one example, some militia personnel were attempting to combat the spread of AIDS by placing under surveillance homosexuals who sought treatment for the disease. Critics quickly raised civil liberties questions about such tactics, contending that even if such methods led to arrests, the practice criminalized what was essentially a medical problem. Other critics addressed the ethical issues stemming from the pervasive militia intrusion into private life.[82]

The ill-equipped militia was poorly prepared to combat the more visible prostitution, increasingly pervasive drug abuse and the AIDS threat of the *perestroika* period. In a sharp break with the past, the militia joined the United Nations' Fund for Drug Abuse Control and Interpol (the International Police Organization) in order to combat international drug trafficking.[83] Yet law enforcers did not automatically receive additional powers to combat the proliferation of narcotics and the increasingly professional business of home brewing. On the contrary, both the new legalism of Soviet reform efforts and fiscal constraints pointed the police in the opposite direction.

CONCLUSION

The Soviet state consistently sought to control rather than rehabilitate the deviant, saddling the militia with contradictory functions. The militiaman's combined role of law enforcer and social worker created numerous problems unknown in most western societies, where the treatment of deviants is more clearly distinguished from their policing. In such societies, alcoholics are not sent to detoxification facilities run by the police, ex-convicts are not directed to police officers for surveillance and job placement, the unemployed are not the responsibility of law enforcement authorities and police do not intervene in homes to remove abused children. Particularly in democratic states with developed social welfare systems, such tasks are generally performed by trained counsellors and/or social workers.

In general, deviants felt the effects of *perestroika* more strongly than did the ordinary citizen. Social deviance was effectively repressed during most of the Soviet period only because the militia possessed the right to intrude into many aspects of private life. Charged with enforcing mass conformity with state-decreed social norms, especially among those who did not instinctively respond to such pressure, militiamen relocated prostitutes, beat up punks and forced young men with long hair to get haircuts. The presence of deviants untouched and unharassed by the militia was thus one of the most striking consequences of *perestroika*. Even the leading Soviet émigré satirist, Vladimir Voinovich, observed in 1990 that long-haired youth and women in mini-skirts were the most visible evidence of societal change in the USSR.[84] Once a showcase of Soviet order and conformity, Moscow in the late 1980s displayed a visible number of deviants for the first time in many decades. Militia authority had so diminished by May Day of 1990 that thousands of individuals were even able to march through Red Square carrying anti-Communist Party and anti-government slogans, undeterred by the capital's massive police contingent.

The increasingly noticeable deviant on Soviet streets was not, however, a consequence of a new-found tolerance on the part of the militia. Like much of *perestroika*, tolerance was ordered from above. Once required to penalize the deviant – a duty more often than not performed with enthusiasm – militiamen were forced to tolerate behavior that they and many of their fellow citizens found objectionable. In the end, *perestroika* provided a curious mix of tolerance and intolerance for deviance. Although Gorbachev's policy of "reconstructing" the Soviet economy and Soviet society allowed for more tolerance of the deviant, it did not remove the militia from the enforcement of morality, as evidenced by the anti-alcohol campaign of 1985–88.

While punks, prostitutes and underworld gamblers were granted limited tolerance,[85] Gorbachev simultaneously sought to eradicate the one accepted and institutionalized form of deviance in Soviet society – alcoholism – soon after he assumed power. Mobilizing the full weight of Soviet law enforcement, he launched the anti-alcohol campaign only to see it boomerang, undermine Communist Party and militia credibility and exacerbate already severe state deficit problems.

Perestroika saw the Soviet Union experience increased polarization and income differentials among citizens at a time when the state's social safety net was being eroded. The conditions gave rise to growing numbers of vagrants, drug addicts, ex-offenders and problem youth. Unfortunately, these "deviants" still had no one to turn to except the militia, who continued to perform the dichotomous role of social workers with sticks until the final days of the Soviet regime.[86] The tens of thousands of offenders released into society during *perestroika* as a result of state decarceration policies overwhelmed the militia, which found itself unable to provide them guidance and/ or employment assistance. Large numbers of drug addicts and alcoholics likewise continued to fall into the hands of militiamen too corrupt to be concerned with their treatment. Although western scholars lament the ineffectiveness of social intervention programs in their societies, the glaring inadequacies of the Soviet approach to deviance during the last decade of Soviet history makes such ineffectiveness look benign.

9   The militia and crime control

Rosy face, shiny revolver
My militia watches over me

Children's Ditty

Low crime rates in the Soviet Union were not the result of a superior police. Rather, the Soviet militia was a central component of an entire system of social, political and economic controls that reduced the possibilities for crime commission in the USSR. The militia enforced measures that restricted individual mobility, removed recidivists from major urban centers and kept released offenders under surveillance. Rather than find panaceas for crime, the authoritarian Soviet state simply created a unique geography of crime in the country, together with a massive imprisoned population which, in actual numbers and on a per capita basis, exceeded that of other industrialized societies.[1]

The geography of crime in the USSR – a pattern unknown outside of the communist world – was the product of the militia's power over citizen's mobility and their place of residence. In most societies, crime rates in urban areas are significantly higher than those in rural communities. In the Soviet Union, by contrast, crime rates in major urban centers were relatively low prior to the *perestroika* era. Not only did the allocation of police resources favor the major cities of the Slavic republics, known criminals were removed from these cities and young unmarried males – the group most likely to commit crime in any society – were denied permits to live in these cities. These "rejects" of the major urban centers settled in suburban communities, the secondary cities of the Soviet Far East and the Far North and rural areas where they were responsible for disproportionately high crime rates.

For many years, the Soviet militia appeared enormously successful in maintaining order and keeping crime rates low. Although the incidence of crime grew noticeably during the last twenty years of the Soviet regime, national crime rates remained significantly lower than those of the United States and most western European countries. The militia was, however, unable to suppress the crime wave that seized the USSR in the late 1980s.

After years of living in a well-ordered, highly policed society, Soviet citizens viewed the unprecedented growth in crime as a visible symbol of societal collapse. The militia's inability to contain the explosion in crime meant the state was no longer able to deliver on one of its fundamental promises to its citizenry: the maintenance of social order. Like their counterparts in the democratizing nations of the former socialist bloc, political authorities in the USSR soon discovered that their law enforcement agencies were better prepared to deal with crowd control and produce confessions than to perform the standard police work needed to apprehend criminals.

CRIME RATES OVER TIME IN THE USSR

Stalin's ruthless use of police power permitted him to suppress an entire generation of professional criminals. Years of internal struggle and the dislocation of millions of people due to civil war, famine and the collectivization of agriculture presented the dictator with a serious crime problem. Like Hitler and Franco, however, Stalin was able to return order to the streets by repressing political offenders and professional criminals alike, sentencing large numbers of the latter to lengthy periods of confinement. Whereas political prisoners faced harsher conditions in the labor camp system known as the *gulag*, members of the criminal underworld were isolated from society in these camps, greatly impairing their ability to train a generation of successors.

After Stalin's death, both political and ordinary offenders were released from labor camps. Upon re-entry into Soviet society, criminals then found it possible to cultivate a younger generation of professionals. As the criminal justice reforms of Khrushchev limited the duration of maximum prison sentences, the cost of crime was also reduced. Crime rates began to rise soon after the dictator's death and grew at a rate that exceeded that of the nation's population growth. Within fifteen years of Stalin's demise, the USSR again faced a noticeable crime problem.[2] Crime grew steadily throughout the Brezhnev years and continued to climb after his death in 1982. Prior to the 1986 congress of the Communist Party of the Soviet Union, even Party leaders publicly admitted that the Soviet Union was experiencing a serious problem of social order.[3]

Although crime rates dipped in 1987, this was probably the result of the strictly enforced anti-alcohol campaign. The 10 percent drop in crime commission in 1987, however, was not sustained.[4] Crime rates rose slightly in 1988, when prohibition was still in force, only to rise precipitously after the campaign was more or less called off in 1989. Crimes then increased in number and seriousness, and a marked number began to be committed with the use of firearms. Registered crime in the USSR rose nearly 32 percent in 1989, 13 percent during the first nine months of 1990 (a period during which serious crime rose by 20 percent), and 22 percent in the first half of 1991.

Crime rates in the individual Soviet republics also continued to rise in 1991, escalating still further following the breakup of the USSR.[5]

Much of the overall growth in crime in the late 1980s was attributable to serious violent offenses, the type of crime least likely to be subjected to statistical manipulation by Soviet law enforcement bodies. Although crime had been on the rise under Brezhnev, the crime wave that accompanied *perestroika* far exceeded the rate of increase noted by Soviet authorities during the preceding decade.[6] Thus, the sudden explosion in criminal activity in the late 1980s did not represent a continuation of an existing trend, but an altogether new phenomenon spawned by the social disorganization and declining police authority of a collapsing state. The disintegrating social order in the USSR cannot, however, be blamed solely on the demoralization of militia personnel during these years, nor on the insufficient number of experienced officers left by the mass dismissals which closed the Brezhnev era. Profound social and economic changes and the diminution of social controls during *perestroika* also played a role in the growth of crime. Together with political unrest, internal refugees and unemployment, these changes created insecurity in a society that had no reserves or programs to deal with such problems.

New criminal justice policies also contributed to the rise in crime. First, the militia arrested far fewer individuals. Between 1986 and 1988, for example, the number of individuals arrested and detained in the USSR dropped almost by one-half, from 749,000 to 402,000.[7] Second, in order to reduce the number of people in hard labor camps, considerably fewer individuals were sentenced to such confinement. Third, large numbers of individuals were released from penal colonies into communities that had neither jobs nor unemployment benefits for them.[8] Finally, organized crime became a significant criminal problem during the late 1980s and in many cases provided the only viable employment for former inmates who found themselves jobless and homeless upon their release from prison.

RECORDING CRIME

As in many other societies, crimes recorded in the Soviet Union reflected the ability of the police to act on those crimes. Nevertheless, the distortion of crime statistics in the USSR was greater than in many other societies due to pressure the Communist Party brought to bear on the militia. Party pressure was evident at every stage of the criminal process – the recording of crime, arrests, investigations and trials – and prompted militiamen to act only in those cases where they were assured of apprehending criminals.

As with the economy, the administration of the criminal justice system was largely driven by Party-determined plans. Regular police operated with arrest quotas, a requirement that frequently led to unusual investigative practices.[9] Technically illegal, arrest quotas were normally delivered to Party authorities without signatures or seals, a practice that continued throughout the *peres-*

troika years. An exposé published in *Izvestiia* in 1989, for example, claimed that minimum performance requirements of militia officials in the region surrounding Alma Ata (the capital of the Kazakh republic), included committing 10 people annually to alcohol treatment, disclosing one firearms charge per month, and prosecuting 14 breaches of passport regulations and 4 violations of motor transport regulations per quarter. According to the article, the specificity of the plan meant that militiamen "quite often have to resort to blatant breaches of regulations in order to achieve their set targets."[10]

Under Party pressure to clear virtually every crime committed, Soviet policemen resorted to devious record keeping in order to hide their inefficiency, such as a two-file system for recording crime. This system, with its two separate sets of records, allowed militiamen to classify burglaries and thefts as "criminal manifestations" when they could not locate any suspects. Such crimes would then be deleted from statistics for the precinct, permitting policemen to achieve desired rates of performance.[11] Many offenses simply went unrecorded, particularly those of theft, economic crime and violations of safety rules. The chances of a case of pickpocketing being recorded, for example, were less than 50 percent; the odds were even lower in cases of petty theft and receipt of stolen property. The extent of underreporting can even be detected in MVD statistics published for the year 1989, which document that, whereas citizens reported 3.9 million crimes to the militia, the latter registered only 2.5 million.[12]

Many assaults that resulted in injury were never recorded as crimes due to a longstanding agreement between the militia and medical personnel. In general, the police were advised of a physical assault only when an individual had sustained a knife wound or gunshot.[13] Policemen were reluctant to record even serious crimes when there was little chance of apprehending the perpetrators. In Georgia, for example, numerous crimes of a certain burglary ring were never recorded, although militiamen went through *pro forma* efforts to investigate individual burglaries.[14] Even a crime as serious as rape was occasionally concealed from the books. In another incident in Georgia, four young men raped a thirteen-year-old girl. When the parents noticed that their daughter was missing, the militiaman on duty neither recorded the fact in his log nor reported it to his superiors. After learning of the rape the next day, the girl's parents were pressured not to report the offense by relatives of the rapists. Meanwhile, the militiaman in question illegally contacted the parents of the four young men. The crime remained unrecorded until two weeks later, when the personnel administration of the republican MVD launched an official investigation after the girl's family insisted that it look into the matter.[15]

Militia personnel who failed to record crimes in the above cases were seriously disciplined, yet the practice of underreporting serious crime was widespread throughout the USSR. According to First Deputy Minister V. Trushin of the USSR MVD, 800 people were punished for failing to report crimes and almost 200 for falsifying documents in the first six months of 1987 alone. Although the Party reduced its pressure on the militia to clear crimes during the *perestroika* era, policemen remained unwilling to record many crimes if there was little chance of apprehending the criminals who committed them.[16]

Militiamen's inability to arrive rapidly at the scene of a crime also inhibited accurate reporting. Poor equipment and overwhelming paperwork often prevented policemen from reaching a crime scene for two to three hours; when two crimes occurred simultaneously, the wait could be even longer.[17] Under such circumstances, militiamen were frequently confined to arresting people who committed offenses in public places where law enforcement personnel and *druzhinniki* were regularly stationed. In one city district, 25 percent of all "recorded crime" occurred, not surprisingly, at the local market.[18]

CLEARING CRIMES

Once the militia registered an offense, they were in the unenviable position of needing to clear it. Prior to *perestroika*, an offense was considered cleared if an individual were arrested, as Soviet courts generally accepted forced and fabricated evidence against suspects, guilty or innocent. Militiamen also found it difficult to solve a large number of crimes because they lacked the equipment – e.g., computers, dispatcher systems, radio equipment, dictaphones, and even gas and police vehicles – needed to perform their jobs effectively.[19] In addition to underreporting the actual number of crimes that occurred in Soviet society, militia personnel often engaged in report padding and illegal investigatory techniques to improve their clearance rates. Individuals detained for one offense might be forced to accept responsibility for another crime or crimes for which no perpetrators had been identified. In the resort city of Evpatoria, for example, two teenagers arrested for theft in 1986 confessed to an unrelated theft that had taken place six months previously. The youths reconsidered their confessions during an adjournment at their trial, claiming they had been forced to confess under physical duress. In the absence of substantiating evidence, however, the youths were nonetheless convicted. As the presiding judge explained: "We cannot allow a situation in which many thefts go unsolved."[20]

Property offenses were among the militia's least solved crimes. According to an official 1990 source, 72.5 percent of personal property thefts for 1989 remained unsolved, as did nearly 70 percent of thefts of state property. The figures for burglary were not much better – only such readily solvable crimes as intentional homicide and rape, often perpetrated by offenders known to the victim, had solution rates above 70 percent.[21] Although these clearance rates were higher than those recorded in the United States, they still fell far short of the guaranteed punishment which the Party promised all offenders.

Prior to the late 1980s, the Party expected the militia to clear 92–5 percent of all recorded crime, an unachievable target for any police force, even with the best of personnel, equipment and community cooperation.[22] When the policy and procedural changes of *perestroika* reduced the pressure to sustain such targets, clearance rates plunged: the militia cleared 90 percent of all reported crimes in 1980; 82 percent in 1985; 50 percent in 1988; and 36 percent in 1989.[23]

In terms of personnel performance, the figures demonstrate a dramatic reduction in the efficiency of individual investigators. If in 1979 every criminal investigator cleared 26 crimes per year, by 1989 they were clearing only 16.8. The USSR was not the only socialist country to experience such a dramatic decline in clearance rates during this period. In Hungary, for example, disclosure rates for crime plummeted after the collapse of the communist system, even though police recording practices did not change substantially.[24]

Various explanations were offered for the militia's declining performance. Some experts maintained that reduced Party expectations of the police, adjustments in the accounting system for clearance rates, increased crime and the heavy militia workload were responsible. Others suggested that illegal militia practices, once responsible for the militia's successes, were now unacceptable. A professor at a higher MVD institute even suggested that the primary cause of the decline in police efficiency was the "wave of apathy and lowered discipline" that had overcome militiamen.[25] No doubt a combination of all these factors was at work.

THE INVESTIGATIVE PROCESS

The investigative process in the Soviet Union was quite different from that known in the United States and represented a middle ground between an inquisitorial and adversarial system. The particular Soviet twist was to make the examining magistrate a part of the prosecution. Criminal investigations conducted by the principal law enforcement agencies in the USSR – the militia, the procuracy and the KGB – served three basic functions: to detect crime that threatened the social, political and economic order; to locate suspects for reported offenses; and to prepare ironclad cases that could not be discredited by defense attorneys in court. The division of responsibility among the three investigative agencies, as discussed in Chapter 4, was determined by the code of criminal procedure. All investigations were overseen by the procuracy, which had different branches responsible for detecting improprieties in the investigative work of each separate agency. Due to the innate conflict between the procuracy's supervisory and prosecutorial roles, however, the system of supervision rarely unearthed legal mistakes made by investigators.

For many years, the Soviet legal system operated on the assumption that it was better to convict ten innocent men than let one guilty man go free.[26] According to this philosophy, the purpose of investigations was not to solicit truth, but to obtain convictions. The militia was under constant pressure to initiate cases; once a case was opened, Party pressure made it almost impossible to drop, even in the face of insufficient evidence or the arrest of the wrong suspect. A case that did not result in conviction and was sent back for reinvestigation by a judge was considered a tragedy for an investigator. Both investigative and judicial personnel feared case dismissal to such a degree that they went to great lengths to avoid such a disposition, including use of fabricated accusations, false testimony and falsified evidence. Conviction was nearly assured in the cases that proceeded to trial because judges feared reprisals from the Party apparatus.[27]

There were two forms of investigation in the Soviet criminal justice system: the *doznanie* (inquiry) and the preliminary investigation. Both served to gather and confirm evidence, leading to the preparation of a written case that was submitted to a judge. The inquiry was the exclusive domain of the militia, which handled investigations of minor crimes. The preliminary investigation, which dealt with more complicated cases, required more sophisticated police work.[28] In some cases, the preliminary investigation was conducted entirely by the militia, but the most serious cases, such as homicide and rape, were handed to the procuracy. As explained in Chapter 4, the latter originally handled almost all criminal investigations in the justice system, a division of labor that ended when new legislation in 1965 made the militia responsible for investigating approximately 80 percent of all crimes, including burglary, aggravated assault and many economic offenses that ordinarily fell within the domain of the OBKhSS. Militia personnel rarely appeared in the courtroom, their involvement in criminal cases being largely confined to investigative work behind the scenes.

Although Soviet judges did not hold the investigatory work of the militia in high regard, they generally accepted paperwork submitted by militiamen as valid. Such credence was not, however, given to their testimony in court. As the chief of the Moscow internal affairs department explained in 1989:

> In many states which are regarded as rule-of-law states the following law applies: Three witnesses are needed to disprove a policeman's evidence. In our country the reverse applies: The evidence of a militiaman can be taken into consideration if it is backed up by three witnesses.[29]

Militia investigators generally did not specialize unless they worked in the OBKhSS or in units devoted to fighting organized crime, burglaries or narcotics. Most investigators worked on a wide variety of crimes, with senior investigators receiving more serious and complex cases than those assigned to beginners. Differentiation in caseload was often more a function of seniority than the nature of the offenses being investigated.

Personnel at all levels were burdened by laborious paperwork, a task that consumed at least 20 percent of investigators' time in the 1970s, rising to 80 percent by 1990.[30] Local forensic laboratories and a national MVD laboratory assisted militia investigators in their work, providing OBKhSS personnel with handwriting expertise and furnishing more technical assistance to other divisions of the MVD. Although criminalistic techniques were advanced at the national level,[31] the situation was quite different at the regional level. Like many American policemen in small towns, Soviet militia personnel outside of large cities did not have the capacity either to collect or properly analyze fingerprints and other crime traces.

Throughout an investigation, emphasis was placed on the psychological aspects of various tasks. Readers of Dostoevsky's *Crime and Punishment* will remember the careful cat-and-mouse game of the prosecutor that eventually leads to Raskol'nikov's confession in the novel. The priority given to psychological techniques in criminal investigation in the USSR, which differed sharply from western investigative practice, remained popular among Soviet policemen. Certain investigators, for example, considered the psychological impact of the timing of a search, an *ochnaia stavka* (a one-on-one confrontation between the offender and the witness at the station house) and the method of interrogation to be of crucial importance.[32]

The search, one of the earliest phases of an investigation, was not clearly defined under Soviet law, thus giving militiamen great flexibility in its use. While searches were supposed to be conducted only if sanctioned by a procurator, the militia statute provided a loophole: a search could be conducted without the permission of a procurator if one were notified within 24 hours. Despite such leeway, militia personnel in the Brezhnev era were known to forge the names of procurators without suffering repercussions. Violations of search procedures were not confined to the Stalin and Brezhnev eras, but continued to occur under Gorbachev. In some cases, illegal searches and seizures by the militia actually served the procuracy's own ends.[33]

Detention was another strong tool of the militia during an investigation. Soviet law permitted three separate kinds of detention: administrative, criminal and post-conviction. Serious offenders like murderers, rapists and thieves could be held in detention facilities for 72 hours while their confinement was sanctioned by a procurator. Offenders then had to be charged within ten days or let go, a procedure that was not always observed. In the late *perestroika* period, procurators began to refuse to sanction the confinement of many individuals detained by the militia – an indication that the latter continued to make many unjustified arrests.[34]

Pre-trial detentions of three to four years were not unknown in the USSR, as the investigation of the "Uzbek mafia" (the group of Party, governmental, law enforcement and trade officials charged with embezzling hundreds of millions of rubles from the Soviet state in the late 1980s) gave no uncertain proof.[35] Although the militia's rationale for such extended detentions as that of former MVD Deputy Minister Iurii Churbanov was the complexity of a given case, legal critics contended the true purpose of such detentions was to remove undesirable individuals from circulation when insufficient evidence existed to convict them.

Lengthy detentions also served political purposes. In the Gorbachev era, for example, a Nagorno-Karabakh activist was detained while under investigation for embezzlement. The investigators could not find sufficient evidence to bring the case to trial and the jurisdiction of the case was transferred to a court in Byelorussia, then a bastion of conservatism. Yet even in Byelorussia the judge dismissed the case for lack of evidence. Although the militia failed to convict the activist, his detention accomplished its primary function – removing the leader from his political constituency for more than a year.[36]

Arrests and detention were also used throughout the Soviet period to intimidate suspects. Without the inducements of a plea bargain system, coercion, rather than promises of leniency, produced the compliance of suspects in the Soviet criminal justice system. The militia conducted the *dopros* (interrogation) of suspects in custody using a variety of techniques. Subtle psychological pressure (such as the proffering of cigarettes to a defendant under intense stress), deception, physical abuse and direct threats of lengthy confinement were regularly used to extract confessions from suspects. In Central Asia, investigators were known occasionally to use drugs to reduce a defendant's resistance during an interrogation.[37]

Intimidation of suspects regularly involved flagrant police abuse. In one reported case, in order to force an elderly secretary to sign a document that falsely accused her director of misappropriating 2,600 rubles, OBKhSS investigators threatened her with three days of confinement. In the face of such a threat, the woman signed the incriminating papers.[38] Similarly, in a murder case in Latvia, militia personnel apprehended two young men who, after two months of detention, confessed to having brutally killed a young girl. Having achieved confessions, investigators chose to ignore the accurate description of the murderer provided by railroad engineers at the site of the crime. They proceeded to stack the police line-up to prejudice the investigation and fed the prosecution's witness detail after detail at the trial in order to "refresh her memory." Although the defendants retracted their confessions in court, claiming they had been produced by physical force, the young men were still convicted of the murder and one was sentenced to death.[39] Before the youth was executed, a multiple recidivist (previously convicted of nine different homicides) confessed to the girl's murder. His testimony was verified and the original accused were subsequently declared innocent.

Unfortunately, the use of brutal techniques produced benefits for police officers: the militia investigators in the Latvian case initially received bonuses for having cleared the homicide and were singled out for exemplary work on Soviet Militia Day.[40] Other cases did not end as happily – Soviet journalist Arkadii Vaksberg documented one investigation in which confessions induced by force led to the sentencing of fourteen innocent individuals, some of whom were executed. The problem of police abuse did not disappear during the Gorbachev period, but did attract increased media attention.[41]

The MVD itself reported that the most frequent violations of investigatory procedures occurred in Ukraine, Georgia, Turkmenistan, Estonia, Tadjikistan and Moldavia.[42] Official data, of course, did not present the whole picture. In Uzbekistan, corruption within the republic's internal affairs and legal organs was so extensive that even the most criminal militia personnel and procurators were not disciplined. Only after Telman Gdlyan and Nikolai Ivanov, the controversial procuratorial investigators from Moscow were sent to clean up the Uzbek mafia in the early 1980s, did heads begin to roll in the republic's internal affairs ministry.[43]

Because the militia retained the upper hand from the moment of a suspect's arrest until the conclusion of the investigation, the very structure of the investigative process contributed to police abuse. Prior to 1989, mentally sound suspects did not have access to a defense attorney during the entire criminal investigation (a period that could last up to 9 months). In 1989, citizens finally attained the right to counsel early in the investigative process, but institutional resistance, high legal costs and an inadequate number of defense attorneys prevented this right from becoming institutionalized before the collapse of the Soviet Union. At the close of the Soviet period, George Feifer's observations on the investigative process in the late 1960s remained relevant:

> That the accused is available for extensive questioning by the investigator is the great difference between Soviet and common law procedure. Under the latter, a man charged can not be further examined; the prosecutor must build its case without him. In Moscow, a man charged faces a long inquisition, and while the prosecution may have a great deal of other evidence to draw upon, it is evident from what goes on in court that inquisition contributes heavily to the preparation of the state's case.[44]

JOINT INVESTIGATIONS

Investigators from the militia and the procuracy often conducted inquiries and preliminary investigations together. Such cooperative efforts included joint visits to crime scenes, joint evaluation of evidence and the staffing of cooperative work brigades used to apprehend criminals and locate missing property. Such cooperative activities became more frequent in the latter decades of the Soviet period, but were fraught with conflict. Not only were relations between the MVD and the procuracy inherently antagonistic, the quality of work produced by militia "organs of inquiry" (their official name within the MVD bureaucracy) was often inferior to that produced by investigative departments of the procuracy. Militia personnel in these organs were slow to initiate cases, paid less attention to procedural requirements, and fulfilled reluctantly – if at all – operational requests from the procuratorial personnel with whom they were expected to cooperate.[45]

In order to overcome militia reluctance to fulfill requests for information and procedural assistance, procuratorial investigators often resorted to subterfuge, bridging boundaries that supposedly separated investigators in the two agencies. For instance, procurators might give instructions to the chief of a militia investigative department, who would then transmit the order to subordinates in his own name.[46] Although militia personnel who handled preliminary investigations were of a higher caliber than those employed in the organs of inquiry, they, too, lacked the sophistication of procuratorial investigators. Investigators in neither institution, however, possessed the kind of legal consciousness needed to establish and maintain a law-based state. MVD investigators generally handled an average of 5.3 cases a month, procuratorial investigators 1.7. The heavy workload of militia investigators led to constant violations of the law as, in addition to their poor legal training, time constraints forced militiamen to reach hasty conclusions. The volume of cases handled by militia investigators, moreover, meant that they could concentrate on only the most serious criminal cases.[47]

The militia also worked with the KGB on the latter's non-political investigations, including cases that involved organized crime, major economic transgressions, hijackings and complex weapons cases.[48] Militia investigators resented the lighter caseloads and superior resources of the KGB, but had no choice but to cooperate with the security police when asked. The parameters of the militia's assistance in such investigations is illustrated by the following story from the Brezhnev era.

During the late 1970s, KGB officials asked a militia officer to help them in the investigation of an economic crime by gaining the confidence of a young Georgian offender. The militia officer had originally arrested the young man, who was found in possession of a large quantity of dollars (it was then illegal for Soviet citizens to possess foreign currency), but no documents. When the suspect categorically refused to talk to KGB personnel, under whose jurisdiction the case fell, they released the young man into the custody of the militia officer, hoping the latter could gain his confidence and discover his partners in crime. The officer did indeed win over the young man, who in conversations at the militiaman's home began to provide information about fellow foreign currency traders. The apartment was bugged and all of their conversations were recorded, although the officer claimed he learned of the listening devices only when the KGB came to remove them. Such effective work paid off – the militia officer in question was subsequently invited to join the KGB.[49]

PERESTROIKA'S IMPACT ON THE INVESTIGATION

Prior to *perestroika*, Soviet courts provided no check on the behavior of investigators or the criminal justice system, nor any disincentives for corrupt and/or shoddy investigative work. Rewards were given for results – convictions – rather than adherence to legal procedures. Under such circumstances, it is hardly surprising that in a poll conducted in the early 1990s, cited in a 1992 collection of essays on Russian judicial reform, 82 percent of the "people's" judges and 95 percent of the higher court judges surveyed considered investigative work in the criminal justice system to be mediocre or even bad.[50]

Efforts to humanize the legal system and demands that militia investigators adhere to legal procedures brought about profound changes in the processing of criminal cases during the *perestroika* era. Prior to 1987, 13 to 17 offenders out of every 100 were released during the preliminary investigation; by 1988–89, the figure had jumped to between 36 and 37. Militia personnel began to release not only minor offenders, but those accused of committing more serious crimes as well. Three times as many individuals accused of physical assault and more than five times as many individuals accused of rape were released during the investigatory stage in 1988, for example, than were released in 1985.[51]

Regarding investigatory procedures, extended questioning was reserved only for serious offenders (a change driven partly by the increase in crime and partly by the decline in the number of investigators) and more individuals were allowed to remain at liberty during their investigations than had been the case in the past. Ironically, at the same time less serious offenders were beginning to be treated more humanely, the maximum period of detention for suspects in serious criminal cases was increased from 9 to 18 months.[52]

These dramatic changes in policy could be attributed in some measure to reduced Party pressure on investigators to meet high clearance rates. Given Gorbachev's emphasis on the rule-of-law state, procurators and judges in the late 1980s began to dismiss cases in which there was inadequate evidence or where clear violations of criminal procedure had occurred. Critics of the militia, however, suggested that the increased rate of dismissals was only an effort to cover up militia inactivity and incompetence.[53]

ORGANIZED CRIME

At the same time the militia was struggling to implement procedural reforms at the end of the 1980s, it found itself fighting a losing battle against organized crime. Soviet officials denied the existence of professional criminality in the USSR for many years, but organized criminal groups mushroomed during the Brezhnev period; by the late 1980s, they posed an undeniable and dangerous threat to Soviet society.

Closely aligned with the ruling elite of the Communist Party, criminal groups operated largely untouched by the police throughout the Brezhnev period, exploiting shortages of consumer goods and infiltrating many aspects of Soviet life.[54] The anti-alcohol campaign of the mid-1980s gave organized crime a further boost, positioning its leaders to exploit the new economic opportunities offered by the nascent market economy of the *perestroika* era. At the close of the decade, Soviet citizens were blaming many ills of Soviet society – including increased shortages of food and consumer goods, violence and visible income differentials – on organized crime.

According to militia investigators, every fifth criminal group had penetrated the apparatus of the state and about one-half of the groups engaged in economic crime had attempted to corrupt Soviet officials. Estimates of the research Institute of the USSR Ministry of Internal Affairs indicate that 25–30 percent of the money derived from criminal economic activity between 1990 and 1993 was used to influence government or state officials. Their efforts were in many cases successful – in 1988, Internal Affairs Minister Aleksandr Vlasov admitted that many senior militia officials were involved in organized crime.[55] Not surprisingly, MVD specialists on the problem were pessimistic about the militia's ability to obliterate professional criminal groups. In the words of one journalist, organized crime was "rooted in the bureaucratization of society, in the administrative–command system, whose methods invariably breed an alternative economy."[56]

Soviet experts never developed a clear operational definition of organized crime, believing it to consist of thousands of criminal groups. Indeed, professional organized crime in the USSR included a range of diverse phenomena. A number of criminal activities – such as prostitution and gambling rings, the manufacture and sale of drugs and extortion – are also common in western societies. In the Soviet Union, however, such endeavors had a distinct Soviet flavor – a consequence of the inadequacies of central planning and the concentration of political and economic power in leading members of the Communist Party. These conditions facilitated such unique Soviet organized criminal enterprises as large-scale embezzlement from the state (epitomized by the Uzbek mafia), the diversion of goods from trading organizations to organized criminal groups and, in the late 1980s, money laundering via newly sanctioned cooperatives.[57]

A symbiotic relationship existed between organized crime and the co-operative movement from the moment the latter was re-legalized in late 1986, when a new law on individual enterprise was introduced in the Soviet Union.[58] Not only did members of organized criminal groups pass the ill-gotten gains of their organizations and the Communist Party *nomenklatura* through cooperatives, they also financed the formation of many such businesses. In the absence of banks, racketeers became financiers, assuming positions in companies in exchange for their investment. As a result, a great number of new private Soviet businesses were criminalized from their inception.[59]

Although cooperatives were the targets of competitors and rival criminal groups, they received scant protection from the militia. Many militiamen refused to protect such businesses because they resented the latters' profits and/or believed their primary responsibility was to protect state institutions. In the late 1980s, unprincipled militia personnel were known to extract as much as 300 rubles a month (a sum in excess of their monthly salary at the time) from cooperative owners. Owners who refused to pay such sums often ended up paying with the "destruction of space, loss of commodities, injury, or even with their [lives]."[60]

Cooperative owners were reluctant to complain to the militia about extortion threats from criminals not only because they were regularly shaken down by policemen themselves, but because they had to violate many laws and regulations in order to stay in business. Their eagerness to minimize contact with law enforcement personnel thus made even honest cooperative owners attractive victims for criminal rackets. Forced to protect themselves – and the crimes perpetrated against them and their families were very serious – cooperative owners resorted to buying weapons on the black market and hiring expensive private guards.[61]

Internal corruption and active intimidation of the militia, together with a lack of institutional resources and anti-racketeering legislation prevented the militia from effectively fighting organized crime. If the police was hamstrung in its ability to control this kind of crime, however, members of professional criminal groups successfully struck at the militia – killing policemen, stealing their uniforms and making off with their weapons. As in the United States, law enforcement bodies were more successful in apprehending individuals at the lower end of criminal organizations than at their upper levels, as the sophistication of professional criminal groups makes it difficult to collect evidence that can sustain convictions in court.[62]

Organized crime represented a genuine threat to the integrity of the Soviet state for several reasons. First, the close connections between the Party apparatus and justice and law enforcement officials and members of organized criminal groups undermined the authority of the Soviet political and legal systems in the eyes of the populace. Second, organized criminals revived the criminal underworld in Soviet society, a force that Soviet authorities could not control. The helplessness of law enforcement in the face of professional criminal groups was a serious blow to the state, which since Stalin's time had experienced few setbacks in the pursuit of its enemies. Third and perhaps most important today, organized crime impeded the growth of legitimate private enterprise and a private economic sector in the Soviet Union.[63]

Using national security as a rationale, the Soviet government brought the KGB into the fight against organized crime in 1989.[64] Only the KGB was considered to have the equipment, sophisticated manpower, experience in surveillance and perceived institutional integrity to effectively battle with professional criminality. Although professional analysis of organized crime and operational coordination remained with the MVD, much of the complex investigative work in this area was transferred to the KGB at that time.

As luck would have it, the latter's new role helped the security police justify its existence in the democratizing USSR. (Its assumption of this role shared certain similarities with the entrance of the American military into the war on drugs in the United States.) Drafting many investigators from its domestic division into the battle against organized crime, the KGB was able to forestall personnel and budget cuts while simultaneously popularizing its image. Critics, however, suggested that the KGB exaggerated the threat of organized crime in order to legitimate itself in the changed Soviet society of *perestroika*. Although such criticism could not be dismissed, organized crime did represent a grave threat to social and political order that the corrupt and ill-equipped MVD could not handle.

In the end, the addition of KGB resources had little overall impact on organized crime due to KGB corruption, poor coordination between the regular and security police, and an unclear division of responsibilities between the two bodies. The failure of MVD–KGB efforts to bring organized crime under control had political, social and economic implications that transcended the specific crime problem and left a dangerous legacy for the post-Soviet states. With the collapse of the state at the end of the 1980s, organized crime became an alternative source of economic and political power in Soviet society. Just as the Sicilian mafia was able to partially replace the state in certain parts of Italy, professional Russian criminal organizations were able to partially usurp economic power in the USSR at a time when the country was attempting to move toward a more democratic and market-oriented system.

CONCLUSION

At the same time that *glasnost'* began to highlight the glaring problems of the Soviet criminal justice system in the late 1980s, crime began to skyrocket due to diminished political control, increased economic hardship, citizens' decreased fear of the state and the diversion of militia resources to manage interethnic conflicts and safeguard public order during rallies and demonstrations.[65] Crime and social disorder in the *perestroika* period were not only social problems, but central issues in the political debates that raged within Soviet society during these years. The militia under Gorbachev strained to simultaneously preserve the state and control crime. Once the unifying ideology of communism was discredited, however, the social contract between the state and the citizenry collapsed and the police lost on both counts.

The Gorbachev period saw the press reveal the full dimension of crime in the USSR as well as corrupt militia practices like unregistered crime, inflated reporting indicators, collusion with criminals, physical abuse, violation of suspects' rights, extraction of false confessions and conviction of innocent people. The press provided glaring exposés of the criminalization of the militia and its contribution to the crime problem, a contribution that became more pronounced with the anti-alcohol campaign and the rise of organized criminal organizations in the late 1980s. These revelations and the concomitant explosion in crime undermined citizen confidence in their personal safety and, more importantly, in the integrity of the Soviet system and its officials. After the revelations of *glasnost'*, Soviet authorities found they could no longer justify a massive and intrusive law enforcement apparatus that had become deeply corrupted and failed to limit crime.

The Soviet criminal justice system did not manage to institutionalize legal safeguards for the accused before the state collapsed, although legal reformers did attempt to improve policing by enhancing militia efficiency in combatting crime, reducing corruption and augmenting procedural protections. Yet these conflicting objectives could not be achieved simultaneously, particularly in an environment in which increasing political polarization, nationalism and fiscal restraints limited the possibilities for innovation and reform. In the end, few legal protections of individual rights against police abuse survived the *perestroika* era and the successor states to the USSR now find themselves needing to institute criminal justice reform during a period of rising crime. The criminalization of emerging private businesses during the Soviet period, together with the links established between the justice system and members of the criminal underworld, also leaves a dangerous legacy for the post-Soviet states, with organized crime now supplanting the militia by means of private security forces in many regions of the former USSR.

10 The political functions of the militia

> Political policing: it reaches out for potential threats in a systematic attempt to preserve the distribution of power in a given society.
>
> Jean-Paul Brodeur[1]

Political functions of the militia were an integral part of law enforcement in the USSR. Until *perestroika*, neither the Soviet law enforcement bureaucracy nor individual militiamen questioned this element of their mandate. For most of the Soviet period, the sheer number of regular policemen and their proximity to the population made it possible to effectively monitor and control the political activity of Soviet citizens, usually in conjunction with the security police. Joint militia–KGB control meant that most subversive political activity in the USSR was prevented before it could escalate to the level of overt political conflict. Since political tasks and undercover activity were central elements of Soviet policing, militiamen were, in the words of Jean-Paul Brodeur, "more deeply involved in crime management than in crime repression."[2]

The political functions of the Soviet militia were often masked from public attention and could be determined only by drawing on a variety of documentary sources, the most important of which were *samizdat* publications circulated by members of human rights groups, cultural and religious dissenters and diverse national groups.[3] *Samizdat* publications confirmed that, whereas the KGB had primary responsibility for controlling groups in opposition to the regime, the militia played an important auxiliary role in protecting state security and enforcing political conformity. Using administrative (and, to a lesser degree, criminal) law, as well as psychiatric confinement, the militia clearly communicated the limits of acceptable political and religious behavior in Soviet society.[4]

Opposition groups under militia and KGB surveillance were unable to evolve into mass political movements in the pre-*perestroika* period. The well-publicized human rights movement in the USSR that began after the arrests of writers Andrei Sinyavsky and Iulii Daniel in 1966 was actually more influential than its numbers suggested, but constant arrests rapidly led to its attrition. Perhaps the largest groups in the USSR considered to be in "opposition" to the regime prior to the Gorbachev era were the Baptist and Pentecostal churches, which together had more than 100,000 followers by the early 1980s.[5] Although political activists emerged from time to time from such national groups as the Crimean Tatars, Ukrainians and Lithuanians, as well as from the Jewish emigration movement, these activists never numbered more than a few thousand prior to *perestroika*.

The militia's wide range of political functions can be traced to the amalgamation of continental, colonial and communist police traditions in Soviet policing, all of which subordinated the interests of citizens to those of the state. Political policing was an integral part of the continental police model, in which the police is used both to control crime and penetrate society on behalf of the state. Police in colonial societies likewise controlled crime while ensuring the obedience of colonized subjects to central rule. In communist states, police went one step further and ensured citizen compliance with official state ideology.

By requiring adherence to both the economic and political objectives of the state, Marxism–Leninism gave law enforcement bodies in the USSR an explicit political mandate, conferring on the militia numerous political functions not found in all authoritarian political systems. The colonial aspects of Soviet law enforcement, moreover, caused these functions to vary from region to region. Outside Slavic and/or Russified regions, for example, the Soviet militia was more concerned with subordinating the population to central rule than in areas where more consensus on Soviet values and communist ideology existed.

After the great violence of the first years of the Bolshevik regime, political control was largely exerted by means of administrative police restraints rather than direct confrontation. The means of such control were both transparent and covert; both means relied extensively on undercover activities as well as conventional licensing and law enforcement techniques. Many of the more indirect tools of control discussed in previous chapters (e.g., the licensing of printing presses, internal passports, parasite laws and surveillance) fulfilled explicit political functions while maintaining social order in Soviet society.

Police, however, can successfully combine security duties with conventional crime control only when they enjoy public sympathy and a considerable degree of legitimacy. [6] In the collapsing Soviet Union, the militia enjoyed neither, finding it impossible to control the social divisions engendered by *perestroika*. On the contrary, the militia's increasingly overt political role during the final years of the Soviet regime intensified citizen hostility towards the police, undermining law enforcement and the Soviet state itself.

THE KGB–MVD RELATIONSHIP AND MILITIA OPERATIONS

The statute that authorized the establishment of the militia required it to assist the KGB in the latter's activities. While militia–KGB cooperation did occur within the context of ordinary criminal cases that fell within the KGB mandate, this cooperation was more often realized in a variety of political situations in which the militia, by virtue of its extensive administrative and licensing controls, could intervene more readily than the KGB. The militia rarely initiated action in political cases, generally acting only on direct instructions from the security police. The personal antagonism of an individual militiaman towards a particular activist or group could, of course, result in harsher action than that demanded by the security police, just as personal sympathy for an activist or group could result in more lenient action. Militia personnel in Leningrad, for example, failed to intervene in demonstrations by nationalist, anti-Semitic members of *Pamiat'* in 1989, just as Moscow police failed to halt an attack by *Pamiat'* members on the offices of the newspaper *Moskovskii komsomolets* in 1992.[7]

When directed to intervene in political situations by the KGB, militia actions were generally limited to harassment, unlawful detention, threats, unjustified arrest and the incarceration of suspects in psychiatric hospitals. In such cases, the militia might prevent the public or a witness from attending the trial of a political activist, search an apartment on the pretext of a fire inspection, intervene in a private religious service, prevent the burial of an exiled national in his homeland or frame a political activist for assaulting a militia officer.[8] Harassment alone could consist of beatings, unauthorized interrogations, verbal threats and/or surveillance.

As described in Chapter 8, the militia used the passport and registration system to intimidate, isolate, and harass dissidents and political activists – denying them residence permits in key locations, questioning them about their passports and registration permits and circumscribing their permanent area of residence. Dissidents and political activists were likewise harassed by means of the parasite laws which, when not used to imprison or exile them abroad, gave the militia grounds for threatening and otherwise harassing individuals considered politically suspect. While the heavy hand of the security police was rarely visible in such incidents, the targeting of such people for particular harassment by the militia indicated that it was performing the dirty work of the KGB.

Finally, the militia's ability to limit individual mobility externally as well as domestically also served political ends. MVD control over foreign passports and travel documents allowed militiamen to impede the foreign travel of individuals deemed politically unreliable, such as Jews seeking to emigrate. The latter were frequently intimidated by verbal insults and guard dogs when they applied for permission to emigrate; religious activists, ethnic minorities and ordinary citizens who sought to visit friends in the west or to emigrate met similar harassment.[9]

In extreme cases, militia personnel committed dissidents, nonconformists and obstinate individuals (people who sought justice at the workplace, for example) to unnecessary psychiatric diagnosis and treatment. Such confinement was governed by secret instructions that had been adopted by both the

USSR Procuracy and USSR MVD in 1972; new regulations that attempted to limit psychiatric abuse by approving the hospitalization only of the mentally ill were issued only under Gorbachev.[10]

In parts of the USSR that were more visible to foreigners, such as the cities of Moscow, Leningrad and Kiev, the techniques of the militia in political cases were generally more subtle, reflecting both the increased sophistication of the militia as well as the greater exposure given to police excesses in these cities. By contrast, nationalist activists or individuals who expressed non-conformist religious or political views in more remote parts of the country were frequently subjected to more physical and verbal police abuse. In Moscow, for example, the organizers of a silent demonstration on Human Rights Day in the late 1970s were merely dragged away from the site of the gathering by the militia. Yet *samizdat* literature attests that Crimean Tatars were forcibly deported for political activities, Georgian religious believers living in Azerbaijan were terrified by the militia and a Catholic church in Moldavia was destroyed with the assistance of the militia.[11]

Geographical variations in the political activities of the militia increased during *perestroika*, the result of significant differences in political activism in the various Soviet republics, as well as conscious decisions of the CPSU national leadership. Thus in the final days of the USSR, relatively small-scale protests were held in major Russian cities, whereas hundreds of thousands of people gathered in many non-Slavic republics to demand greater political autonomy and even independence. Either as a result of local instructions or the central government's transfer of additional MVD personnel to such republics, more violent police methods were generally used against protesters in non-Slavic areas of the USSR in the later Gorbachev years.

UNSANCTIONED PUBLIC PROTESTS

In the post-Stalin period, public protests were sporadic and touched on a broad range of social and political issues, presaging the more overt political activity of the *perestroika* years. Between 1956 and 1983, the militia played a significant role in subduing over 400 collective protests reported in *samizdat*, the western and Soviet press and eyewitness accounts published by Soviet émigrés. The subject of these protests reflected the issues that would come to the fore with such force under Gorbachev: human rights, nationality issues and cultural expression. By helping to suppress such activities, the militia did not eliminate the social forces behind them, but merely postponed the threat they posed to the Soviet regime. The fact that unsanctioned public protests increased noticeably in the years immediately preceding Gorbachev's rise to power (see Tables 10.1 and 10.2) indicates that *perestroika* simply allowed forces that had been percolating within Soviet society to surface openly.

The regime's response to the protests documented in Tables 10.1 and 10.2 depended on the composition of the leadership of the CPSU at the time and

Table 10.1 Chronological distribution of unsanctioned public demonstrations by number of participants, 1953–83

Number of Participants	1953–64	1965–74	1975–83	Total
Less than 10	—	7	10	17
10s	4	67	131	202
100s	18	66	44	128
1,000s	8	18	11	37
10,000s	1	1	4	6
100,000s	—	1	1	2
Unknown	1	14	2	17
Total:	32	174	203	409

Source: Ludmilla Alexeeva and Valery Chalidze, *Mass Unrest in the USSR*, vol. 1 (Washington, D.C.: Office of Net Assessments, 1985), 222

Table 10.2 Breakdown of reasons for demonstrations, 1953–83

Reason	Number of Meetings and Demonstrations
Economic	3
Political	8
Human Rights	194
National	119
Cultural	70
Peace	4
Fascist	11
Total	409

Source: adapted from Ludmilla Alexeeva and Valery Chalidze, *Mass Unrest*, vol. 1, 224

the level of oppositional political activity involved. The years of Stalinist repression left a very passive population; consequently, the militia confronted few public demonstrations in the first decade after Stalin's death. Alexeeva and Chalidze report a mere 32 demonstrations during this time period, generally small, most of which concerned national, political and cultural matters. According to these authors, about one-half of the public demonstrations that occurred during these years were dispersed by the militia, often with the use of force and the assistance of Soviet Army troops.[12]

Militia treatment of political demonstrators was milder in the first post-Stalin period than during the Brezhnev era, when the regime adopted a differentiated approach to unplanned mass public action. In the words of Alexeeva and Chalidze, the new approach "depended on the site of the action, on its character, and on the general direction of Soviet domestic and foreign policy at the moment of a given action."[13] Although the regime exhibited a consistent reluctance to introduce troops into such situations throughout the Brezhnev era, it was generally impatient with public action that did not take place under governmental control.[14] Despite consistent law enforcement responses to demonstrations in the Brezhnev years, the number of demonstrations and mass meetings in the USSR grew dramatically between 1965 and 1974 – over five times as many demonstrations were held during this period than in the preceding decade. Proportionately more of these protests concerned human rights questions than in the past, and many involved hundreds, if not thousands, of individuals.

The militia rarely played an active role in dispersing public gatherings, confining itself to impeding demonstrators from reaching or participating in protests and singling out individual leaders for reprisal afterwards.[15] During the early Brezhnev period, however, the militia faced serious problems in defusing large-scale demonstrations in areas where national tensions ran high. In April 1965, for example, a demonstration of 100,000 youths and students occurred in Yerevan, the capital of Armenia. The protest, motivated by nationalist sentiment, was dispersed with fire hoses and volunteer militia (who were reported to have beaten demonstrators). Possibly the most famous riot of the Brezhnev era occurred in the late 1960s after a soccer match in Uzbekistan. Despite careful advance planning by the militia and local Party authorities, large-scale riots ensued after the game provoked Russian–Uzbek hostility among the spectators. The disturbances quickly spread beyond the sports arena and the militia and other law enforcement bodies were unable to contain the conflict. Troops were eventually called in and many lives were lost. In the aftermath of the riots, hundreds of individuals were prosecuted and many Party and law enforcement personnel were purged for having failed to forestall the disturbances.[16]

If the militia had problems peacefully defusing demonstrations fueled by nationalist sentiment, neither was it successful in containing violence precipitated by militia brutality. In the early 1960s, for example, two individuals' deaths at the local militia station in two separate cities resulted in worker protests. In Aleksandrov, a town near Moscow, workers struck at the plant of the deceased worker. Similarly motivated protests in Murom, a town 150 kilometers southwest of Nizhnii Novgorod, destroyed local militia buildings. These acts of specifically directed violence were suppressed by special troops and followed by mass arrests of demonstrators, some of whom later received the death sentence.[17] Such reactions to militia abuse were not confined to the Khrushchev years and continued under Brezhnev. In Dneprodzerzhinsk in 1972, for example, the militia's enforcement of anti-alcohol laws during a wedding party resulted in the destruction of the local militia and city Party committee (*gorkom*) buildings. The militia shot at crowds during this incident, with the result that at least ten people were killed and even more wounded.[18]

By the final years of the Brezhnev period, the number of planned protests had increased, but skillful militia techniques were able to reduce their size, particularly in Slavic areas. More demonstrations featured tens rather than hundreds of demonstrators because participants were prevented from joining such protests. Better intelligence on planned protests and enhanced coordination between the KGB and the militia permitted the latter to deter demonstrators through the use of threats and sanctions. Before a scheduled Jewish demonstration at Babi Yar, site of a mass grave of Nazi holocaust victims in Kiev, in the mid-1970s, for example, Muscovites arriving at the Kiev train station and airport were detained by the local militia. Some participants were put on a train and accompanied back to Moscow by militia units. Similar actions were implemented by the militia in other parts of the country in the late 1970s and early 1980s to prevent other Jewish commemorative efforts.[19]

The militia did not deter Jewish activists alone. Calculated efforts were made to prevent human rights activists from joining demonstrations on 10 December each year to mark Human Rights Day. Among other tactics, militiamen visited activists' apartments and warned them not to leave home that day, streets were cordoned off to prevent access to the demonstration site and volunteer militia were mobilized in large numbers to prevent people from assembling.[20]

In the late 1970s and early 1980s, more than 200 meetings and demonstrations concerning national and human rights questions were held in the USSR, yet none escaped police control. The presence of the militia and other law enforcement bodies contained such protests and militiamen were generally able to disperse demonstrators without recourse to extraordinary force, although beatings and skirmishes did occur at some of the more acrimonious protests. In several cases individuals were arrested on the spot and subsequently tried for such offenses as hooliganism.[21] Overall, however, the militia gradually learned to diffuse rather than confront political conflict during the post-Stalin period.

PLANNED STATE DEMONSTRATIONS

The militia exercised control not only over public protests, but also over orchestrated political expressions of the Soviet state. Although responsibility for organized mass gatherings and demonstrations on such state holidays as 7 November, May Day and Soviet Army Day was assigned to special supervisory personnel at militia headquarters,[22] the maintenance of public order at such events was considered too important to be left to the militia alone. Thus militiamen, together with large numbers of citizen auxiliaries, worked with Party, state and social organizations for months in advance of such demonstrations in order to ensure that no political embarrassments occurred.

Despite advance planning, embarrassing incidents did occur and occasionally public riots were even reported. One former militia officer recalled the case of a drunken demonstrator who collapsed with a portrait of Lenin at a May Day parade during Brezhnev's rule. While the man might have escaped severe punishment under less visible circumstances, the importance attached to public ceremonies meant that he could not merely be fined for disturbing the public order. Following established procedure for such state events, the militia official responsible for the case reported to the KGB and the man was subsequently handed over to the security police for prosecution on political charges.[23]

LABOR UNREST

The militia handled worker unrest less frequently than public protests in the post-Stalinist period. In general, managers of an enterprise tried to settle a labor dispute before the militia was called in. If their negotiation attempts failed, Party and local governmental authorities might intervene. Although the KGB was notified concerning any labor conflict, militia and KGB personnel were not actively employed until negotiations failed; special troops were then summoned only if the militia could not settle such a conflict on its own.[24]

In the limited number of cases in which it did intervene, the militia used a variety of techniques, most of which were directed at diffusing tensions or isolating strike leaders. If the police had prior knowledge of a worker protest, for example, they might mobilize volunteer militia units to participate in patrols to assure calm around the enterprise. Militiamen would often enter factory premises during strikes to calm crowds or remove recalcitrant workers to the local precinct, where they were known to use physical force during interrogations. The militia's role in strikes, however, sometimes appeared more active than was actually the case, as KGB agents dressed as militiamen often conducted the interrogations of labor activists at local militia station houses.[25]

ARTISTIC EXPRESSION

The militia helped to control personal expression in Soviet society by limiting artistic as well as written expression, a function seen in the treatment of non-conformist artists in Moscow during the mid-1970s. In September 1974, the western press and a small coterie of intellectuals were advised of an exhibit of 24 unofficial artists to be held in a vacant lot in southwestern Moscow. The exhibit lasted only briefly, as bulldozers soon appeared on the pretext that the area was being prepared for landscaping. Militiamen then rushed at the artists, roughed them up and stamped on their works. A *New York Times* correspondent lost his front tooth in the mêlée and five artists beaten by militiamen were subsequently arrested for hooliganism.[26]

Militia techniques in this sphere sometimes proved counterproductive. On this occasion, the militia accomplished its objective – closing down the art exhibit – at the price of an international sensation. The visibility of the militia's strong-arm tactics in this case had far-reaching implications: the second Party secretary for Moscow was held responsible for the fiasco, removed from his post and sent into diplomatic exile as the USSR Ambassador to North Vietnam. Two weeks later, a mass exhibit of politically motivated art was held in Izmailovo park at which 65 artists exhibited their work. The militia permitted this subsequent exhibit – attended by 15,000 people – to proceed without disruption.[27]

RELIGIOUS ACTIVITY

Strong repression of religious activity in the Stalinist period was replaced by more targeted repression after the dictator's death. Although Soviet law permitted the performance of services and rites of religions recognized by the regime, it prohibited services outside of established places of worship. Religious education was also prohibited and parents were barred from providing their children religious training even in the home. Established religions were infiltrated by the security police; less organized religions, such as the Baptists and Pentecostals (which could not be readily controlled by a compromised leadership), were singled out for more intense reprisals.

Although the KGB conceived and executed anti-religious police actions, the militia enforced the limits on permissible religious expression in Soviet society. Some of the more common techniques used by the militia in this area, such as disrupting religious services, fining religious leaders, halting religious burials and destroying churches and clandestine printing presses, have already been discussed in previous chapters. However, these were not the only methods used in the state's assault on the exercise of religion. Militiamen were also known to turn worshippers away from pilgrimage sites and to assault those who reached such sites. Religious processions in Lithuania and the Slavic republics received similar treatment. On the day of one planned Catholic procession in Lithuania in the 1980s, for example, quarantines were announced in the community and the militia blocked the road that was to be used for the procession. The organizers of the celebration were then arrested and subsequently tried in court.[28]

Religious ceremonies such as funerals and weddings sometimes evoked more dramatic reactions from the militia. For example, militiamen occasionally dispersed wedding parties by means of bulldozers; in one Ukrainian community, the police went so far as to cordon off a village to prevent guests from attending a wedding.[29] More violent means were used to disrupt unauthorized outdoor religious services. In 1978, a meeting of young Baptists was disrupted by tractors that began to clear the forest during prayers. Militiamen and auxiliary citizen personnel then provoked a fight and, despite the lack of resistance on the part of the Baptists, some were transported to the militia station in cars while others were physically manhandled and threatened with firearms. Such incidents were widespread – *samizdat* literature is filled with cases of militia harassment of Baptist and Pentecostal worshippers, some of whom were killed in such incidents.[30]

As mentioned previously, militia personnel also initiated cases against religious believers who gave unauthorized religious education to their children. Although criminal and alcoholic parents were more frequently the target of such state intervention, the militia occasionally took such action against Baptist parents. The militia's function did not end with instituting legal procedures against the parents, but extended to returning Baptist children to state childrens' homes after their escape and return to their families. Adult religious activists were sometimes even confined in mental hospitals.[31]

Unable to find relief within their own country, religious believers sometimes tried to take refuge in foreign embassies. There they encountered special militia units dressed in regular uniforms who were assigned control of the entryways of all offices and residential complexes of foreign governments.[32] A *samizdat* document of a religious believer vividly brings to life the political role and attitudes of militiamen who guarded foreign embassies:

> I came to the Canadian embassy. When I approached . . . the militiaman who was standing there ran to me and started shouting all kinds of curses. . . . Then with all his strength he began to hit me around the head. An open wound developed. I cried "Why do you beat me?" He screamed back, "I will kill you, you vile creature. . . ." Then another shouted "Beat him so he loses consciousness."[33]

When the author of this account returned to his home town, the links between embassy-based militia units and the KGB became all too clear: the man was immediately summoned to the local KGB office for questioning.

POLITICAL VENDETTAS

The political functions of the militia did not always involve the suppression of dissidents and religious believers, but often promoted the personal political interests of individual politicians. KGB and Party personnel both regularly deployed militia personnel to harass whistleblowers on corrupt practices and to collect incriminating materials on political rivals. When Boris Yeltsin was the first Party secretary of Moscow, for example, he instructed Moscow district militia inspectors to get after his political enemies saying "See if those sons of bitches are getting up to anything."[34] Although officials were called to account for manipulating law enforcement under *perestroika*, such activities were carried on with impunity for most of the 74-year existence of the Soviet regime. In fact, reporting of the *perestroika* years revealed how deeply entrenched this practice was.

In the Voroshilovgrad province of Ukraine, both the KGB chief and the first Party secretary were dismissed in 1987 after using the militia to get rid of an investigative journalist from the newspaper *Soviet Miner*. The journalist, who had been studying the violation of safety standards in local mines, was arrested after being "trailed by a 'capture group' . . . from the Voroshilovgrad militia."[35] Whereas *Pravda* reported the vigorous militia interrogation of the journalist after he was first arrested, only an obscure Soviet publication announced the journalist's death several months later, when the young man failed to recover from the brutality of his militia interrogation.[36]

PERESTROIKA AND THE MILITIA'S POLITICAL FUNCTIONS

The dissolution of the Soviet state cannot be understood without insight into the political functions of the militia during the *perestroika* period. While the militia was not the only force deployed by the Soviet state to maintain order and central control as the USSR spun out of control, the militia remained the most immediate level of contact between the state and the citizenry. Its failure to enforce central authority during this crucial period was certainly a contributing factor to the eventual collapse of the USSR. Confronting the diverse conflicts of the *perestroika* period would have been difficult for a well-equipped law enforcement body in a society where the police enjoyed legitimacy, but it was an impossible task for a beleaguered tool of a ruling political party that had lost legitimacy.

During the Gorbachev era, political forces and movements that would have taken a full generation to develop in any other society arose within a single year. The Soviet state found itself simultaneously challenged by the emergence of civil society, potent nationalist movements, ethnic conflict and labor strikes; many of these phenomena occurred most forcefully outside of the Russian republic. Labor unrest posed a particular problem for the regime because it disputed the legitimacy of the communist system and the colonial state.[37] Together with other law enforcement bodies, the militia was asked to adjust to informal social movements while suppressing ethnic conflict.

One of *perestroika*'s greatest challenges to the militia was the need to adjust and regulate informal groups which developed by the thousands in Soviet society under Gorbachev. Many of these associations, such as independent theatrical groups or stamp societies, were of little concern to the authorities. Other such groups, however, including rock bands, political discussion groups and ecological movements, publicly expressed concerns that transcended what had long been traditional limits on expression in Soviet society. Although most informal groups made significant efforts to avoid provoking a violent response from law enforcement bodies, the Soviet government, long accustomed to dominating all social and political activity, responded to social change in the way most familiar to it: with the militia.

In the late 1980s, militiamen were deployed to monitor informal groups, control labor strikes and patrol national protests – their resources rapidly stretched to the breaking point. Unequipped to deal with protest organized outside of the state, the militia sometimes exacerbated the level of tension in Soviet society by crude and even violent handling of political protests. Yet militiamen did not always intervene in ethnic conflict on behalf of the central government. Rather, militia personnel of indigenous national groups several times sided with their ethnic group against the USSR Ministry of Internal Affairs during the late 1980s.[38]

During the initial stages of *perestroika*, the militia used aggressive law enforcement techniques against members of different political movements in

Moscow and the Baltic republics. Members of such groups were followed, individual activists taken into custody and meetings dispersed by expelling people from the various facilities where meetings were held.[39] The militia treated those people it perceived as dissidents, such as Sergei Grigoryants, editor of the independent magazine *Glasnost'* and a former Soviet political prisoner, particularly harshly.

Once Grigoryants began to publish *Glasnost'*, for example, he began to be shadowed by the militia and threatened with prosecution for violating the internal passport laws. In 1988, after a year of publication, the militia ransacked his office and removed the equipment he needed to publish the magazine. His office was again ransacked in 1993, this time by *Pamiat'* members, who proceeded undeterred by the militia.[40]

Consistently harsh treatment was also applied to members of the explicitly anti-communist political group, the Democratic Union. In 1988, the Moscow militia thwarted a demonstration by the group, dragging off members who refused to leave the demonstration site. Another militia confrontation with the group occurred in central Moscow in late 1989. In 1990, Union member Sergei Kuznetsov was tried in court for slandering a militiaman. Several Russian commentators on the trial suggested that Kuznetsov had been framed by the militia because the political and justice systems were hostile to the Democratic Union, which they perceived to be an overt opposition movement.[41]

The attitude of many militiamen towards new political activity in Soviet society was expressed in an article entitled "How to Fight with Informals?" that appeared in a Leningrad militia newspaper in 1989.[42] The article advised militia personnel to infiltrate groups, identify individual members of such movements, prepare reports and initiate criminal cases against groups. Traditional militia operational methods, such as surveillance, harassment, and arrest were regularly deployed against those who sought to form the basic elements of civil society during the early years of *perestroika*. Under visible assault by state authorities, however, members of informal groups rapidly became demoralized.[43]

By the final years of the Soviet period, there was no consistency in the way the militia treated political protests and informal groups. At times policemen tried to accommodate themselves to the democratization of Soviet society, a process they themselves acknowledged was difficult, yet no established procedures determined which public meetings should be granted demonstration permits and which denied. Law enforcement thus remained largely arbitrary in this area. Certainly there was more tolerance of protests by 1988, when a new law on the subject – "On the Procedure of Organizing and Holding Rallies, Meetings, Street Processions and Demonstrations in the USSR" – was established by an *ukaz* of the Presidium of the USSR Supreme Soviet.[44] Yet, as Ernest Ametistov, a liberal jurist subsequently appointed to the Russian Constitutional Court, commented at the time:

> In the Baltic republics there are authorized meetings on the most burning political and national problems with many thousands taking part; Moscow

authorities ban a meeting devoted to the events in Czechoslovakia, while those in Leningrad shut their eyes to the gatherings of the *Pamiat'* movement, whose slogans are in direct opposition to the Constitution.[45]

At moments when political liberalism prevailed under Gorbachev, the militia permitted a contained level of public political expression. In June 1988, for example, the main directorate of the Moscow militia asserted that "if a meeting or demonstration is permitted it will take place without interference from the militia."[46] Tolerance was generally extended to demonstrators as long as they did not become too vociferous or challenge the militia's authority. Unaccustomed to the impassioned protests of Jewish "refuseniks," Crimean Tatars and other informal groups, however, the militia often imposed administrative sanctions on demonstrators in Moscow and other locales.[47]

When the Gorbachev government adopted a more conservative line, more violent tactics were used against demonstrators, particularly by members of the OMON, as demonstrated by the attack on the Vil'nius television station in January 1991. Attacks against protesters could be particularly aggressive when they coincided with such Communist events as October Revolution or May Day parades.[48] Despite oscillations in policy, the militia in Russia and many other areas of the USSR became more tolerant of large-scale public protests during the last four years of the regime's existence, a phenomenon previously unknown in Soviet society.

MILITIA REACTION TO NATIONALISM AND ETHNIC CONFLICT

Ironically, just as the militia was learning to tolerate political demonstrations, its colonial functions were again much in evidence as MVD troops joined the army in attempting to repress regional resistance to central rule. The extent and frequency of the militia's cooperation with the armed forces, the KGB and other internal troops in the late 1980s had not been seen in the USSR since the initial years of the Soviet regime.

The militia alone was rarely able to control the increasing number of ethnic disturbances that broke out throughout the country and internal troops and the military were repeatedly called in to contain such strife. Militiamen were neither brutal suppressors nor heroes of the moment in such conflicts. Rather, they manned the state's initial line of defense against dissolution and were none too successful in the task. In the late Soviet period, the major areas of nationalist protest and ethnic conflict were the Baltics, Moldavia, the Caucasus, Central Asia and Ukraine. Other areas, such as Tatarstan and North Ossetia, experienced short-term ethnic conflicts that were successfully contained. Although the militia strategy varied from region to region, as in other failing empires, the decolonization process frequently produced violent policing.[49]

Nationalist movements in Latvia, Lithuania and Estonia were all peaceful, but focused on independence and secession from the Soviet Union. In response to this challenge to the authority of the central state, both local and USSR MVD militia personnel used violent means in an attempt to suppress these movements. Local militia personnel did not always act on the orders of central authorities, but in support of their own interests – many militia personnel employed in the Baltic republics were Slavs who were not eager to see these states attain independence. With encouragement from Moscow, they blocked protests and harassed demonstrators. As independence movements in these states gained momentum in 1991, militiamen used increased force against them. On New Year's Day 1991, OMON units of the Ministry of Internal Affairs stormed the Latvian Interior Ministry and killed four people; the maneuver was followed by OMON attacks on border posts. The OMON attacks in Lithuania during the same period galvanized the nationalist movement in the republic; such attacks continued throughout 1991 until the Baltic states achieved independence following the unsuccessful coup in August of that year.[50]

The political agenda of the population of Ukraine also provoked violent intercessions by the local militia. As late as 7 November 1990, for example, militiamen in Kiev severely beat students who attempted to thwart a military parade commemorating the anniversary of the October Revolution.[51] Political aspirations in Moldavia were an additional source of bloodshed and prompted the introduction of militia and OMON personnel into that republic. Efforts by the Gagauz, a group of Christianized Turks, to secede from Moldavia in 1990 led the militia – with the assistance of tens of thousands of citizen volunteers – to cordon off the region inhabited by these people. The central government, to whom the Gagauz turned for protection, responded by sending in MVD troops, units that were later accused by the Moldavian leadership "of virtually encouraging the leaders of the Gagauz separatists."[52] The Gagauz conflict foreshadowed the even more serious conflict that broke out in the Dniester region in eastern Moldavia in June 1991, when the Soviet government answered calls for assistance from the region's majority Slavic population by flying OMON units into the area.[53] Introduction of MVD personnel preceded that of Soviet military personnel, who remained in the Dniester region after Moldavia became independent.

In the Central Asian republics, ethnic hostilities generally served as the pretext for militia intervention. As in Moldavia and the Nagorno-Karabakh region of Azerbaijan, ethnic conflict sometimes coincided with territorial disputes. The ethnic conflict that occurred in the Fergana Valley of Uzbekistan in 1989, however, was not purely ethnic in nature, as discontent with Soviet government policies and a collapsing economy had contributed to tension in the area. When militia and MVD troops were brought in to control the conflict between the local population and Meskhetian Turks, law enforcement units were scorned by the rioters. According to an Uzbek newspaper, armed groups drove around the *oblast'* Party committee building and made fun of the militiamen there. Subsequent rioting in the Uzbek city of Parkent led to even more violence by and against the militia in 1990, when militiamen fired on a group of more than 5,000 demonstrators. According to one analyst, "before the violence was over the building of the district administration of internal affairs had been burned" and a militia officer killed.[54]

The unwillingness of the Soviet government to remove itself from conflicts in the border regions of the USSR increased the level of violence and instability in these republics, exacerbating rather than calming political hostilities in the late *perestroika* years. In the end, the colonial reaction of using the police to suppress ethnic and national disorder left Russia with an unstable periphery once the USSR ceased to exist.

CONCLUSION

The militia's reaction to pro-democratic protesters and ethnic violence during the *perestroika* years illustrated a major dilemma of the Gorbachev era: how to liberalize Soviet society while maintaining social order and central governmental control. If *glasnost'* were to proceed, political controls within the Soviet Union needed to be reduced, the role of the KGB diminished and militia tactics for dealing with political and religious activity changed.[55] In order for the USSR to move towards a more democratic system, the Communist Party apparatus and the KGB had to learn to perceive the militia as a professional law enforcement body and not as a tool for performing the less savory tasks of political control. The reverse, however, occurred. The militia was increasingly thrust into a political role, one from which its 70-year legacy of political functions and legislative mandate to assist the KGB prevented its escape.

Unfortunately, the forms of policing that provided the basis for Soviet law enforcement – the continental, colonial and communist police models – ensured a heightened political role for the militia during times of political conflict. Thus it was the militia, not the security police, that actively defended the Soviet government against threats to its authority and domination in the turbulent years of the late 1980s and, later, defended the Yeltsin government from the challenge mounted by opposition forces within the Russian parliament in October 1993. The ever more pronounced political role of the regular police remained a major obstacle to the democratic transformation of Soviet society while the USSR remained a state and left a serious legacy of conflict and bloodshed for its successor states.

Conclusion

Beginning with the Bolshevik Revolution of 1917, the Soviet militia functioned as part of a centrally controlled law enforcement apparatus designed to produce a highly ordered state. This apparatus, with its sensitivity to the wishes of the Communist Party, worked to endow the heterogeneous society of the USSR with a veneer of uniformity. Soviet citizens were held in check by a police body that combined overt operations with undercover techniques which coopted or compromised the majority of the population. The vulnerable status of the individual in the system enhanced state control over the citizenry as a whole, ensuring a high degree of political and social conformity among the population. Extensive police controls resulted in lower crime rates than those found in most other industrialized countries and deterred overt acts of political resistance against the state.

Ironically, Marxist analyses of policing shed some light on the nature of the Soviet militia. Marxist scholars such as Maureen Cain and Isaac Balbus have strongly challenged the orthodox view of the police as a neutral body that prevents and controls crime, arguing instead that it is a fundamental institution of the ruling class to maintain its power.[1] Although class analysis has been applied insightfully to policing in both democratic and authoritarian societies, the argument is more complicated to apply to the Soviet Union, where the regular police was envisioned as the protector of worker and peasant interests, but acted as an instrument of the *nomenklatura* class of the Communist Party of the Soviet Union.

The militia in the post-revolutionary period was explicitly established as an agent of Bolshevik ideology. In accordance with Marxist theory, the militia was to shape the populace into the desired class structure: worker and peasant interests were to be defended, those of all other classes, repressed. Militia personnel drawn from worker and peasant classes were crucial actors in the process of molding Soviet society to fit Bolshevik ideology. Although the state never officially renounced its ideological commitment to a worker and peasant state, the class bias of law enforcement did become less apparent after several decades of Soviet rule. Nevertheless, even at the end of the Soviet period individuals were still excluded from law enforcement careers if they had "inappropriate" class origins.

Perhaps, however, the nature of the Soviet state is of more relevance to the militia than the latter's class origins or original ideological mission. The Soviet state denied the concept of citizenship that lay at the basis of the Enlightenment. While the concept of citizen rights significantly shaped governance (and policing) in western Europe and many parts of the Anglo-Saxon world, individuals in communist states were regarded as objects of state control rather than autonomous individuals. The USSR neither developed a legal framework to control its law enforcement agencies, nor allowed civil liberties to develop in the country. The state's penetration of private life crushed civil society, leaving no area of cultural, personal or economic life outside the surveillance of the state. In the absence of legal guarantees of civil rights, the Soviet citizen's only protection against the power of the state was its corruption and inefficiency.

During seventy-four years of Soviet rule, the militia was transformed from a militarized body suppressing political opposition to a law enforcement body responsible primarily for social and economic order. This transformation was similar to that which has been observed in the police forces of other industrialized societies: over time, a distance was gradually established between the police and the nation's political structure. Yet, because the Soviet militia functioned as a tool of the Communist Party, the relationship between the militia and the political structure in the USSR remained much closer than in democratic societies, allowing the Party to close that distance at the end of the Soviet era and direct the militia once again to suppress political opposition.

Despite its final effort to democratize during the *perestroika* years, the Soviet militia remained an authoritarian police force which retained elements of continental, colonial and communist police traditions. These elements remain present in the transitional police forces of the newly independent states today, even in the absence of Marxist ideology, the Communist Party and the Soviet state.

During *perestroika*, Communist Party General Secretary Mikhail Gorbachev attempted to reverse the relationship between the Soviet state and citizen. Instead of tolerating the arbitrary exercise of police power, he hoped to establish a socialist, law-based state in which institutions and individuals would be subordinate to the law. The state, however, faced the dilemma of how to liberalize while maintaining order and centralized control. Citizen access to the courts was expanded during the Gorbachev era and, for the first time in Soviet history, individuals were able to contest such militia actions as the denial of a registration permit. Yet the idea of a socialist rule-of-law state arrived too late in the Soviet Union; the Party quickly lost its legitimacy during *perestroika* and could not spearhead a campaign for the renewal of the police and justice system.

As a result of Gorbachev's reforms, the social and political conformity long sought by the Communist Party rapidly crumbled as individuals lost their fear of the state. Workers struck, crime rates escalated and ethnic conflict erupted almost daily. The once seemingly invincible militia, demoralized by corruption and personnel purges, proved unable to stabilize Soviet society and, despite the regime's massive diversion of resources to control escalating political unrest, the control apparatus as a whole could not keep pace with the changes occurring in the society around it. At a crucial moment in Soviet history, the militia failed to perform its basic function: control of the citizenry.

Not only did the militia lose credibility among those it policed, it lost credibility among those charged with executing its orders. The departure of numerous personnel at the end of the 1980s evidenced a serious morale problem and left the police without the qualified, experienced personnel needed to fulfill the body's ever more difficult duties (a problem which has only intensified since the collapse of the USSR). In the late *perestroika* period, moreover, when central political authority no longer prevailed, non-Slavic militia officers actively sided with republican interests against the Soviet state in many of the republics.

As the USSR began to splinter, militiamen became executors of the policies of a weak state, one which could not even guarantee their security. Record numbers of militiamen were attacked and killed by fellow citizens in the late 1980s as they sought to control nationalist movements, ethnic violence and increasingly vicious criminals. By the time the regime collapsed, Soviet citizens could no longer count on the most fundamental law enforcement services needed to protect them from rising crime and the operations of ever-expanding organized criminal groups.

Deteriorating police performance increasingly prompted many people to take policing into their own hands by creating private police forces and citizen militias independent of the Communist Party. These new forms of law enforcement, together with the efforts of the Soviet republics to exert more control over their ministries of internal affairs, were part of a general trend away from centralized control toward greater republican and regional sovereignty in the country. Decentralization occurred, however, without the consciousness or framework of legal norms that sustain democratic societies and democratic police forces.[2]

POST-SOVIET POLICING

After the communist regimes of Eastern Europe collapsed, an acute examination of past policing techniques occurred in Hungary, Germany, Poland and Czechoslovakia. The attention given to policing in these countries was based on the conviction that close scrutiny of existing police practices was vital to democratization.[3] Not surprisingly, many police methods were deemed incompatible with a democratic society in these nations, among them covert policing techniques, forced citizen collaboration with law enforcement bodies and the practice of planning the administration of justice. The former socialist states of the region have tried different reform approaches in order to limit police intrusion into private life. Poland has replaced many of its regular policemen, preferring inexperienced beginners to corrupt professionals insensitive to legal norms. West Germany has forced former East German policemen to adopt West German police techniques (in Berlin, police from the former German Democratic and Federal republics are paired in patrols). Hungary has abolished the network of informants that served as the foundation for undercover police work in that country, and Czechoslovakia, in destroying its secret police apparatus, has set a precedent for the ordinary police in the contemporary Czech and Slovak republics.

The destruction of the communist system in the former Soviet Union has not been so thorough. The contemporary Russian state, together with many other successor states to the USSR, failed to exploit the impetus for change that followed the unsuccessful coup attempt and subsequent breakup of the Soviet Union in 1991.[4] Reformers have been more successful in removing symbols of state coercion such as the statue of Feliks Dzherzhinsky (the founder of the Soviet security police) before the KGB headquarters in Moscow than in restructuring law enforcement bodies. The superstructure of the Soviet state has collapsed, but the institutions of the Soviet period remain very much intact; the commitment to democratization and political change on the part of certain internal affairs personnel has yet to be matched by the kind of institutional changes that would promote a more open and accountable police. The continued executive practice of issuing classified normative acts, some of which directly affect citizens' rights and freedoms, offers concrete evidence of the unchanged institutional environment.[5]

The police forces of post-Soviet states remain true to the continental police model in their structure, functions and operations. Unlike several post-communist nations in Eastern Europe, the range of functions performed by the police in the newly independent states of the former USSR has not contracted. Several of these states have adopted new statutes on the regular police that grant the police the same duties it possessed in the Soviet period. Despite general acknowledgement of the fact that the passport and registration system violates basic human rights, most of these states have also preserved this significant militia control over the populace.

Even more disconcerting, police forces in some of these states have used their new-found independence to secure or enhance their power at the expense of citizens' rights. In Russia, for example, the former Supreme Soviet Committee on Defense and Security was dominated by security, interior ministry and military industrial personnel (only a few of whom were inclined to reform) and the March 1992 Law on Security identified internal affairs organs as part of the security apparatus.[6]

The 1994 report of Russian Ombudsman Sergei Kovalëv documented two major violations committed by law enforcement personnel in 1993. First, following the attack on the parliament in October 1993, many individuals, including former deputies and staff members, who left the Russian "White House" were beaten by members of the militia in the courtyards of neighboring homes and on the streets. Brutal beatings also occurred at several police stations and at militia headquarters at Petrovka 38. Many of the detained later claimed that militiamen had shouted anti-Semitic and anti-Caucasian insults at them. Second, during the state of emergency which followed, approximately 10,000 individuals were expelled from Moscow by the militia, most of them non-Russian. The ombudsman's office has suggested that these expulsions resembled an ethnic cleansing.[7]

Informants and undercover techniques are still used widely to detect criminals and penetrate society in most of the successor states to the USSR. Having failed to incorporate the concept of civil liberties into law enforcement, police operations in these states – in bonafide continental tradition – continue to emphasize the supremacy of the state over the individual. In Kazakhstan, the powers of law enforcement agencies have been enhanced and the militia is now authorized to perform twenty-four different types of operations, including secret entry to apartments, houses and offices of private enterprises. The new Russian law on police operations, separate from that on state security, gives law enforcement personnel great latitude in the use of investigative methods and institutes only weak legal safeguards against police abuses, including the misuse of deadly force.[8]

Russian society, moreover, has yet to create a real division of political powers or to develop any kind of popular legal consciousness. Militiamen retain the right to engage in surveillance activity, monitor mail, eavesdrop on telephone conversations and other forms of communication and to use technical devices that are not life-threatening in order to monitor citizen behavior. It is small comfort that the Russian militia can employ such methods only with the permission of the courts or the Procuracy.[9]

The political functions associated with the continental police model also remain intact in many of the newly independent states; militiamen continue to suppress ethnic disorder, police political protests and monitor members of political opposition groups. In certain Central Asian countries, Interpol (acting under the authority of the Ministry of Internal Affairs) has been used to locate Uzbek dissidents who have taken refuge in Kazakhstan. Such dissidents have then been detained and returned to Uzbekistan, where they were subjected to political repression.[10] And although the Communist Party is no longer the life force of these states, several of these countries have yet to recognize an individual's right to political expression without state intervention.

Although a unified Ministry of Internal Affairs no longer controls policing in the entire territory of the former USSR, republican ministries of internal affairs remain. Most of these bodies remain unchanged from their Soviet incarnations and continue to manage law enforcement in the newly independent states with the same personnel, the same mandate and many of the same laws of Soviet times. Coordination of law enforcement among these states, moreover, is now being justified by the threat of organized crime, which has rapidly moved to exploit the porous borders between them. Although vital, such cooperation threatens in the short-run to reestablish ties that existed at the national ministerial level during the Soviet period.

It is an altogether disturbing fact that the law enforcement bureaucracies of the successor states to the USSR have the power to perpetuate Soviet police traditions in the absence of the Communist Party of the Soviet Union and its system of social controls. The state's penetration of private life through the security police and the militia remains a fact of life in most post-Soviet states. The Tadjik legislature, for example, passed a new law on the militia in 1992 that requires state bodies, labor collectives and official and public associations to assist the regular police in its activities – continuing communist practice in the absence of communist ideology.[11] Cooperation between law enforcement agencies and the military also endures in many of these nations. In Russia, armed forces personnel were first directed to perform police work in January 1991.[12] By continuing to combine these different parts of the state control apparatus, the Russian state remains wholly within the continental tradition.

The communist element of policing in post-Soviet states should eventually disappear with the delegitimation of basic communist ideology. Property relations of the communist regime, however, remain extant in most of these countries, particularly with respect to land ownership, with state- and publicly-owned property in these nations only gradually being privatized. Thus it is highly likely that state paternalism will endure even in the absence of regimes structured to deliver all essential social services to the population.

Finally, the post-Soviet police forces of the successor states have also inherited the law enforcement problems of the Soviet period. Independence has not eliminated the causes of endemic corruption, the lack of legal consciousness or the severely limited technical capabilities of the police. (While the number of Russian militia officers may have recently increased, the quality of their professional training has declined.)[13] In fact, many of these problems have been exacerbated by the collapse of the imperial center.

Growing state corruption and organized crime in the successor states also have had major repercussions on law enforcement in the former Soviet republics. In 1993, for example, Russian police officials suggested that 13,000 internal affairs employees were directly collaborating with organized criminal groups and many more were accepting bribes from so-called "mafias." In Krasnodar and Dagestan, militia personnel have even beaten up judges.[14] In only two months in late 1994, 324 violations committed by Ukrainian MVD personnel were publicly disclosed and 43 criminal cases were initiated against MVD employees.[15] The poor salaries of militiamen, flourishing corruption at top leadership levels of the successor states and the difficulties of surviving hyperinflation have made police corruption as severe a problem, if not more so, than it was at the close of the Soviet regime. Lastly, numerous militia personnel are leaving for the private sector. The head of the Russian State Duma Committee on Security, Viktor Iliukhin, estimates that there are now approximately 100,000 individuals working in private security forces controlled by organized crime. These bodies continue to exist without any legal norms to regulate their conduct.[16]

The process of privatization in the successor states has also been criminalized since its inception. Many investors who have participated in privatization came from the former shadow economy, that is, in the past they acted as speculators, racketeers and extortionists. According to estimates of the Russian Ministry of Interior in mid-1993, 40,000 enterprises were controlled or established by organized criminal groups, with law enforcement personnel complicit in much of this illegal activity.[17] Privatization, moreover, is occurring against a background of severe economic and political crisis – almost one-half of the former Soviet republics are now party to serious interethnic conflict or civil war. Under such conditions, observance of legal norms is continually subordinated to the survival of the state and its citizens.

Given the newly independent states' financial straits, shortages of militia cars, typewriters, telecommunications equipment and even gasoline are more serious problems today than they were for the Soviet militia during the waning days of the USSR. Such underequipped police forces are a poor match for increasingly sophisticated, well-equipped professional criminal organizations. As Iliukhin's State Duma committee has noted, the state is now competing with such organizations for experienced law enforcement personnel, with criminal groups able to offer more attractive salaries. The police forces of most of the successor states remain severely understaffed and it is difficult to locate replacements for departing personnel, a situation that threatens to endure for some time to come.

THE COLONIAL LEGACY

In addition to their continental and communist heritage, the structure and composition of post-Soviet police institutions represent one of the most concrete legacies of Soviet colonialism. Slavs enjoyed a visible presence in the militia forces of all former republics of the USSR, a staffing pattern required to reenforce the authority of the central Russian state. While some of the newly independent states of the region have forced Slavic (or Russified) personnel off their police forces, many others lack qualified replacements for law enforcement bodies.[18] Slavic personnel continue to operate in the security police of most Central Asian nations; the same situation largely holds for the militias of these countries.

As in other parts of the world, colonial relationships continue between the former imperial center and the periphery of the Soviet empire, largely because many former Soviet republics did not acquire autonomy – economic or otherwise – with independence. Unlike the Baltic states and Ukraine, not all of these new countries fought, or even sought, to become sovereign nations, a status they achieved as a result of the collapse of the empire. Russia's assertion that it has a legitimate right to intervene in these countries on behalf of the twenty-five million Russians living outside Russia's borders adds additional weight to the colonial character of the relations between the former imperial center and the "near abroad."

The law enforcement policies of the central Russian government are also exacerbating internal tensions among different ethnic groups within Russia itself, a problem it shares with most other successor states to the USSR. The refusal of Tatarstan and Chechn'ia to sign the Federation Treaty in March 1992 is just one example of the fact that many regions of Russia still consider themselves to be in a colonial relationship with Moscow. The attack on Chechn'ia by Russian forces in December 1994 will be perceived as further evidence that the Russian state is determined to subordinate these ethnic groups. Attempts of the Russian militia and procuracy to maintain control over law enforcement in these regions without the input of the local legal bodies only confirms their perceptions of the imperial nature of Russian rule.

THE POST-SOVIET FUTURE

To date, most of the newly independent states have been unable to reconceptualize policing. While it may be premature to expect major restructuring of law enforcement agencies and practices in these nations, their failure to address one of the more important authoritarian legacies of the Soviet period inhibits their ability to democratize. The future development of police forces in the successor states will depend on the type of societies that emerge in these countries. Twenty years from now, it is unlikely that these fifteen countries will have similar police forces. The more western parts of the former Soviet Union may well strive to implement European models of policing, while many of the Islamic countries of Central Asia may eschew western legal models and follow law enforcement models closer to Turkish and/or Iranian experience. Whatever course they follow, the communist legacy of the Soviet regime and, in many cases, the colonial legacy of Russian rule, will continue to weigh heavily on law enforcement in these nations for years to come.

Sadly, many of the newly independent states seem to have traded one form of violence for another. Whereas once state repression was accentuated and civilian violence relatively insignificant, today nearly one-half of the former Soviet republics cannot control crime or ethnic and nationalist violence within their borders. If these countries continue to live in a state of war for a protracted period, it is possible they may choose the Hobbesian alternative and create authoritarian governments (with authoritarian police forces) in order to put an end to constant conflict. Should such a scenario prevail, the continental police tradition will be further perpetuated in these nations.

If, however, the new states of the region succeed in creating individual property and distributing it with some equity within their societies, they will create a bulwark against unlimited state authority. These nations would then have the opportunity to develop civil societies and civil liberties and gradually require that their police forces operate according to the rule of law.

Movement away from communist property relations should force these states to accept the idea that certain areas of human conduct are outside the purview of government and state regulation and thereby reduce the degree of interventionist policing known in the former Soviet Union. While it is too early to be assured of either of these two scenarios, law enforcement in most of the former Soviet republics is clearly in a precarious state.[19] The morale of law enforcement agencies is at an all-time low – they can neither control escalating crime, nor handle the increasingly sophisticated activities of organized criminal groups which threaten not only their own societies, but those of many other nations in the world. With the declining authority of the security police and the army in these nations, only the militia remains, affecting the ability of the successor states both to stabilize and control organized crime. Far from being of interest only to specialists on the region, or an impediment to democratization, the current condition of militia operations in the Soviet successor states is thus an issue of global concern.

Appendix

INTERVIEWS WITH FORMER POLICE PERSONNEL

The interviews conducted for this book with Soviet émigrés who had formerly worked in the Soviet militia and the USSR Ministry of Internal Affairs and other branches of the Soviet justice system were accomplished in two stages. The first stage of interviews was conducted with a broad range of former lawyers who had worked in the Soviet justice system and in Soviet enterprises. These interviews, conducted as part of the author's research on a previous book, were directly applicable to the work and were held in Israel, Canada and the United States in 1980 and 1981. The second round of interviews was undertaken in Israel in the spring of 1987 and involved only individuals who had worked in the militia. Although one of these interviewees was an individual the author had met on a prior trip to Israel, the remaining seven individuals had not been previously interviewed. Many individuals in this second group had worked in different parts of the *militsiia*, such as the *ugolovnyi rozysk* (criminal investigative branch), the OBKhSS (economic crimes branch) and the GAI (automobile division).

The first set of interviewees were located primarily through an advertisement in *Novoe russkoe slovo*, the leading Russian-language émigré newspaper in the United States. The advertisement solicited résumés from former criminal justice personnel, legal advisors at enterprises and arbitrators, informing readers that an American professor in Washington, D.C., was conducting research on the operation of Soviet law and would pay for interviews with émigré Soviet lawyers. No name or telephone number was given in the advertisement; résumés were sent to a postal box in Washington, D.C. Over 40 résumés were received in response to the advertisement. The individuals who responded came from all parts of the Soviet Union and had more diverse experience than the Soviet lawyers the author had initially found through the grapevine. The overwhelming majority of respondents resided in New York, permitting the first round of interviews to be concentrated in that city.

After the success of the advertisement in the United States, a similar advertisement was placed in the leading Israeli émigré newspaper in the

Russian language, *Nasha strana*, two and one-half months prior to the author's planned trip there. The wording of the advertisement was identical to that placed in the United States, except that a special request was made for Soviet lawyers who had worked in Central Asia and the Caucasus. Résumés were again sent to a postal box and then forwarded to the author in the United States. This second advertisement produced over 40 replies from a diverse group of lawyers with experience in all parts of the USSR. Most respondents resided in or near Jerusalem or Tel Aviv, making almost every one easily accessible to the author during her stay in Israel.

The responses to these advertisements came in many forms and revealed much about the individuals who replied. Some provided very detailed résumés; others tried to sell themselves, proclaiming the uniqueness of their information, while still others – obviously hesitant about participating in the project – provided only limited information about themselves. The hesitancy of certain respondents was no doubt due to their doubts about their potential usefulness to the project, concern about the security of family members living in the USSR and skepticism about the scientific value of the research. A few individuals who responded wondered whether the advertisement was some kind of *provokatsiia* (provocation) on the part of either American or Soviet agents – a fact they admitted with amusement after completing the interview. In Israel, where less emphasis is placed on résumés, the information provided by respondents was often sketchier – sometimes written in faint pencil on a postcard. Needless to say, such respondents were not selected for the study.

The offer of pay did not appear to be a strong motivation among the respondents selected for interviews. Many interviewees seemed pleased that their knowledge and time were valued; almost none asked in advance what the payment would be and some even tried to decline compensation for an experience that they found enjoyable. This sharply contrasted with the author's experience with certain former Soviet defense attorneys and procurators located through recommendations, whose agreement to participate in an interview was largely motivated by the prospect of compensation.

The selection of people to be interviewed was a long and careful process. In the United States, a Soviet émigré who could discern more about the personalities and experiences of the respondents than the author was instrumental in the selection process. Those individuals who responded carelessly, appeared motivated primarily by the prospect of financial remuneration or exaggerated their career accomplishments were eliminated. Interviews conducted in 1987 in Israel were arranged by Konstantin Mirozhnik, an experienced researcher knowledgeable about individuals with specialized expertise who had worked previously on several émigré interview projects. He provided invaluable assistance in selecting respondents, as well as arranging and facilitating interviews in Israel.

No matter how careful the selection of interviewees, a bias was nevertheless introduced into the study by using a sample of Jewish émigrés who had chosen three different countries as their permanent place of residence after their emigration from the USSR. Fortunately, subsequent revelations in the Soviet press of the *perestroika* era confirmed much of the information initially obtained from these interviews. The only major difference between the information gleaned from émigré interviews and that provided by the Soviet press was that former Jewish *militsiia* personnel did not feel that a distinct police subculture existed in the former USSR, whereas Soviet literature supported its existence. This discrepancy can perhaps be explained by the fact that Jews were such a minority in the Soviet militia that they may have been excluded from the police community.

THE INTERVIEWEES

Although almost all were Jewish, the interviewees chosen for this study came from very different social, cultural and professional backgrounds. Western, or Ashkenazi, Jews and Sephardic Jews native to Central Asia and the Caucasus were both represented in the sample. Some of these former militia personnel – especially those who emigrated from the Baltic republics – came from privileged merchants' families; others came from the working class. Some had entered policing immediately after high school, while others had chosen a law enforcement path after an earlier, related career.

The individuals interviewed ranged in age from 27 to 77. Together, these individuals possessed over 1,000 years of experience in almost all of the republics of the USSR dating back to the early years of the Stalinist period. The sample contained former militia employees who had worked in major cities as well as in towns and rural settlements. Most of these individuals had experience in specialized areas of policing, such as investigations and vehicular work; a few had conducted daily patrols.

While they were not at the bottom of the police hierarchy, no one in the sample interview group had obtained a rank higher than *militsiia* captain. The presence of only lower- and mid-level personnel in the sample could be expected to invalidate any generalizations about the nature of the Soviet administrative, criminal and civil justice systems drawn from the interviews. Information provided by middle-level personnel was, however, remarkably consistent with that provided by lower echelon personnel and that which appeared in the official police journal, *Sovetskaia militsiia* (a journal that became available to foreigners during the *perestroika* era). The principal difference between information provided by personnel at different levels of the police hierarchy was that higher-placed officials cited cases involving higher-level Party officials; individuals of higher rank were also more aware of and involved in the corruption that pervaded the militia and the MVD.

THE INTERVIEWS

Prior to the interview, most individuals completed a biographical question-naire that solicited information about their nationality, social background, education, Komsomol and Party membership, marital status, work ex-perience, income and reasons for emigration. Most interviewees filled out this form carefully, enabling the author to avoid repetition and to probe more deeply into their experience in the Soviet justice system during the interview session. Interview questions concerned the work conditions and experiences of each former militia employee, examining, among other things, their relationships with fellow workers and the Communist Party. Interviewees were asked to cite specific examples that illustrated the modes of police operations in the USSR and the different influences that affected their work as policemen.

Interviews were conducted in a variety of settings – in the private home of friends or family, an interviewee's home, a hotel room or an office. In general, it was preferable to conduct interviews in the private home of friends or family because such locales assured those being interviewed that the research was academic, not governmental, consequently allowing them to be more forthcoming about their experiences in the militia. When interviews were held in individuals' homes, however, interviewees often became distracted by family members, personal memorabilia and a desire to feed their guest. Despite the gastronomic pleasures, the author's research objectives made her encourage meetings away from interviewees' homes.

All meetings with former Soviet lawyers were preceded by a certain amount of informal discussion about their lives in emigration, sometimes touching upon their lives in the USSR, the nature of the research project and the author's previous residence in the USSR. The author would often then familiarize herself with the information they had provided in the biographical questionnaire (in Israel, not all questionnaires were completed prior to the interview). The conversation would then proceed to questions about in-terviewees' career choices, the nature of their work in the militia and their reasons for emigrating. Interviews were generally tape recorded after par-ticipants signed an agreement with the author that guaranteed them anonym-ity and stipulated that the recording would be made available to the scholarly community only upon receipt of the author's permission. Tape recorded interviews lasted from one and one-half to approximately three and one-half hours. To obtain this amount of taped conversation required a considerably longer duration of time – from one-half to an entire day – due to digressions that were not worth recording or incidents that individuals chose to share with the author off the record. In the few cases where interviews were of longer duration, the author found that participants often became repetitive without imparting much additional information.

The author's research budget permitted the transcription of only a limited number of the interviews. In some cases it was thus possible to work from written texts of interviews, while in others the author simply listened to tapes of the interviews which had been organized and catalogued.

INTERVIEW QUESTIONS

1 What does a militia officer's day look like?
2 What are the main activities of the *detskaia komnata* (children's room)?
3 Are there special problems faced by female militia personnel?
4 To what extent do militia officers carry weapons? To what extent do they use weapons and how strict are the controls over their use?
5 How much is militia work affected by the campaign-style approach employed in other sectors of Soviet life?
6 Is the militia likely to emphasize certain kinds of activities while neglecting others?
7 Do administrative–organizational changes have an effect on the day-to-day activities of the ordinary militiaman?
8 To what extent is the militia involved in domestic conflicts, or to what extent do rank-and-file militiamen choose to avoid such conflicts?
9 How pervasive is the problem of bribery and extortion among the local militia as opposed to members of the militia hierarchy?
10 To what extent do members of the *militsiia* at the local level cooperate with members of the KGB?
11 To what extent do conflicts between the procuracy and the MVD affect the daily operations of militia work and the investigation of criminal activity?
12 Do the periodic infusions of new personnel from the Communist Party and the Komsomol have a noticeable effect on the operation of the *militsiia*?
13 Does the legacy of the Stalinist period impede militia operations?
14 To what extent does the militia receive the necessary cooperation from the citizenry in order to carry out its social order and crime control functions?
15 What is the relationship between the criminal investigative branch (*ugolovnyi rozysk*) and the public order branches of the *militsiia*, such as the *uchastkovyi inspektor*?
16 What kind of housing and other perquisites are provided to the militia?
17 Is it possible to leave the militia? What kind of career opportunities are available to those individuals who leave?
18 Does the militia have its own subculture? How does this subculture manifest itself?
19 Do militiamen have prejudices that affect their operations? What attitudes do militiamen have towards different ethnic groups?
20 What was the ethnic composition and social origin of the militia in your area?
21 What were the different styles of policing employed in different parts of

the urban community? How did urban policing differ from that in rural areas?

22 To what extent did the militia use force on suspects? How has this practice changed since the Stalinist period?

23 What was the relationship between the militia and prostitutes in the community?

24 What was the relationship between the officer on the beat and the supervising officer? How did members of the local militia relate to personnel in the criminal investigative branch (*ugolovnyi rozysk*) and the economic crimes division (OBKhSS)?

25 What were the manifestations of militia stress (i.e., drug use, alcohol, high divorce rates)?

Glossary

administrative organs: the department of the Secretáriat of the Central Committee of the Communist Party of the Soviet Union responsible for overseeing law enforcement; during the *perestroika* era this department was renamed the State and Law Department

Basmachi: Islamic resistance to Soviet rule in Central Asia during the years 1918–22

bezprizornye: homeless youth, a phenomenon that created a recurring law-and-order problem in Soviet society during the early Soviet period, World War II and again during the *perestroika* era

bizhi: individuals without direction

bomzhi: individuals without permanent homes

Cheka: the first name given to the secret police in the Soviet regime, established as a special organ of police repression immediately after the October 1917 revolution (the name "Cheka" is an acronym derived from the first letters of the official Russian name of this organ, the All-Russian Extraordinary Commission); the secret police was subsequently known as the GPU (State Political Administration), OGPU (Unified State Political Administration), NKVD (People's Commissariat of Internal Affairs), and KGB (Committee on State Security)

CPSU: Communist Party of the Soviet Union

dopros: interrogation

doznanie: inquiry

druzhinniki: unpaid auxiliary citizen policemen

GAI: state automobile inspectorate

glasnost': the policy of openness in the Soviet press and mass media under Gorbachev

GOVD: city-level organs of internal affairs

ispolkom: the executive committee, or the lowest-level body of local government

KGB: Committee on State Security, otherwise known as the security police

kharakteristika: a character reference, including an evaluation of an individual's political reliability, required for all employment and for admission to university in the USSR

kolkhoz: collective farm

Komsomol: Communist youth organization

krai: large administrative region, ranked above *oblast'*

kulaks: rich peasants purged under Stalin

militsiia: the name for the regular Soviet police

MOOP: Ministries for the Defense of Public Order (the ministry responsible for the regular and security police during the period 1962–68)

MVD (Ministry of Internal Affairs): the ministry that oversaw the militia in the USSR (it retains its name and function in most former Soviet republics today)

nadzor: administrative surveillance, an additional penalty imposed on released prisoners after their completion of a labor camp sentence; such surveillance placed additional restrictions on the travel and associations of ex-prisoners and was sometimes used to impose a curfew on these individuals

NEP: New Economic Policy, the economic policy that encouraged limited private enterprise pursued by the Soviet government in the period 1921–28

nomenklatura: the system of higher-level appointments in Communist Party organs and the Soviet government; appointments to such positions were subject to Party approval (individuals in the higher levels of the Party apparatus were said to belong to the *nomenklatura*)

NKVD: People's Commissariat of Internal Affairs, a police organ established in 1918 which underwent numerous changes in name and functions until 1948, when it was renamed the Ministry of Internal Affairs (MVD)

OBKhSS: the militia unit assigned to combat the theft of state- and publicly owned property

obkom: *oblast'* committee of the CPSU

oblispolkom: executive committee of the *oblast'* regional government

ochnaia stavka: the one-on-one confrontation between a suspect and a witness during a criminal investigation

OGPU: Unified State Political Administration, the name given to the security police organ established by Soviet law in November 1923; the OGPU was directly associated with the mass repressions connected with the collectivization of Soviet agriculture during the late 1920s and early 1930s; it was absorbed into the NKVD in July 1934

OMON: special-purpose militia detachments first deployed in the USSR in 1988

OVIR: the militia body that issued foreign passports and emigration documents

Pamiat': an anti-Semitic, Russian nationalist organization that came into being during the final years of the Soviet period

parasite: an individual who was not gainfully employed in the USSR; individuals were so defined after receiving three warnings from the militia that they must find employment

perestroika: the policy of economic and political renewal of Soviet society initiated by Communist Party First Secretary Mikhail Gorbachev in the late 1980s

politsiia: the Tsarist police; also the word used by the Soviet regime for police in capitalist societies

prokuratura: the procuracy, probably the most important element of the Soviet legal apparatus, responsible for representing the state in civil and criminal cases and overseeing the observance of law by the courts, the militia and at the workplace

Pravda: the official newspaper of the CPSU Central Committee

pravovoe gosudarstvo: law-based state; the concept of a socialist law-based state was articulated under *perestroika* and envisioned that individuals and institutions in the Soviet system would be subordinate to the law

propiska: the certificate of registration of a citizen's domicile that was an integral part of the internal passport system in the USSR

propusk: a permission form that provided an individual the right to enter a particular installation

raboche-krestiianskaia militsiia: the workers' and peasants' militia established by the Bolshevik regime immediately after the 1917 revolution

raikom: the district committee of the Communist Party

raiispolkom: the executive committee of the urban or rural district government

rezhimnyi goroda: Soviet cities that were closed to new inhabitants

RSFSR: Russian Soviet Federated Socialist Republic

RUKH: the movement for Ukrainian national renewal that became a political force in Ukrainian politics in the late 1980s

samizdat: unofficial writings illegally circulated in the Soviet Union; Soviet citizens were prosecuted for the preparation, possession and/or dissemination of *samizdat* materials

samogonovarenie: home brewing, or the illegal production of alcohol, generally in an individual's home

shabashniki: wildcat workers; individuals who performed temporary work off-budget in various locales without formal contracts

Shariia: traditional Islamic criminal law

soviet: at the local level, an executive body; at the national level (the USSR Supreme Soviet), a legislative body

speculation: the purchase and resale of goods for profit

spetsmilitsiia: a special branch of the militia that served closed institutions and/or cities in the USSR

spetsproduktsiia: special products treated as security items by the Soviet regime

toksimania: dependence on non-traditional addictive substances such as glue

uchastkovyi inspektor: the local district inspector of the militia – the officer on the beat

uchëty: the records kept by the militia on problem individuals in the community with known pasts (e.g., criminals, hooligans, prostitutes, individuals with a history of alcoholism)

ugolovnyi rozysk: the criminal investigative unit of the militia

vedomstvennaia militsiia or *vedomstvennaia okhrana*: the departmental guard, militia units that guarded enterprises and other Soviet institutions

vnevedomstvennaia okhrana: the non-departmental guard, militia units that existed in both civilian and militarized forms

vnutrennye voiska: the internal troops of the Ministry of Internal Affairs

Whites: supporters of the tsarist regime that opposed the Bolsheviks during the Russian Civil War (1918–22); the Whites lost their last footholds in the Far East in 1918, but continued to fight limited battles with the Soviet regime until 1922

Notes

INTRODUCTION

1 Otwin Marenin, "Police Performance and State Rule," *Comparative Politics* 18, no. 1 (1985): 101.
2 On Gorbachev's objectives, see V. Kudriavstev, "Pravo i demokratiia," *Izvestiia*, 4 October 1986. On the social contract between the Soviet state and its citizens, see James R. Millar, "The Social Legacies and the Aftermath of Communism," in *The Social Legacy of Communism*, ed. James R. Millar and Sharon L. Wolchik (Washington, D.C.: Woodrow Wilson Press; and Cambridge, England: Cambridge University Press, 1994); and Robert Sharlet, *Soviet Constitutional Crisis: From De-Stalinization to Disintegration* (Armonk, New York: M.E. Sharpe, 1992), 15–54.
3 Nikolai Popov, "Krizis doveriia – krizis vlasti," *Ogonëk*, no. 7 (1990): 3.
4 Marenin, "Police Performance and State Rule," 102.
5 For a description of the fate of the KGB in the Russian Federation following the dissolution of the USSR, see J. Michael Waller, *Secret Empire: The KGB in Russia Today* (Boulder, Colorado: Westview Press, 1994), ch. 1.
6 For examples of western literature on democratic police forces, see David H. Bayley, *Forces of Order: Police Behavior in Japan and the United States* (Berkeley: University of California Press, 1976) and *Patterns of Policing: A Comparative International Analysis* (New Brunswick, New Jersey: Rutgers University Press, 1985); George E. Berkley, *The Democratic Policeman* (Boston: Beacon Press, 1969); Maureen E. Cain, *Society and the Policeman's Role* (London: Routledge and Kegan Paul, 1973); and Herman Goldstein, *Policing a Free Society* (Cambridge, Massachusetts: Ballanger Publishing Company, 1976).

John Brewer differentiates democratic police from other types of police forces in *The Police, Public Order and the State: Policing in Great Britain, Northern Ireland, the Irish Republic, the USA, Israel, South Africa and China* (New York: St. Martin's Press, 1988).

The only exceptions to western scholars' primary focus on democratic police forces are the significant number of studies of fascist policing, among them Shlomo Aronson, *Beginnings of the Gestapo System: The Bavarian Model in 1933* (Jerusalem: Israel University Press, 1969); Edward Crankshaw, *Gestapo: Instrument of Tyranny* (London: Putnam, 1956); Jacques Delarue, *The Gestapo: A History of Horror* (New York: Morrow, 1964); and Hsi-Huey Liang, *The Rise of Modern Police and the European State System from Metternich to the Second World War* (Cambridge, England, and New York: Cambridge University Press, 1992).

Policing in authoritarian societies of Latin America has yet to be studied extensively and is only now beginning to be of interest to scholars in Brazil, Mexico and Venezuela.

1 THE SOURCES OF SOVIET POLICING

1 David M. Anderson and David Killingray, "Consent, Coercion and Colonial Control: Policing the Empire, 1830–1940," in *Policing the Empire: Government Authority and Control, 1830–1940*, ed. David M. Anderson and David Killingray (Manchester: Manchester University Press, 1991), 1.

2 The Soviet model of policing is extensively analyzed in the theory of totalitarianism. This theory describes a total state in which a single political party imposes a chosen ideology and ensures the perpetuation of its power by failing to provide civil liberties to its citizens, enforcing its will by means of a police apparatus. For a discussion of the attributes of a total, or totalitarian state, see Giuseppe de Vergotinni, *Diritto Costituzionale Comparato* (Padova: Cedam, 1991), 888–9.

3 Valeria Votchal, "The Movement Toward Conflict Management in the Former Soviet Union," *Forum National Institute for Dispute Resolution* (Winter 1993): 19.

4 Jean-Paul Brodeur, "High Policing and Low Policing: Remarks about the Policing of Political Activities," *Social Problems* 30, no. 5 (1985): 512.

5 For a detailed analysis of the continental police tradition, see David H. Bayley, *Patterns of Policing: A Comparative International Analysis* (New Brunswick, New Jersey: Rutgers University Press, 1985); and R.I. Mawby, *Comparative Policing Issues: The British and American Experience in International Perspective* (London: Unwin Hyman, 1990), especially 24–6. On the advent of private policing in the twentieth century, see, for example, Clifford D. Shearing and Philip C. Stenning, *Private Policing* (Newbury Park, California: Sage, 1987).

6 Knut Sveri, "Human Rights and the Right of the Police to Use Physical Force," (paper presented at international Conference on Social Changes, Crime and Police, Eotvos Lorand University, Hungary, 1–4 June 1992).

7 Bayley discusses the difference between specialized and unspecialized police forces and the historical background behind this difference. See Bayley, *Patterns of Policing*, 12.

8 Mawby, *Comparative Policing Issues*, 26–7.

9 ibid., 25, 40.

10 Jean-Paul Brodeur, "Undercover Policing in Canada: Wanting What is Wrong," *Crime, Law, and Society* 18 (1992): 122.

11 For a discussion of the USSR's lack of a legal framework to regulate covert policing, see T. Kolganova, "Nuzhna li nam agentura?" *Sovetskaia militsiia*, no. 1 (1991): 48. Yevgenia Albats, "Shadowy Figures," *Moscow News*, no. 14 (5–12 April 1992), discusses the impotence Soviet citizens felt in the face of the regime's police apparatus.

12 See Brodeur, "Undercover Policing in Canada," 122–3; and Jean-Jacques Rousseau, *The Social Contract and Discourse on the Origin of Inequality* (New York: Washington Square Press, 1967), 55.

13 As quoted by R.I. Mawby in *Comparative Policing Issues*, 26. Mawby cites the 1969 reprint of Fosdick's 1915 monograph: R.B. Fosdick, *European Police Systems* (Montclair, New Jersey: Patterson Smith, 1969).

14 See Donald D. Barry, ed. *Toward the "Rule of Law" in Russia? Political and Legal Reform in the Transition Period* (Armonk, New York: M.E. Sharpe, 1992).

15 See the analysis of this constitution in Paolo Biscaretti di Ruffia and Gabriele

Crespi Reghizzi, *La Costituzione Sovietica del 1977* (Milano: Fott. A. Giuffrè Editore, 1979).

16 Louise Shelley, "Soviet Criminal Law and Justice: Are There or Were There Secrets?" in *The Soviet Sobranie of Laws: Problems of Codification and Non-Publication*, ed. Richard M. Buxbaum and Kathryn Hendley, University of California at Berkeley Research Series, no. 78 (1991): 140–55.

17 For an account of the rise of state paternalism, see B. Chapman, *The Police State* (London: Pall Mall Press, 1970).

18 See Lajos Szamel, "Constitutional State and Security," *Selections from the Former Articles of the Security Review* (Budapest: Security Review of the Home Office, 1992), 18. (Hungary uses the British term "Home Office" to refer to its ministry of internal affairs.)

19 ibid.

20 On the state's assumption of policing duties in the nineteenth century, see Mawby, *Comparative Policing Issues*, 26–7. On state regulation of commerce and industry, see Otwin Marenin, "Police Performance and State Rule," *Comparative Politics* 18, no. 1 (1985).

21 Mawby, *Comparative Policing Issues*, 44, 61.

22 For a description of the attributes of colonial police recruits, see Anderson and Killingray, "Consent, Coercion and Colonial Control," 12.

23 Alec Nove, *The Soviet System in Retrospect: An Obituary Notice*, Fourth Annual Averell Harriman Lecture (New York: Columbia University Press, 1993), 24.

24 Mawby, *Comparative Policing Issues*, 27–9.

25 ibid., 29.

26 See Anderson and Killingray, "Consent, Coercion and Colonial Control," 9. Among the customs outlawed in Central Asia were bride purchase and the kidnapping of an intended bride prior to marriage. The practice of resolving family disputes through the mediation of community leaders in the Central Asian steppes was also suppressed to ensure that no alternative source of legal authority existed outside of the Soviet state.

27 Ronald Weitzer, "Policing Northern Ireland Today," *Political Quarterly* 58, no. 1 (January–March 1987): 89.

28 Mawby, *Comparative Policing Issues*, 40–1.

29 See in particular Book II of Jean-Jacques Rousseau's *The Social Contract* (note 12 above) on the limits on sovereign power.

30 See Charles Donohue, Jr, "Reflections on the Comparative Law of Property," in *Encyclopedia Britannica* (forthcoming).

31 See Votchal, "The Movement Toward Conflict Management," 19.

2 THE FORMATION OF THE MILITIA

1 Rex A. Wade, *Red Guards and Workers' Militias in the Russian Revolution* (Stanford: Stanford University Press, 1984), 40– 1.

2 ". . . 'A takzhe ne eli semechek'," *Sovetskaia militsiia*, no. 4 (1990): 35.

3 M.N. Eropkin, *Razvitie organov militsii v sovetskom gosudarstve* (Moscow: Vysshaia Shkola MOOP, 1967), 12.

4 See Neil Weissman, "Policing the New Order: The Soviet Militsiia, 1917–1928" (paper presented at the sixteenth annual meeting of the American Association for the Advancement of Slavic Studies, New York, 1984), 19.

5 ibid.; and Neil Weissman, "Regular Police in Tsarist Russia, 1900–1914," *The Russian Review* 44 (1985): 45–68.

6 For a description of additional volunteer militia duties in the early postrevolutionary period, see Eropkin, *Razvitie organov militsii*, 15–16.

7 ibid., 11–12, documents the joint policing efforts of the Red Army and the Red Guard.
8 On the attempted suppression of anarchist groups in Moscow, see ibid., 111–13. On the Tambov uprising, see Wade, *Red Guards and Workers' Militias*, 308.
9 Weissman, "Policing the New Order," 8.
10 ibid., 8.
11 The congress was a meeting of the *gubispolkomy*, or executive committees of the *gubernii*. In the early post-revolutionary period, the country was divided into *gubernii*, as it had been during the Tsarist period. (*Gubernii* were roughly equivalent to states in administrative status.) They were later abolished in the Soviet period and replaced by *oblasti*, which were slightly smaller in size. For the resolution adopted by the congress, see Eropkin, *Razvitie organov militsii*, 17–18. See also S. V. Bilenko, *Sovetskaia militsiia Rossii (1917–1930)* (Moscow: Akademiia MVD SSSR, 1976), 24–5.
12 David H. Bayley, *Forces of Order: Police Behavior in Japan and the United States* (Berkeley: University of California Press, 1976), 35.
13 See Eropkin, *Razvitie organov militsii*, 19.
14 Robert Conquest, *The Soviet Police System* (New York: Praeger, 1968), 30.
15 On the duties of the newly created criminal investigative branch, see Eropkin, *Razvitie organov militsii*, 20. A special unit also existed in the militia to fight banditry; see V. Polubinskii, "Georgii Tylner," *Sovetskaia militsiia*, no. 11 (1990): 38. On the control of speculation, see N. Panchenko, ". . . I vsiudu merkantilynyi dukh," *Sovetskaia militsiia*, no. 5 (1991): 39. For a discussion of the role criminal law played in the socialist economy, see A. Malygin, "Kak poiavilos' postanovlenie o militsii?" *Sovetskaia militsiia*, no. 9 (1990): 35.
16 On the formation of the departmental guard, see Malygin "Kak poiavilos' postanovlenie," 20, 31. On the merger with the NKVD, see ibid., 44.
17 See Weissman, "Policing the New Order," 8. In the early 1920s, 35 percent of the militia in Moscow was drawn from the working class, whereas in Siberia the figure was only 10 percent, with the rest coming from peasant backgrounds. In Saratov, 30 percent of militia personnel were demobilized soldiers. See Bilenko, *Sovetskaia militsiia Rossii*, 45.
18 A. Malygin and M. Misailov, "Munitsipal'naia i federal'naia militsiia," *Sovetskaia militsiia*, no.4 (1991): 10.
19 Bilenko, *Sovetskaia militsiia Rossii*, 45–6.
20 V. Maksimov, *Sluzhba postovogo militsionera* (Moscow: NKVD, 1925), 8–9, 34–5.
21 On the initiation of basic educational programs, see ibid., 47–8. V. Polubinskii notes that the first head of the militia criminal investigative unit (UR) was subsequently transferred to the Cheka in "Shit i mech pravoporiadka," *Agitator*, no. 20 (1987): 23–5.
22 Eropkin, *Razvitie organov militsii*, 40.
23 Neil Weissman, "Prohibition and Alcohol Control in the USSR: The 1920s Campaign Against Illegal Spirits," *Soviet Studies* 38, no. 3 (1986): 361.
24 See Weissman, "Policing the New Order," 12–15.
25 ibid., 8.
26 On the goals of early militia training programs, see N.I. Timofeev, "Deiatel'nost' kommunisticheskoi partii Ukrainy po obucheniiu kadrov militsii respubliki," *Trudy Kievskoi vysshei shkoly*, no. 9 (1975): 10. The Byelorussian statistics are cited in Eropkin, *Razvitie organov militsii*, 37–44.
27 Eropkin, *Razvitie organov militsii*, 16. See also Peter H. Solomon, "Criminal-ization and De-Criminalization in Soviet Criminal Policy," *Law and Society Review* 16, no. 1 (1981– 82): 16–17.
28 Weissman, "Policing the New Order," 16–17.

29 On the duties of the transport militia, see N.A. Shchelokov, *Sovetskaia militsiia* (Moscow: Znanie, 1971), 64.

30 Robert Conquest, *The Soviet Police System* (New York: Praeger, 1968), 13.

31 David H. Bayley, *Patterns of Policing: A Comparative International Analysis* (New Brunswick, New Jersey: Rutgers University Press, 1985), 205. On the use of the militia in the Civil War, see *Sputnik krasnogo militsionera* (Moscow: Zagotkhoza militsii respubliki, 1924), 3. For a discussion of the Central Asian situation, see A.M. Mukhamedov, *Slavnyi put'* (Askhabad: Turkmenistan, 1965), 33–71; T.A. Dzalilov, *Stranitsy istorii militsii Khorezma i Bukhary* (Tashkent: Uzbekistan, 1970), 16–70; Ia. Motylev and E. Lysenko, *Soldaty poriadka* (Dushanbe: Efron, 1967), 37–40; T. Dzalilov, *Vernye otchizne* (Tashkent: Uzbekistan 1968), 68–119.

32 See Center for Research on Criminal Justice, *The Iron Fist and the Velvet Glove*, 2d ed. (Berkeley: Center for Research on Criminal Justice, 1977), 28–30. For an extensive treatment of this topic, see, for example, Sidney L. Harring, *Policing a Class Society: The Experience of American Cities, 1865–1915* (New Brunswick: Rutgers University Press, 1983); and Wilbur Miller, *Cops and Bobbies: Police Authority in New York and London, 1830–1970* (Chicago: University of Chicago Press, 1977).

33 See Eropkin, *Razvitie organov militsii*, 28, 30.

34 David M. Anderson and David Killingray, "Consent, Coercion and Colonial Control: Policing the Empire, 1830–1940," in *Policing the Empire: Government, Authority and Control, 1830–1940*, ed. David M. Anderson and David Killingray (Manchester: Manchester University Press, 1991), 2.

35 Dzalilov, *Vernye otchizne*, 55–6.

36 Anderson and Killingray, "Consent, Coercion and Colonial Control," 7.

37 Dzalilov, *Stranitsy istorii militsii*, 13–14.

38 See Gregory J. Massell, *The Surrogate Proletariat: Moslem Women and Revolutionary Strategies in Soviet Central Asia, 1919–1929* (Princeton: Princeton University Press, 1974); and Louise Shelley, "Female Criminality in the 1920s: A Consequence of Inadvertent and Deliberate Change," *Russian History* 9, pt. 3 (1982): 265–84.

39 Massell, *The Surrogate Proletariat*, 14.

40 See P. F. Nikolaev, *Omskaia militsiia v pervye gody sovetskoi vlasti (1917–1923)* (Omsk: Arkhivnyi otdel UVD ispolkoma Omskogo oblastnogo soveta deputatov trudiashchikhsiia, 1959), 42–9; and idem, *Sovetskaia militsiia Sibiri (1917–1922)* (Omsk: Zapadno-sibirskoe knizhnoe izdatel'stvo, 1967), 228–53.

41 Weissman, "Prohibition and Alcohol Control in the USSR," 349–68.

42 Peter Juviler, *Revolutionary Law and Order* (New York: Free Press, 1976), 26.

43 ibid.

44 See Nikolaev, *Omskaia militsiia*, 66–8, for a discussion of materials relating to grain requisitions, located in the Omsk state archives.

45 Conquest notes, "By 1931, the militia in the USSR were organized in Chief Administrations under the Councils of People's Commissars of the Union Republics, with local militia organs still in dual subordination" (Conquest, *The Soviet Police System*, 31).

46 See ibid., 16; and Merle Fainsod, *How Russia Is Ruled*, rev. ed. (Cambridge: Harvard University Press, 1970), 452–3.

47 Conquest, *The Soviet Police System*, 18.

48 See, for example, Hannah Arendt, *The Origins of Totalitarianism* (New York: Harcourt Brace Jovanovich, 1979); and C.J. Friedrich and Zbigniew Brzezinski, *Totalitarian Dictatorship and Autocracy* (Cambridge, Massachusetts: Harvard University Press, 1965).

49 Fainsod, *How Russia is Ruled*, 73.
50 ibid.
51 See G. Shelud'ko, *Sovetskaia militsiia na strazhe obshchestvennogo poriadka* (Kiev: Vishcha shkola, 1982), 23.
52 V. Nekrasov, "Nikolai Ezhov," *Sovetskaia militsiia*, no. 2 (1990): 21–2.
53 Ronald Hingley, *The Russian Secret Police* (London: Hutchinson, 1970), 188.
54 V. Nekrasov, "Sergei Kruglov," *Sovetskaia militsiia*, no. 5 (1990): 18.
55 See Hingley, *The Russian Secret Police*, 202.
56 Nekrasov, "Sergei Kruglov," 22.
57 V. Nekrasov, "Lavrentii Beriia," *Sovetskaia militsiia*, no. 3 (1990): 18–24 and no. 4 (1990): 40–6.
58 V. Nekrasov, "Nikolai Dudurov," *Sovetskaia militsiia*, no. 6 (1990): 18.
59 See Smolensk Archives, WPK #90 and #351.
60 Among the works that document the role of the army and the Cheka in collectivization, see especially Robert Conquest, *The Harvest of Sorrow* (New York: Oxford University Press, 1986).
61 G.A. Bogomolov *et al.*, *Vekhi trudnykh budnei* (Saratov: Privolzhskoe knizhnoe izdatel'stvo, 1963), 53.
62 Smolensk Archives, WPK #93, provides this information in the notes of an NKVD meeting. On intensified political education of militiamen during collectivization, see Bogomolov *et al.*, *Vekhi trudnykh budnei*, 52.
63 As quoted in Cronid Lubarsky, "On the Soviet Passport System," *Papers on Soviet Law*, no. 3 (1981): 43.
64 For the decree that reestablished the passport system, see "On The Establishment of a Unified Passport System and Compulsory Registration of Passports," *Sobor zakonov SSSR*, 1932, no. 84, item 516.

   B.M. Babiia, *Sovetskii zakon i grazhdanin* (Kiev: Naukov dumka, 1980), 107, cites justifications for reintroducing the system. On repeat violations of passport laws, see N.A. Apiian, *Na strazhe pravoporiadka i zakonnosti* (Erevan: Izdatel'stvo Erevanskogo universiteta, 1979), 132–3.
65 "Moscow Youth Paper's Article on Camps Described," Foreign Broadcast Information Service, *Daily Report: Soviet Union*, 3 March 1988, Annex, 9.
66 Anderson and Killingray, "Consent, Coercion and Colonial Control," 6.
67 Merle Fainsod, *Smolensk Under Soviet Rule* (Cambridge: Harvard University Press, 1958), 195–209.
68 On the use of militiamen in World War II, see I.M. Logivenenko, "Uchastie rabotnikov militsii v velikoi otechestvennoi voine," *Trudy Kievskoi vysshei shkoly*, no. 9 (1975): 15; and D. Skiliagin *et al.*, *Dela i liudi Leningradskoi militsii* (Leningrad: Lenizdat, 1967), 181. Citizen complaints about the militia during the war are cited in Eropkin, *Razvitie organov militsii*, 67–8.
69 Logivenenko, "Uchastie rabotnikov militsii," 18–19.
70 See Hingley, *The Russian Secret Police*, 184–6.
71 In many areas criticism of the militia during the *perestroika* era was more verbal than physical. In Moldavia, however, physical abuse predominated.
72 Logivenenko, "Uchastie rabotnikov militsii," 18.
73 ibid., 19.
74 Hingley, *The Russian Secret Police*, 204.
75 Clive Emsley, *Policing and Its Context, 1750–1870* (New York: Schocken Books, 1983), 114.
76 See Robert Reiner, "The Politicization of the Police in Britain", in *Control in the Police Organization*, ed. Maurice Punch (N.Y.: Paul Mall Press, 1970), 143.
77 Brian Chapman, *The Police State* (London: Pall Mall Press, 1970), 114.
78 See ibid., 115, for Chapman's definition of the general mandate of the police.

3 THE POST-STALINIST MILITIA

1 Charles Reith, as cited in George E. Berkley, *The Democratic Policeman* (Boston: Beacon Press, 1969), 18.
2 See the statement of A.M. Iakovlev on the law of the Stalinist period in "Kakim dolzhno byt' pravovoe gosudarstvo?" *Literaturnaia Gazeta*, 6 June 1988.
3 Robert Conquest, *Power and Policy in the USSR: The Study of Soviet Dynastics* (New York: St. Martin's Press; and London: MacMillan, 1961), 440–7.
4 ibid., 212–17.
5 Nikolai Zhusenin, "History Club: Some Episodes from a Criminal Life," *Nedelia* (22–28 February 1988), as cited in "Lavrentiy Beria's Crimes, Arrest Recounted," Foreign Broadcast Information Service, *Daily Report: Soviet Union* (hereafter FBIS, *Daily Report*), 2 March 1988, 60.
6 Rachel A. Connell, "New Evidence on Beria's Downfall," Cold War International History Project Bulletin 1 (Spring 1992): 17.
7 See "History Club," 61.
8 V. Nekrasov, "Sergei Kruglov," *Sovetskaia militsiia*, no. 5 (1990): 18–26. This chapter relies heavily on several articles written by Nekrasov, an employee of the USSR Ministry of Internal Affairs who had privileged access to the ministry's archives during the *perestroika* years. The author has no reason to doubt the accuracy of Nekrasov's information, but must note that, as of the writing of this book, independent scholars have yet to verify this information in the MVD archives.
9 See V. Nekrasov, "Nikolai Dudurov," *Sovetskaia militsiia*, no. 6 (1990): 17–25, in which he cited Dudurov's memoirs.
10 See Amy W. Knight, *The KGB: Police and Politics in the Soviet Union* (New York: Allen & Unwin, 1988), 48.
11 Barbara Raffel Price, *Police Professionalism* (Lexington, Massachusetts: D.C. Heath, 1977), 23–56.
12 See Robert Reiner, *The Politics of the Police* (New York: St. Martin's Press, 1985), 4.
13 The 1962 statute on the *militsiia* was not published, but circulated to a limited audience in *Spravochnik po zakonodatel'stvu dlia rabotnikov organov prokuratury, suda i ministerstva vnutrennykh del*, Vol. 2, pt. 1 (Moscow: Iuridicheskaia literatura, 1971), 304–11.
14 Nekrasov, "Nikolai Dudurov," 18.
15 ibid.
16 See "N.R. Mironov Reviews Reformation of Soviet Punitive Agencies; Stalin and Vyshinskiy Blamed for Past Abuses," *Survey of the Soviet Press* (hereafter *SSP*), no. 351 (13 March 1964): 10; and Conquest, *The Soviet Police System*, 24–5. The executive committee (*ispolkom*), or chief executive organ, of *oblasti* and *kraiia* oversaw these administrations of internal affairs. In towns and districts, militia departments were subordinate to the respective *ispolkom* of the town or *raion*. (*Oblast-* and *krai*-large regions – administrative subdivisions below that of a union republic – ranked above the *raion*, or district, subdivision.)
17 Nekrasov, "Nikolai Dudurov," 25.
18 V. Nekrasov, "Vadim Tikunov," *Sovetskaia militsiia*, no. 8 (1990): 20–1.
19 ibid., 22–4.
20 Nekrasov, "Vadim Tikunov," 30.
21 Nekrasov, "Nikolai Dudurov," 19.
22 See, for example, "RSFSR Militia Interviewed on Drive Against Using Bread as Livestock Feed", *SSP* 278 (1 October 1962): 24–5; "RSFSR Ukase Stipulates 3-Year Minimum Sentence for Feeding Bread to Livestock," *SSP* 311 (27 May

1963): 66–7; and "RSFSR Deputy Prosecutor Calls for Legal Crackdown on All Thefts and Waste of Grain Products," *SSP* 334 (1 November 1963): 76–9.

23 See Harold Berman, *Justice in the USSR*, rev. ed. (Cambridge, Mass.: Harvard University Press, 1982), 291–8. The parasite laws were later applied by the militia against such dissidents as the great poet Iosif Brodsky in 1964.

24 See ibid., 285–98.

25 Nekrasov, "Nikolai Dudurov," 24.

26 Some criminal elements masked their criminal activity by joining the *druzhinniki*. See, for example, "'Crude' Actions by Volunteer Guardsmen in Arkhangelsk Scored," *SSP* 162 (27 June 1960): 20–4.

27 See, for example, "Previous 'Softness' Toward Three Killers Brings Dismissal of Militia Workers," *SSP* 88 (19 January 1959): 41–2; "Hooligans in Riga Find 'Tenderhearted' Public Defenders; Militia Department Rebuked for 'Liberalism' and 'Spinelessness' in Launching Investigations," *SSP* 225 (18 September 1961): 60–1; and "Moscow City Police Chief Fired as Failure," *SSP* 273 (27 August 1962): 42.

28 "'Izvestiya' Reassures Skeptical Readers that Militia is Still in Good Graces Despite Press Criticism," *SSP* 282 (29 October 1962): 47.

29 See Amy Knight, "Soviet Politics and the KGB–MVD Relationship," *Soviet Union* 11 (1984): 163–4.

30 "Party and Government Decree Aimed at Improving Work of Militia; 'Soviet Militia Day' to be Observed Annually," *SSP* 280 (15 October 1962): 13.

31 V. Nekrasov, "Nikolai Shchelokov," *Sovetskaia militsiia*, no. 9 (1990): 15–16.

32 Knight, "Soviet Politics and the KGB–MVD Relationship," 157–81.

33 "'Brezhnev's Special Favour' Protected Corrupt," British Broadcasting Corporation Monitoring, *Summary of World Broadcasts: USSR* (hereafter BBC Monitoring, *SWB: USSR*), SU/0144, 6 May 1988, B/1.

34 In 1969, criminal charges were brought against 300 ministry personnel; in the following six months, cases were initiated against an additional 260. See Nekrasov, "Nikolai Shchelokov," 17.

35 Peter Kruzhin, "Political Organs Created in the MVD," *Radio Liberty Research Bulletin*, 30 December 1983.

36 Nekrasov, "Vadim Tikunov," 17, 24.

37 See "Polozhenie o sovetskoi militsii," adopted by the USSR Council of Ministers on 8 June 1973, published in *Svod Zakonov SSSR*, Vol. 10, no. 385, 236–47.

38 See note 13 above for a discussion of the publication of the 1962 statute.

39 See G.P. Shelud'ko, *Sovetskaia militsiia na strazhe obshchestvennogo poriadka* (Kiev: Vishcha shkola, 1982), 23.

40 Nekrasov, "Nikolai Shchelokov," 18.

41 See, for example, Liudmila Alekseeva, *Istoriia inakomysliia v SSSR* (Benson, Vermont: Khronika Press, 1984).

42 See Peter H. Juviler, *Revolutionary Law and Order* (New York: Free Press, 1976), 103.

43 On militia surveillance of so-called "parasites," see L.N. Gusev and A.A. Bakhitov, "O rezultatakh sotsiologicheskikh issledovaniia o retsidivistov i drugikh otkloniashikh ot sotsial'nogo poleznogo truda," *Informatsionnye soobshcheniia VNIIOP pri MOOP*, no. 35 (1971). On the immunity of Communist Party members, the militia could not investigate Party members for criminal offenses without the permission of the relevant Party organization.

44 For information on procedural improvements under Brezhnev, see Nekrasov, "Nikolai Shchelokov," especially 17–19.

45 Samuel Walker, *Popular Justice: A History of American Criminal Justice* (New York: Oxford University Press, 1980), 61.

46 "Georgian TV, Radio Chief Denounces Corruption, Unequal Law Enforcement,"

Joint Publications Research Service, *USSR Report* (hereafter JPRS, *USSR Report*), 10 December 1982, 54. For a later account of the same problem, see Nikolai Popov, "Krizis doveriia – krizis vlasti," *Ogonëk*, no. 7 (1990): 2–4.

47 "Vlasov writes on Perestroyka, Crime Rate," Moscow TASS, as cited in FBIS, *Daily Report*, 5 April 1988, 48. On the initiation of the Andropov anti-corruption campaign in the early 1980s, see Elizabeth Teague, "Andropov Cleans up the Militia," *Radio Liberty Research Bulletin*, 9 November 1983, 3; and "The Police and Openness," *Current Digest of the Soviet Press* (hereafter *CDSP*) 39, no. 52 (1988): 25. (The latter source translates a Soviet article published in 1988 that revealed new information about the campaign.)

48 "V Politburo Tsk KPSS," *Pravda*, 11 December 1982.

49 Kruzhin, "Political Organs Created in the MVD," 3.

50 On Fedorchuk's appointment, see Nekrasov, "Nikolai Shchelokov," 22. Knight, *The KGB*, 89, discusses his previous service in the KGB.

51 "Vsesoiuznoe soveshchanie," *Pravda*, 26 January 1983, 2.

52 See N. Kipman, "O kompetentnosti i professionalizme," *Sovetskaia militsiia*, no.4 (1990): 22.

53 Dismissals of MVD personnel in 1983 are documented in A. Vlasov, "Na strazhe pravoporiadka," *Kommunist*, no. 5 (1988), 47. On the link between corruption in trade organizations and the militia, see M. Vidov, "'Khoziain goroda,'" *Sovetskaia militsiia*, no. 9 (1990): 39.

54 Nekrasov, "Nikolai Shchelokov," 21–2.

55 ibid.

56 For a review of the charges against Churbanov and his associates, see Nataliya Gevorkyan, "On the Eve of the Trial," *Moscow News*, no. 36 (1988); and Victor Loshak, "Churbanov, Yakhyayev and Others," *Moscow News*, no. 37 (1988), 4. Dmitrii Likhanov, "Koma," *Ogonëk*, nos. 1–4 (1989), provides an analysis of the trial and its role in the anti-Brezhnev campaign. For specifics of the sentencing, see Michael Dobbs, "Brezhnev Kin Jailed for 12 Years," *Washington Post*, 31 December 1988; and Aleksandr Borin, "Eshchë raz o 'Churbanovskom prot-sesse,'" *Literaturnaia gazeta*, 8 March 1989. Arkady Vaksberg, *The Soviet Mafia* (New York: St. Martin's Press, 1991), 127, discusses the interest the trial held for the Soviet population.

57 Kruzhin, "Political Organs Created in the MVD," 6–7.

58 In 1986, Gorbachev replaced Kunaev, the ethnic Kazakh First Party Secretary of Kazakhstan, with a Russian. The appointment resulted in mass protests un-anticipated by Gorbachev.

59 February 1990 interview with a scholar from the Institute of State and Law, Moscow, who worked closely with the MVD during this period.

60 See Knight, "Soviet Politics and the KGB–MVD Relationship," 180; and Kruzhin, "Political Organs Created in the MVD."

61 On the reduction of police divisions, see "Strict Reckoning," *Literaturnaia gazeta*, 29 August 1984. On the restructuring of police patrols, see V.V. Fedorchuk, "Militia Day Address," Soviet television, 10 November 1983, as reported in BBC Monitoring, *SWB: USSR*, SU/7491, 10 November 1983, B/1.

62 See "MVD Official Discusses New Structural Measures," FBIS, *Daily Report*, 7 April 1988, 44, for a discussion of the adverse press coverage of militia activities. At the time, most accounts of bribe-taking concerned payoffs to militiamen by black market traders and cooperative owners.

63 See, for example, O. Utitsin, "Prestizh militseiskikh pogon," *Leninskoe znamia*, 8 September 1988.

64 See V. Zimin, "O bednom OMONe zamolvite slovo," *Iuridicheskaia gazeta*, no. 15 (1991), for a discussion of Lithuanian and Latvian investigations of OMON activities in these republics during the late Gorbachev era.

65 See "Interior Minister Interviewed by Yugoslav Journal," FBIS, *Political Affairs Report*, 1 July 1988. Vlasov had been a member of the Central Committee since 1981. He began his career as first Party secretary of Irkutsk *oblast'* at the age of 29 and then became an inspector of the CPSU Central Committee. After a stint on the staff of the Central Committee, he assumed the post of first Party secretary of Rostov *oblast'*, the fifth largest in the USSR.

66 See "Fedorchuk Assigned to Soviet Army Inspectorate," FBIS, *Daily Report*, 11 March 1986, S1.

67 Yuri Feofanov, "Mob Wars," *Moscow News*, no. 44 (1988).

68 Conversation with militia officers in Moscow, October 1989.

69 See, for example, "'Vzgylad' Shows Attack on Liberal Writers," *RFE/RL Daily Report*, 29 January 1990.

70 See Killingray and Anderson, 9.

71 See Mikhail Belikov *et al.*, "Not to be Repeated," *Moscow News*, no. 17 (1989).

72 See, for example, "Secession Proclaimed in Moldavia's Eastern Area," *RFE/RL Daily Report*, 4 September 1990; and "Estonian MVD Chief on Ministry's Role," FBIS, *Daily Report*, 13 August 1990.

73 See "New Latvian Minister of Internal Affairs," *RFE/RL Daily Report*, 14 May 1990.

74 See November 1990 draft law of the Estonian Republic, "On the Police," Russian translation (author's archive); and "Moldavia to Create Depoliticized Republican Police," *RFE/RL Daily Report*, 6 December 1990, 7.

75 See "Bakatin Supports Baltic Independence," *RFE/RL Daily Report*, 19 February 1991, 4.

76 See "Conference on Internal Political Organisation of the MVD," BBC Monitoring, *SWB: USSR*, SU/0142, 4 May 1988, B/5; Francis X. Clines, "Moscow Victors Act to Promote Freer Markets," *New York Times*, 22 March 1990. The goal of removing Party influence from the police was not limited to democratic activists; it was also an issue in numerous strikes in the late *perestroika* era. A major demand of striking Kievan workers in July 1990, for example, was the depoliticization of the militia. See *Glasnost in Jeopardy: Human Rights in the USSR*, A Helsinki Watch Report (New York and Washington, D.C.: Human Rights Watch, 1991), 50.

77 "Political Organs to be Disbanded in the MVD," *RFE/RL Daily Report*, 21 March 1990.

78 "Depoliticization in Uzbek Town," *RFE/RL Daily Report*, 27 July 1990, documents the resistance this process met in certain militia organizations. For an account of the divisive nature of the issue among militia personnel themselves, see "O Partii i politorganakh," *Sovetskaia militsiia*, no. 6 (1990): 7.

79 "Nashi liudi v parlamente," *Sovetskaia militsiia*, no. 4 (1990): 9.

80 For the 1989 figures, see Joseph Serio, ed. and trans., *USSR Crime Statistics and Summaries, 1989 and 1990*, Vol. 1 (Chicago: Office of International Criminal Justice, University of Illinois at Chicago, 1992), 47. For the 1990 figures, see B. Vasil'ev and A. Pokrovskii, "Politupravlenie zakryto. Nuzhen novyi 'vospitatel,'" *Izvestiia*, 15 December 1990.

81 See "Ryzhkov Announces Measures to Strengthen Law and Order," *RFE/RL Daily Report*, 15 October 1990, 3.

82 Bill Keller, "Gorbachev Given Direct Authority Over his Cabinet," *Washington Post*, 26 December 1990.

83 See Michael Dobbs, "Gorbachev Ousts Minister of Interior," *Washington Post*, 3 December 1990.

84 David Remnick, "KGB Given Powers Over Businesses," *Washington Post*, 27 January 1991.

85 On joint army–militia patrols, see Serge Schmemann, "Kremlin's Troops to Join

Police on Patrol in Major Soviet Cities," *New York Times*, 26 January 1991; and Francis X. Clines, "Soviets Increase Patrols by Army, Extending Crackdown to 86 Cities," *New York Times*, 6 February 1991. On the deployment of OMON troops, see "More Military Units Sent into Moldavia," *RFE/RL Daily Report*, 15 March 1991, 5; and "Discussions Held, But Results Unclear," *RFE/RL Daily Report*, 4 January 1991, 3. On the substantial increase in government funding for the militia during this period, see "MVD Budget Increased," Radio Free Europe/ Radio Liberty, *Soviet/East European Report* 8, no. 34 (10 June 1991): 4.

86 For a contemporary account of the coup, see Bill Keller, "Old Guard's Last Gasp," *New York Times*, 22 August 1991.

87 "Dunayev Speaks on Militia's Role," FBIS, *Daily Report*, 10 September 1991, 76–8.

88 "KGB's 'Supersecret Spetznaz' Functions Viewed," FBIS, *Daily Report*, 18 September 1991, 24.

89 Keller, "Old Guard's Last Gasp."

90 The transfer of responsibilities from the USSR to the RSFSR MVD began well in advance of the formation of the Commonwealth of Independent States. For example, Russian President Yeltsin issued a decree on 20 October 1991 that ordered all internal security troops of the USSR located on Russian territory to be transferred to Russian jurisdiction. See "O vnutrennykh voiskakh MVD RSFSR," *Vedomosti s"ezda narodnykh deputatov RSFSR i Verkhognogo Soveta RSFSR*, no.46 (1991): item 1564.

91 Eric H. Monkkonen, *Police in Urban America, 1860–1920* (Cambridge: Cambridge University Press, 1981).

92 Although dramatic, the kind of structural realignment and recruitment policies needed to restore militia credibility in the USSR in the late 1980s proved possible in the United States, where the nature of policing underwent profound change following the race riots and anti-war demonstrations of the 1960s.

4 THE ORGANIZATION AND MANAGEMENT OF SOVIET POLICING

1 David H. Bayley, *Patterns of Policing* (New Brunswick, New Jersey: Rutgers University Press, 1985), 69.

2 The VV (*vnutrennye voiska*) combined the functions of the American national guard and marshall service and was also responsible for certain functions relating to the maintenance of social order.

3 A.E. Lunev, *Upravlenie v oblasti administrativno–politicheskoi deiatel'nosti* (Moscow: Iuridicheskaia literatura, 1979), 130.

4 See I. Zeldes, "The History and Organization of Police in the USSR" (paper presented at the annual meeting of the Academy of Criminal Justice Sciences, 1985).

5 Lunev, *Upravlenie*, 128–30.

6 "Militsiia," in *Iuridicheskii entsiklopedicheskii slovar'*, ed. A.Ia. Sukharev (Moscow: Sovetskaia entsiklopedia, 1984), 174–5.

7 See, for example, V. Rudnev and S. Mostovshchikov, "'K' upalo, 'G' – propalo, kto ostalsiia v KGB?," *Izvestiia*, 29 December, 1991; and "Yeltsin Dismisses Security, Interior Officials," Foreign Broadcast Information Service, *Daily Report: Soviet Union* (hereafter, FBIS, *Daily Report*), 21 January 1992, 49.

8 See Lunev, *Upravlenie*, 131.

9 ibid., 69.

10 N.A. Shchelokov, *Sovetskaia militsiia* (Moscow: Znanie, 1971), 65.

11 A. Vlasov, "Na strazhe pravoporiadka," *Kommunist*, no. 5 (1988): 48.

12 On staffing and militia subunits at the municipal level, see V.G. Kutushev, *Sotsial'noe planirovanie v organakh vnutrennykh del* (Saratov: Izdatel'stvo Saratovskogo universiteta, 1983), 51. At levels of the militia bureaucracy above that of the city, one deputy was responsible for political affairs, which included relations with the Communist Party apparatus and the KGB.

13 "Moscow Vice," text of "48 Hours" (New York: CBS News broadcast, 30 May 1990).

14 See Kutushev, *Sotsial'noe planirovanie*, 70, for information on militia staffing in rural areas. The work of precinct inspectors is explored in some detail in chapters 7 and 8.

15 Classified analysis of crime reports was carried out by the Ministry of Internal Affairs, which collected materials not only from the militia, but from the GAI and the fire service. See *Papers on Soviet Law*, vol. 3, ed. Leon Lipson and Valery Chalidze (New York: Institute of Socialist Law, 1981), 63–131.

16 Closed institutions and cities in the USSR were those in which highly classified scientific research, often with military applications, was conducted. Individuals working in such institutions were limited in their personal associations and such cities were, as a rule, closed to foreigners – some were even closed to other Soviet citizens.

   Spetssudy, or "special courts," had jurisdiction over the cases of individuals living in closed cities. For more information on *spetssudy*, see Moscow Helsinki Work Group, *Document 75: A Chronicle of Human Rights in the USSR*, no. 33 (January–March 1979): 44–5; and G. van den Berg, "Special Courts in the USSR: Their Nature and Activities," *Review of Socialist Law* 8, no. 3 (1982): 237–50.

17 For information on the number of departmental guard employees, see V. Yasmann, "The Power of the Soviet Internal Security Forces," Radio Free Europe/Radio Liberty, *Report on the USSR* (hereafter RFE/RL, *Report on the USSR*), 26 October 1990, 13.

   The original statute issued upon the creation of this guard was published as *Polozhenie o vedomstvennoi militsii i instruksiia o poriadke ee organizatsii i deiatel'nosti*, ed. I.F. Kiselev (Moscow: Izdatel'stvo NKVD, 1929). The sub-sequent militia statute which governed the work of this force can be found in *Sovetskoe administrativnoe pravo* (Moscow: Iuridicheskaia literatura, 1981), 390. For documentation on where the departmental guard was employed in Moscow, see Shchelokov, *Sovetskaia militsiia*, 66–7.

18 Discussion of the military units of the extra-departmental guard are conspicuously absent from Soviet police literature.

19 Responsibilities of the extra-departmental guard are outlined in a resolution of the USSR Council of Ministers dated 18 February 1966. See "Model Statute on Extra-Departmental Guards attached to the *Militsiia*", in *Spravochnik po zakonodatel'stvu dlia rabotnikov organov prokuratury, suda i ministerstva vnutrennykh del*, vol. 2 (Moscow: Iuridicheskaia literatura, 1971), 404–11. This guard was not bound to a single installation; its mandate included inspecting the work of the departmental guards, reviewing protective measures of consumer cooperatives and other rural organizations, as well as providing the latter with technical assistance. On its work protecting churches during the *perestroika* era, see "Militia work in protecting property and combating theft of alcohol," British Broadcasting Corporation Monitoring, *Summary of World Broadcasts: USSR* (hereafter BBC, *SWB: USSR*), SU/0141, 3 May 1988, B/4.

20 "Internal Troops to Retain Central Command," *RFE/RL Daily Report*, 23 November 1990, 6.

21 ibid.

22 On the 1990 expansion of the internal troops, see Yasmann, "the Power of the Soviet Internal Security Forces," 14. Their deployment in various hot spots of

ethnic tension is documented by, among others, "MVD Troops Role Viewed," FBIS, *Daily Report*, 8 November 1990, 80–81; "MVD General on Role of Internal Troops," *RFE/RL Daily Report*, 14 June 1991, 6; and "Situation Tense at Latvia's Press Building," *RFE/RL Daily Report*, 4 January 1991, 3.

23 See Harold J. Berman, *Soviet Criminal Law and Procedure: The RSFSR Codes*, 2d ed. (Cambridge, Mass.: Harvard University Press, 1972), 84.

24 See ibid., 241–2, for the legislation passed in the early 1960s. L.A. Bykov and G.A. Kvelidze, *Prokurorskii nadzor za ispolneniem zakonov v deiatel'nosti organov doznaniia i predvaritel'nogo sledstviia MVD* (Tbilisi: Sabchota sakartvelo, 1975), 3, document the change effected by the 1965 law. Article 126 of the RSFSR Code of Criminal Procedure specified those crimes for which the procuracy retained sole investigatory responsibility; see Berman, *Soviet Criminal Law*, 241–2.

25 See M. Maliarov, *Prokurorskii nadzor v SSSR*, 2d ed. (Moscow: Iuridicheskaia literatura, 1969), 93; and S.A. Pashin, *Kontseptsiia sudebnoi reformy v Rossiiskoi Federatsii* (Moscow: Respublika, 1992), 26.

26 N. Slavutskaia, "Vzaimootvetsvennost'," *Moskovskaia pravda*, 16 November 1988, 3.

27 January 1989 interview with Leningrad procurator conducted during Helsinki Watch mission to the USSR.

28 Sh.K. Vakhitov, "Mesto sledstvennogo apparata v sisteme gosudarstvennykh organov," *Sovetskoe gosudarstvo i pravo*, no. 2 (1988): 70. The appearance of this article in the leading Soviet law journal at a crucial moment during *perestroika* legal debates suggests that others in the legal community supported this view.

29 An October 1987 discussion with a member of the USSR MVD reform commission in Moscow revealed MVD support for dividing militia investigative and operational branches within the ministry. For the resolution adopted on this score by the 1988 Party conference, see "O pravovoi reforme," *Literaturnaia gazeta*, 6 July 1988, 5. For information on the proposal to unite militia, procuratorial and KGB investigators into one body, see "Demokratizatsiia i zakonnost'," *Pravda*, 14 March 1988, 4.

30 "MVD General Alleges KGB Control of MVD," *RFE/RL Daily Report*, 15 October 1990, 6.

31 See "Pugo Promoted," *RFE/RL Daily Report*, 5 February 1991, 4.

32 See H. Oda, "The Communist Party of the Soviet Union and the Procuracy," in *Law and the Gorbachev Era*, ed. Donald D. Barry (Dordrecht: Martinus Nijhoff, 1988), especially 131.

33 See B.A. Viktorov, *Pravovye osnovy deiatel'nosti organov vnutrennykh del* (Moscow: Iuridicheskaia literatura, 1979), 66–9.

34 "Vlasov Attends Meeting on MVD Political Organs," FBIS, *Daily Report*, 27 April 1988, 42.

35 See S.N. Imashev, "V stroi sozidatelei," *Sovetskaia militsiia* no. 6 (1982): 16.

36 For a detailed discussion of the *nomenklatura* system, see Michael Voslensky, *Nomenklatura: The Soviet Ruling Class* (Garden City, New York: Doubleday, 1984).

37 See, for example, I.I. Petkova, "Nauchnaia konferentsiia po problemam razvitiia organov vnutrennykh del," *Sovetskoe gosudarstvo i pravo*, no. 11 (1977): 144–6. The article discusses a conference on the activities of the CPSU within internal affairs organs.

38 See Elizabeth Teague, "Andropov Cleans up the Militia," *Radio Liberty Research Bulletin*, 9 November 1983, 3.

39 "Conference on Internal Political Organisation of the MVD," BBC, *SWB: USSR*, SU/0142, 4 May 1988, B/5–6.

40 See "Zampolit! Zampolit? Zampolit . . .," *Sovetskaia militsiia*, no. 3 (1990): 28.

41 See "Militiamen Support Depoliticization," *RFE/RL Daily Report*, 23 August 1990, 6.

42 On the restructuring ordered by Gorbachev, see "Gorbachev Decree on Military–Political Organs," *RFE/RL Daily Report*, 5 September 1990, 3. The MVD's response to the decree is documented in B. Vasil'ev and A. Pokrovskii, "Politupravlenie zakryto. Nuzhen novyi 'vospitatel'," *Izvestiia*, 15 December 1990, 8.

43 "Who Controls the MVD and KGB?" *RFE/RL Daily Report*, 9 August 1990, 5.

44 See "USSR Security Council Membership," *RFE/RL Daily Report*, 13 March 1991, 4.

45 "Estonian Daily Analyzes Kalugin Affair," FBIS, *Daily Report*, 16 August 1990, 43.

46 See "Pugo Wants More Power," *RFE/RL Daily Report*, 20 December 1990, 5.

47 See "CPSU Activities Suspended," FBIS, *Daily Report*, 30 August 1991, 31.

48 See Aleksandr Gurov and Iurii Shchekochikhin, "Okhota na L'va ili boi s ten'iu," *Literaturnaia gazeta*, 23 May 1990, 12.

49 See Victor Yasmann, "MVD Budget Increased," Radio Free Europe/Radio Liberty, *Soviet/East European Report*, 10 June 1991, 4.

50 See Oleg Aksënov and Valerii Kulik, "Riskovye liudi," *Sovetskaia militsiia*, no. 1 (1991): 1.

51 Leonid Miloslavsky, "Militia Initiative," *Moscow News*, no. 32 (1989): 5.

52 See Mikhail Tsypkin, "Worker's Militia: Order Instead of Law," Radio Free Europe/Radio Liberty, *Report on the USSR*, 17 November 1989, 14; and "Russian Interior Minister Outlines Plan," FBIS, *Daily Report*, 13 November 1989, 85.

53 Tsypkin, "Worker's Militia," 16.

54 See ibid. and the following letters in the liberal weekly *Nedelia*: "Zachem nam militsionery–lubiteli," *Nedelia* no. 31 (1989); and "Moia militsiia menia sberezhet," no. 44 (1989).

55 See "Municipal Militia being formed in Dushanbe," *RFE/RL Daily Report*, 13 March 1990, 5; and "Municipal Militia Established in Dushanbe," *RFE/RL Daily Report*, 4 April 1990, 9.

56 On rural practices, see "Munitsipal'naia militsiia," *Nedelia*, no. 1 (1990): 4. For the Simferopol and Volgograd budgets, see "Munitsipal'naia militsiia budet," *Sovetskaia militsiia*, no. 8 (1990): 50; and "Municipal Militia Formed in Volgograd," *RFE/RL Daily Report*, 19 September 1990, 6, respectively.

57 See, for example, "Gorbachev Reorganizes Moscow Police," *RFE/RL Daily Report*, 27 March 1991, 3; Francis X. Clines, "Fighting Protests, Gorbachev Orders Moscow Controls," *New York Times*, 27 March 1991; and "Moscow Decides to Establish its Own Militia," *RFE/RL Daily Report*, 10 April 1991, 7.

58 "Moscow Decides to Establish its Own Militia," 7.

59 See V. Bezrukov, "Militseiskii kooperativ 'bar'er'," *Sovetskaia militsiia*, no. 8 (1990): 47–8.

60 N. Lashkevich, "Chem zaniaty chastnye detektivy," *Izvestiia*, 17 November 1990.

61 See Aleksandr Kuleshov, "Sovetskie Pinkertony," *Nedelia*, no. 34 (1989): 8–9; "Ex-KGB Officer Joins Private Investigative Association," *RFE/RL Daily Report*, 25 April 1990, 6; and V. Volkihin, "Reket ni pri chem," *Pravda Ukrainy*, 4 November 1988, 3.

62 For an extensive treatment of this topic, see *Private Policing: Implications for Social Control*, ed. Clifford D. Shearing and Philip C. Stenning (Newbury Park, California: Sage, 1987).

63 See Yasmann, "MVD Budget Increased," 4.

64 Dmitrii Demidov, "Eda v odnom otdel'no vziatom raione," *Nedelia*, no. 48 (1991): 2.

65 For the draft law, see "Zakon Soiuza Sovetskikh Sotsialisticheskikh Respublik o sovetskoi militsii, proekt," *Izvestiia*, 15 June 1990, 2. The debate on the law is reflected in A. Brilliantov and A. Smol'ianinov, "Konkretno, po punktam," *Sovetskaia militsiia*, no. 12 (1990): 40–2.

66 See "Zakon Soiuza Sovetskikh Sotsialisticheskikh Respublik o sovetskoi militsii," *Izvestiia*, 16 March 1991, 2.

67 "Russian Constitutional Court Annuls KGB/MVD Merger," *RFE/RL Daily Report*, 15 January 1992, 1.

68 "Chronology of Yeltsin's First Year," FBIS, *Daily Report*, 26 June 1992, 13.

69 See, in particular, Anderson and Killingray, "Consent, Coercion and Colonial Control," 18.

5 ALLOCATION, RECRUITMENT AND TRAINING OF MILITIA PERSONNEL

1 As cited in V.G. Kutushev, *Sotsial'noe planirovanie v organakh vnutrennykh del* (Saratov: Izdatel'stvo Saratovskogo universiteta, 1983), 40.

2 See Ellwyn R. Stoddard, "Blue Coat Crime," in *Thinking About Police*, ed. Carl B. Klockars (New York: McGraw Hill, 1983), 338.

3 David H. Bayley, *Patterns of Policing* (New Brunswick, New Jersey: Rutgers University Press, 1985), 47.

4 For an in-depth examination of the role of the Soviet constitution in Soviet society, see Robert Sharlet, *Soviet Constitutional Crisis: From De-Stalinization to Disintegration* (Armonk, N.Y.: M.E. Sharpe, 1992).

5 See in particular James Q. Wilson, *Varieties of Police Behavior: The Management of Law and Order* (Cambridge, Mass.: Harvard University Press, 1968), 17–34.

6 See David M. Anderson and David Killingray, "Consent, Coercion and Colonial Control," in *Policing the Empire: Government, Authority and Control, 1830–1940*, ed. David M. Anderson and David Killingray (Manchester: Manchester University Press, 1991), 6; R.I. Mawby, *Comparative Policing Issues: The British and American Experience in International Perspective* (London: Unwin Hyman, 1990), 27–30; and M. Brodgen, "The Emergence of the Police – The Colonial Dimension," *British Journal of Criminology* 27, no. 1 (1987): 4–14.

7 High crime rates in rural areas were often a consequence of the resettlement of released criminals in these communities, as the registration system administered by the militia did not allow such people to settle in major cities. The Russian nationalist writer, Valentin Rasputin, a member of Mikhail Gorbachev's presidential council, wrote critically of this situation in his novel *Pozhar* (Arson).

8 M.M. Babaev, "Kriminologicheskaia otsenka sotsial'no ekonomicheskikh i demograficheskikh faktorov," *Sovetskoe gosudarstvo i pravo*, no. 6 (1972): 97–102.

9 See "Interior Minister Interviewed by Yugoslav Journal," Joint Publication Research Service, *Soviet Union: Political Affairs* (hereafter, JPRS, *Political Affairs*), "Official Use Only" edition, 1 July 1988, 4; and "Soaring Crime Turns Soviets Toward Interpol," *Christian Science Monitor*, 13 July 1989; and A. Diatlov and E. Zhirnov, "Skol'ko sluzhit v militsii," *Komsomol'skaia pravda*, 12 July 1989.

10 Bureau of Justice Statistics, U.S. Department of Justice, *Sourcebook of Criminal Justice Statistics* (Washington, D.C.: U.S. Government Printing Office, 1988), Table 1.53, 88. This table cites a ratio of 2.2 policemen for every 1,000 residents in the United States as of October 1987.

11 "Interior Minister Interviewed by Yugoslav Journal," 4.

12 For the Moscow figure, see Natalia Dzhalogoniia, "Komu stoiat' na strazhe

poriadka," *Moskovskie novosti*, no. 34 (23 August 1987). The New York figure is documented by the Federal Bureau of Investigation, U.S. Department of Justice, *Uniform Crime Reports for the U.S., 1992* (Washington, D.C.: U.S. Government Printing Office, 1992), Table 78, 331. On the Moscow transit population, see "Moscow Internal Affairs Head Interviewed," Foreign Broadcast Information Service, *Daily Report: Soviet Union* (hereafter, FBIS, *Daily Report*), 3 March 1989, 60.

13 The Leningrad ratio is cited in "Council of Ministers Presidium Discusses Crime," FBIS, *Daily Report*, 19 October 1990, 44. The Gorky figure is documented by Leonid Miloslavsky, "Militia Initiative," *Moscow News*, no. 32 (1989).

14 The personnel makeup of private police services was a far cry from what had been anticipated in Soviet society. See Aleksandr Kuleshov, "Sovetskie pinkertony," *Nedelia*, no. 34 (1989). On the membership of dismissed militia personnel of the bar, see V. Savitsky, "Ways of Restructuring the Legal System: The Prestige of the Bar," *Current Digest of the Soviet Press* (hereafter *CDSP*), 39 no. 12 (1987): 7–8. Information on militia involvement in violence in Uzbekistan was provided by a Central Asian scholar at the Institute of State and Law, USSR Academy of Sciences, in a September 1989 interview in Moscow. On the quality of replacement recruits, see N. Kipman, "O kompetentnosti i professionalizme," *Sovetskaia militsiia*, no. 4 (1990): 22.

15 A. Fatula and T. Lisitsyna, "'Proshu uvolit' menia . . . ,'" *Sovetskaia militsiia*, no. 5 (1990): 46–7.

16 See, for example, "Depoliticalization of Lithuanian Militia Viewed," FBIS, *Daily Report*, 1 March 1990, 93.

17 A. Fatula and T. Lisitsyna, "'Proshu uvolit' menia . . . ,'" 47.

18 "Officers Air Housing Problems with Officials," FBIS, *Daily Report*, 13 August 1990, 89.

19 See Dzhalogoniia, "Komu stoiat' na strazhe poriadka." In 1990, 4,000 vacancies existed on the Moscow militia force. See Andrei Rudakov, "Prestupnost' v Moskve: domysly i real'nost'," *Nedelia*, no. 11 (1990).

20 Antonina Grigo, "Let Justice Prevail," JPRS, *Soviet Union: Political Affairs*, 2 December 1981, R15–24.

21 Dzhalogoniia, "Komu stoiat' na strazhe poriadka."

22 "Some Conscripts to Trade Fatigues for Militia Uniforms," *RFE/RL Daily Report*, 12 July 1990, 8.

23 The importance of military ties among militia personnel is indicated by N. Shchelokov in "Sluzhit' narodu – vysshee prizvanie," *Kommunist voorozhennykh sil*, no. 21 (1977): 72.

24 G. Kononov, "The Quality of Ideological Work: The Word is Dearer than the Ruble," *Current Digest of the Soviet Press* (hereafter *CDSP*), no. 34 (1982): 23.

25 Two anthologies used for such training were *Narodnomu druzhinniku* (Moscow: Znanie, 1973); and B.M. Babiia, *Sovetskii zakon i grazhdanin* (Kiev: Naukov dumka, 1980). On the actual level of citizen participation in volunteer policing, see William Zimmerman, "Mobilized Participation and Soviet Dictatorship", in *Politics, Work and Daily Life in the USSR*, ed. James R. Millar (Cambridge: Cambridge University Press, 1987), 337–9.

26 See, for example, "Municipal Militia Being Formed in Dushanbe," *RFE/RL Daily Report*, 13 March 1990, 5.

27 See "Conference on Internal Political Organisation of the MVD," British Broadcasting Corporation Monitoring, *Summary of World Broadcasts: USSR* (hereafter BBC, *SWB: USSR*), SU/0142, 4 May 1988, B/5–6. A September 1989 interview with an MVD specialist at the Institute of State and Law, USSR

Academy of Sciences in Moscow provided information on salary disparities and resentment of Communist Party personnel in the MVD at the time.

28 September 1989 interview with Soviet militia official in Moscow.

29 For militiamen salaries, see David Lane, *Soviet Economy and Society* (New York: New York University Press, 1985), 174; and Dzhalogoniia, "Komu stoiat' na strazhe poriadka." For information on the tax exempt status of militia employees, see "Interior Minister Interviewed by Yugoslav Journal," 4. The 1990 tax reform is documented in "USSR Law on Income Taxes Published," FBIS, *Daily Report*, 16 May 1990, 61–3. For line personnel, the full tax rate became 13 percent, for upper level officers, 15 percent.

30 Bakatin himself discussed the relationship between poor compensation and crime in "Bakatin Interviewed on Crime 'Crisis,'" FBIS, *Daily Report*, 19 July 1989, 101. An October 1987 interview with a militia official in Moscow provided the salary figure for a precinct inspector. The survey is cited in Fatula and Lisitsyna, "'Proshu uvolit' menia . . .,'" 51–2.

31 On government expenditures related to salary increases, see Fatula and Lisitsyna, "'Proshu uvolit' menia . . .,'" 52; "MVD Budget Increased," *RFE/RL Daily Report*, 5 March 1991, 5; and "MVD Budget Increased," Radio Free Europe/Radio Liberty, *Soviet/East European Report* 8, no. 34 (10 June 1991): 4. Regarding salaries paid by private police services, see "Cooperatives Arm Themselves Against Racketeers," FBIS, *Daily Report*, 4 April 1989, 69.

32 On the Novosibirsk incident, see V. Nikolaev, "'Samozakhvat,'" *Sovetskaia militsiia*, no. 8 (1990): 73. Militia housing in Moscow is described in Iurii Kokorin, "Da, obshchaga," *Sovetskaia militsiia*, no. 1 (1991): 40–2; and Kirill Stoliarov, "Kuda smotrit militsiia," *Nedelia*, no. 39 (1989).

33 V. Karasik, "Kakaia militsiia nam nuzhna?" *Sovetskaia militsiia*, no. 5 (1991): 18.

34 Iu.M. Kozlov, et al., *Upravlenie v oblasti administrativno–politicheskoi deiatel'nosti* (Moscow: Iuridicheskaia literatura, 1979), 194.

35 See, for example, A. Arbuzkin and A. Mikhailov, "Poimite nas pravil'no . . .," *Sovetskaia militsiia*, no. 7 (1990): 38.

36 These rules are discussed in general terms by L.M. Kolodkin in "Pravovoe regulirovanie raboty s kadrami organov vnutrennykh del," *Pravovedenie*, no. 1 (1983): 27–34.

37 See Vladimir Dichev, "Mestu sluzhby izmenit' nel'zia," *Sovetskaia militsiia*, no.7 (1990): 28–30; and "Ishchet zhenshchina," *Sovetskaia militsiia*, no.1 (1991): 15.

38 April 1992 interview with Dr. Eduard Raska, director of the newly established Estonian Academy for Public Safety.

39 See Michael Dobbs, "State of Emergency Imposed After Riots in Soviet Republic," *Washington Post*, 6 June 1990; and Alan Cooperman, "Pro-Moscow Police Jeer Latvian Leader," *Washington Post*, 29 January 1991.

40 "Bakatin Interviewed on Crime 'Crisis,'" FBIS, *Daily Report*, 19 July 1989, 98.

41 N.A. Shchelokov, "V bor'be za novogo cheloveka," *Agitator*, no. 20 (1976): 33; and Iu.M. Churbanov, "Deiatel'nost' KPSS po formirovaniiu i vospitaniiu kadrov sovetskoi militsii," *Voprosy istorii KPSS*, no. 8 (1981): 31.

42 Churbanov, "Deiatel'nost' KPSS," 31.

43 For a discussion of legal training at MVD institutes, see V.P. Sal'nikov and V.F. Kazachenko, "Pravovoe vospitanie i pravovaia kul'tura v sisteme organov MVD SSSR," *Pravovedenie*, no. 1 (1980): 54–8. Footage of the 1989 television documentary "Cops" complements descriptions of physical training found in Soviet texts. "Cops" (New York: Fox Television, broadcast 15 July 1989).

44 "Ostatochnyi printsip i vlast' ankety," *Sovetskaia militsiia*, no. 9 (1990): 20.

45 ibid., 29.

46 Fatula and Lisitsyna, "'Proshu uvolit' menia . . .,'" 22, 49.
47 ibid., 49.
48 See "Ostatochnyi printsip," 30; and Fatula and Lisitsyna, "'Proshu uvolit' menia . . .,'" 52.
49 Fatula and Lisitsyna, "'Proshu uvolit' menia . . .,'" 29.
50 See S.N. Imashev, "V stroi sozidatelei," *Sovetskaia militsiia*, no. 6 (1982): 16; and V. Fedorchuk, "Neuklonno ukrepliat' pravoporiadok," *Kommunist*, no. 12 (1985): 69.
51 Arkady Vaksberg, *The Soviet Mafia* (New York: St. Martin's Press, 1991), 105.
52 See ibid., 170, for Churbanov's accusations against Krylov. On the latter's suicide, see Eduard Cherkover, "Do i posle vystrela v sebia," *Nedelia*, no. 9 (1989): 17.
53 Churbanov, "Deiatel'nost' KPSS," 33.
54 January 1989 discussion with senior MVD officials during author's visit to the USSR with a Helsinki Watch delegation.
55 A. Vlasov, "Na strazhe pravoporiadka," *Kommunist*, no. 5 (1988): 47.
56 B.D. Ledin and N. Perfil'ev, *Kadry apparata upravleniia v SSSR* (Leningrad: Nauka, 1970), 153.
57 See "Ostatochnyi printsip," 29.
58 See V.N. Kudriavtsev, "Pravo i demokratiia," *Izvestiia*, 4 October 1986; A. Iakovlev and I. Gamaiunov, "V pol'zu spravedlivosti," *Literaturnaia gazeta*, 24 September 1986; and "Ostatochnyi printsip," 30.
59 On the pairing of junior and senior militiamen, see S. Markov, "Stroka v raport," *Sovetskaia militsiia*, no. 5 (1982): 32. The author examined a militia conduct code for the city of Kaliningrad – published in *samizdat* and smuggled to Holland – in July 1988.
60 Samuel Walker, *Popular Justice* (New York: Oxford University Press, 1980), 226.
61 ibid., 246.
62 Jerome Skolnick, *Justice Without Trial* (New York: Wiley, 1967), ch. 11.
63 Kutushev, *Sotsial'noe planirovanie*, 135. Forty-eight percent of those surveyed commented that superiors should pay more attention to subordinates and their opinions.
64 In 1989, for example, the U.S.–USSR Initiatives organization ran a training program for Soviet militiamen. See Dick Ward, "Policing Perestroika," *C.J. International* 5, no. 4 (1989).
65 Kutushev, *Sotsial'noe planirovanie*, 144.
66 ibid., 47.
67 The 1983 national survey documented by Kutushev shows that 37.9 percent of those surveyed felt that more frequent group recreation would have improved interpersonal relations within the collective. ibid., 135.
68 Richard J. Lundman, ed., *Police Behavior* (New York: Oxford University Press, 1980), 225.
69 Peter K. Manning and Lawrence J. Redlinger, "Invitational Edges of Corruption: Some Consequences of Narcotic Law Enforcement," in *Policing: A View From the Street*, eds. Peter K. Manning and John van Maanen (Santa Monica: Goodyear Publishing Co., 1978), 153.
70 See S.A. Pashin, *Kontseptsiia sudebnoi reformy v Rossiiskoi Federatsii* (Moscow: Respublika, 1992), 10. In the late Soviet period, the cases of only about one-third of those arrested were subsequently dropped; the chance of conviction in court was 99.8 percent. A far greater proportion of arrest cases in the United States was dropped during the same time period, but nearly all cases that were prosecuted resulted in convictions. (Approximately 1 percent of criminal felony cases result in acquittals in the United States. See Bureau of Justice Statistics, U.S. Department of Justice, *The Prosecution of Felony Arrests, 1988* [Washington, D.C.: U.S. Government Printing Office, 1992], 3.)

71 "Figures for Crime Against Militia Disclosed," FBIS, *Daily Report*, 16 March 1990, 85.

72 For information on militia car theft, see Lidiia Grafova, "Dama s sobachkoi, no bez avtomobilia," *Literaturnaia gazeta*, 1 January 1987. On militia involvement in trading other stolen merchandise, see "Georgian Party First Secretary Urges Crackdown on Tbilisi's Criminals," *CDSP*, no. 4 (1986): 10. On murders committed by militiamen, see "Figures for Crime Against the Militia Disclosed," 85.

73 For an analysis of how police regulation of illegal goods and services in capitalist societies contributes to police corruption, see Ellwyn R. Stoddard, "Blue Coat Crime," in *Thinking About Police*, ed. Carl B. Klockars (New York: McGraw Hill, 1983), 338–9.

74 See "Bakatin Confirmed Interior Minister," FBIS, *Daily Report*, 11 July 1989, 46.

75 V. Borisovskii, "S tochki zreniia kadrovika," *Sovetskaia militsiia*, no.9 (1990): 14.

76 Fatula and Lisitsyna, "'Proshu uvolit' menia . . .,'" 21. A regulation that increased militiamen's vulnerability required one officer to stay in a police car when summoned to the scene of a violent domestic dispute (ibid., 21). In the same article, the authors report that 93 percent of younger MVD employees were dissatisfied with service in the militia due to the lack of legal and social protections (ibid., 54).

   For a personal account of a militiaman's disappointment with police work, see I. Chukhin, "Ia b' v militsiiu poshel . . .," *Sovetskaia militsiia*, no. 10 (1990). Chukhin was a lieutenant colonel in the militia and a people's deputy of the RSFSR.

77 For homicide data for 1989, see Joe Serio, ed. and trans., *USSR Crime Statistics and Summaries, 1989 and 1990*, vol. 1 (Chicago: Office of International Criminal Justice, 1992). For information about suicides among MVD personnel for the same year, see "Suicides in the Militia," *RFE/RL Daily Report*, 12 April 1990, 5.

   On the demonstration by Leningrad militiamen, see "Leningrad Militiamen Dismissed for Disobedience," FBIS, *Daily Report*, 2 May 1989, 48; and Yuri Kupin, "The Colonel Apologizes," *Moscow News*, 13 August 1989.

   On the Supreme Soviet law, see "Draft Law on Strikes Published," *RFE/RL Daily Report*, 18 August 1989.

78 On militiamen's long hours, see "Crime Wave, Glasnost' Spur MVD Resignations," FBIS, *Daily Report*, 2 May 1989, 55–6. The lack of overtime pay for militia personnel is documented by Stoliarov, "Kuda smotrit militsiia." Attrition among militia personnel in 1989 is described in Fatula and Lisitsyna, "'Proshu uvolit' menia . . .,'" 53.

79 Fatula and Lisitsyna, "'Proshu uvolit' menia . . .,'" 53.

80 See "Internal Affairs Ministry Holds Conference," FBIS, *Daily Report*, 12 September 1989, 54, 64.

81 June 1989 interviews with members of the association of Lithuanian lawyers in Vil'nius.

6 MILITIA OPERATIONS

1 Staff of the Commission on Security and Cooperation in Europe, *Human Rights and Democratization in the Newly Independent States of the Former Soviet Union* (Washington, D.C.: Commission on Security and Cooperation in Europe, 1993), 48.

2 See William Ker Muir, Jr., *Police: Street Corner Politicians* (Chicago: University of Chicago Press, 1977), ch. 14.

3 October 1987 interview with MVD official in Moscow.

4 "Chto mozhet' chego ne mozhet militsiia," *Izvestiia*, 4 August 1990.

5 ibid. Numerous interviews with former and practicing Soviet law enforcement personnel also confirmed the enormity of paperwork in a Soviet policeman's life; such interviews support a great deal of the information related in this chapter. See appendix for further details about in-person interviews.

6 Author's observations during visits to the USSR in 1987 and 1989; these impressions were later confirmed by discussions with Soviet law enforcement personnel.

7 K. Nikitin, "On Guard Over Order," *Current Digest of the Soviet Press* (hereafter *CDSP*) 23, no. 45 (1971): 21–2, documents the institution of round-the-clock patrols in 1970. R.K. Rybal'chenko, *Upravlenie v oblasti vnutrennykh del* (Kharkov: Kharkovskii iuridicheskii institut, 1977), 9, cites the 90 percent figure for crime reported during evening hours.

8 See Richard V. Ericson, *Reproducing Order: A Study of Police Patrol Work* (Toronto: University of Toronto Press, 1982), ch. 1 for a discussion of police work routines in western societies. For descriptions of daily militia work in the USSR, see V.A. Slavin, "Ob usloviiakh imushchestvennoi otvetstvennosti organov militsii za vred, prichinennyi grazhdanam v sfere administrativnoi deiatel'nosti," *Trudy Moskovskoi vysshei shkoly militsii*, no. 1 (1977): 75; and G. Bondarenko and I.V. Mart'ianov, *Sovetskoe administrativnoe pravo* (Lvov: Vishcha shkola, 1977), 57.

For annual administrative violations processed by the militia, see Ger Van den Berg, *The Soviet System of Justice: Figures and Policy* (Dordrecht, The Netherlands: Martinus Nijhoff, 1985), 35. For the 1987 Moscow figures on the unemployed and those placed in jobs by the militia, see "Moscow MVD Briefs Press on Holiday Activities," Foreign Broadcast Information Service, *Daily Report: Soviet Union* (hereafter FBIS, *Daily Report*), 7 January 1988, 52.

9 See Sergei Zamoshkin, "Can the Militia Shoot Back?" *Moscow News*, no. 31 (1989): 4; V. Borovikov, "Zachem militsioneru pistolet?" *Sovetskaia militsiia*, no. 9 (1990): 53–4; and "Proposed Law on Weapons," *Radio Free Europe/Radio Liberty Daily Report* (hereafter *RFE/RL Daily Report*), 8 August 1991, 5.

10 In a September 1994 interview with Russian ombudsman Sergei Kovalëv in Washington, D.C., he noted that his office was investigating the militia practice of two militia officers colluding to kill an individual and then covering up their behavior. On homicides committed by police in Latin America, see, for example, Raul Zaffaroni, "The Right to Life and Latin American Penal Systems," *Annals of the American Academy of Political and Social Science* 56 (November 1989): 57–67.

11 See Kirill Stoliarov, "Kuda smotrit militsiia," *Nedelia*, no. 39 (1989): 16.

12 See "Khronika odnogo dezhurstva," *Sovetskaia militsiia*, no. 8 (1990): 57.

13 On *uchastki* and militia posts, see I. Pudalov, "'Ministr' mikroraiona," *Verchniaia Moskva*, 18 August 1988. For more information on the *koban* system in Japan, see David Bayley, *Forces of Order: Police Behavior in Japan and the United States* (Berkeley: University of California Press, 1976), ch. 2.

14 On the equipment situation of a Moscow precinct, see "Precinct Police Officer," *CDSP* 39, no. 23 (1987): 19. "Khronika odnogo dezhurstva," *Sovetskaia militsiia*, 56, documents the institution of direct oversight of precinct officers in 1985.

15 For information on mobile militia units and their creation, see A. Platayev, "To Serve the People Faithfully," Joint Publications Research Service, *USSR: Political and Sociological Affairs* (hereafter JPRS, *USSR*), 8 March 1983, 46–7; and "Kazakh Police, Volunteers Halt Food Theft, Black Marketeering," JPRS,

USSR, 15 February 1983, 8. On the activities of such units in Moscow, see John Simpson, "Moscow Cops," *World Monitor* (January 1990): 55–9.

16 V. Tolstov, "Poriadok na ulitsakh," *Izvestiia*, 16 January 1984.

17 On the use of reserve police in the United States, see Martin Alan Greenberg, *Auxiliary Police* (Westport, Connecticut: Greenwood, 1984), 171. On the use of *druzhinniki* in the USSR, see "Recruitment into Voluntary Militia Groups," British Broadcasting Corporation Monitoring, *Summary of World Broadcasts: USSR* (hereafter BBC Monitoring, *SWB: USSR*), SU/7254, 10 February 1983, B/5; and "Lieutenant-General Elisov, interview on Moscow Radio, 14 March 1985," as reported in BBC Monitoring, *SWB: USSR*, SU/7606, 31 March 1984, B/1.

18 Both militia and auxiliary units turned a blind eye to this kind of harassment. See "Local Guardsmen Accused of Arbitrary Arrest and Brutality," *Survey of the Soviet Press* (hereafter *SSP*) 141 (1 February 1960), 39–41; "'Crude' Actions by Volunteer Guardsmen in Arkhangel'sk Scored," *SSP* 162 (27 June 1960), 20; "Kirgiz Gathering of Volunteer People's Guards Criticizes Decrease in Numbers and Legal Violations Among Guardsmen," *SSP* 179 (24 October 1960), 15–16; "Nikolaev *Druzhinniki* Leaders Indicted for Brutality, Rape and Embezzlement as Result of Investigations Pressed by *Komsomol'skaya Pravda*," *SSP* 210 (5 June 1961), 32–3; "Guardians of Order," *CDSP* 23, no. 44 (1971): 22; "People's Volunteer Militia Aides," *CDSP* 28, no. 32 (1976): 18; "Unsealed Railroad Car," *CDSP* 32, no. 52 (1980): 16–17; Bill Keller, "Moscow's East Side Story: Teen-Age Toughs," *New York Times*, 7 March 1987; and Arthur Werner, "The Activities of the Voluntary Citizens' Police" (paper presented at Third International Sakharov Hearings, Washington, D.C., 1979).

19 See "Fighting Teenage Crime in Estonia," *CDSP* 36, no. 31 (1984): 24; Iu.M. Churbanov, *Tovarishch militsiia* (Moscow: Molodaia gvardiia, 1980), 143; and M. Ivanov, "Legal University: People's Militia: Business and Concerns," JPRS, *USSR*, 16 April 1984, Annex, 8–13.

20 Interview with former militia officer in Israel, March 1987.

21 The new legislation was jointly adopted by the MVD and the Central Committee of the Komsomol. See Churbanov, *Tovarishch militsiia*, 135, concerning the difficulties of implementing the resolution.

22 See Werner, "The Activities of the Voluntary Citizens' Police."

23 See, for example, B.A. Viktorov, *Pravovye osnovy deiatel'nosti organov vnutrennykh del* (Moscow: Iuridicheskaia literatura, 1979), 129–30; "Sluzhit' narodu – vysshee prizvanie," *Kommunist vooruzhennykh sil*, no. 21 (1977): 70–1; and P.P. Osipov, ed., *Kompleksnoe izuchenie sistemy vozdeistviia na prestupnost'* (Leningrad: Izdatel'stvo Leningradskogo gosudarstvennogo universiteta, 1978), 143.

24 On army–militia patrols, see "Police Patrols Increased," *RFE/RL Daily Report*, 6 February 1991, 5; "No Joint Patrols in Leningrad," *RFE/RL Daily Report*, 15 February 1991, 7; "Moiseev on Army's Changing Role," *RFE/RL Daily Report*, 13 March 1991, 6; "Cossacks Patrol Siberian Cities," Radio Free Europe/Radio Liberty, *Soviet/East European Report* 8, no. 26 (1 April 1991): 3.

On the ability of the Baltic states and Ukraine to avoid instituting such patrols, see, for example, "No Joint Patrols in Riga," *RFE/RL Daily Report*, 4 February 1991, 4; and "Lvov Forms own Militia Patrols," *RFE/RL Daily Report*, 31 January 1991, 6.

25 A 1988 survey of the residents of Nikolaev (a town in Russia) reported that nearly 70 percent of those surveyed claimed they had never seen their militia inspector. V. Mel'nik, "Eshche raz ob uchastkovym," *Iuzhnaia pravda*, 26 July 1988. See also A. Vlasov, "Na strazhe pravoporiadka," *Kommunist*, no. 5 (1988): 48.

On the worsening manpower crisis in the late 1980s, see "Precinct Police Officer," 18.

26 On the émigré survey in the United States, see the following article based on the Soviet Interview Project: James R. Millar, "Prospects for Economic Reform: Is (Was) Gorbachev Really Necessary?" in *Political, Economic and Security Prospects for the 1990s*, ed. J.J. Lee and Walter Korter (Austin, Texas: LBJ School of Public Affairs, 1991), 81, table 4.

On the evaluation of the citizen–militia divide by Soviet militiamen themselves, see E.P. Petrov, R.A. Safarov and S.S. Strel'nikov, "Obshchestvennoe mnenie i sovetskaia militsiia," *Sovetskoe gosudarstvo i pravo*, no. 7 (1981): 75–6; and S.A. Pashin, ed., *Kontseptsiia sudebnoi reformy v Rossiiskoi Federatsii* (Moscow: Respublika, 1992), 12. (The latter publication was issued by the Russian Federation Supreme Soviet.)

27 On the Olympic-related cleanup, see "A Hard Look at Prostitution in the USSR," *CDSP* 39, no. 11 (1987), 2. For more information on prostitution in Moscow, see "Detective on problem of prostitution in Moscow, BBC Monitoring, *SWB: USSR*, SU/0030, 19 December 1987, B/12. An October 1987 interview with a senior MVD official in Moscow confirmed that recorded crime dropped significantly during such special occasions.

28 Interview with former Jewish activist in Israel, March 1987.

29 For an analysis of how western police forces are influenced by political trends, see Otwin Marenin, "Police Performance and State Rule," *Comparative Politics* 18 (October 1985): 105.

30 On joint visits of different militia divisions to apartment complexes, see V. Kul'batskii, "Na pravil'nyi put'," *Sovetskaia militsiia*, no. 6 (1982): 21–23. On coordinated vehicular operations of the militia, see N. Arestov, "Zaslon na dorogo," *Sovetskaia militsiia*, no. 5 (1982): 48–49.

31 Interview with émigré defense counsel in New York, 1981.

32 See, for example, Yuri Feofanov, "Ours Not to Reason Why?" *New Times*, no. 10 (1990): 33.

33 See, for example, J. Michael Waller, "Russia's Legal Foundations for Civil Repression," *Demokratizatsiya* 1, no. 3 (1993): 111–12.

34 See especially Gary T. Marx, *Undercover: Police Surveillance in America* (Berkeley: University of California Press, 1988).

35 Marx, *Undercover*, 188. On the lack of constitutional safeguards against undercover police work in the USSR, see T. Kolganova, "Nuzhna li nam agentura?" *Sovetskaia militsiia*, no.1 (1991): 48.

36 Marx, *Undercover*, 148–52.

37 "Militia Bill Approved, Split on Law Enforcement," FBIS, *Daily Report*, 8 June 1990, 35–6.

38 See Merle Fainsod, *Smolensk under Soviet Rule* (Cambridge, Mass.: Harvard University Press, 1958), 162.

39 Yevgeniya Albats, "Shadowy Figures," *Moscow News*, no. 14 (April 1992). Although Albats's article concerns KGB informants, this author's personal interviews with numerous Soviet militia personnel revealed a similar rate – lower, yet significant – of forced citizen cooperation in undercover militia operations.

40 Albats, "Shadowy Figures."

41 See G.P. Shelud'ko, *Sovetskaia militsiia na strazhe obshchestvennogo poriadka* (Kiev: Vishcha shkola, 1982), 27–8.

42 See Neil Weissman, "Regular Police in Tsarist Russia, 1900–1914," *Russian Review* 44 (January 1985): 49.

43 Albats, "Shadowy Figures."

44 Fainsod, *Smolensk under Soviet Rule*, 162.

45 Interview with émigré defense counsel in New York, 1981.

46 Roman Solchanyk cites the Ukrainian *samizdat* report in "Kiev Authorities Seek Informers to Assist Police in Combating Crime," *Radio Liberty Research Bulletin*, 8 December 1981, 1. The *Izvestiia* article was penned by E. Parkhomovskii, "Ne zvonite anonimno," *Izvestiia*, 16 January 1982.

47 See, for example, Lidiia Grafova, "Neuchto bez anonimki," *Literaturnaia gazeta*, 10 February 1988. Another negative view of anonymous denunciations was expressed by the former director of the Institute of State and Law, who subsequently became vice president of the Soviet (now Russian) Academy of Sciences, see V.N. Kudriavtsev, "The Presumption of Innocence No Longer A 'Bourgeois Invention,'" BBC Monitoring, *SWB: USSR*, SU/0149, 12 May 1988, B/5.

48 See the discussion of anonymous tips and their usefulness in "Interior Minister Interviewed by Yugoslav Journal," JPRS, *USSR*, 1 July 1988, 6.

49 See Marx, *Undercover*, 2.

50 Militia Bill Approved, Split on Law Enforcement, 35–36.

51 For a discussion of how Party members were brought to trial in the USSR, see Robert Sharlet, "The Communist Party and the Administration of Justice in the USSR," in *Soviet Law After Stalin*, vol. 3, ed. Donald B. Barry, F.J.M. Feldbrugge, and Peter Maggs (Alphen aan de Rijn, The Netherlands: Sijthoff & Noordhoff, 1979), 376–8.

Concerning the involvement of Party members in serious crimes in the Caucasus and Central Asia, see Arkadii Vaksberg, "Pravde v glaza," *Literaturnaia gazeta*, 17 December 1986, 13; and Louise Shelley, "Party Members and the Courts: Exploitation of Privilege," in *Ruling Communist Parties and their Status under Law*, ed. D.A. Loeber (Dordrecht, The Netherlands: Martinus Nijhoff, 1986), 75–90.

Continued Party interference on behalf of Party members is reported in Iuri Feofanov, "Ot komandy po telefonu k komande po megafonu," *Izvestiia*, 24 May 1990. His contention was supported by a series of Uzbek movies produced in the late 1980s that depicted serious crimes committed by Uzbek Party officials. One such film addressed the rapes of young girls by a regional Party secretary and their subsequent self-immolation.

For information on the consequences of prosecuting Party members without Party approval, see Louise I. Shelley, "Soviet Courts as Vehicles for Political Maneuver," *Soviet Union* 13, no. 2 (1986): 163–86; and Ol'ga Chaikovskaia, "Obizhaites' na menia, ne obizhaites'," *Literaturnaia gazeta*, 22 October 1986, 12.

52 "Nuykin Calls Bureaucracy Reform's Adversary," FBIS, *Daily Report/Annex*, 5 February 1988, 5.

53 James Q. Wilson, *Varieties of Police Behavior* (New York: Atheneum, 1974), 286.

54 See ibid., 140–226. Soviet police did demonstrate a service style of policing by providing educational lectures and traffic safety instruction. However, these activities were highly ideological in nature and were not a primary function of the militia.

Not only did Soviet militia not practice genuine service policing, crime victims in the USSR, as in many other nations (including the United States and certain Latin American countries), were often treated badly by law enforcement bodies. In the Soviet Union, this occurred largely because the state emphasized collective over individual rights. Victims' rights movements that have recently emerged in so pronounced a fashion in western societies were never a major concern in the USSR. In general, a victim's only option was to press for prosecution and be represented by a defense attorney in court.

55 Interviews with former and active Soviet militia personnel, together with articles

published in the militia journal *Sovetskaia militsiia*, support the existence of two operational styles among militiamen.

56 "Kidnapping of Minor 'Bride' by Militiaman and Accomplices Illustrates Tenacity of Turkmen Feudal Bey Customs," *SSP* 364, 12 June 1964, 63.

57 Louise Shelley, "Internal Migration and Crime," *Canadian Slavonic Papers* 23, no. 1 (1981): 83.

58 October 1980 interview with former Soviet militia official in Chicago. Supporting information was provided by émigré attorneys in Israel.

59 See Wayne Di Franceisco and Zvi Gitelman, "Soviet Political Culture and 'Covert Participation' in Policy Implementation," *American Political Science Review* 78 (September 1984): 605–7, which discusses sample questions 269–71 of Gitelman's émigré survey as well as variables 1076–7 of the Soviet Interview Project conducted at the University of Illinois (the so-called "Millar project": see James R. Millar, "History, Method, and the Problem of Bias," *Politics, Work and Daily Life in the USSR*, ed. James R. Millar (Cambridge, England: Cambridge University Press, 1987), 3–30).

60 One example of the consequences of such subordination was seen in Nagorno-Karabakh, when an Armenian militia official, after delivering the body of an Azeri slain in the region to his family, commented that his fate should be the fate of all Azeris. "Coming Apart," television show produced by Hedrick Smith (New York: Public Broadcasting Service, May 1990).

61 See *Conflict in the Soviet Union: Black January in Azerbaidzhan* (New York: Helsinki Watch/Memorial, 1991), 7; "MVD Officer on National Relations Among Troops," FBIS, *Daily Report*, 4 February 1988, 40; and "Sumgait Officials' Censure Published," FBIS, *Daily Report*, 31 March 1988, 33–4.

62 See, for example, "'Unusual Situation' After Journalists Attempt to Exchange Records," New Service of the BBC, SU/0033, 23 December 1987, B/1.

63 As Jonathan Rubenstein has noted, "A policeman's principal concern is to physically control the people he is policing" (idem, *City Police* [New York: Farrar, Straus and Giroux, 1972], 302).

7 THE MILITIA AND DAILY LIFE

1 "Statistics on Authorized Absenteeism Cited," Foreign Broadcast Information Service, *Daily Report: Soviet Union* (hereafter FBIS, *Daily Report*), 13 May 1988, 64.

2 Louise I. Shelley, "Recent Changes in Soviet Legislation: Administrative Law and Educational Reforms," *Fifth International Sakharov Hearings*, ed. Allan Wynn (London: Andre Deutsch, 1986), 24.

3 See, for example, "Poll on Attitudes to Economic Reforms," FBIS, *Daily Report*, 19 June 1992, 37.

4 Clifford D. Shearing and Philip C. Stenning, "Say 'Cheese:' The Disney Order that is Not so Mickey Mouse," in *Private Policing*, ed. Clifford D. Shearing and Philip C. Stenning (Newbury Park, California: Sage, 1987), 319.

5 *Pamiatka krasnogo militsionera* (Moscow: Achinskaia gosudarstvennaia tipografiia, 1924) discussed the functions of the post militiaman, including his political responsibilities. See also *Sputnik krasnogo militsionera* (Moscow: Zagotkhoza, 1924).

6 V.A. Pomerantsev, I.L. Liubimov, comp. I.F. Kiselev, ed., *Deistvuiushchie rasporiazheniia po militsii postanovleniia tsirkyliary, prikazy i instruktsii sistematicheskii sbornik s poiasneniiami*, 2d ed. (Moscow: NKVD RSFSR, 1928).

7 Interviews with Dr. Boris Levin (Chief, Section on Drug Abuse, Institute of

Sociology, USSR Academy of Sciences) in Moscow, October 1987. Levin is now head of Drug and Alcohol Research at the Institute of Sociology.

8 Administrative Code of the RSFSR, *Vedomosti Verkhovnogo Soveta RSFSR*, no. 27 (5 July 1984): item 1341.

9 "Polozhenie o sovetskoi militsii," *Spravochnik po zakonodatel'stvu dlia rabotnikov organov prokuratury, suda i ministerstva vnutrennykh del*, vol. 2, pt. 1 (Moscow: Iuridicheskaia literatura, 1971), 304–11.

10 Despite longstanding enforcement of administrative measures, the RSFSR adopted its first Administrative Code only in June 1984. Failure to codify the law had, in effect, only served to enhance police controls over Soviet society. The Code went into effect on 1 January 1985. See *Vedomosti Verkhovnogo Soveta RSFSR*, no. 27 (note 8 above).

11 Special instructions were issued to the militia in 1964 that detailed who could be registered in Moscow and under what conditions. These regulations, provided only to law enforcement personnel at the time, can be found in *Spravochnik po zakonodatel'stvu dlia rabotnikov organov prokuratury, suda i ministerstva vnutrennykh del*, vol. 3 (Moscow: Iuridicheskaia literatura, 1972), 369–85. A copy of 1975 legislation on registration in Moscow can be found in Radio Free Europe/ Radio Liberty, *Arkhiv samizdata* (hereafter *Arkhiv samizdata*), no. 4855 (September 1983). Similar instructions were issued in order to virtually close Leningrad, capitals of the Soviet republics and certain major port and industrial centers to future settlers. Employees of the passport divisions of these major centers were forbidden to register almost all new settlers except those who obtained work in the KGB, the militia or enterprises that could grant them a registration permit. See Cronid Lubarsky, "On the Soviet Passport System," *Papers on Soviet Law*, no. 3 (1981): 47–9.

12 See, for example, "Kakim dolzhno byt' pravovoe gosudarstvo," *Literaturnaia gazeta*, 8 June 1988; and Hiroshi Oda, "Law Enforcement Agencies;" Louise I. Shelley, "Soviet Criminal Law and Justice: Are There or Were There Secrets;" and Peter Juviler, "Secret Justice and Personal Rights," in *The Soviet Sobranie of Laws: Problems of Codification and Non-Publication*, Research Series #78, ed. Richard M. Buxbaum and Kathryn Hendley (Berkeley: International and Area Studies, 1991). These articles address the issue of the impact of unpublished laws on both law enforcement and individuals.

13 Such entries appeared in a form understandable only by law enforcement authorities.

14 B.M. Babiia, *Sovetskii zakon i grazhdanin* (Kiev: Naukov dumka, 1980), 109.

15 As A.P. Korenev has noted, "[N]ormative acts empowering the police to demand the presentation of documents in order to verify the observance of the rules of the passport system do not contain a list of the grounds for such verification" (A.P. Korenev, "The Rights of the Soviet Police and Socialist Legality," *Soviet Law and Government*, no. 22 (1984): 81–94).

16 "What Do the Militia Do?" *Moscow News*, no. 50 (1988): 11.

17 N.A. Apiian, *Na strazhe pravoporiadka i zakonnosti* (Erevan: Izdatel'stvo Erevanskogo universiteta, 1979), 217.

18 See Viktor Zaslavsky and Yuri Luryi, "The Passport System and Changes in Soviet Society," *Soviet Union*, no. 6 (1979): 138. At the time, the law was issued only to administrative offices that enforced passport regulations.

19 Olympiad S. Ioffe and Peter B. Maggs, *Soviet Law in Theory and Practice* (London, Rome, New York: Oceana, 1983), 251.

20 See A. Krivoruchko and V. Iakovlev, "Razreshenie na svidanie," *Literaturnaia gazeta*, 25 November 1987, 13.

21 See Article 198 of the Criminal Code of the RSFSR, amended, *Vedomosti Verkhovnogo Soveta RSFSR*, no. 49 (1982): item 1821.

22 The most notable dissident case was probably that of Anatolii Marchenko, who was sent to a labor camp in 1975 for violating passport regulations three times. For information on ex-offenders being returned to camps for similar violations, see Iu.V. Solopanov and V.E. Kvashis, *Retsidiv i retsidivisty* (Moscow: Iuridicheskaia literatura, 1971).

23 Two-thirds of all Soviet émigrés surveyed by the Soviet Interview Project reported contact with the militia concerning their residence permits. See Barbara A. Anderson and Brian D. Silver, "The SIP [Soviet Interview Project] General Survey Sample," in *Politics, Work and Daily Life in the USSR*, ed. James R. Millar (Cambridge: Cambridge University Press, 1987), variable 1071, 354–71.

24 See, for example, T. Merzliakova, "Izgoi po ... zakonu sovmestima sistema propiski c pravami cheloveka," *Izvestiia*, 6 February 1991; and "Nash pratikum," *Sovetskaia militsiia*, no. 12 (1990): 39.

25 Information on the staffing of the Leningrad passport division was provided by Cathy Fitzpatrick, then a staff member of Helsinki Watch, who in 1989 spent a month with a Canadian broadcasting crew filming the Leningrad militia.

26 See "Nash pratikum," 39.

27 As cited in "Session Approves Law on Refugees, Migrants," FBIS, *Daily Report*, 22 June 1992, 53. (The FBIS item is a translation of an article by ITAR-TASS parliamentary correspondent Alexey Tabachnikov.)

28 Interviews with Soviet law enforcement personnel and human rights figures in Moscow, September 1990.

29 "Constitutional Watchdog Rules Against Residence Permits," *RFE/RL Daily Report*, 29 October 1990, 5.

30 "Poll on Attitudes to Economic Reforms," 37.

31 Helsinki Watch Report, *Toward the Rule of Law: Soviet Legal Reform and Human Rights under Perestroika* (New York: U.S. Helsinki Watch Committee, 1989), 5, 18–19.

32 "Daily Life of Estonian Militia," Joint Publications Research Service, *USSR Report: Political and Sociological Affairs*, 19 February 1986, 72.

33 Interview with one of the dissidents who sheltered Amal'rik, New York, 1987.

34 Interviews with Soviet law enforcement personnel in Moscow, October 1987 and September 1989.

35 These periodic campaigns had been a fact of life in the USSR since the late Stalin period. For a description of the beginning of such a campaign, see Apiian, *Na strazhe pravoporiadka*, 165. For information about lax enforcement of permit laws in Moscow in the late Soviet period, see Andrei Rudakov, "Prestupnost' v Moskve: Domysly i real'nost'," *Nedelia*, no. 11 (1990).

36 B.A. Viktorov, *Pravovye osnovy deiatel'nosti organov vnutrennykh del* (Moscow: Iuridicheskaia literatura, 1979), 126.

37 As described in detail in Chapter 6, administrative personnel of residential buildings were required by statute to assist the militia in enforcing passport and registration regulations. Such designated personnel included the heads of housing offices; housing administrators; apartment house and hotel managers; chairmen of housing construction trusts; homeowners; and directors and managers of sanatoria, rest homes, pensions, tourist parks and hospitals. With such a body of informants at its disposal, the militia could assure the smooth functioning of the elaborate passport system.

38 See, for example, Celestine Bohlen, "Itinerant Workers Spark Debate," *Washington Post*, 17 August 1985; and "Private Sector Thrives in the Soviet Countryside," *Current Digest of the Soviet Press* (hereafter *CDSP*) 37, no. 24 (1985): 1.

39 "Private Sector Thrives," 2–3. For a further discussion of *shabashniki*, see Patrick Murphy, "Soviet *Shabashniki*: Material Incentives at Work," *Problems of Communism* 34, no. 6 (1985): 54.

40 For a description of the Moscow regulation on food stores, see Celestine Bohlen, "In Moscow's Food Stores, Panic and then Empty Shelves," *New York Times*, 27 May 1990. P. Remizov, "Ispolkom Mossoveta razreshil obyskivat'," *Moskovskii vypusk*, 9 February 1991, details the joint monitoring of cars, airports and railroad stations by various militia units in Moscow. The militiaman from Tiumen' is quoted in "What Do the Militia Do?" 11 (see note 16 above). For more on militia protection of food supplies, see "Kirghizia Prohibits Export of Consumer Goods, *RFE/RL Daily Report*, 8 March 1990, 9; and "Moscow Militia Blocks Goods Flow from City," FBIS, *Daily Report*, 9 January 1992, 52.

41 G.P. Shelud'ko, *Sovetskaia militsiia na strazhe obshchestvennogo poriadka* (Kiev: Vishcha shkola, 1982), 32.

42 See Dmitrii Likhanov and Pavel Krivtsov, "Bez vesti," *Ogonëk*, no. 19 (1989): 32.

43 During the Brezhnev period, the Soviet government attempted to improve the service of the militia information bureaus. See Apiian, *Na strazhe pravoporiadka*, 165. Shelud'ko, *Sovetskaia militsiia*, 32–3, confirms that citizens used the passport division files to locate lost relatives and that this division cooperated with operational units of the militia regarding suspicious characters. According to numerous interviews with émigrés and Soviet legal personnel conducted by the author in Moscow, Israel and the United States in the late 1980s, passport division personnel were supposed to identify husbands who consistently refused to pay alimony by making an entry in their internal passports.

44 B. Il'chenko, "Propal bez vesti," *Sovetskaia militsiia*, no. 5 (1991): 23.

45 "Soviet Reporter in New York Finds It's a Driver's Delight," *New York Times*, 7 March 1988.

46 Shelud'ko, *Sovetskaia militsiia*, 33–4.

47 See A.E. Lunev, *Upravlenie v oblasti administrativno–politicheskoi deiatel'nosti* (Moscow: Iuridicheskaia literatura, 1979), 179–88.

48 M. Lichagina, "Letter to the editor," *Literaturnaia gazeta*, 10 February 1988.

49 See, for example, "The New and Improved Supreme Soviet and the Institutionalization of Human Rights Reform," presentation of Supreme Soviet delegation before the Commission on Security and Cooperation in Europe, Vienna, 28 November 1989.

50 Helsinki Watch Report, *Toward the Rule of Law*, 136–7.

51 Ger Van den Berg, *The Soviet System of Justice: Figures and Policy* (Dordrecht, The Netherlands: Martinus Nijhoff, 1985), 47.

52 On the isolation of people with venereal disease, see L.L. Popov and A.P. Shergin, *Upravlenie grazhdanin otvetstvennost'* (Leningrad: Nauka, 1975), 16. For further information on how the militia tracked AIDS patients, see Oleg Moroz, "Otverzhennye," *Ogonëk*, no. 16 (April 1990), 28.

53 N.A. Shchelokov, *Sovetskaia militsiia* (Moscow: Znanie, 1971), 44–6.

54 For more on gun registration in the USSR, see Valerii Rudnev, "Esli u vas est' ruzh'e," *Nedelia*, no. 19 (1990). Sanctions imposed for the failure to register or properly maintain fire arms are detailed in the Administrative Code of the RSFSR, *Vedomosti Verkhovnogo Soveta RSFSR*, no. 27 (1984): item 909, and Article 218 of the RSFSR Criminal Code (for a translation of the latter, see Harold J. Berman, *Soviet Criminal Law and Procedure: The RSFSR Codes*, 2d ed. [Cambridge, Massachusetts: Harvard University Press, 1972]). Shelud'ko, *Sovetskaia militsiia*, 29, discusses those cases in which militiamen were to confiscate weapons and ammunition from their legal owners. For information concerning the theft of arms from the militia and the army, see Louise I. Shelley, "Inter-Personal Violence in the U.S.S.R.," *Violence, Aggression and Terrorism*, no. 2 (1987): 49–50; V.D. Malkov, "Khishchenie ognestrel'nogo oruzhiia boevykh pripasov i vzryvchatykh veshchestv," Ph.D. diss., Higher School of the USSR Ministry of Internal Affairs,

Moscow, 1969; and "Supply of Weapons to Uzbek Criminals Reported," FBIS, *Daily Report*, 12 October 1989, 63.

55 On religious and political *samizdat*, see *Arkhiv samizdata* 29 (1983): item 4994. An October 1980 interview with a Soviet émigré who had worked as a criminalistics expert on classified militia projects provided details on the attribution of *samizdat* publications to specific typewriters. Mark Hopkins, *Russia's Underground Press: The Chronicle of Current Events* (New York: Praeger, 1983), 99–101, provides information concerning the confiscation and destruction of printing equipment that had not been registered with the militia.

56 See, for example, Celestine Bohlen, "Amid Soviets' Changes: Who Owns the Papers?" *New York Times*, 11 June 1990. Interviews with human rights activists, labor activists and Baltic nationalists in Washington, D.C., and the former Soviet Union in 1989 and 1990 confirmed that the Communist Party continued to assert control over printing facilities during the *perestroika* era.

57 Helsinki Watch Report, *Civil Society in the USSR* (New York: U.S. Helsinki Watch Committee, 1990), 31.

58 See David Remnick, "General Ordered Attack, Gorbachev Tells Assembly," *Washington Post*, 15 January 1991; and *idem*, "Soviet Troops Seize Latvia's Newspaper Publishing Plant," *Washington Post*, 3 January 1991.

59 *Civil Society in the USSR*, 30–1.

60 D. Aripov, "Vozbuzhdenie ugolovnogo dela po prestupleniiam sostavliaiushchim preezhitki feodal'nogo byta," in *Voprosy kriminalistiki i sudebnoi ekspertizy* (1962): 66–9. (This journal was published irregularly in Dushanbe, Tadjikistan, then Frunze, capital of the Tadjik Soviet Socialist Republic.)

61 See Yuri Feofanov, "The Fourth Dimension," *CDSP* 22, no. 27 (1970): 27–8.

62 ibid.

63 See, especially, Shelud'ko, *Sovetskaia militsiia*, 23; and B. Sharov, *Vedomstvennaia militsiia, eë organizatsiia i rabota* (Moscow: NKVD RSFSR, 1928).

64 See T.K. Zarubitskaia, "Organy vnutrennykh del v sisteme okhrany sotsialiticheskoi sobstvennosti," in *Pravovye i organizatsionnye mery bor'by s pravonarusheniiami protiv sotsialisticheskoi sobstvennosti*, ed. B.K. Babaev *et al.* (Gorky: Gorkovskaia vysshaia shkola, 1982), 118; and V. Anishchenko, "Rhodonite Up His Sleeve," *CDSP* 34, no. 32 (1982): 17–18.

65 V.M. Olnev, "Prirodookhranitel'naia deiatel'nost' i organy vnutrennykh del," in *Pravovye i organizatsionnye mery*, 160–1.

66 Albert J. Reiss, Jr., "The Legitimacy of Intrusion Into Private Space," in *Private Policing*, ed. Clifford D. Shearing and Philip C. Stenning (Newbury Park, California: Sage, 1987), 25.

67 Departmental guard units were governed by the same regulations as were regular militia units, while non-departmental guard units were governed by a separate statute. For this latter statute, see "Statute on Non-Departmental Guards Attached to Militia of MOOP RSFSR," in *Spravochnik po zakonodatel'stvu dlia rabotnikov organov prokuratury, suda i ministerstva vnutrennykh del*, vol. 2, pt. 1 (Moscow: Iuridicheskaia literatura, 1971), 410–11.

8 POLICING THE DEVIANT: SOCIAL WORKERS WITH STICKS

1 V. Fokin, "209-a ne rabotaet," *Sovetskaia militsiia*, no. 4 (1991): 49.

2 The USSR Academy of Sciences, for example, sponsored a conference on deviance outside of Moscow in April 1990 to which this author was invited.

3 See V. Bobrov *et al.*, "Paspivochnaia u stanka," *Vecherniaia Moskva*, 24 January 1989.

4 See, for example, E. Zikibaev, "Trebuetsiia obedinenie usilii," *Kazakhstanskaia Pravda*, 15 June 1988; and D. Beknazarov, "Konets plantatsiiam durmana," *Kommunist Tadzhikistana*, 28 July 1988.

5 Iu. Churbanov, *Tovarishch militsiia* (Moscow: Molodaia gvardiia, 1980), 151.

6 A. Vlasov, "Na strazhe pravoporiadka," *Kommunist*, no. 5 (1988): 54–5, 57.

7 See "Insidious Grams of Drugs," *Current Digest of the Soviet Press* (hereafter *CDSP*) 39, no. 2 (1987): 1; and Liudmila Tkacheva, "Kto spasët narkoman," *Komsomolets kubani*, 5 March 1988.

There were significant geographic variations in drug addiction in the USSR. In 1989 in Turkmenia, for example, 129.9 out of every 100,000 residents were registered addicts; the comparable figure for Byelorussia for the same year was 4.8. See "USSR Drug Addiction Prevalence Quantified," Foreign Broadcast Information Service, *Daily Report: Soviet Union* (hereafter, FBIS, *Daily Report*), 11 January 1989, 83. The number of registered addicts rose dramatically in the 1980s, in part due to more careful record keeping. Mikhail Levin, "I tak narkomania," *Ogonëk*, no. 23 (1988): 18, reports that the number of drug addicts in the national USSR registry rose by 28 percent between 1980 and 1986 and that the number of cases of *toksikomania* (abuse of non-traditional drugs such as glue) doubled.

8 Iu.I. Veselov, "Sluzhatelei vysshei shkoly militsii shefstvuiut nad trudnovo-spituemymi," in *Preduprezhdenie beznadzornosti i pravonarushenii sredi nesovershennoletnikh*, ed. M.K. Makharov (Omsk: Omskaia vysshaia shkola militsii, 1969), 103–4.

9 "Behind Another's Back: Parasitism Has No Place in Our Life," *CDSP* 21, no. 37 (1969): 19.

10 See V. Nekrasov, "Vadim Tikunov," *Sovetskaia militsiia*, no. 8 (1990): 22.

11 In the 1980s, drug users developed a homemade narcotics mixture from pre-scription drugs. This mixture, which once comprised only 2 percent of drug confiscations in Moscow, represented 30 percent of all drug seizures in the capital by the late 1980s. See interview with Moscow police official in "Eschë raz o narkomanii," *Izvestiia*, 23 November 1987.

12 On the Afghanistan supply connection, see Rensselaer W. Lee III and Scott B. MacDonald, "Drugs in the East," *Foreign Policy*, no. 90 (Spring 1993): 89–107; and Rensselaer W. Lee III, "Soviet Narcotics Trade," *Society* 28, no. 5 (July 1991): 46–52.

On drug cultivation in the Caucasus and Central Asia, see, for example, "Increased Drug Trade Expected, Antidrug Campaign Urged," FBIS, *Daily Report*, 29 May 1992, 49.

13 October 1989 interview with Igor' Karpets, director of the All-Union Institute for the Study of the Causes and Development of Measures for the Prevention of Crime (Vsesoiuznyi institut po izucheniiu prichin i razrabotke mer preduprezhdeniia prestupnosti) of the USSR Procuracy, Moscow.

14 According to statistics cited in B.M. Levin and M.B. Levin, *Narkomaniia i narkomany* (Moscow: Prosveshchenie, 1991), there were 8,104 registered addicts and practitioners of *toksimaniia* in the USSR in 1960; 24,995 in 1970; 36,186 in 1980 and 47,947 in 1986. Figures for western societies are generally not as precise because of the absence of drug addict registries in these nations, but publications such as *Drug Abuse in America: Problem in Perspective*, Second Report of the National Commission on Marijuana and Drug Abuse (Washington, D.C.: Government Printing Office, 1973), and R.L. Hartnall, "Current Situation Related to Drug Abuse Assessment in European Countries," *Bulletin on Narcotics* (January–June 1986): 71–76, document that drug abuse was far more widespread in the west during the same time period.

15 On the necessity of education for drug prevention in the USSR, see Tkacheva, "Kto spasët narkoman."

16 "Bakatin Interviewed on Crime 'Crisis,'" FBIS, *Daily Report*, 19 July 1989, 101.

17 See, for example, "Discusses 'Narco-Mafia,'" FBIS, *Daily Report*, 26 February 1988, 62; Vlasov, "Na strazhe pravoporiadka," 55; and "Soviet Drug Scene Gets Heavy Coverage," *CDSP* 39, no. 2 (1987): 3.

18 On the Kuban, see Tkacheva, "Kto spasët narkoman." Regarding the creation of the Georgian drug commission, see A.A. Gabiani, *Narkotizm vchera i segodniia* (Tbilisi, Georgia: Sabchota sakartvelo, 1988), 248–57.

19 See "Technical Equipment Problems," FBIS, *Daily Report*, 26 February 1988, 61; and "Discusses 'Narco-Mafia,'" 62.

20 "Technical Equipment Problems", 61.

21 The *Pravda* article noted: "The law enforcement mechanism is sometimes ineffectual with regard to pinpointing and unmasking drug dealers and traffickers and the people responsible for organizing and maintaining drug dens operating in Armenia, Estonia, Lithuania, and Volgograd, Kemerovo, Cheliabinsk, and Saratov *oblasti*." See translation in "Technical Equipment Problems."

22 See "Measures to Combat Drug Problem Reported," FBIS, *Daily Report*, 12 September 1989, 66.

23 See Peggy McInerny, "Narcotics Trafficking in the USSR," Kennan Institute for Advanced Russian Studies Meeting Report 8, no. 8 (1991).

24 See, for example, "Moscow Lawmen Stage Daily Roundups of Workers Buying Liquor During Workday," *CDSP* 37, no. 21 (1985): 14.

25 "Reduced Penalties Encourage Home Brewing in Gomel Province," *CPSP* 36, no. 11 (1984): 31–2.

26 ". . . A nachalos' s 'p'ianoi' kampanii," *Rossiiskie militseiskie vedomosti*, no. 3 (1991): 8.

27 On police monitoring of alcohol consumption, see "Fedorchuk on Police's Anti-Drinking Role," *CDSP* 37, no. 22 (1985): 10–11; and "Dal'she, dal'she . . . Dal'she?" *Vechernyii Leningrad*, 28 September 1988. For arrest figures during the campaign, see *Statisticheskie dannye o prestupnosti i pravnarusheniiakh po SSSR* (Moscow: MVD USSR glavnyi informatsionnyi tsentr, 1989), 19. One to two percent of these arrests were for criminal violations, the remainder were for administrative violations.

   A September 1987 interview with Dr. Boris Levin, chief of the section on drug abuse of the Institute of Sociology of the USSR Academy of Sciences, Moscow, provided information on the numbers of people placed in sobering-up facilities.

28 See "Anti-Alcohol Campaign Said to 'Run Dry,'" FBIS, *Daily Report*, 16 January 1986, R4.

29 In one region of the USSR, only 10 percent of the men surveyed in a poll were willing to participate in militia raids to detect illegal production and sale of alcohol. See Vladimir Treml, "A Noble Experiment? Assessing Gorbachev's Anti-Drinking Campaign," (paper presented at fall conference of the Washington, D.C., chapter of the American Association for the Advancement of Slavic Studies, Washington, D.C., September 1986).

30 See, for example, Anatolii Rubinov, "Otchevo blagoukhaiut muzchiny, ili o parfiumernom sposobe bor'by s alkogolizmom," *Literaturnaia gazeta*, 12 November 1986.

31 Estimate of Boris Levin (see note 27) in an October 1989 interview in Moscow.

32 ibid.

33 See T. Durasova, "'Optimalist' v trekh litsakh," *Leningradskii rabochii*, 6 January 1989.

34 B. Levin and M. Levin, *Krutoi povorot* (Moscow: Sovetskaia Rossiia, 1989).

35 See, for example, I. Sikorskii, "Mesto zhitel'stva aerovokzal," *Vozdushnyi transport*, 10 November 1988.
36 "Pravda dlia izbrannykh," *Strana i mir*, no. 4 (1985): 35.
37 See Article 209–1 of the RSFSR Criminal Code in Harold J. Berman, *Soviet Criminal Law and Procedure: The RSFSR Codes*, 2d ed. (Cambridge, Massachusetts: Harvard University Press, 1972), 187. For a *perestroika*-era consideration of the legal requirement to work, see Igor Granikin, "Nuzhna li trudovaia povinnost'," *Nedelia*, no. 18 (1990).
38 "Krepit' Pravo," *Krokodil*, no. 26 (1985): 3.
39 See "Contemporary Issues: Wish to Change Places," FBIS, *Daily Report*, 11 July 1988, 83; and "Pravda dlia izbrannykh," 35.
40 David Remnick, "Painful Topic Confronts Soviets: Homelessness at Home," *Washington Post*, 21 February 1988. For a discussion of the procedure that allowed the militia to detain the homeless, see G.P. Shelud'ko, *Sovetskaia militsiia na strazhe obshchestvennogo poriadka* (Kiev: Vishcha shkola, 1982), 18.
41 See Remnick, "Painful Topic," for a description of vagrants in Tashkent in 1988. The estimate of the percentage of vagrants who were ex-offenders is derived from T.M. Kafarov and Ch.T. Musaev, *Bor'ba s posiagatel'stvom na obshchestvennyi poriadok* (Baku: Elm, 1983), 178.
42 A. Lebedev, "The Bottom Layer," *CDSP* 39, no. 14 (1987): 1.
43 For information on the reluctance of enterprise managers to hire vagrants, see G. Gvetadze, "Georgian Minister of Internal Affairs Interviewed," Joint Publications Research Service, *USSR Report: Political and Sociological Affairs*, 3 August 1984, 38. "Behind Another's Back" (see note 9 above) provides information on how vagrants managed to leave jobs and elude militia detection.
44 Lebedev, "The Bottom Layer," 3.
45 USSR Ministry of Internal Affairs press release no. 559, 30 November 1989, documents the 18–29 age bracket for parasites in the period 1985–88. Lebedev, "The Bottom Layer," 3, provides information on the transmission of venereal disease and tuberculosis by parasites. For a discussion of the sociological study of crime in the Moscow *oblast'* during the 1980s, see K.K. Goryainov, "Some Results of Studying Cases of Parasitism," *CDSP* 36, no. 5 (1984): 14. A.I. Smirnov *et al.*, *Prestupnost' i pravonarusheniia v SSSR* (Moscow: Iuridicheskaia literatura, 1990), 84, cites the percentage of parasites among total offenders in the USSR in 1988. The declining use of parasite laws after *perestroika* meant that by 1989, only 5 percent of offenders were defined as parasites while 31.2 percent were defined as unemployed.
46 On the militia's purported lack of powers, see *Prestupnost' i pravonarushenia*, 19.
47 I.L. Petrukhin, "Zaderzhanie i arest," *Sovetskoe gosudarstvo i pravo*, no. 8 (1989): 75–6.
48 Lebedev, "The Bottom Layer," 3.
49 See Andrea Stevenson Sanjian, "Prostitution, the Press and Agenda-Building in the Soviet Policy Process," in *Soviet Social Problems*, ed. Anthony Jones, Walter D. Connor and David E. Powell (Boulder: Westview, 1991), 270–95.
50 On the special Moscow militia unit, see B. Chubar, "Iz zhizni putan, reketirov, kidal i prochikh," *Zhurnalist* (August 1989): 11. On arrests of ordinary prostitutes, see Nikolai Krivomazov and Georgii Ovcharenko, "A domoi prikhodili na tsipochkakh," *Ogonëk*, no. 15 (1987): 30. For information on prostitutes bribing militiamen, see "Eva ischet Adama s valiutoi," *Sovetskaia militsiia*, no. 1 (1990): 38.
51 For more on the Riga registration system, see "Tougher Anti-prostitution Measures Urged," FBIS, *Daily Report*, 13 May 1988, 52–3. On the establishment of moral division in other cities of the USSR, see "Sochi Gorkom Leader on Battle

Against Graft," FBIS, *Daily Report*, 12 May 1988, 55. "A Hard Look at Prostitution in the USSR," *CDSP* 39, no. 11 (1987): 2, documents the existence of a prostitute registry at the 69th militia precinct in Moscow.

52 "A Hard Look at Prostitution in the USSR," *CDSP*, 2.

53 ibid.

54 "Eva ishchet Adama s valiutoi," 37.

55 In September 1989 the author overheard militiamen chasing whores away from the centrally located "Natsional" Hotel in Moscow. Regarding publications on Moscow prostitutes, see "Eva ishchet Adama s valiutoi," 38–9.

56 "Tougher Anti-Prostitution Measures Urged," 53.

57 On scam operations in Estonia, see "Militia Abets Robbery of Finnish Tourists," FBIS, *Daily Report*, 19 May 1988, 31. Interestingly, police officials complained that they did not have the right to enter flats where brothels were sometimes organized. See "Detective on problem of prostitution in Moscow," British Broadcasting Corporation Monitoring, *Summary of World Broadcasts: USSR* (hereafter BBC, *SWB: USSR*), SU/0030, 19 December 1987, B/23.

58 Nekrasov, "Vadim Tikunov," 22 (see note 10 above), documents the creation of these rooms under Khrushchev. For the categories of crime handled by such centers, see "Instruktsiia ob organizatsii detskoi komnaty militsiia," Decree of the USSR Ministry of the Defense of Public Order, 19 August 1968, no. 542, in *Spravochnik po zakonodatel'stvu dlia rabotnikov organov prokuratury suda i ministerstva vnutrennykh del*, vol. 2, pt. 2 (Moscow: Iuridicheskaia literatura, 1972), 573. Additional information on the location and activity of children's rooms can be found in N.I. Gukovskaia, A.I. Dolgova and G.M. Minkovskii, *Rassledovanie i sudebnoe razbiratel'stvo del o prestupleniiakh nesovershennoletnikh* (Moscow: Iuridicheskaia literatura, 1974), 73–5, 90–5; and M. Kasymova and P. Arenberg, *Preduprezhdenie pravonarushenii nesovershennoletnikh* (Tashkent: Fan, 1972), 95–107.

59 M.N. Eropkin, *Upravlenie v oblasti okhranu obshchestvennogo poriadka* (Moscow: Iuridicheskaia literatura, 1965), 204; and "Letters to Pravda Ukrainy," *CDSP* 22, no. 50 (1971): 23–4.

60 See "Instruktsiia ob organizatsii," 574–6.

61 V. Pechersky, "The Prosecutor and Adolescents," *CDSP* 37, no. 6 (1985): 18–19.

62 "Juvenile Delinquency in One Moscow Precinct: Problems and Causes," Radio Liberty, Audience Research and Program Evaluation Division, Background Report #10–76, 6 July 1976.

63 See, for example, V. Andriyanov, "Patrons in Name Only," *CDSP* 22, no. 50 (1971): 23; and Joseph Serio, trans., *USSR Crime Statistics and Summaries, 1989 and 1990* (Chicago: Office of International Criminal Justice, University of Illinois at Chicago, 1992), 30.

64 "Ideologiia rukopashnogo boia," *Smena*, 20 January 1989.

65 Kasymova and Arenberg, *Preduprezhdenie*, 95.

66 V.S. Orlov, *Podrostok i prestuplenie* (Moscow: Izdatel'stvo Moskovskogo gosudarstvennogo universiteta, 1969), 185.

67 V. Soskov, "Chetvertyi raz v pervyi klass," *Moskovskaya pravda*, 25 August 1988.

68 Petrukhin, "Zaderzhanie i arest," 76; "Instruktsiia ob organizatsii," (note 58) 573.

69 See, for example, M. Mikhailov, "Siuzhet bez montazha i bez kupiur," *Leningradskaia pravda*, 12 February 1989.

70 For information on crimes committed by youth in the USSR during the Brezhnev era, see "The Adult's Responsibility," *CDSP* 21, no. 40 (1969), 20; E. Raska, "Profil' zhizhennykh orientatsii kak sub"ektivnyi faktor prestupnosti molodezhi," *Sovetskoe pravo*, no. 3 (1978): 185; and Anastasia Gelishchanov,

"Juvenile Crime in the Georgian SSR," *Radio Liberty Research Bulletin*, no. 25 (1979).

For documentation of the percentage of violent crimes committed by youth in the USSR in the early 1970s, see V.N. Kudriavtsev *et al.*, *Lichnost' prestupnika* (Moscow: Iuridicheskaia literatura, 1971), 111. In the United States during the same period the figure was approximately 13 percent. See U.S. Department of Justice, *Sourcebook of Criminal Justice Statistics* (Washington, D.C.: U.S. Government Printing Office, 1978), 511.

"Evening in Dzerzhinsk City," Joint Publications Research Service, *USSR Report: Political and Sociological Affairs*, (hereafter JPRS, *USSR: Political and Sociological Affairs*), 18 July 1986, 77–84, provides information about the behavior of youth gangs at the end of the Soviet period.

For examples of criticisms of militia performance *vis-à-vis* juvenile offenders, see "Inadequate Crime Prevention Work with Young People, Adults' Bad Example Decried," *CDSP* 36, no. 31 (1984): 4; Iu.P. Shchekochikhin, "Po komy zvonit kokol'chik," *Sotsiologicheskie issledovaniia*, no. 1 (January–February 1987): 81–93; and Richard B. Dobson, "Youth Problems in the Soviet Union," in *Soviet Social Problems*, ed. Anthony Jones, Walter D. Connor, and David E. Powell (Boulder, Colorado: Westview Press, 1991), 227–51.

71 See Resolution of the Presidium of the USSR Supreme Soviet, "On the Procedure for Applying the Decree of the Presidium of the USSR Supreme Soviet of June 12, 1970, 'On Probationary Sentencing to Deprivation of Freedom with Mandatory Assignment of the Convicted Person to Work,'" *Vedomosti Verkhovnogo Soveta RSFSR*, no. 24 [1526] (17 June 1970): items 205, 281–3.

72 N. Yemelin, "Helping by Trusting," *CDSP* 21, no. 46 (1969): 22.

73 For more on ex-convicts' return to crime after release from prison, see K. Ergashev, "To Jointly Eradicate Malice," JPRS, *USSR: Political and Sociological Affairs*, 7 May 1982, 91. On crime by ex-convicts in the town Nikolaev, see B. Mel'nik, "Eshche raz ob uchastkovom," *Iuzhnaia pravda*, 26 July 1992, 3.

74 See D.N. Bakhrakh, *Mery administrativnogo i obshchestvennogo vozdeistviia na pravonarushitelei* (Moscow: Pravda, 1971), 19–20.

75 *Arkhiv samizdata* 29, no. 3302 (1978) documents the treatment of Lev Luk'ianenko after his release from prison on political charges.

76 Lev Yudovich, "Administrative Surveillance – A Means of Police Repression," *Radio Liberty Research Bulletin*, no. 454 (1983); and *Arkhiv samizdata* 29, no. 3302. The latter source provides information on how the militia limited the contacts of dissidents in exile. For an account of how the militia used *nadzor* restrictions to return dissidents to prison, see Anatoly Marchenko, *From Tarusa To Siberia*, ed. Joshua Rubinstein (Walled Lake, Michigan: Strathcona, 1980).

77 Louise I. Shelley, "Crime in the Soviet Union," in *Soviet Social Problems*, ed. Anthony Jones, Walter Connor and David Powell (Boulder, Colorado: Westview Press, 1991), 252–69.

78 M. Podgorodnikov, "Rezonans kak chelovek stanovit'siia brodiagoi," *Literaturnaia gazeta*, 21 October 1987.

79 "MVD Discusses Problems of Ex-Offenders," *RFE/RL Daily Report*, 9 August 1989.

While on a Helsinki Watch mission to the USSR in January 1989, the author held discussions on this topic with the head of the MVD Institute (a special research division separate from the MVD Academy), who expressed a desire to eliminate *propiska* regulations because they proved counterproductive to rehabilitation.

80 Bill Keller, "Russia's Restless Youth," *New York Times Magazine*, 26 July 1987, 50.

81 See "Homo Sovieticus: A Rough Sketch," *Moscow News*, no. 11 (1990).
82 On militia surveillance of AIDS patients, see Oleg Moroz, "Otverzhennye," *Ogonëk*, no. 16 (April 1990): 28. For examples of protests against this practice, see L. Asaulova, "Rezus otritsatel'nyi," *Sovetskaia militsiia*, no. 9 (1990), 73; and V. Kulagin, "Takoi strannyi rozysk," *Izvestiia*, 8 March 1989.
83 See "Customs Official on Cooperation in Drug Wars," FBIS, *Daily Report*, 19 October 1988, 11; and "Fees for USSR Joining Interpol Discussed," FBIS, *Daily Report*, 25 April 1990, 66.
84 Vladimir Voinovich (dinner address at the Kennan Institute for Advanced Russian Studies, Woodrow Wilson International Center for Scholars, Washington, D.C., 25 April 1990.)
85 See, for example, Dmitry Sidorov and Victor Turshatov, "Stepping out into the Night," *Moscow News*, no. 38 (1988).
86 See, for example, M. Tagieva, "Mezhdy proshlym i budushchim," *Turkmenskaia iskra*, 15 January 1989.

9 THE MILITIA AND CRIME CONTROL

1 For a fuller discussion of this topic, see Louise Shelley, "The Geography of Soviet Criminality," *American Sociological Review* 45 (February 1980): 111–22.
2 A.I. Smirnov *et al.*, *Prestupnost' i pravonarusheniia v SSSR* (Moscow: Iuridicheskaia literatura, 1990), 20.
3 See, for example, D.I. Patiashvili, "For a Model City – Exemplary Order in Everything", Foreign Broadcast Information Service, *Daily Report: Soviet Union* (hereafter FBIS, *Daily Report*), 15 January 1986, R13–15, in which the first Party secretary of the Georgian Republic acknowledges the crime problem in his republic.
4 Smirnov *et al.*, *Prestupnost' i pravonarushenia*, 26.
5 For documentation of the drop in crime rates during 1988, see V.V. Luneev, "Prestupnost' v SSSR za 1988g: statistika i kommentarii kriminologa," *Sovetskoe gosudarstvo i pravo*, no. 8 (1989): 85. On the increased use of weapons in crime commission during the late 1980s, see "Srochno kupliu oruzhie," *Sovetskaia militsiia*, no. 9 (1990): 55; and "Ryzhkov Interviewed on Plans to Combat Crime," FBIS, *Daily Report*, 9 October 1990, 51. In the latter article, USSR Prime Minister Nikolai Ryzhkov claimed that 4,600 crimes were committed with guns in the first eight months of 1990. Increased use of guns in crime commission was in part attributable to the illegal gun trafficking that grew out of the Afghan war and in part to increased thefts from militia and military arsenals.
  Crime rates for 1989, 1990 and 1991 are documented in the following sources: 1989: *Prestupnost' i pravonarusheniia*, Table 1, 11. 1990: "Rhyzhkov Interviewed on Plans," 51. 1991: S.A. Pashin, ed., *Kontseptsiia sudebnoi reformy v Rossiiskoi Federatsii* (Moscow: Respublika, 1992), 8.
  Concerning individual Soviet republics, the crime rate in Russia alone rose over 33 percent in the first three months of 1992 as compared to the same period in 1991. See "Russia Targets Jobless Youth in Crime Prevention Drive," Radio Free Europe/Radio Liberty, *Daily Report*, 21 May 1992, 2.
6 The growth in serious violent crime in the late 1980s is discussed in A. Alekseev, "Itogi i prognozy," *Sovetskaia militsiia*, no. 5 (1990): 7. See Smirnov *et al.*, *Prestupnost' i pravonarusheniia*, 5, 10–11, for information on crime rates in the Brezhnev period as a whole.
7 "Bakatin Interviewed on Crime 'Crisis,'" FBIS, *Daily Report*, 19 July 1989, 99.
8 See "Volny apatii v more stereotipov," *Sovetskaia militsiia*, no. 8 (1990): 13; and "Interior Minister dismisses rumors of planned pogrom," British Broad-

casting Corporation Monitoring, *Summary of World Broadcasts: USSR* (hereafter, BBC, *SWB: USSR*), SU/0165, 31 May 1988, i.

9 According to a Soviet émigré defense counsel whom the author interviewed in New York in 1980, one investigator desperate to fulfill his arrest quota in the Stalin era rounded up women who had survived abortions, which were then illegal.

10 The *Izvestiia* article is translated in "Police Criticized in Filling Set Arrest Quotas," FBIS, *Daily Report*, 5 April 1989, 85. In another incident described in the article, a journalist observed the investigative branch of the Moscow administration of internal affairs receive a six-meter list of suspects. Soon after the list was delivered, a deputy MVD colonel began to pressure investigators to charge all "suspects" on the list by the end of the month.

11 I thank Peter Solomon for his insights on this practice.

12 See Ger Van den Berg, *The Soviet System of Justice: Figures and Policy* (Dordrecht, The Netherlands: Martinus Nijhoff, 1985), 14, for estimates on the likelihood of certain crimes being recorded. I. Servetskii, "Komu nuzhen otkaznoi," *Sovetskaia militsiia*, no. 11 (1990): 54, documents that 3.9 million crimes were reported to the militia in 1989. Smirnov *et al.*, *Prestupnost' i pravonarusheniia*, 15, table 7, documents that the militia registered 2.5 million crimes the same year. Even if the two figures resulted from different criteria for identifying crime, the wide disparity between them indicates that a vast number of criminal acts were not officially recorded.

13 The author learned of this agreement between militia and medical personnel in numerous interviews with former militia personnel in the United States and Israel between 1980 and 1987 (see Appendix). See also A. Lazarev, "A kogda lovit' prestupnikov?" *Nedelia*, no. 43 (1989).

14 See *Zariia vostoka* article of 5 March 1983, translated as "Special Committee Investigates Corruption in Georgian MVD," Joint Publications Research Service, *USSR: Political and Sociological Affairs*, 7 April 1983, 45–6.

15 ibid., 47.

16 On the disciplining of militia personnel in 1987, see "The Police and Openness," *Current Digest of the Soviet Press* (hereafter *CDSP*) 39, no. 52 (1988): 25. The author personally discovered the continued reluctance to record crimes without suspects during *perestroika* when a close friend was brutally raped in a Moscow suburb in 1989. The case was recorded and investigated only after the woman's husband filed a complaint with the procuracy. When militiamen finally arrived at their apartment to take a report, the officers complained of the impossibility of their workload due to the contemporary crime wave. Their complaint was affirmed by Minister of Internal Affairs Vadim Bakatin that same year when he claimed "the organs of inquiry and investigation have, figuratively speaking, become choked." "Bakatin Interviewed on Crime 'Crisis,'" 99.

17 A. Lazarev, "A kogda lovit' prestupnikov?"

18 F. Ivanov, "Operatsiia bez sekreta," *Izvestiia*, 5 February 1989. Bribery, of course, also worked to prevent militiamen from reporting all crimes committed in their full view, especially those at markets. See, for example, "Militiamen Ignore Profiteering at Nazran Market," FBIS, *Daily Report* 27 July 1988, 45. Given the endemic shortages in the Soviet economy, militiamen also hesitated to move against people who sold needed consumer goods at such markets, even if they did so illegally (October 1989 interview with Soviet law enforcement personnel, Moscow).

19 See "Internal Affairs Ministry Holds Conference," FBIS, *Daily Report*, 12 September 1989. To cite an example of poor militia equipment, in 1990 it was discovered that one-half of all communications devices installed in railroad cars to summon militia personnel were not operational. See "MVD Statistics on Railroad Crime Reported," FBIS, *Daily Report/ Supplement*, 11 May 1990, 4.

20 Smirnov *et al.*, *Prestupnost' i pravonarusheniia*, 19.
21 See ibid. for 1989 theft figures. On burglaries, see "The Writer and Society: Watch Out for Report Padding," *CDSP* 38, no. 42 (1986): 19.
22 See, for example, "What do the Militia Do?" *Moscow News*, no. 50 (1988).
23 Smirnov *et al.*, *Prestupnost' i pravonarusheniia*, 19.
24 For Soviet investigator figures, see "Volny apatii," 12. For a discussion of the changes which occurred in the Hungarian police at this time, see Sandor Pinter, "The Effect of Social Changes on the Police," in Louise Shelley and Jozef Vigh (Chur: Switzerland: Harwood Academic Publishers, 1995), 109–17.
25 "Volny apatii," 12.
26 In a *perestroika*-era survey of 305 judges in Stavropol *oblast'* that was conducted by legal researchers, 40 percent of the judges surveyed rejected the following statement: "It is better to acquit ten innocent people than convict one innocent person." Pashin, *Kontseptsiia sudebnoi reformy*, 20.
27 See "Pravosudie i glasnost'," *Literaturnaia gazeta*, 30 March 1988, 13. During the mid-1960s, judges sent back only 2 percent of all cases investigated by the procuracy and invalidated only 13 percent of militia cases for lack of evidence. See N. Zhogin, "Rol' i mesto sledstvennogo apparata v SSSR," *Sotsialisticheskaia zakonnost'*, no. 4 (1969): 19.
28 D.S. Karev and N.M. Savgirova, *Vozbuzhdenie i rassledovanie ugolovnykh del* (Moscow: Vysshaia shkola, 1967), 18.
29 "Moscow Internal Affairs Head Interviewed," FBIS, *Daily Report*, 3 March 1989, 60.
30 The 1970 figure is cited in S.V. Borodin, *Protsessual'nye akty predvaritel'nogo rassledovaniia: primernye obratzsy* (Moscow: Iuridicheskaia literatura, 1972); the 1990 figure in O. Aksenov, "Nabolelo," *Sovetskaia militsiia*, no. 7 (1990): 40.
31 One Russian criminalistics expert formerly employed by a national research institute of the USSR MVD has even published an article on innovative criminalistics techniques in a publication put out by the U.S. Federal Bureau of Investigation (interview with Dr. Ilya Zeldes, Fargo, South Dakota, October 1980).
32 See, for example, G.G. Shikhantsov, "Metody psikhologicheskogo izucheniia sledstvennoi deiatel'nosti," *Voprosy gosudarstva i prava*, vol. 1 (Minsk: 1969), 211–20; A.P. Derbenev, "O psikhologicheskikh priemakh doprosa na predvaritel'nom sledstvii," *Pravovedenie*, no. 1 (1981): 86–90; and E. Varutin, "Kak my isportili nastroenie liudiam," *Molodëzh Estonii*, 6 May 1988.
33 The police search was defined in Article 168 of the RSFSR Code of Criminal Procedure; see Harold J. Berman, *Soviet Criminal Law and Procedure: The RSFSR Codes*, 2d ed. (Cambridge, Mass.: Harvard University Press, 1972), 256. The lack of clarity in the definition of the term 'search' permitted the militia excessive leeway in how it conducted searches, a problem the author discussed in a September 1994 interview with Russian ombudsman Sergei Kovalëv. For a technical description of the initiation of a Soviet militia search, see V.G. Kitchenko, "K voprosu ob osnovanii k proizvodstvu obyska," *Trudy Kievskoi vysshei shkoly*, no. 9 (1975): 116.

The following *perestroika*-era story reveals the ways in which illegal searches served the aims of the procuracy. During the highly charged 1990 investigation of the state cooperative ANT, which was accused of transporting tanks across the Soviet Union for illegal export and sale, the home of the cooperative directors was searched illegally and documents and property were seized without justification. When the procuracy – the oversight body that monitored the legality of militia investigations – was queried about the legitimacy of the militia's unauthorized search and illegal removal of private property, the procurator assigned to the case replied, "We would have confiscated them anyway" (Yuri Teplyakov, "Who Needed the Tanks?" *Moscow News*, no. 13 [1990]).

34 Mikhail Paleev, member, USSR Supreme Soviet Subcommittee on Judicial Reform (oral presentation at a conference for leading legal officials of the Commonwealth of Independent States sponsored by the U.S. Information Agency, Washington, D.C., 10 July 1992).

35 See I.L. Petrukhin, "Zaderzhanie i arest," *Sovetskoe gosudarstvo i pravo*, no. 8 (1989): 73–81.

36 Discussion with human rights activists in Moscow, October 1989.

37 See Petrukhin, "Zaderzhanie i arest." Interviews with former militia prisoners in Moscow and the United States during the 1980s confirmed the militia's use of drugs on suspects in Central Asia.

38 Galina Silina, "Osoboe mnenie," *Literaturnaia gazeta*, 24 December 1986.

39 "Verdict in Murder Trial Based on Coerced Confessions Overturned by Lucky Accident; Defense Lawyers Complaisance Scored," *CDSP* 38, no.42 (1986): 5–6.

40 ibid.

41 See Arkadii Vaksberg, "Pravde v glaze," *Literaturnaia gazeta*, 17 December 1986, 13. Dmitrii Likhanov cites several incidents of police abuse during the *perestroika* years in "Bronirovannye mundiry," *Ogonëk*, no. 7 (1987): 30–1. In one case, a factory worker in Karelia was kicked so brutally by investigators that his spleen had to be removed. In another incident, militiamen placed a gas mask over the head of a metalworker until he lost consciousness; in a third case, militiamen beat a criminal suspect over the head with a four-pound ball until his head was cut open.

In the latter case, *obkom* and MVD officials acted to protect the abusive investigator even after his conduct was publicized by *Izvestiia* when the paper received an anonymous letter of complaint. See "Posle anonimki," *Izvestiia*, 13 June 1986.

In 1994, the newly created office of the Russian Ombudsman continues to document militia abuses in Russia.

42 "Internal Affairs Official on Failings, Tasks," FBIS, *Daily Report*, 28 April 1988, 59.

43 Gdlyan and Ivanov achieved fame for their attacks on organized crime in the late 1980s and were elected to the USSR Congress of People's Deputies in 1989. When they subsequently made claims that internal corruption in the Communist Party reached as high as Politburo member Egor Kuz'mich Ligachëv, the Procuracy of the USSR initiated an investigation against the two men. Although threatened with prosecution, they were never charged. See Otdel kommunisticheskogo vospitaniia 'LG,' "Politika i pravo," *Literaturnaia gazeta*, 24 May 1989, 13; "Reaction to Commission's Findings on Gdlyan Case," FBIS, *Daily Report*, 24 May 1989, 41–6; and "Prosecutor's Office Issues Corruption Warning," FBIS, *Daily Report*, 8 May 1990, 38.

44 George Feifer, *Justice in Moscow* (London: Bodley Head, 1964), 88.

45 On joint investigative efforts by the militia and procuracy, see G.I. Panteev and A.M. Chepul'chenko, "Vzaimodeistvie organov doznaniia i predvaritel'nogo sledstviia v protsesse rassledovaniia prestuplenii," *Trudy Kievskoi vysshei shkoly*, no. 7 (1973): 218–19; and A.V. Dulov, *Takticheskie operatsii pri rassledovanii prestuplenii* (Minsk: Izdatel'stvo Belorusskogo gosudarstvennogo universiteta, 1979), 30. Kh.S. Tadzhiev discusses the poor work and uncooperativeness of militia investigators in "Obespechenie prokurorom vzaimodeistviia organov doznaniia i predvaritel'nogo sledstviia," in *Pravovoe regulirovanie obshchest-vennykh otnoshenii* (Moscow: Institut gosudarstva i prava, 1976), 78.

46 See Pashin, *Kontseptsiia sudebnoi reformy*, 26.

47 For more on the heavy workload of militia investigators during the 1980s, see

"USSR Judicial, Legal Problems Examined," FBIS, *Daily Report/Annex*, 18 April 1990, 6. "Volny apatii" documents that the number of crimes investigated by the criminal investigative branch of the militia rose by 98.5 percent between 1979 and 1990. Pashin discusses the legal violations and poor decisions of militia investigators in Pashin, *Kontseptsiia sudebnoi reformy*, 13, 21.

48 See, for example, "Petropavlosk Criminals Arrested, Weapons Seized," FBIS, *Daily Report*, 12 October 1989, 61.

49 Interview with former Soviet militia officer in Israel, 1981.

50 Pashin, *Kontseptsiia sudebnoi reformy*, 10.

51 "Volny apatii," 13.

52 "Ukaz presidiuma Verkhnogo Soveta RSFSR," 11 December 1989, no. 50, Art. 1470. This *ukaz* amended Article 97 of the RSFSR Code of Criminal Procedure to institute the 18-month maximum detention period.

53 "Volny apatii," 13.

54 See Viktor Turshatov, "Organized Crime," *Moscow News*, no. 39 (1988).

55 Vlasov's admission can be found in "Vlasov Holds Talk with Writers, Journalists," FBIS, *Daily Report*, 27 April 1988, 42. The MVD research institute figures are cited by Svetlana P. Glinkina in "Privatizatsiya and Kriminalizatsiya: How Organized Crime is Hijacking Privatization," *Demokratizatsiya* 2, no. 3 (Summer 1994): 385.

56 Gennady Khohkryakov, "The Shadow Economy and the Administrative—Command System," *Moscow News*, no. 46 (1988).

57 See, for example, Iurii Shchekochikhin and Aleksandr Gurov, "Lev prygnul," *Literaturnaia gazeta*, 20 July 1988.

58 See "Pravda Carries Law on Individual Labor Activity," Joint Publications Research Service, *USSR: National Affairs*, 26 November 1986, R1–8.

59 On money laundering and the financing of businesses by criminal groups, see Shchekochikhin and Gurov, "Lev prygnul;" and L.L. Fituni, "CIS: Organized Crime and Its International Activities," (monograph prepared by the Center for Strategic and Global Studies, Russian Academy of Sciences, Moscow, 1993), 62.

60 "Cooperatives Arm themselves Against Racketeers," FBIS, *Daily Report*, 4 April 1989, 69. "A Touchstone of Cooperation," *Moscow News*, no. 9 (1989), describes militiamen's resentment of the profits earned by cooperatives. Interviews with Russian police in fall 1989 confirmed that militiamen believed their duty was to protect state, not private, enterprises.

61 See E. Lukin, "Mafia: Prizraki i priznaki," *Ekonomicheskaia Gazeta*, no. 48 (November 1988); and Georgii Ovcharenko, "Pokupaiu pistolet," *Pravda* 23 March 1989, 6.

62 Vladimir Sokolov describes attacks on the militia by professional criminal groups in "Bandokratiia," *Literaturnaia gazeta*, 17 August 1988. For a description of the Soviet militia's legal successes in sighting such groups, see Anatoli Volobuev, "Soviet Union – Combatting Organized Crime Problems and Perspectives," *C.J. International* 5, no. 6 (1989): 14.

63 Lukin, "Mafia: Prizraki i priznaki."

64 See, for example, "KGB Chief on Role in Beating Racketeering," FBIS, *Daily Report*, 8 June 1989, 55–6; and Iu. Nikiforov, "Za mafiiu dolzhny vziat'siia i chekisty," *Nedelia*, no. 14 (1989).

65 See "Bakatin Interviewed on Crime 'Crisis,'" 98.

10 THE POLITICAL FUNCTIONS OF THE MILITIA

1 Jean-Paul Brodeur, "High Policing and Low Policing: Remarks about the Policing of Political Activities," *Social Problems* 30, no. 5 (1983): 513.

2 ibid., 514.
3 Much of the information about militia abuses of human rights first made available by *samizdat* was subsequently confirmed by official literature of the *perestroika* period.
4 For a description of how the militia used criminal law for political purposes, see *Arkhiv samizdata* 5 (1980): no. 3845. For information about the militia's role in confining dissidents to psychiatric hospitals, see *idem* 19 (1982): no. 4637 and 13 (1986): no. 5644; and A. Novikov, S. Razin, and M. Mishin, "Assignment in Response to a Disturbing Letter: A Closed Subject: For Many Years Now Psychiatric Science and Practice Have Been Shut Off from Glasnost Behind a High and Impenetrable Wall. Meanwhile Crimes Have Been Committed Behind that Wall," *Komsomol'skaia pravda*, 11 November 1987, 4, as cited in Foreign Broadcast Information Service, *Daily Report: Soviet Union* (hereafter FBIS, *Daily Report*), 20 November 1987, 45–51.
5 On the human rights movement, see Ludmilla Alexeyeva and Paul Goldberg, *The Thaw Generation: Coming of Age in the Post-Stalin Era* (Boston: Little, Brown, 1990), 124–36. For membership estimates of the Baptist and Pentecostal churches, see Liudmilla Alekseeva, *Istoriia inakomysliia* (Benson, Vermont: Khronika Press, 1984), 171–202.
6 Ronald Weitzer, "Policing a Divided Society: Obstacles to Normalization in Northern Ireland," *Social Problems* 33, no. 1 (1985): 53.
7 Information on the 1989 incident was provided by a member of the Leningrad procuracy during an interview in October of that year. See Liudmilla Alexeyeva and Catherine A. Fitzpatrick, *Civil Society in the USSR* (New York: Helsinki Watch, 1990), 73–9, for more information about *Pamiat'* activities during this period. For documentation of the *Moskovskii komsomolets* incident, see "Armed Pamyat Members Threaten Journalists," FBIS, *Daily Report*, 15 October 1992, 23.
8 For documentation of cases in which the militia prevented the public and/or witnesses from attending political trials, see *Arkhiv samizdata* 8 (1984): no. 5167; and 43 (1983): no. 5077. Ibid. 5 (1977): no. 2852 describes an apartment search conducted on the pretext of a fire inspection; ibid. 33 (1983): no. 5036 documents how the militia prevented the burial of a Crimean Tatar in his homeland. For further information on police treatment of Crimean Tatars, see Aishe Seit-muratova, "Soviet Persecution of the Crimean Tatars," in *The Fifth International Sakharov Hearing Proceedings*, ed. Allan Wynn (London: Andre Deutsch, 1986), 107–9.

For information on the framing of political activists for assaulting a police officer, see *Arkhiv samizdata* 12 (1986): no. 5638.
9 *Arkhiv samizdata* 1 (1979): no. 3436, and 23 (1982): no. 4667.
10 For cases of psychiatric confinement of dissidents and non-conformists by the militia, see, "Assignment in Response to a Disturbing Letter," 47–48; and *Arkhiv samizdata* 19 (1982): no. 4637; 21 (1982): no. 4650; and 13 (1986): no. 5644. For the 1972 regulations, see ibid. 21 (1977): no. 2954. The regulations that sought to curb such abuse are discussed in Bill Keller, "Mental Patients in Soviet Union to get New Legal Rights," *New York Times*, 5 January 1988.
11 See *Arkhiv samizdata* 12 (1978): 3186; 32 (1978): no. 2831; 20 (1981): no. 4308; and 3 (1978): no. 3324.
12 Ludmilla Alexeeva and Valery Chalidze, *Mass Unrest in the USSR*, vol. 2 (Washington, D.C.: Office of Net Assessments, 1985), 360.
13 ibid.
14 ibid.
15 ibid., vol. 1, 144.
16 For documentation of the 1965 Yerevan demonstration, see ibid. The Uzbek riot

is discussed in Boris Kamenetsky and Alexandra Alexandrovna, "Ispoved zhenshchiny," *Kontinent*, no. 38 (1983): 209–20.

17 Alexeeva and Chalidze, *Mass Unrest*, vol. 2, 331.

18 *Arkhiv samizdata*, 32 (1973): no. 1437.

19 Alexeeva and Chalidze, *Mass Unrest*, vol. 2, 361–2.

20 ibid., 366–7.

21 See, for example, Alekseeva, *Istoriia inakomysliia*, 340.

22 G. Tumanov, *Organizatsiia upravleniia v sfere okhrany obshchestvennogo poriadka* (Moscow: Iuridicheskaia literatura, 1972), 174–5.

23 See the discussion of an émigré interview project in Louise Shelley, "Interviews mit Emigrierten Sowjetischen Juristen," *Osteuropa* (October 1984): 796–803.

24 Alexeeva and Chalidze, *Mass Unrest*, vol. 2, 272.

25 ibid., 258, 275, 277.

26 See Christopher Wren, "Russians Raid an Exhibit of Modern Art with Bulldozers," *New York Times*, 16 September 1974; and Robert Toth, "Art in the Ring of the Cutthroats," *Los Angeles Times*, 17 September 1974.

27 *Chronicle of Current Events*, no. 34 (31 December 1974): 34–5. (See Mark Hopkins, *Russia's Underground Press: The Chronicle of Current Events* (New York: Praeger, 1983), 176, for a table of contents of the issues of this *samizdat* publication.) The author personally attended the second art exhibit.

28 Alexeeva and Chalidze, *Mass Unrest*, vol. 2, 320–8.

29 ibid., 320, 323.

30 See Alexeeva, *Istoriia inakomysliia*, 178, for an account of the militia's disruption of the 1978 Baptist meeting of youth from Omsk, Kokchevavskoi and Tselinograd *oblasti* in Isilkuskii *raion*. For additional accounts of militia harassment of Baptists and Pentecostals, see *Arkhiv samizdata* 30 (1972): no. 1117; 41 (1972): no. 1167; 47 (1973): no. 1370; 25 (1980): no. 4007; and 20 (1981): no. 4308.

31 Regarding cases instituted against religious parents and oversight over their children, see *Arkhiv samizdata* 36 (1974): no. 1817. For accounts of the psychiatric hospitalization of adult believers, see Michael Bourdeaux, "The Church in the USSR – Prospects under the New Leadership," in *Fifth International Sakharov Hearing*, ed. Allan Wynn (London: Andre Deutsch, 1986), 61.

32 When the author visited Moscow in October 1987 and stayed at the American embassy, her passport was registered with the branch of the militia assigned to the embassy.

33 *Arkhiv samizdata* 23 (1976): no. 2171.

34 "Energichno vesti perestroiku," *Pravda*, 13 November 1987.

35 "KGB Man Fired for Hounding Newsman," *Current Digest of the Soviet Press* (hereafter *CPSP*) 39, no. 1 (1987): 1; see also "Chebrikov Reports Dismissal of Province KGB Head for Masterminding Illegal Actions against Journalist," ibid., 20.

36 Malcolm Haslett, "Current Affairs Talks: KGB Death Plot Sensation," British Broadcasting Corporation Central Talk Features, Caris Talk no. 137 (19 October 1987).

37 David Killingray and David M. Anderson, "An Orderly Retreat? Policing the End of Empire," in *Policing and Decolonisation Politics: Nationalism and the Police: 1917–65*, ed. David M. Anderson and David Killingray (Manchester: Manchester University Press, 1992), 10.

38 See, for example, the account of Georgian militia fighting Soviet Army troops in Tbilisi in April 1989 in Mikhail Belikov et. al, "Not to be Repeated," *Moscow News*, no. 17 (1989). For a further discussion of the MVD role in Georgia, see Cathy Cosman, *Glasnost in Jeopardy: Human Rights in the USSR* (New York, Helsinki Watch, 1991), 65–6.

39   See, for example, Bill Keller, "Soviets Beginning to Crack Down on the Unofficial Political Clubs," *New York Times*, 29 November 1987.

40   For more on the Grigoryants story, see "Soviet Police Shadow Unofficial Publication," *The New York Times*, 14 August 1987; and Bill Keller, "Soviet Close a Magazine Extolling Openness," *New York Times*, 19 May 1988. A 1993 interview with Dr. Michael Waller in Washington, D.C., following the latter's meeting with Grigoryants, confirmed the details of these incidents.

41   For information on the Democratic Union's 1988 and 1989 clashes with the police, see respectively, Bill Keller, "Moscow Police Thwart Rally by Opposition Group," *New York Times*, 12 June 1988; and A. Vasil'ev, "Pushkinskaia ploshchad' v 19:00," *Trud*, 1 November 1989. For more on the Kuznetsov trial in 1990, see "Television Joins Media Defense of Kuznetsov," *RFE/RL Daily Report*, 8 January 1990, 4.

42   S. Miliukov, "Kak borot'siia s 'neformalami'?" *Leningradskaia militsiia*, no. 10 (11 March 1989).

43   See, for example, Elizaveta Bokova, "Miloserdiia proshu; Ispoved' neformala," *Literaturnaia gazeta*, 14 June 1988.

44   "O poriadke organizatsii i provedeniia sobranii, mitingov, ulichnykh shestvykh i demonstratsii v SSSR," Presidium of the Supreme Soviet of the USSR, *ukaz* no. 9306-XI, 28 July 1988. For more on the difficulties militiamen experienced in adjusting to democratization see A. Andrusenko, "Moskva sevognia: vzgliad s petrovki, 38," *Sovetskaia kultura*, 22 October 1988. On increased police tolerance of demonstrations, see Bill Keller, "In Moscow, Tolerance of Protests," *New York Times*, 8 June 1988.

45   Leonid Miloslavsky, "Lessons in Street Democracy," *Moscow News*, no. 36 (1988).

46   "Militia Spokesman Warns Against Disturbances," FBIS, *Daily Report*, 22 June 1988, 41.

47   ibid.; see also "Militia Censured for Acts Against Demonstrators," FBIS, *Daily Report*, 30 June 1988, 58.

48   See, for example, "Riot Police Beat Leningrad Demonstrators," *RFE/RL Daily Report*, 8 November 1990, 5.

49   See Killingray and Anderson, "An Orderly Retreat?" 13.

50   On militia attitudes and actions towards the Baltic independence movements, see Rein Taagepera, "Estonia's Road to Independence," *Problems of Communism* 38 (November–December 1989): 16; and Gary Lee, "Latvia Militia Cordon Prevents Riga Protest," *Washington Post*, 19 November 1987. For documentation of the 1 January 1991 and subsequent OMON attacks in Latvia, see "Black Berets Storm Latvian Interior Ministry," *RFE/RL Daily Report*, 3 January 1991, 3; Saulius Girnius, "In Lithuania A Tense Peace as Soviet Military Harasses Citizenry," Radio Free Europe/Radio Liberty, *Soviet/East European Report* 8, no. 35 (20 June 1991): 1–2; and "And Policemen in Latvia," *RFE/RL Daily Report*, 18 July 1991, 4.

51   "Kiev Demonstrators 'Severely' Beaten," FBIS, *Daily Report*, 8 November 1990, 82.

52   "Moldavian Soviet Seeks Solution," FBIS, *Daily Report*, 8 November 1990, 80.

53   "USSR OMON Units Sent to Moldavia," FBIS, *Daily Report*, 10 June 1991, 8.

54   James Critchlow, "Uzbekistan: A Changed Political Climate," *RFE/RL Soviet/East European Report* 8, no. 31 (20 May 1990): 1. On the Fergana Valley riots in 1989, see *idem*, "The Crisis in Uzbekistan," *RFE/RL Soviet/East European Report* 6, no. 32 (1 August 1989).

55   For a comparative perspective on this problem, see the discussion of the change in American police tactics for handling domestic political activity in U.S. society during the mid- to late 1960s in Isaac D. Balbus, *The Dialectics of Legal*

Repression: Black Rebels Before the American Courts (New Brunswick, New Jersey: Transaction Books, 1982), ch. 5.

CONCLUSION

1 See Maureen E. Cain, *Society and the Policeman's Role* (London: Routledge & Kegan Paul, 1973); and Isaac D. Balbus, *The Dialectics of Legal Repression: Black Rebels Before the American Criminal Courts* (New Brunswick, New Jersey: Transaction Books, 1982).

2 Several noted specialists have examined the legal framework that underlies democratic societies and police forces, among them see Egon Bittner, *The Functions of Police in Modern Society* (Cambridge, Massachusetts: Oelgeshlager, Gunn & Hain, 1980); Clive Elmsley, *Policing and Its Context, 1750–1870* (New York, Schocken Books, 1983); Hsi-Huey Liang, *The Rise of Modern Police and the European State System from Metternich to the Second World War* (Cambridge, England: Cambridge University Press, 1992); Robert Reiner, *The Politics of the Police* (New York: St. Martin's Press, 1985); and Albert J. Reiss, Jr., *The Police and the Public* (New Haven: Yale University Press, 1971).

3 See the proceedings of a 1992 conference in Hungary that examined issues of policing: Jozsef Vigh and Geza Katona, eds, *Social Changes, Crime and Police* (Budapest: Eotvos Lorand University, 1993).

4 It may be that part of the reason Russia has been unable to reform its law enforcement agencies is that certain elements of the militia, as well as the Alpha Division of the KGB, sided with Yeltsin against the coup perpetrators in August 1991. MVD troops again supported the Russian president in October 1993, when they helped to storm the Russian parliament building; their support subsequently earned the MVD both material benefits and political protection in the Yeltsin regime. Ironically, the prodemocracy stance of these groups in the MVD and security police may have shielded more conservative coworkers from harsh reprisals.

5 See "Human Rights Committee Chairman Describes Abuses," Foreign Broadcast Information Service, *Daily Report: Eurasia* (hereafter FBIS, *Daily Report*), 1 September 1994, 7.

6 For the composition of the Supreme Soviet committee, see J. Michael Waller, "Russia's Security and Intelligence Services Today," *ABA National Security Law Report* 15, no. 6 (June 1993): 5. For more information on the 1992 Law on Security, see *idem*, "Russia's Legal Foundations for Civil Repression," *Demokratizatsiya* 1, no. 3 (1993): 111.

7 "O sobliudenii prav cheloveka i grazhdanina v Rossiiskoi Federatsii za 1993 god" (report of the Office of the Russian Ombudsman presented at a meeting of the Human Rights Commission under the President of the Russian Federation, Moscow, 14 June 1994).

8 On police powers in Kazakhstan, see "New Law Boosts Powers of Police," FBIS, *Daily Report*, 26 October 1994, 41. For the text of the new Russian law, see "Ob operativno-rozysknoi deiatel'nosti v Rossiiskoi Federatsii," Russian Federation Law 892, *Vedomosti s"ezda narodnykh deputatov Rossiiskoi Federatsii i Verkhovnogo Soveta Rossiiskoi Federatsii*, no. 17 (23 April 1992): 1222–3. Information on the weak safeguards this law contains against police abuses was provided by Russian ombudsman Sergei Kovalëv in a September 1994 interview in Washington, D.C.

9 "Ob operativno-rozysknoi deiatel'nosti."

10 September and October 1994 interviews with Central Asian human rights figures in Washington, D.C.

11 See "Law on Militia," Foreign Broadcast Information Service, *Daily Report: Central Eurasia/Laws*, 1 September 1992, 113.

12 "On Cooperation between the Police and Units of the USSR Armed Forces in Ensuring Law and Order in Combatting Crime," decree of the President of the Union of Soviet Socialist Republics, translated in "Are Police–Army Patrols Constitutional?" *Current Digest of the Soviet Press* (hereafter *CDSP*) 18, no. 5 (1991): 7.

13 "MVD Personnel Chief Astapkin Discusses Militia, Crime," FBIS, *Daily Report*, 13 October 1994, 47–8.

14 On Russian militia cooperation with organized criminal organizations, see "'Alarm, jetzt kommen die Russen,'" *Der Spiegel*, no. 25 (1993): 105. On Krasnodar and Dagestan, see "Revamped Justice System Suffers Birth Pangs," *CDSP* 36, no. 34 (1994): 10.

15 "Radchenko on Crime Problem, MVD," FBIS, *Daily Report*, 14 November 1994, 67.

16 July 1994 interview with Viktor Iliukhin, Moscow.

17 Svetlana P. Glinkina in "Privatizatsiya and Kriminalizatsiya: How Organized Crime is Hijacking Privatization," *Demokratizatsiya* 2, no. 3 (Summer 1994): 388.

18 See, for example, Michael J. Beckelhimer, "Estonia's Men in Blue," *The Baltic Observer* 59, no. 15 (16–22 April 1993): 6.

19 In Russia, politicians of the left and the right agree that the socioeconomic situation, rather than the MVD, is most to blame for the current crime situation. See "Softer Version of Law Against Organized Crime Adopted," FBIS, *Daily Report*, 28 November 1994, 31.

Bibliography

RUSSIAN BOOKS

Alekseeva, Liudmila. *Istoriia inakomysliia v SSSR*. Benson, Vermont: Khronika Press, 1984.

Apiian, N.A. *Na strazhe pravoporiadka i zakonnosti*. Erevan, Armenia: Izdatel'stvo Erevanskogo universiteta, 1979.

Babaev, B.K. *et al*, eds *Pravovye i organizatsionnye mery bor'by s pravonarusheniiami protiv sotsialisticheskoi sobstvennosti*. Gorky, Russia: Gorkovskaia vysshaia shkola, 1982.

Babiia, B.M. *Sovetskii zakon i grazhdanin*. Kiev, Ukraine: Naukov dumka, 1980.

Bakhrakh, D.N. *Administrativno–pravovye mery bor'by s p'ianstvom*. Moscow: Iuridicheskaia literatura, 1973.

—— *Mery administrativnogo i obshchestvennogo vozdeistviia na pravonarushitelei*. Moscow: Pravda, 1971.

Bilenko, S.V. *Sovetskaia militsiia Rossii (1917–1930)*. Moscow: Akademiia MVD SSSR, 1976.

Bogomolov, G.A., *et al*. *Vekhi trudnykh budnei*. Saratov, Russia: Privolzhskoe knizhnoe izdatel'stvo, 1963.

Bondarenko, G.P., and I.V. Mart'ianov. *Sovetskoe administrativnoe pravo*. Lvov, Ukraine: Vishcha shkola, 1977.

Borodin, S.V. *Protsessual'nye akty predvaritel'nogo rassledovaniia: primernye obratzsy*. Moscow: Iuridicheskaia literatura, 1972.

Bykov, L.A., and G.A. Kvelidze. *Prokurorskii nadzor za ispolneniem zakonov v deiatel'nosti organov doznaniia i predvaritel'nogo sledstviia MVD*. Tbilisi, Georgia: Sabchota sakartvelo, 1975.

Churbanov, Iurii. *Tovarishch militsiia*. Moscow: Molodaia gvardiia, 1980.

Churbanov, Iurii, *et al*. *Upravlenie v oblasti administrativno–politicheskoi deiatel'nosti*. Moscow: Iuridicheskaia literatura, 1979.

Dulov, A.V. *Takticheskie operatsii pri rassledovanii prestuplenii*. Minsk, Byelorussia: Izdatel'stvo BGU (Beyolrusskogo gosudarstevnnogo universiteta), 1979.

Dzalilov, T.A. *Vernye otchizne*. Tashkent, Uzbekistan: Uzbekistan, 1968.

—— *Stranitsy istorii militsii Khorezma i Bukhary*. Tashkent, Uzbekistan: Uzbekistan, 1970.

Eropkin, M.N. *Upravlenie v oblasti okhranu obshchestvennogo poriadka*. Moscow: Iuridicheskaia literatura, 1965.

—— *Razvitie organov militsii v sovetskom gosudarstve*. Moscow: Vysshaia Shkola MOOP, 1967.

Gukovskaia, N.I., A.I. Dolgova, and G.M. Minkovskii. *Rassledovanie i sudebnoe razbiratel'stvo del o prestupleniiakh nesovershennoletnikh*. Moscow: Iuridicheskaia literatura, 1974.

Kafarov, T.M., and Ch.T. Musaev. *Bor'ba s posiagatel'stvom na obshchestvennyi poriadok*. Baku, Azerbaijan: Elm, 1983.

Karev, D.S., and N.M. Savgirova. *Vozbuzhdenie i rassledovanie ugolovnykh del*. Moscow: Vysshaia shkola, 1967.

Kasymova, M., and P. Arenberg. *Preduprezhdenie pravonarushenii nesovershennoletnikh*. Tashkent, Uzbekistan: Fan, 1972.

Kiselev, I.F., ed. *Polozhenie o vedomstvennoi militsii i instruksiia o poriadke eë organizatsii i deiatel'nosti*. Moscow: Izdatelst'vo NKVD, 1929.

Kozlov, Iu.M., et al. *Upravlenie v oblasti administrativno–politicheskoi deiatel'nosti*. Moscow: Iuridicheskaia literatura, 1979.

Kudriavtsev, V.N., et. al., *Lichnost' prestupnika*. Moscow: Iuridicheskaia literatura, 1971.

Kutushev, V.G. *Sotsial'noe planirovanie v organakh vnutrennykh del*. Saratov, Russia: Izdatel'stvo Saratovskogo universiteta, 1983.

Ledin, B.D., and N. Perfil'ev. *Kadry apparata upravleniia v SSSR*. Leningrad: Nauka, 1970.

Levin, B., and M. Levin. *Krutoi povorot*. Moscow: Sovetskaia Rossiia, 1989.

—— *Narkomaniia i narkomany*. Moscow: Prosveshchenie, 1991.

Lunev, A.E. *Upravlenie v oblasti administrativno–politicheskoi deiatel'nosti*. Moscow: Iuridicheskaia literatura, 1979.

Makharov, M.K. *Preduprezhdenie beznadzornosti i pravonarushenii sredi nesovershennoletnikh*. Omsk, Russia: Omskaia vysshaia shkola militsii, 1969.

Maksimov, V. *Sluzhba postovogo militsionera*. Moscow: NKVD pri zagotkhoze militsii respubliki, 1925.

Maliarov, M.P. *Prokurorskii nadzor v SSSR*. 2d ed. Moscow: Iuridicheskaia literatura, 1969.

Malkov, V.D. "Khishchenie ognestrel'nogo oruzhiia boevykh pripasov i vzryvchatykh veshchestv. "Kandidat avtoreforat, Vysshaia shkola MVD SSSR, Moscow, 1969.

Motylev, Ia., and E. Lysenko. *Soldaty poriadka*. Dushanbe, Tajikistan: Efron, 1967.

Mukhamedov, A.M. *Slavnyi put'*. Askhabad, Turkmenistan: Turkmenistan, 1965.

Narodnomu druzhinniku. Moscow: Znanie, 1973.

Nikolaev, P.F. *Omskaia militsiia v pervye gody sovetskoi vlasti (1917–1923)*. Omsk, Russia: Arkhivnyi otdel UVD ispolkoma Omskogo oblastnogo soveta deputatov trudiashchikhsiia, 1959.

—— *Sovetskaia militsiia Sibiri (1917–1922)*. Omsk, Russia: Zapadno–Sibirskoe knizhnoe izdatel'stvo, 1967.

Orlov, V.S. *Podrostok i prestuplenie*. Moscow: Izdatel'stvo Moskovskogo gosudarstvennogo universiteta, 1969.

Osipov, P.P., ed. *Kompleksnoe izuchenie sistemy vozdeistviia na prestupnost'*. Leningrad: Izdatel'stvo Leningradskogo gosudarstvennogo universiteta, 1978.

Pamiatka krasnogo militsionera. Moscow: Achinskaia gosudarstvennaia tipografiia, 1924.

Pashin, S.A. *Kontseptsiia sudebnoi reformy v Rossiiskoi Federatsii*. Moscow: Respublika, 1992.

Pomerantsev, V.A., and I.L. Liubimov, comp. I.F. Kiselev, ed. *Deistvuiushchie rasporiazheniia po militsii postanovleniia tsirkyliary, prikazy i instruktsii sistematicheskii sbornik s poiasneniiami*. 2d ed. Moscow: NKVD RSFSR, 1928.

Popov, L.L., and A.P. Shergin. *Upravlenie grazhdanin otvetstvennost'*. Leningrad: Nauka, 1975.

Pravovoe regulirovanie obshchestvennykh otnoshenii. Moscow: Institut gosudarstva i prava, 1976.

Rybal'chenko, R.K. *Upravlenie v oblasti vnutrennykh del*. Kharkov, Ukraine: Kharkovskii iuridicheskii institut, 1977.

Sharov, B. *Vedomstvennaia militsiia, eë organizatsiia i rabota*. Moscow: NKVD RSFSR, 1928.

Shchelokov, N.A. *Sovetskaia militsiia.* Moscow: Znanie, 1971.

Shelud'ko, G.P. *Sovetskaia militsiia na strazhe obshchestvennogo poriadka.* Kiev, Ukraine: Vishcha shkola, 1982.

Skiliagin, D., *et al. Dela i liudi Leningradskoi militsii.* Leningrad: Lenizdat, 1967.

Smirnov, A.I *et al.,* eds, *Prestupnost' i pravonarusheniia v SSSR.* Moscow: Iuridicheskaia literatura, 1990.

Solopanov, Iu.V., and V.E. Kvashis. *Retsidiv i retsidivisty.* Moscow: Iuridicheskaia literatura, 1971.

Sovetskoe administrativnoe pravo. Moscow: Iuridicheskaia literatura, 1981.

Spravochnik po zakonodatel'stvu dlia rabotnikov organov prokuratury, suda i ministerstva vnutrennykh del. Vol. 2, pt. 1. Moscow: Iuridicheskaia literatura, 1971.

Spravochnik po zakonodatel'stvu dlia rabotnikov organov prokuratury, suda i ministerstva vnutrennykh del. Vol. 3. Moscow: Iuridicheskaia literatura, 1972.

Sputnik krasnogo militsionera. Moscow: Zagotkhoza militsii respubliki, 1924.

Statisticheskie dannye o prestupnosti i pravnarusheniiakh po SSSR. Moscow: MVD USSR glavnyi informatsionnyi tsentr, 1989.

Tumanov, G. *Organizatsiia upravleniia v sfere okhrany obshchestvennogo poriadka.* Moscow: Iuridicheskaia literatura, 1972.

Viktorov, B.A. *Pravovye osnovy deiatel'nosti organov vnutrennykh del.* Moscow: Iuridicheskaia literatura, 1979.

NON-RUSSIAN BOOKS

Alexeeva, Ludmilla and Valery Chalidze. *Mass Unrest in the USSR.* vol.2 Washington, D.C.: Office of Net Assessments, 1985.

Alexeyeva, Ludmilla and Paul Goldberg. *The Thaw Generation:Coming of Age in the Post-Stalin Era.* Boston:Little Brown, 1990.

Alexeyeva, Ludmilla and Cather A. Fitzpatrick. *Civil Society in the USSR.* New York: Helsinki Watch, 1990.

Anderson, David M., and David Killingray, eds. *Policing the Empire: Government, Authority and Control, 1830–1940.* Manchester, England: Manchester University Press, 1991.

—— *Policing and Decolonisation Politics: Nationalism and the Police, 1917–65.* Manchester, England: Manchester University Press, 1992.

Arendt, Hannah. *The Origins of Totalitarianism.* New York: Harcourt Brace Jovanovich, 1979.

Aronson, Shlomo. *Beginnings of the Gestapo System: The Bavarian Model in 1933.* Jerusalem: Israel University Press, 1969.

Balbus, Isaac D. *The Dialectics of Legal Repression: Black Rebels Before the American Criminal Courts.* New Brunswick, New Jersey: Transaction Books, 1982.

Barry, Donald D., ed. *Law and the Gorbachev Era.* Dordrecht, The Netherlands: Martinus Nijhoff, 1988.

—— ed. *Toward the "Rule of Law" in Russia? Political and Legal Reform in the Transition Period.* Armonk, New York: M.E. Sharpe, 1992.

Barry, Donald B.; F.J. Feldbrugge; and Peter Maggs, eds. *Soviet Law After Stalin.* vol.3 Aplen ann den Rijn, The Netherlands: Sijthoff & Noordhoff, 1979.

Bayley, David H. "1975. The Police and Political Development in Europe. "In *The Formation of National States in Western Europe.* Edited by Charles Tilly. Princeton: Princeton University Press, 1975.

—— *Forces of Order: Police Behavior in Japan and the United States.* Berkeley: University of California Press, 1976.

—— *Patterns of Policing: A Comparative International Analysis.* New Brunswick, New Jersey: Rutgers University Press, 1985.

Berkley, George E. *The Democratic Policeman.* Boston: Beacon Press, 1969.

Berman, Harold J. *Soviet Criminal Law and Procedure: The RSFSR Codes.* 2d ed. Cambridge, Massachusetts: Harvard University Press, 1972.

Berman, Harold J. *Justice in the USSR.* rev. ed. Cambridge:Harvard University Press, 1982.

Brewer, John. *The Police, Public Order and the State: Policing in Great Britain, Northern Ireland, the Irish Republic, the USA, Israel, South Africa and China.* New York: St. Martin's Press, 1988.

Bittner, Egon. *The Functions of Police in Modern Society.* Cambridge, Massachusetts: Oelgeshlager, Gunn & Hain, 1980.

Buxbaum, Richard M., and Kathryn Hendley, eds. *The Soviet Sobranie of Laws: Problems of Codification and Non-Publication.* Research Series #78. Berkeley: International and Area Studies, 1991.

Cain, Maureen E. *Society and the Policeman's Role.* London: Routledge & Kegan Paul, 1973.

Center for Research on Criminal Justice. *The Iron Fist and the Velvet Glove.* Berkeley: Center for Research on Criminal Justice, 1977.

Chapman, Brian. *The Police State.* London: Pall Mall Press, 1970.

Colton, Timothy. *Commissars, Commanders and Civilian Authority: The Structure of Soviet Military Politics.* Cambridge, Massachusetts: Harvard University Press, 1979.

Conflict in the Soviet Union: Black January in Azerbaidzhan. New York: Helsinki Watch/Memorial Report, 1991.

Conquest, Robert. *Power and Policy in the USSR: The Struggle for Stalin's Succession, 1945–1960.* New York: St. Martin's Press, 1967.

—— *The Soviet Police System.* New York: Praeger, 1968.

—— *The Harvest of Sorrow.* New York: Oxford University Press, 1986.

Cosman, Cathy, ed. *Glasnost in Jeopardy:Human Rights in the USSR.* New York: Helsinki Watch, 1991.

Crankshaw, Edward. *Gestapo: Instrument of Tyranny.* London: Putnam, 1956.

Delarue, Jacques. *The Gestapo: A History of Horror.* New York: Morrow, 1964.

Emsley, Clive. *Policing and Its Context, 1750–1870.* New York: Schocken Books, 1983.

Ericson, Richard V. *Reproducing Order: A Study of Police Patrol Work.* Toronto: University of Toronto Press, 1982.

Fainsod, Merle. *Smolensk Under Soviet Rule.* Cambridge, Massachusetts: Harvard University Press, 1958.

—— *How Russia Is Ruled.* 6th ed. Cambridge: Harvard University Press, 1970.

Feifer, George. *Justice in Moscow.* London: Bodley Head, 1964.

Friedrich, C.J., and Zbigniew Brzezinski. *Totalitarian Dictatorship and Autocracy.* Cambridge, Massachusetts: Harvard University Press, 1965.

Gabiani, A.A. *Narkotizm vchera i segodniia.* Tbilisi, Georgia: Sabchota sakrtvelo, 1988.

Goldstein, Herman. *Policing a Free Society.* Cambridge, Massachusetts: Ballanger Publishing Company, 1976.

Greenberg, Martin Alan. *Auxiliary Police.* Westport, Connecticut: Greenwood, 1984.

Harring, Sidney L. *Policing a Class Society: The Experience of American Cities, 1865–1915.* New Brunswick: Rutgers University Press, 1983.

Helsinki Watch Report. *Toward the Rule of Law: Soviet Legal Reform and Human Rights under Perestroika.* New York: U.S. Helsinki Watch Committee, 1989.

—— *Civil Society in the USSR.* New York: U.S. Helsinki Watch Committee, 1990.

Hingley, Ronald. *The Russian Secret Police.* London: Hutchinson, 1970.

Hopkins, Mark. *Russia's Underground Press: The Chronicle of Current Events.* New York: Praeger, 1983.

Ioffe, Olympiad S., and Peter B. Maggs. *Soviet Law in Theory and Practice*. London, Rome, New York: Oceana, 1983.

Jones, Anthony; Walter D. Connor; and David E. Powell, eds. *Soviet Social Problems*. Boulder, Colorado: Westview, 1991.

Juviler, Peter. *Revolutionary Law and Order*. New York: Free Press, 1976.

Klockars, Carl B., ed. *Thinking About Police*. New York: McGraw Hill, 1983.

Knight, Amy W. *The KGB: Police and Politics in the Soviet Union*. New York: Allen & Unwin, 1988.

Lane, David. *Soviet Economy and Society*. New York: New York University Press, 1985.

Liang, Hsi-Huey. *The Rise of Modern Police and the European State System from Metternich to the Second World War*. Cambridge, England: Cambridge University Press, 1992.

Locke, John. *The Second Treatise on Government*. New York: Macmillan, 1952.

Lundman, Richard J., ed. *Police Behavior*. New York: Oxford University Press, 1980.

Marchenko, Anatoly. *From Tarusa To Siberia*. Edited by Joshua Rubinstein. Walled Lake, Michigan: Strathcona, 1980.

Marx, Gary T. *Undercover: Police Surveillance in America*. Berkeley: University of California Press, 1988.

Massell, Gregory J. *The Surrogate Proletariat: Moslem Women and Revolutionary Strategies in Soviet Central Asia, 1919–1929*. Princeton: Princeton University Press, 1974.

Mawby, R.I. *Comparative Policing Issues: The British and American Experience in International Perspective*. London: Unwin Hyman, 1990.

Millar, James R., ed. *Politics, Work and Daily Life in the USSR*. Cambridge: Cambridge University Press, 1987.

Millar, James R., and Sharon L. Wolchik, eds. *The Social Legacy of Communism*. Washington, D.C.: Woodrow Wilson Center Press; and Cambridge, England: Cambridge University Press, 1994.

Miller, Wilbur R. *Cops and Bobbies: Police Authority in New York and London, 1830–1970*. Chicago: University of Chicago Press, 1977.

Monkkonen, Eric. *Police in Urban America, 1860–1920*. Cambridge: Cambridge University Press, 1981.

Muir, Jr., William Ker. *Police: Street Corner Politicians*. Chicago: University of Chicago Press, 1977.

Nove, Alec. *The Soviet System in Retrospect: An Obituary Notice*. New York: Harriman Institute, Columbia University, 1993.

Price, Barbara Raffel. *Police Professionalism*. Lexington, Massachusetts: D.C. Heath, 1977.

Reiner, Robert. *The Politics of the Police*. New York: St. Martin's Press, 1985.

Reiss, Jr., Albert J. *The Police and the Public*. New Haven: Yale University Press, 1971.

Rousseau, Jean-Jacques. *The Social Contract and Discourse on the Origin of Inequality*. New York: Washington Square Press, 1967.

Rubenstein, Johnathan. *City Police*. New York: Farrar, Straus and Giroux, 1972.

di Ruffia, Paolo Biscaretti, and Gabriele Crespi Reghizzi. *La Costituzione Sovietica del 1977*. Milano: Fott. A. Giuffrè Editore, 1979.

Sharlet, Robert. *Soviet Constitutional Crisis: From De-Stalinization to Disintegration*. Armonk, New York: M.E. Sharpe, 1992.

Shearing, Clifford D. and Philip C. Stenning, eds. *Private Policing*. Newbury Park, California: Sage, 1987.

Shelley, Louise and Jozsef Vigh, eds. *Social Changes, Crime and the Police*. Chr:Switzerland: Harwood Academic Publishers, 1995.

Skolnick, Jerome. *Justice Without Trial*. New York: Wiley, 1967.

Staff of the Commission on Security and Cooperation in Europe. *Human Rights and Democratization in the Newly Independent States of the Former Soviet Union.* Washington, D.C.: Commission on Security and Cooperation in Europe, 1993.

Stead, Philip John. *The Police of France.* New York: Macmillan, 1983.

Vaksberg, Arkady. *The Soviet Mafia.* New York: St. Martin's Press, 1991.

Van den Berg, Ger P. *The Soviet System of Justice: Figures and Policy.* Dordrecht, The Netherlands: Martinus Nijhoff, 1985.

de Vergotinni, Guiseppe. *Diritto Costituzionale Comparato.* Padova: Cedam, 1991.

Vigh, Jozsef, and Geza Katona, eds. *Social Changes: Crime and Police.* Budapest: Eotvos Lorand University, 1993.

Voslensky, Michael. *Nomenklatura: The Soviet Ruling Class.* Garden City, New York: Doubleday, 1984.

Wade, Rex A. *Red Guards and Workers' Militias in the Russian Revolution.* Stanford: Stanford University Press, 1984.

Waller, Michael. *Secret Empire: The KGB in Russia Today.* Boulder, Colorado: Westview Press, 1994.

Walker, Samuel. *Popular Justice: A History of American Criminal Justice.* New York: Oxford University Press, 1980.

Wilson, James Q. *Varieties of Police Behavior: The Management of Law and Order.* New York: Atheneum, 1974.

JOURNALS

A survey of the following journals was conducted for the time periods indicated next to the title:

Agitator, 1982–87

Arkhiv samizdata (Munich: Radio Free Europe/Radio Liberty), 1972–86

British Broadcasting Corporation, *Summary of World Broadcasts* (BBC, *SWB*), 1985–91

Current Digest of the Soviet Press (*CDSP*), 1982–93

Foreign Broadcast Information Service (FBIS), *Daily Report: Soviet Union* (subsequently *Daily Report: Central Eurasia*), 1984–92

Iuridicheskaia gazeta, 1991–92

Joint Publications Research Service (JPRS), *USSR Report: Political and Sociological Affairs,* 1981–92

Kommunist, 1982–88

Literaturnaia gazeta, 1982–92

Moscow News, English edition, 1988–92

Nedelia, 1989–92

Ogonëk, 1987–92

Radio Free Europe/Radio Liberty (RFE/RL), *Daily Report,* 1982–94

Sovetskaia militsiia, 1990–92

Sovetskoe gosudarstvo i pravo, 1972–92

Survey of the Soviet Press (*SSP*), 1959–64

Vedomosti Verkhovnogo Soveta RSFSR, 1972–91

Index